NOVEL AND ROMANCE 1700–1800

NOVEL AND ROMANCE

1700 – 1800

A Documentary Record

Edited by

IOAN WILLIAMS

Lecturer in English Literature
University of Warwick

LONDON: ROUTLEDGE & KEGAN PAUL

First published 1970
by Routledge & Kegan Paul Limited
Broadway House, 68–74 Carter Lane
London, E.C.4
Printed in Great Britain
by Butler & Tanner Ltd
Frome and London
© Ioan Williams 1970
SBN 7100 6595 7

006102

Contents

v

CONTENTS

Preface

The documents collected in this volume trace the development of novel-criticism during one of the most formative periods of the history of fiction, from 1700 to 1800. The material gathered here includes prefaces to collections, translations and original novels; essays written for journals modelled on the *Spectator;* passages from miscellanies and from books written primarily for some purpose unconnected with the novel; reviews from the monthly reviews; and introductions to the collected works of certain authors. The various important pamphlets are represented by selected passages from Charles Gildon's *An Epistle to Daniel Defoe* (Nos. 10 and 12) and the anonymous *An Essay on the New Species of Writing . . .* (No. 35). Comments by foreign authors have only been included when they refer to novels that were written in English and published in England; and reviews of foreign novels have only been admitted when they relate to translations rather than to the original texts. The one exception to this rule is No. 8, Bishop Huet's essay, translated as *The History of Romances.*

Every reader familiar with the full range of source material will have in mind one or more items which might have been included. The criticism of Henry Fielding is the most obvious lacuna. It became apparent during the process of compilation that if Fielding's comments on the novel were included their bulk would be disproportionate, and the decision was taken to publish them separately, together with his remarks on other literary subjects. Meanwhile, the most important of his statements about the novel, in the text of *Joseph Andrews* and *Tom Jones,* are already freely available, and will form a background against which the material included in the volume should be seen.

When the contents of the volume had been decided, there remained the question of how they should be presented. The relative scarcity of comment during the early years of the century and the widely different nature of the sources made it difficult to obtain a well-balanced volume. It appeared that there was a very strong argument for presenting the material in sections divided according to source or subject-matter. The essays from the essay-journals, traditionally conservative and concerned to preserve an ideal of middle-class behaviour in a changing world, are radically different from the work of the reviewers, who were expected to be more willing to accept each variation on the new form on its own merits. Similarly, the translator who was introducing a foreign work to the public was writing in terms completely different from those used by a writer like Horace Walpole, who was explaining his creative approach. Moreover, certain preoccupations cut across divisions according to source and suggested a grouping under titles like 'The Aim of Fiction', or 'Realism of Character'.

A third possibility was to present the material in the order in which it was written. Because the volume covers years of criticism and creative writing, this seemed the best. The impulse to emphasize distinctions in source and subject-matter gave way before the need to show the relationship between the development of criticism and the development of fiction. On the other hand, an attempt has been made in the Introduction to consider the material from points of view which are not brought out by the chronological presentation.

THE TEXT

The choice of texts has been governed to some extent by convenience, although in all cases either a first edition or an authoritative contemporary or modern edition has been used. For editorial footnotes authoritative modern editions have been used when available; otherwise references have been made to contemporary or original editions. Square brackets have been used to indicate omissions from the text and editorial insertions. Finally, the fact that a footnote is taken from the original and has not been inserted by the editor is indicated by the presence after it of the initials [o.n.] within square brackets.

Acknowledgements

There are certain books which everyone who is concerned with eighteenth-century fiction must be grateful for, and to which I owe a particular debt. Among these are the catalogues of Andrew Block and W. H. McBurney. B. C. Nangle's indices to *The Monthly Review* (1930) enabled me to identify the authors of passages in that periodical. I owe a great deal to A. D. McKillop's *Samuel Richardson, Printer and Novelist* (1936), a book which it would be difficult to overpraise, and I wish to mention R. D. Mayo's *The English Novel in the Magazines 1740–1851* (1962), as a book which contains the best that has yet been written on certain aspects of eighteenth-century criticism of prose fiction.

I owe more personal debts to Mr. K. Gransden and Mr. C. Rawson of the University of Warwick and to Mr. K. Stubbs of the University of Exeter, who provided me with information which I could not have obtained for myself. I should like to thank the staff of the University of Warwick Library and especially Miss A. Cooper for the help which she has given me. And, finally, I should like to mention my gratitude to my wife, though only she can be aware of its proper extent.

Introduction

Eighteenth-century criticism of prose fiction in England falls into two sections, dividing at the year 1740. The century began with the rejection of the previously popular heroic romance. The first forty years was a period of great activity and experiment, but was marked by a lack of confidence on the part of the novelists and a generally hostile attitude on the part of the critics, who were offended by the frivolity and immorality of much contemporary fiction. This period ended suddenly with the publication of Samuel Richardson's *Pamela* (1740) and Henry Fielding's *Joseph Andrews* (1742), which was partly stimulated by his rival's success. These two writers consolidated their achievement with *Clarissa* (1748) and *Tom Jones* (1749). Together they demonstrated that fiction could be popular and yet have artistic and intellectual appeal. However, there then followed such an enormous increase in the production of fiction that many observers felt that the novel was a threat to cultural and moral standards. Some commentators attacked the new genre on the basis of the theoretical position provided by Richardson. Others, more interested in the novel itself than in its effects on the public, attempted to describe its characteristics and formulate its rules. Between 1740 and the end of the century a great deal of discussion went on and very positive advances were made towards the serious consideration of prose fiction as a branch of literature on equal terms with poetry and drama. During the later decades of the century the debate became more intensive, with the development of thorough and regular reviewing by literary journals. At the same time, however, discussion began to be more stereotyped and repetitive. The fiction written during the last twenty years of the century did not stimulate new thinking as that of Richardson and Fielding had done. The dominant form was the Gothic romance, which seems only to have called forth rather weary repetitions of Aristotelean criteria and a nostalgic looking-back to the more challenging works of the mid-century.

The positive achievement of the mid-century critics resulted from their attempts to apply to the novel criteria borrowed from other types of criticism. Writers who were familiar with the long history of epic criticism turned naturally to Aristotle's *Poetics* for a terminology with which to treat this new form. Aristotle had defined poetry as the imitation of the actions of men and had said that the work of art consisted of six parts: fable; manners; sentiments; diction; music; and decoration. Of these six parts, according to his *Poetics*, the first three were the more important and the fable was the most important of all. On the basis of these remarks, and the trend of Aristotle's argument in general, most eighteenth-century critics agreed in treating prose fiction as if it were poetry without the ornament of verse. Furthermore, working from Aristotle's division of poetry into the two broad categories of tragedy and comedy, they constructed a theory of kinds which rested on a distinction between the serious and the non-serious, the first containing tragedy, epic and serious romance, the second dramatic comedy, burlesque and anti-romance. For a long time naturalistic prose fiction suffered from this system of division. It was included with the non-serious forms and especially associated with the anti-romance. However, the system had a strong influence on the theory of the fiction writers themselves. The authors of the French heroic romances attempted to complete the framework of genres by writing what they thought of as prose epics. Fénelon followed them with his *Télémaque* (1699), which was closely modelled on the *Odyssey*. Finally, Fielding united the serious and the non-serious with his idea of the comic epic in prose, on the analogy of Homer's lost comic verse-epic, the *Margites*.

Fielding's discussion of his own principles in the Preface to *Joseph Andrews* and the introductory chapters of *Tom Jones* ensured that critics who were interested in the technical aspects of his work would tend to discuss it in Aristotelean terms, even if they were not otherwise disposed to do so. This was helpful: critics needed some kind of pattern into which they could fit the totally new form of literature, and Aristotle provided it. On the other hand, the tendency to discuss the work of art in terms of its component parts as Aristotle described them ultimately came to have a stultifying effect. In particular, the emphasis on plot as the design-bearing element, which grew out of Aristotle's treatment of fable or myth, distracted attention from other sources of significance. The tendency to think of the novel's structure as depending on the relationship between the incidents in a story discouraged critics from thinking of the novel as a unity in any other sense. Fielding himself was moved by his admiration for order and arrangement to praise Charlotte Lennox's *The Female Quixote* (1752) at the expense of *Don Quixote*. For works like *Tristram Shandy* (1760–7), and even for *Clarissa*, the Aristotelean terminology was completely inadequate.

By the end of the eighteenth century, critics badly needed a new approach to prose fiction, but in the absence of another Richardson or Fielding they lacked the stimulus to find it. In dealing with contemporary works, the monthly reviewers were aware that there was a decline from the standards of the earlier writers, but were at a loss to say why. They discussed the Gothic romances of Mrs. Radcliffe and her imitators as they had earlier discussed the more naturalistic novels, falling back on the criterion of 'imitation of nature' to express the difference between them. There was much criticism written during the last twenty years of the century, and several writers approached the novel with sensitivity and respect. But many of the most interesting comments were not made by the critics, but by the novelists themselves, or by writers who were dealing with prose fiction casually, in connection with other subjects. In the monthly reviews there was surprisingly little of interest. This situation continued until after 1800, and even the novels of Scott failed to stimulate new thinking. It was not until the third decade of the nineteenth century, with such writers as Victor Hugo, George Sand, Bulwer Lytton and Charles Dickens, that a totally new system of criticism began to come into existence.

THE DECLINE OF THE HEROIC ROMANCE

The first passage in this collection is the translator's Preface to one of the most famous of the French heroic romances, Madeleine de Scudéry's *Artamène* (1649–53). This may serve to remind the English reader that discussion of prose fiction in eighteenth-century England followed an intensive debate about the merits and characteristics of the heroic romance. Although never fully domiciled in England, it threw its shadow over the discussion of prose fiction in this country. Its sudden decline in popularity and respectability during the early years of the century indicates an important change which was taking place. The appearance of the heroic romance in seventeenth-century France accompanied the formulation of neo-classic doctrine and was the result of a serious attempt by writers of high standing to bring romance within the bounds of the neo-Aristotelean system of kinds. Its rejection in early eighteenth-century England amounted to a rejection of neo-classicism as it affected prose fiction and marked the end of one phase of the long debate between Ancient and Modern.[1] Issues which continued to be of importance in the discussion of poetry and drama were settled almost without debate when the heroic romance was decisively

3

rejected in favour of forms which related more closely to the conditions of ordinary life.

Out of its context the theory which underlay the heroic romance has a surprisingly modern air. Madeleine de Scudéry's ideas, as she states them in the Preface to her *Ibrahim* (1641), seem close to those of much later writers:

> But amongst all the rules which are to be observed in the completion of these workes, that of true resemblance is without question the most necessary; it is, as it were, the fundamentall stone of this building, and but upon which it cannot subsist; without it nothing can move, without it nothing can please: and if this charming deceiver doth not beguile the mind in *Romanzes*, this kind of reading disgusts, instead of intertaining it: I have laboured then never to eloigne myself from it, and to that purpose I have observed the manners, customes, Religions, and inclinations of people: And to give a more true resemblance to things, I have made the foundations of my work Historicall, my principall personages such as are marked out in the true History for illustrious persons, and the warres effective.[2]

'True resemblance', however, the keystone of neo-classic doctrine, referred to the imitation of a generalized human nature rather than the conditions of ordinary life, and the historical background which was intended to give an appearance of truth was distorted so as to comply with the contemporary ideas of seemliness and propriety. Heroic romance praised itself for its superiority over history proper in being able to give a 'perfect pattern of virtuous Love and truly merited Honour'.[3] An aristocratic form, it addressed itself to the 'most necessary men',[4] was constructed on an antiquated psychology and appealed to an audience which felt that the representation of things as they were should be confined to the comedy and the anti-romance. Charles Gildon's *Defence of Love in Tragedies* (1694), contains an analysis of the function of heroic love which applies as much to the romance as to the heroic drama:

> ... it must be granted that Love in its Nature, must inspire Noble and more August Thoughts and Sentiments, than *Grief* or *Terror*. For the Soul is more dilated, and exerts its noblest Faculties more in Love, than in *Sorrow* or *Fear*; which both contract the soul and its Operations. Love pushes a Generous Mind on to Great Actions, to render itself more agreeable and taking to the Object of his Desires

than Others. Wheras *Grief* and *Fear* are opposites to all that's Great and Noble. All the steps of Love are Great, and much akin to that Glory *Rapin* will have the only object of an Hero's Passion; for Admiration is the first Illustrious Step by which a man mounts to Love: and to secure *Admiration*, a Man must perform something extraordinary: For, 'tis not the Beauty or Manly Fabrick of the Body that are suppos'd capable alone of making that Impression on an *Heroine*, (for such must the Mistress of an Hero be). 'Tis his Acts that render him Admirable and Charming in her Eye. And indeed common Experience will so convince us that a Person of Quality that has Signaliz'd himself by any Noble Deeds, shall gain the fair much easier than a Son of the Earth unknown to Fame and yet not born to Reputation.[5]

Romances based on this ethos were popular in England during the later part of the seventeenth century. The works imported from France and imitated in England by Robert and Roger Boyle, Nathaniel Ingelo, Sir George Mackenzie, amused readers like John Dryden, Dorothy Osborne and Mrs. Pepys. If we may accept the evidence of Clara Reeve, they were eagerly received at reading parties well into the eighteenth century.[6] As the century wore on, however, they came to be judged in terms of their suitability as reading matter for 'a Son of the Earth unknown to Fame', and condemned for presenting a ridiculous picture of human life and inculcating standards of behaviour which had no validity outside their own artificial world. Even by 1692 the situation had begun to change. The exclusively aristocratic audience which the writers of romance and epic were addressing had begun to disappear and a new class of readers to emerge. Some indication of this process of change is preserved in this collection in the piece reproduced from *The Athenian Mercury* (No. 3). This writer was concerned about the possible effects of fiction which was long and time-consuming and directed towards the stimulation of an aristocratic ethos. The readers of *The Athenian Mercury* had their living to earn, and their self-appointed adviser evidently felt that for them long romances were unsuitable reading.

BETWEEN ROMANCE AND NOVEL: 1700–40

By 1785, when Clara Reeve published her dialogue-essay, *The Progress of Romance*, critics were agreed in distinguishing between the novel and the romance as between realistic and idealistic fiction, though the term 'romance' was still used in a more general sense, as in the title of Clara Reeve's essay. Clara Reeve wrote: 'The Romance is an heroic fable, which treats of fabulous persons and things. The Novel is a picture of real life and manners, and of the time in which it is written.'[7] William Congreve (No. 2), in the Preface to his *Incognita* (1692), discusses novel and romance in very similar terms, but the 'Novel' to which Congreve refers is the short *nouvelle*, turning on an intrigue or love-situation, which was most successfully written by Aphra Behn and which flourished side by side with the heroic romance, providing entertainment to an aristocratic audience. Clara Reeve's distinction between novel and romance was the result of a long process of development. As late as 1740 Lord Chesterfield informed his son (No. 24) that the novel was 'a little gallant history, which must contain a great deal of love and not exceed one or two small volumes' and 'a kind of abbreviation of a Romance; for a romance generally consists of twelve volumes, all filled with insipid love nonsense, and most incredible adventures'. Chesterfield, writing in the year in which Richardson published *Pamela*, summarized the remarks of the majority of commentators between 1700 and 1740. He was unaware of the capacity of prose fiction to make a serious demand on the attention.

The state of contemporary fiction during this period did not encourage the production of a coherent theory. The decline in the prestige of the heroic romance, followed by the proliferation of scandalous chronicles, *romans à clef*, fabulous journeys, *nouvelles* and other miscellaneous forms—all, according to the prevalent critical theory, 'illegitimate' and outside the range of recognized kinds—discouraged serious study. Consequently critical comment is scarce. Writers who did comment on fiction tended, like Shaftesbury in his *Characteristics* (1711), to attack it because it was ridiculous or indecent.[8] A typical expression of moderate opinion is found in a book by John Clarke (1730), who claimed to introduce the reader to the methods and materials of literary and scientific study. Clarke thought that romances were 'generally very indiscreetly and foolishly Writ' and had 'a strong Tendency to corrupt and debauch the Mind with silly Mischievous Notions of Love and Honour, and other Things relating to the Conduct of Life'.[9] There were only two romances which he could heartily recommend—*Don Quixote* and *Télémaque*. The modern reader might think that he could have extended his list, but he was sufficiently unusual in finding anything to praise at all.

The novelists themselves did little to increase public respect for their art. Many writers prefaced their attempts to excite interest in sordid sexual situations with transparently insincere claims that their work was satirical, exemplary or simply the literal truth, which demonstrated the workings of Providence and warned the reader about the dangers of vice. Mrs. Manley was unusual in concerning herself with theory at all (No. 5.) She set the 'novel' against the heroic romance, attacked both the latter and historical novels, and applied the criteria of probability and propriety in conjunction with demands for psychological detail and natural dialogue. Antoine Prévost (No. 22) made the usual claim that his story was true, and supported it with convincing geographical detail and accredited historical witness, but he also tried to attract the attention of the more discerning reader by suggesting that he might accept the story as an instructive fiction. Daniel Defoe, in the Preface (No. 9) to *The Adventures of Robinson Crusoe* (1719), also asserted that his story was true, but insisted that it possessed a moral design, and his evasiveness earned him the reproof administered by Charles Gildon in the *Postscript* (No. 12) to his *Epistle to Daniel Defoe* (1719):

> I think we may justly say, that the Design of the Publication of this Book was not sufficient to justify and make Truth of what you allow to be Fiction and Fable; what you mean by *Legitimating*, *Invention* and *Parable*, I know not; unless you would have us think, that the Manner of your telling a Lie will make it a Truth.

Defoe's case was unusual only because he was a writer of exceptional ability. In the case of other writers it is obvious at the first glance that they have a crude and inadequate conception of the relationship between action and design and lack a clear sense of artistic purpose. The decline of the heroic romance, incapable of fulfilling the demands of early eighteenth-century readers, was not followed by the emergence of a single dominant fictional form. Writers who wished to avoid the charges of frivolity and immorality tried to do so by pretending that they were not writing fiction at all. In such a situation a theory of fiction was not likely to emerge, and as far as most commentators were concerned novel and romance remained on the outskirts of literature, to be treated perfunctorily, merely with reference to their potential moral danger. A great deal of experimenting was carried out by the writers of the period, but until 1740 no single work had appeared which contained a coherent and integral design and which could claim to be treated seriously by its readers.

THE IMPACT OF SAMUEL RICHARDSON

The subject of Richardson's impact on contemporary criticism of fiction falls into two sections, the first relating to the initial reception of *Pamela* and *Clarissa*, the second to the process of development and hardening which the novelist's own idea of fiction went through up to the publication of *Sir Charles Grandison* (1754). A study of Richardson's theory leads to a consideration of the conservative attitudes towards prose fiction which made themselves felt from the middle of the eighteenth century and which rested almost entirely on his creative achievement.

The facts about the reception of *Pamela* are well known: it was acclaimed with a spontaneous burst of enthusiasm; it was praised from the pulpit, imitated, parodied, and used as a tag to sell a wide variety of articles; it was read by people in every section of society and discussed with excitement. Before publication Richardson was rather unsure about the book's reception and took the precaution of providing himself with letters of recommendation and praise, which he published with the novel. Later, when he was more confident, he continued this device as a means of defending his aims and techniques against all possible criticism. The introductory material to the first and second editions of *Pamela* builds up to a crescendo of praise which is maintained against all objections.

The modern reader is likely to find *Pamela* crude and naïve in relation to Richardson's later work and to object to the excessively enthusiastic and sometimes prurient tone of the letters which the author reproduced as prefatory material. Richardson's contemporaries felt, however, that his novel had actually achieved what previous writers had merely claimed, in combining pleasure with ethical instruction and depicting life with triumphant vividness. The Editor's Preface to *Pamela* (No. 23) summarizes the novel's claims to the attention of readers of all ranks and interests: it claims to divert, entertain, instruct and improve, to 'raise a Distress from *natural* Causes, and to excite Compassion from proper Motives'. The Editor's assertions are supported by the letter-writers presented in the following pages. The first of them takes care to praise the device of letter-writing because it leads to authenticity, provides an adequate medium for psychological analysis and stresses the moral and social use of Pamela's example in the state of contemporary degeneracy. The second letter-writer seems more involved with the material of the story. His approach is personal: 'I have interested myself in all her Schemes of Escape; been alternately pleas'd and angry with her in her Restraint; *pleas'd* with the little Machinations and Contrivances she set on foot for her Release, and *angry* for suffering her Fears to defeat them. . . .' This is an innocent commentator, incapable of perceiving the irony that has always been evident in the *Virtue Rewarded* of the novel's subtitle. Pamela, he comments, even though she is attracted by her importunate lover, makes no attempt to inflate his passion: 'A glorious Instance of Self-Denial! Thus her very Repulses became Attractions: the more she resisted, the more she charm'd; and the very Means she used to guard her Virtue, the more endanger'd it, by inflaming his Passions.'

The prefatory material to the second edition (No. 25) shows no slackening of enthusiasm, although it does indicate that more thought had taken place as to the precise nature of *Pamela's* originality. It also shows a determination on the part of the author to deal promptly and effectively with any attempt at criticism. Aaron Hill's answer here to the anonymous letter-writer (whose complaints were not vindictive or far-reaching) is merely a forerunner of Richardson's own defence in the *Gentleman's Magazine* (No. 32). In the second edition praise is freely given for liveliness, simplicity and naturalness of depiction. Emphasis is given to the appropriateness of the epistolary form and the aptness of the style. Aaron Hill takes care to counter possible criticism on the grounds of lowness of subject and style:

Why does the Author's Modesty mislead his Judgement, to suspect the Style wants Polishing?—No, Sir, there is an *Ease*, a *natural Air*, a dignify'd *Simplicity*, and measured Fullness, in it, that, resembling Life, outglows it! He has reconciled the *Pleasing* to the *Proper*. The *Thought* is every-where exactly *cloath'd* by the *Expression*: And becomes its Dress as roundly, and as close, as *Pamela* her Country-habit.

After disposing of the importunate criticism of the 'anonymous gentleman', Hill goes on to clarify the basis of his enthusiasm:

Longinus, I remember, distinguishing by what Marks we may know the *Sublime*, says, it is chiefly from an Effect that will follow the Reading it: a delightfully-adhering Idea, that clings fast to the Memory; and from which it is difficult for a Man to disengage his Attention.—If *this* is a Proof of the *Sublime*, there was never *Sublimity* so lastingly felt, as in PAMELA!

Thousands of readers, apart from the over-enthusiastic Hill, welcomed
Pamela as something entirely new in the domain of prose fiction and
felt justified in so recognizing it on the grounds of its evident moral
value. Moreover, *Pamela* was capable of arousing feelings of elevated
pathos; it expanded the soul and at the same time expanded the realm
of fiction. Low in subject and style, the novel made a serious aesthetic
appeal and made it obviously, without recourse to satire. It gave criticism the stimulus needed before it could begin the long process of
adaptation to prose fiction.

The publication of *Clarissa* in 1747–8 more fully justified the claims
that had been made for Richardson. Contemporary readers felt that
the subject, the sordid setting and the painful suffering, were raised to
sublimity by the character of the heroine. The author of the pamphlet
Remarks on Clarissa, Addressed to the Author (1749), thought by some
to have been Sarah Fielding, showed that she realized and appreciated
Richardson's central purpose:

> The death of Clarissa is, I believe, the only Death of the Kind in any
> Story; and in her Character, the Author has thrown into Action
> (if I may be allowed the Expression) the true Christian Philosophy,
> shewn its force to enoble the human Mind, till it can look with
> Serenity on all human Misfortunes, and take from Death itself its
> gloomy horrors.[10]

Clarissa aroused similar feelings in a wide range of contemporaries,
men and women more moderate than Aaron Hill, as intelligent and
reasonable as William Warburton and Fielding, not all of whom were
prepared to commit themselves to approval of its predecessor. The
comments of the French writers Diderot and Rousseau are well
known;[11] so is the praise of Samuel Johnson, who remarked in conversation with Boswell that *Clarissa*, of all books, shows most knowledge of the human heart.[12] Less well known is the reaction of Fielding,
by this time the author of *Joseph Andrews* as well as *Shamela*, who
praised the novel in his *Jacobite's Journal* and wrote a personal letter to
his rival, telling him that Clarissa's letter to Lovelace after her rape
'is beyond anything I have ever read' and adding: 'God forbid that the
Man who reads this with dry eyes should be alone with my daughter
when she hath no assistance within call.'[13]

This reception increased Richardson's confidence, and we see its
direct result in the altered tone of the Preface to the second and later
editions of the novel. In his first Preface (No. 26) Richardson is clearly

on the defensive and very apprehensive about possible complaints that his novel is too long. He takes care to justify his mode of narration and to outline a simple moral. By the time that he wrote the Preface to the second edition (1751, No. 38), his attitude was entirely changed. In 1748 he had felt obliged to publish the Preface which he seems to have solicited from William Warburton; later he dropped it, with very little excuse. Warburton's Preface (No. 28) was warm in its praise, but it did not allow Richardson what he felt was his full measure of originality. Firstly, though praising the novelist's epistolary method, Warburton suggested that it was in some degree inferior to 'the more artificial composition of a story in one continued Narrative'. Secondly, he suggested that the type of fiction which Richardson was writing had its origin in France. After Richardson had rejected the piece, Warburton altered it to apply to Fielding and Marivaux and found a place for it in a footnote to his edition of Pope.[14] If he had read carefully the prefatory matter to *Pamela*, where Aaron Hill explicitly denied the relevance of French fiction to Richardson's unique work, he might have succeeded better in pleasing the author for whom it was first intended.

The relation between the work of Marivaux and Richardson occurred to other writers besides Warburton. Von Haller, author of the piece reprinted in the *Gentleman's Magazine* (No. 32), compared the two in order to stress Richardson's seriousness of purpose. Marivaux's *Marianne* he found amusing, but '*Clarissa* not only amuses, but instructs; and the more effectually, as the writer paints nature, and nature alone'. This is the point which is most heavily laboured in the Preface to the second edition of the novel, where Richardson warns us about expecting from his work the kind of amusement which we might receive from 'a *light Novel*, or *transitory Romance*', and says that he rather designed 'To investigate the highest and most important Doctrines not only of Morality, but of Christianity, by shewing them thrown into action in the conduct of the worthy characters. . . . ' This Preface is a natural sequel to his reply to the objections voiced by Von Haller, and it was followed in turn by the Concluding Note to *Sir Charles Grandison*, where he makes his final statement about fiction.

This Note really belongs to the history of conservative criticism in the eighteenth century rather than to an account of Richardson's reception and development. Written some time after the publication of *Tom Jones* and *Roderick Random*, it contains Richardson's only published reflection on the novels of his great contemporaries:

The Editor of the foregoing collection has the more readily under-taken to publish it, because he thinks human nature has often, of late, been shewn in a light too degrading; and he hopes, from this series of letters, it will be seen, that characters may be good without being unnatural. Sir Charles Grandison himself is sensible of imperfections, and, as the reader will remember, accuses himself more than once, of tendencies to pride and passion, which it required his utmost caution and vigilance to reign in. . . .

Notwithstanding this, it has been observed by some, that, in general, he approaches too near the faultless character, which critics censure as above nature; yet it ought to be observed, too, that he performs no one action which is not in the power of any man in his situation to perform; and that he checks and restrains himself in no one instance in which it is not the duty of a prudent and good man *to* restrain himself.[15]

This was written after Samuel Johnson's important conservative state-ment in *Rambler*, 4 (No. 33), and no doubt it was partly a result of the stand which Johnson had already taken. The Concluding Note to *Sir Charles Grandison*, however, is very much in harmony with the novel itself; it reflects Richardson's hardened conservatism and confident assertion of his own formula against naturalistic criticism and the success of his rivals.

This increased conservatism and self-approbation was unfortunate, because it led the novelist from *Clarissa* to *Sir Charles Grandison*. It also provided a firm basis for the conservatism of other critics. The publica-tion of *Pamela* and *Clarissa* had transformed the status of the novel in England—had, indeed, transformed the novel itself. Richardson's theory was not entirely original and was not likely to encourage very daring critical thought, but his practice made the novel a force to be considered in the moral and in the aesthetic world. It was Richardson's conscious intention, fully documented in the Concluding Note to *Clarissa*, to expand the realm of fiction and to bring his own work into line with contemporary ideas about Christian tragedy. The heightened effects of *Clarissa* and the vein of sentiment which he exploited became potent stimuli in their own right and contributed to the development of Gothic and sentimental fiction. By the end of the century critics had realized this and had begun to compare what Richardson had actually done with what he had claimed to do. In the middle years of the cen-tury, however, there was widespread agreement about the positive effects of his achievement and critics frequently cited his formula for the mixture of imitation and instruction. There were, after all, one, two, and later three works of fiction which could be admitted into the family, the boarding school and the drawing-room, and this had not been so before.

AFTER RICHARDSON: THE CONSERVATIVE REACTION
TO THE NOVEL

Richardson's great success, followed immediately by that of Fielding and Smollett, had one effect he could not possibly have anticipated and which radically affected the attitude of critics to the new form. The public response to the great novels of the 1740's and 1750's stimulated an enormous increase in novel-writing, together with the machinery for its distribution in the circulating libraries. Plagiarism and the revamping of works already published became widespread, and the demand grew so fast that even the most enterprising booksellers, with the most industrious hacks in their employ, could not keep pace. The fiction which resulted was aptly described by one reviewer of the 1790's as 'a horrible mass of hurtful insignificance'.

There was a widespread belief that this fiction was morally and intellectually dangerous.[16] In the 1750's writers in the essay-periodicals, retailing wild stories about seductions and elopements, began to speak in terms of the perversion of the female imagination and the disintegration of middle-class standards of behaviour. In the farce *Polly Honeycombe* (1760) George Colman depicted a novel-reading miss defying all social conventions and parental authority, determined to make her day-to-day life resemble the plot of a very bad novel. The situation may not have been as Colman suggests, but it was believed to be so, and as the century wore on writers to whom the novel itself was of no interest came to think that it had to be discussed in books on morality, marriage and health. Mary Hays, herself a novelist in a very small way, thought (No. 91) that careful mothers could minimize the dangers besetting novel-reading daughters. Others were more pessimistic and, like the French surgeon quoted in *The Monthly Review* in 1773, were seriously worried about the effects of novel-reading on the female mind and on the reproduction of the race.

One result of the widespread concern about the quality and effects of contemporary fiction was the tendency to look back with nostalgia to the heroic romance. Even before Charlotte Lennox had published her attack on the romance (No. 43), some writers had begun to forget that it projected a ludicrous image of human life. William Whitehead, for example, came to think of the works of Scudéry and Calprenède as the product of a golden age, when writers took care to present a pure and elevated idea of life. Whitehead's view was reiterated by Anna Barbauld (No. 69) in 1773, by Vicessimus Knox (No. 74) in 1778, and became a platitude of late eighteenth-century conservative criticism.

Not all conservatives, however, were reactionary, and many critics were content to base their theory on the example of Richardson, contrasting his practice with that of Fielding or Smollett. Tradition has it that it was the publication of *Tom Jones* and *Roderick Random* which provoked Johnson to write in the *Rambler* (No. 33) the first substantial attack on realism of character and action. In this article Johnson admits the potential of the novel form as distinct from the romance. However, because he thinks that the novel is directed at 'the young, the ignorant, and the idle', he is preoccupied with the dangers involved in its attraction for unformed minds. Asserting that mere imitation of life is not a legitimate end of art, he emphasizes the importance of examples of a 'perfect idea of virtue', after the manner of Richardson. Most dangerous of all, he declares, is the character in whom good and evil qualities are mixed, whose virtues woo the innocent to admire their vices. This is the 'mixed' character who, after Johnson's discussion, was to be a frequent subject of debate.

Johnson's attack on the mixed character is surprising in view of the fact that he was fully aware of the arguments which had been going on for a century about realism of character in the drama and the epic poem. Aristotle himself had distinguished between the moral beauty of a character and his poetic beauty, and there had been many critics to explain that the latter depended on the extent to which that character and his actions were integrated with the moral design of the whole work. Both Dryden and Pope, among many others, had defended the mixed character in the epic poem on the grounds that Homer and Virgil hold up vice to the abhorrence of their reader.[17] Johnson's argument, by comparison with that of Dryden and Pope, is confused. Johnson equates 'promiscuous description' of life with the absence of moral design. In connection with the epic, he would probably have been prepared to admit that the selection of 'those parts of nature, which are most proper for imitation' depended on the nature of the artist's overall design. In the *Rambler* article he wrote as if he discounted the possibility of all but the crudest type of design. He overstressed the power of example and would permit the depiction of vice only when it was made repugnant, firmly setting himself against realism of character.

A discussion of the dangers of the mixed character is an almost invariable feature of conservative criticism in the eighteenth century, by far the greater part of which appears in the numerous essay-journals. John Hawkesworth, author of *The Adventurer* (No. 46), rejected mere didacticism and the accumulation of exemplary character and said that it was necessary to interweave plot and moral in significant action. In spite of this sophisticated attitude, he went on to state that 'The relation of events becomes a moral lecture, when vicious actions produce misery . . . [and] the combat of virtue is rewarded with honour'. Henry Mackenzie, whose attitude in general was enlightened and liberal, ended his paper in *The Lounger* (No. 77) with a solemn warning about the dangers of introducing a mixed character even when it is designed to have a moral effect. Because he felt that the reader was insensibly drawn to imitate the character whom he admired, he followed Johnson and Hawkesworth, and in turn was followed by others, in thinking that the mixed character presented a peculiar danger and encouraged people to think that they could compensate for specific vices with specific virtues. These writers indirectly paid a high compliment to the novelists in arguing as if the intimate relationship between their subject-matter and the life of the ordinary reader were strong enough to overcome moral training and even the moral design of the works themselves. Their arguments now seem reactionary and irrelevant. At the time they were produced by a real sense of urgency and a determination to come to grips with the problems that the novel presented.

Critics were also concerned about the more indirect effects of works which could be claimed to be innocuous or morally beneficial. Mrs. Barbauld, for example, was afraid that constant exposure to scenes of exciting pathos might in time weary the sympathies and end by producing callousness; and that the heightened and artificial picture of suffering virtue might create expectations which life could not realize. Meanwhile, writers who had fully assimilated Richardsonian principles were beginning to look again at the work of the master and to question the morality of depicting vice even for a good purpose. Oliver Goldsmith, annoyed at the popularity of *Tristram Shandy*, spoke out strongly (No. 55) against the depiction of any kind of vice, rejecting even the ancient plea that fiction represented vice punished and virtue rewarded:

'Granted. But will the greater number of readers take notice of these punishments and rewards? Are not their minds carried to something else?' Vicessimus Knox, writing in 1778 (No. 74), criticized Richardson for depicting the rape of Clarissa, though he admitted that the author wrote 'with the purest intention of promoting virtue'. James Beattie, a more intelligent critic, directed his attention to the character of Lovelace, arguing (No. 76) that while the novelist should not attempt to make his characters too perfect, Richardson had created a villain who was dangerously attractive and whose graces might even lead the innocent reader to imagine 'that a character so highly ornamented must have been a favourite of the author'.

Achilles and Macbeth, Beattie thought, are rendered harmless to the innocent reader by the fact that their criminal conduct is 'described and directed in such a manner, by the art of the poet, as to show, that it is hateful in itself, and necessarily productive of misery, both to themselves, and to mankind'. Yet it is very hard to see, on the evidence that Beattie produces, that the element of design is not present in the work of Richardson also. Lovelace's behaviour to Clarissa is certainly hateful in itself and productive of misery to himself and others.

Beattie concludes his essay with an apology for having considered the subject of prose fiction: 'Let not the usefulness of Romance-writing be estimated by the length of my discourse upon it. Romances are a dangerous recreation.' In this he is typical of many of his contemporaries, who discussed the novel only because they felt obliged to take some account of the most disturbing and prominent literary issue of their day. Their attitude differed from that of critics before 1740 because they had seen that the novel which depicted life as it was or might be lived in their own society was a form to be respected. They also had a sense of urgent concern at the proliferation of trashy fiction and the serious effect that it seemed to be having. Consequently they were unwilling to come to grips with purely literary problems and when they did apply the literary criteria which they had learnt from their study of other forms, they rarely applied them consistently. The epic poem and the Shakespearian play were distant in time and manners, but the work of Fielding was uncomfortably close, raising vital moral questions and sometimes reflecting a disturbing disparity between reality and the orthodox moral scheme.

THE DEVELOPMENT OF THEORY

Respect for the novel gradually increased throughout the century, in spite of conservative opposition, and writers began to acknowledge the qualities required to produce outstanding works of fiction. A reviewer of *The History of Tom Fool* (1761) said (No. 54) that good novels required a measure of genius in their composition which put them in a higher rank than the work before him:

> A tolerable share of sense, and a turn for observation, will carry one a good way in making just remarks, and pertinent reflections on men and manners; but it requires the peculiar abilities of a genius to give proper and consistent sentiments to his characters, and to throw his materials together into a form that may be admired, for the beauty of its composition, when the characters and incidents have lost their novelty.

Later in the century Henry Mackenzie (No. 77) and Richard Cumberland (No. 96) pointed out that the writing of a good novel presented peculiar problems which were at least as difficult to overcome as those presented by any other literary form. In 1796 John Moore, like Mackenzie and Cumberland, himself a novelist, in his Introduction to an edition of the works of Smollett, gave a reasonable discussion of all the conservative objections to the novel and a statement of the special benefits it could provide. Gradually a body of reasonable argument in defence of the novel began to develop. The old objections lasted into the nineteenth century, even gaining strength after the Evangelical movement, but by that time they were associated with an extreme religious position.

As a respectful attitude became more established, critics began to give serious attention to the problems of classification created by the increase in the output and the range of fiction. Richard Hurd threw the weight of his authority on to the conservative side with the argument that the novel, lacking verse, was an 'illegitimate' and motley form, outside the domain of literary kinds, but few voices echoed his. Increasingly critics tended to bring the novel within the existing frame of reference and to describe it with the terms at their disposal—both of which were derived from Aristotle. James Beattie (No. 76), for example, who produced the most consistent attempt to divide the new field into classes and types (1783), began by distinguishing the novel from other prose forms on the grounds that they employed fiction as a means to a satirical or an allegorical end.[18] Beattie divided what he thought was the novel proper into two main groups, serious romance and comic romance, both of which he called 'poetical' because their main end was imitation. These two groups he further divided into those which followed the 'historical' or purely sequential arrangement and those which began *in media res*. Thus he arrived at four basic categories, which he illustrated by referring to four different novels: the serious historical (*Robinson Crusoe*); the serious poetical (*Clarissa*); the comic historical (*Gil Blas*); and the comic poetical (*Tom Jones*)— but more properly, according to Beattie, called the Comic Epic Poem. Less thorough attempts at classification were made by other writers, but always on similar grounds, which persisted well into the next century and appeared with little change in John Dunlop's *History of Fiction* (1816).

Statements about structure and technique tended to be made most often in discussion of Fielding. Richardson provided the terms in which his own work had to be discussed. Smollet wrote (No. 49) in defiance of one of the most important of the Aristotelean dicta. He argued that the novel is 'a large diffused picture, comprehending the characters of life, disposed in different groupes, and exhibited in various attitudes, for the purpose of an uniform plan' and that 'a principal personage' was required to attract the reader's attention and unify the incidents by virtue of his own importance. This was not encouraging to the critic who remembered the authoritative statement in the *Poetics* that 'A fable is not one, as some conceive it to be, merely because the hero of it is one'. On the other hand, Fielding had read the *Poetics* at least as well as the commentators, and a stream of critics directed public attention to the fact that his great work was composed in strict accordance with the 'rule' that a fable 'being the imitation of an action, should be an imitation of an action that is one and entire, the parts of it being so connected that if any one of them be either transposed or taken away the whole will be destroyed or changed . . .'. This was remarked as soon as *Tom Jones* appeared. Although the writer who reviewed the novel for *The London Magazine* (No. 30) did not have much space for comment, he did say:

> This piece, like all such good compositions, consists of a principal history, and a great many episodes or incidents; all which arise naturally from the subject, and contribute towards carrying on the chief plot or design.

The writer of the pamphlet *On the New Species* (No. 35) missed the opportunity for a commentary on this aspect of his author's work and left it for Arthur Murphy (No. 62), in his Introduction to the collected edition of Fielding's work (1762), to make the definitive statement about Fielding's structural achievement. Whatever injustice Murphy may have done Fielding's character, he gave an excellent account of the novels, exceeding any previous commentator in length and depth of analysis. Murphy was prepared to consider *Tom Jones* 'in the same light in which the ablest critics have examined the *Iliad*, the *Aeneid*, and the *Paradise Lost*, namely, with a view to the fable, the manners, the sentiments, and the stile'. His essay is the most sustained piece of work on Aristotelean principles that appeared during the century. He considers the four features of his subject in order, beginning with the fable, touching on the variety of character and style and the fitness of expression to character, drawing out each aspect in a detailed comparison with the novels of Marivaux.[19]

Murphy's praise was echoed in an essay which Beattie composed in 1762 and published fourteen years later (No. 61), where he said that the plots of *Tom Jones* and *Amelia* 'would bear to be examined by Aristotle himself, and, if compared with those of Homer, would not greatly suffer in the comparison'. Beattie thought that in this respect Fielding was superior even to Cervantes, in that 'his most perfect unity' was achieved 'by natural means, and human abilities, without any machinery:—while his great master Cervantes is obliged to work a miracle for the cure of Don Quixote'. Later, Henry Pye (No. 79) used the language of Aristotle himself to describe Fielding's 'inimitable comic epopee' and James Burnet, Lord Monboddo (No. 70), announced that the perfect structure of *Tom Jones* entitles Fielding to be called 'one of the greatest poetical geniuses of his age'. Such praise is ample evidence that eighteenth-century critics were prepared to recognize ability and to adjust their inherited terminology to the unfamiliar medium of prose fiction.

A subordinate issue which attracted the attention of critics throughout the period was the debate about the relative merits of the epistolary and the narrative methods of telling a story. Very soon after the publication of *Pamela* critics were aware of the importance of Richardson's technical innovation and the part which it played in his success. One of his correspondents was sharp-sighted enough to perceive that the epistolary method was not suitable for every kind of story. Mrs. Donellan, though she told him (No. 34) 'The epistolary style is yours,

'tis speaking, 'tis painting', also warned him that it might prove unsuccessful in the case of *Sir Charles Grandison*. Richardson's mode was
praised in the *Gentleman's Magazine* (No. 32), where it was said that
the narrative method led to implausibility:

> Romances in general, and *Marivaux's* among others, are wholly
> improbable; because they suppose the history to be written after
> the series of events is closed by the catastrophe; a circumstance,
> which implies a strength of memory, beyond all example and prob-
> ability, in the persons concerned. . . . Or rather it implies a yet more
> improbable confidence and familiarity between all these persons and
> the author.

This is a rather naïve objection, but it is counterbalanced by the
writer's realization that the epistolary form requires us to accept an
uncommon taste for letter-writing and unusual willingness to transcribe minute events and details of conversation. The *Monthly* reviewer
of Mrs. Sheridan's *Memoirs of Miss Sidney Bidulph* (No. 56) took up a
similar position: 'Under correction of the critics', he expressed great
admiration 'of this kind of dramatic writing; where every character
speaks in his own person, utters his feelings, and delivers his sentiments warm from the heart', though he felt obliged to remark that
novels composed in this way 'necessarily appear prolix and redundant'.
Prolixity gave other commentators concern. James Beattie (No. 76)
observed that the form enabled the writer to create and maintain
suspense and to please by variety of effect, but pointed out that 'unless
the fable be short and simple, this mode of narration can hardly fail to
run out into an extravagant length, and be encumbered with repetitions'. John Moore (No. 99) chose to stress the need for distinguishing
between letters written by different characters, in illustration of which
he cited Rousseau's failure and Richardson's success. Richard Cumberland brought to his discussion of the subject (No. 96, III, 1) his experience as a novelist who had used both forms. He neatly summarized
the advantages and disadvantages of both methods of narration, and
concluded: 'Upon the whole, I should conjecture that the writer is best
accommodated by the one, and the reader most gratified by the other.'

Although comparatively minor points, like the relative merits of
narrative forms, were frequently and well discussed, issues of more
far-reaching importance met with much less consideration. One of the
most surprising examples of this failure is the absence of any coherent
thinking about the relationship between the technical features of a

work and its moral design. Conservative critics tended to confuse the element of design with the subject-matter. Most managed to avoid the simplicity of the Rev. Philip Skelton, who advised Richardson (No. 45) 'to stuff your works with adventures, and wedge in events by way of primings, especially when wit and humour happen to be scarce'. On the other hand, few rose above the idea suggested by Smollett's description of his purpose in the Preface to *Roderick Random* (No. 27), or Fanny Burney's declaration in the Preface to *Evelina* (No. 73). One of the predominant ideas was most appealingly expressed by Addison in the *Tatler* (1709), where he confessed his preference for fictitious history over real history on the grounds that it enables us to describe the perfect pattern of Divine justice, which is not otherwise perceptible in the temporal world.[20]

No one in the later part of the century argued quite so naïvely as Addison, but many did believe that the purpose of fiction was to strengthen virtue by providing an encouraging example. Even Smollett, in the Dedication to *Ferdinand Count Fathom* (No. 49), defended himself by pleading that he was showing vice meeting with proper punishment, although he was outraging the tenets of conservative criticism in depicting a villain as the hero of his story. Among the novelists, Courtney Melmoth (No. 71) was unusual in disclaiming responsibility for the vice of his characters, and the translator of *Werter* (No. 75) was almost alone in warning his readers about the danger of not distinguishing the author from the work. James Beattie (No. 61) made the basic observation that the author's design must be evident throughout the whole texture of a work, in the control and direction, and the same point was elaborated by Richard Cumberland (No. 96, VI, 1), who informed his readers that 'the spirit of the author will be seen in the general moral and tendency of the piece, though he will allot to every particular character its proper sentiment and language'.

Comments like these are casual and undeveloped; and they often exist side by side with statements of opinion with which they are inconsistent. Most of the intelligent remarks about the structure or style of novels were made by the novelist-critics, such as Cumberland, Mackenzie and Moore, who were under no obligation to present a coherent body of theory. Other writers were no less casual in their manner and often motivated by prejudice and suspicion.

The fact that Cumberland and Moore, two of the most sensible of the critics, were writing at the very end of the century indicates that there had been no lessening of interest in the problems which the novel presented. They were followed by others, such as John Dunlop, who studied the novel with objectivity and interest and carried criticism over into its next phase of development. Yet after the middle years of the century there were no new subjects for discussion, or any new lines of approach. Conservative writers like Anna Seward went on elaborating the Johnsonian position; writers less narrowly dogmatic went on discussing the topics which had interested their predecessors. The one major change which occurred was the development of regular and intensive reviewing by the monthly magazines. The established journals, the *Gentleman's Magazine*, *The Monthly Review*, *The Critical Review*, had always noticed fiction, but during the later decades of the century they were reviewing new publications more frequently and more thoroughly, and had been joined by a number of other organs, such as *The Analytical Review* (1788) and *The British Critic* (1793), for which novel-reviewing was an important activity. Thus the novel came to receive a great deal of close attention. Some of the reviews were brief and abrupt, but others, which dealt with the work of writers like Charlotte Smith, Ann Radcliffe, William Godwin and Fanny Burney, attempted to be something more than mere notices and frequently used the novel or romance concerned as a basis for generalization about the genre to which it belonged.

The reviewers often wrote with sensitivity and taste. They treated new novels with fairness and objectivity and took care to discriminate between the average stock of the circulating library and the serious attempt at literature. Yet their reviews too often consisted of rather weary repetition of the statements of earlier writers. The kind of general comment which was frequently made during these years is exemplified by a passage from a review of *The Denial* ... in *The Monthly Review* for 1790 (No. 88):

> The story of a novel should be formed of a variety of interesting incidents; a knowledge of the world, and of mankind, are essential requisites in the writer; the characters should be always natural; the personages should talk, think, and act, as becomes their respective ages, situations, and characters; the sentiments should be moral, chaste, and delicate; the language should be easy, correct, and elegant, free from affectation, and unobscured by pedantry; and the narrative should be as little interrupted as possible by digressions and episodes of every kind: yet if an author chuses to indulge, occasionally, in moral reflections, in the view of blending instruction with

amusement, we would not wish, altogether, to frustrate so good a design. . . .

The reviewers looked back on the novels of the mid-century as the high point of English fiction, and considered the fiction of their own day to represent a departure from the standards of Richardson, Fielding and Smollett. Yet they failed to distinguish between the work of these writers and that of their own contemporaries on anything but a superficial level. They thought of the novel as a sum of its parts—apt description, coherent action, accurate depiction of manners and character, lively sentiments, pure language—and they were content to praise a work possessing any combination of these features. Consequently, while they often stated that the romances of Mrs. Radcliffe were in a different class from the novels of Fielding, the basis of their distinction was merely the degree to which either writer imitated nature, a criterion which had been used so often, in so many contexts throughout the century, that it had lost its precision and usefulness.

The situation of these reviewers shows nothing more clearly than the degree of their dependence on the activity of the creative artists for ideas on which to construct their theory. This was so throughout the century. Richardson not only made fiction respectable, but also provided a basis for criticism from which the novel as it was practised by other writers could be attacked, Fielding gave a great impetus to criticism which depended on Aristotelian classification and terminology. The positive achievement of contemporary critics was in adapting themselves to the attitudes of these two writers. The negative aspect of their activity was their incapacity to adjust to other works, like *Tristram Shandy*, or to continue their own development past the point reached early in the second half of the century. In the period which followed the rejection of the romance there was no stimulus to the kind of serious criticism which the romance itself encouraged. The novelists lacked confidence and often integrity, leaving a wide gap between their claims and their performance. The mechanical criticism of the reviewers at the end of the century must be partly attributed to the state of contemporary fiction. In particular, the writers of the Gothic romances, concentrating on effects of beauty, sublimity, awe or terror, rather than subordinating them to an overall design, encouraged critics to think of fiction as mere entertainment. During the great period of eighteenth-century fiction, novelists assimilated into their work ideas which were of major importance in their intellectual and moral context and critics reacted with energy and ability. The theory formulated during that period was sufficiently flexible to last into the next century. After the 1820's novelists made new claims for their art and fiction became the vehicle of advanced thought. Only then did critics acquire a new sense of urgency and importance and only then did they begin to relate the work of the novelists to the lives of their readers and make a proper place for the novel in the contemporary system of thought.

1 From the translator's Preface to *Artamène ou le Grand Cyrus*, 1691

Artamène . . . was by Madeleine de Scudéry (1607–1701), who also wrote *Ibrahim* . . . (1641), *Clélie* (1656–60) and *Almahide* (1660). *Ibrahim* . . . was translated in 1652; *Clélie* was translated in part between 1655 and 1656 and was completed between 1656 and 1661, and was again translated between 1677 and 1678; *Almahide* appeared in English in 1677. *Artamène* . . . was first translated between 1653 and 1655, but the Preface reproduced below is taken from the octavo edition of the 1653–5 translation, published in 1691.

TO THE READER

That most Incomparable *Romance*, so well known under the Title of ARTAMENES, or the Grand CYRUS, having withdrawn itself for some time from the Publick, for want of another Impression, is now sent forth a Second time, in hopes to meet the same Reception which the Former had, as well for the Fame of the Author, as the Noble Subject of the History: Of which it may be truly said, That never any thing was Writ with more Wit and Passion, than this may justly claim; and therefore not unworthy the most Ingenious and Refin'd Understandings. For our Author has so laid his Scenes throughout the whole Work, as to touch at the most Remarkable Affairs of his Time. For the Intrigues and Miscarriages of War and Peace are better, many times, laid open and Satyriz'd in a *Romance*, than in a downright History, which being oblig'd to name the Persons, is often forc'd for several Reasons and Motives to be too partial and sparing; while such disguis'd Discourses as these, promiscuously personating every Man, and no Man, take their full liberty to speak the Truth. Other Writers of this nature there are, who to tickle the ears of their Readers, make it their Business to embellish their Works with strange and forced Inventions, not carying for a Reputation farther than among the Ignorant, which are indeed the greater Multitude. These Men deceive their Readers, and by representing to their Fancies the Imitation of Impossibilities, lead them into the wrong Path of following Example; which never can be design'd to put us upon more than is in the Power of Mortals to perform: Whereas Monsieur SCUDERY, a Person of great Understanding, profuse Fancy, and clear Judgment, pursues exactly the Truth of History in most things; and where he deviates a little, 'tis only to accomplish his Particular Worthy, with the Virtues of Many: urging nothing either improbable, or impossible. And therefore you shall find the Author himself making an early Protestation in the Person of *Chrysantes*, That all was pure Truth which should be related in the History of *Artamenes*; and that if he should chance to fail, or lessen the Truth, it was the Modesty of *Artamenes*, which had accustom'd him to speak part of his Glory, and never to aggrandize the Greatness of his Atchievements.

If you ask what the Subject is; 'Tis the Height of Prowess, intermix'd with Virtuous and Heroick Love; consequently, the Language Lofty, and becoming the Grandeur of the Illustrious Personages that speak; so far from the least fully of what may be thought Vain or Fulsom, that there is not any thing to provoke a Blush from the most modest Virgin; While Love and Honour are in a Seeming Contention, which shall best instruct the willing-ear with most Delight.

As for the Alteration made in the Bulk of the Volumes, we consulted the Practice highly approv'd in *France* and other places beyond Sea, and lately much in use in *England*, of contracting cumbersome Folio's into a far lesser Compass, chiefly for the convenience of the Reader, by reducing them into so many smaller Divisions, as render them much more portable than before, and consequently less troublesome Companions for those that travel, or when their leisure hours invite 'em to delightful Conversation, under the pleasing Shades of Summer, with the Renowned *Artamenes*.

[. . . . .]

2 Preface to *Incognita*, 1691

by WILLIAM CONGREVE

Reader,

Some Authors are so fond of a Preface, that they will write one tho' there be nothing more in it than an Apology for its self. But to show thee that I am not one of those, I will make no Apology for this, but do tell thee that I think it necessary to be prefix'd to this Trifle, to prevent thy overlooking some little pains which I have taken in the Composition of the following Story. Romances are generally composed of the Constant Loves and invincible Courages of Hero's, Heroins, Kings and Queens, Mortals of the first Rank, and so forth; where lofty Language, miraculous Contingencies and impossible Performances, elevate and surprize the Reader into a giddy Delight which leaves him flat upon the Ground whenever he gives of, and vexes him to think how he has suffer'd himself to be pleased and transported, concern'd and afflicted at the several Passages which he has Read, *viz.* these Knights Success to their Damosels Misfortunes, and such like, when he is forced to be very well convinced that 'tis all a lye. Novels are of a more familiar nature; Come near us, and represent to us Intrigues in practice, delight us with Accidents and odd Events, but not such as are wholly unusual or unpresidented, such which not being so distant from our Belief bring also the pleasure nearer us. Romances give more of Wonder, Novels more Delight. And with reverence be it spoken, and the Parallel kept at due distance, there is something of equality in the Proportion which they bear in reference to one another, with that betwen Comedy and Tragedy; but the *Drama* is the long extracted from Romance and History: 'tis the Midwife to Industry, and brings forth alive the Conceptions of the Brain. *Minerva* walks upon the Stage before us, and we are more assured of the real presence of Wit when it is delivered *viva voce*——

> *Segnius irritant animos demissa per aurem,*
> *Quam quæ sunt oculis subjecta fidelibus, & quæ*
> *Ipse sibi tradit spectator.*——
>
> Horace.[1]

Since all Traditions must indisputably give place to the *Drama*, and since there is no possibility of giving that life to the Writing or Repetition of a Story which it has in the Action, I resolved in another beauty to imitate *Dramatick* Writing, namely, in the Design, Contexture and Result of the Plot. I have not observed it before in a Novel. Some I have seen begin with an unexpected accident, which has been the only surprizing part of the Story, cause enough to make the Sequel look flat, tedious and insipid; for 'tis but reasonable the Reader should expect it not to rise, at least to keep upon a level in the entertainment; for so he may be kept on in hopes that at some time or other it may mend; but the 'tother is such a balk to a Man, 'tis carrying him up stairs to show him the Dining-Room, and after forcing him to make a Meal in the Kitchin. This I have not only endeavoured to avoid, but also have used a method for the contrary purpose. The design of the Novel is obvious, after the first meeting of *Aurelian* and *Hippolito* with *Incognita* and *Leonora*, and the difficulty is in bringing it to pass, maugre all apparent obstacles, within the compass of two days. How many probable Casualties intervene in opposition to the main Design, *viz.* of marrying two Couple so oddly engaged in an intricate Amour, I leave the Reader at his leisure to consider: As also whether every Obstacle does not in the progress of the Story act as subservient to that purpose, which at first it seems to oppose. In a Comedy this would be called the Unity of Action; here it may pretend to no more than an Unity of Contrivance. The Scene is continued in *Florence* from the commencement of the Amour; and the time from first to last is but three days. If there be any thing more in particular resembling the Copy which I imitate (as the Curious Reader will soon perceive) I leave it to show it self, being very well satisfy'd how much more proper it had been for him to have found out this himself, than for me to prepossess him with an Opinion of something extraordinary in an Essay began and finished in the idler hours of a fortnight's time: for I can only esteem it a laborious idleness, which is Parent to so inconsiderable a Birth. I have gratified the Bookseller in pretending an occasion for a Preface; the other two Persons concern'd are the Reader and my self, and if he be but pleased with what was produced for that end, my satisfaction follows of course, since it will be proportion'd to his Approbation or Dislike.

3 From *The Athenian Mercury*

Saturday, December 17, 1692

The Athenian Mercury was set up in 1692 (at first under a slightly different title) by John Dunton (1659–1733), in collaboration with a group of writers which included Samuel Wesley, father of John and Dunton's brother-in-law. Swift and Sir William Temple were contributors. The publication was primarily designed to answer the questions of readers.

Quest. 2. Whether 'tis lawful to read Romances?

Answ. Every one grants that 'tis lawful to read Quintus Curtius, or Xenophon's *Life of Cyrus*, in both of which the Loves as well as Wars of two great Monarchs are describ'd. . . .[1] And if so, we think 'tis not easie to assign a reason why the same Stories mayn't be read, when the Heroes are made greater, and their Actions more compleat and lively than before, as in a good Romance they generally are, and particularly in the *Grand Cyrus*, and *Cassandra*: Tho' we think then that the Reading these Books may be lawful, and have some Convenience too, as to forming the Minds of Persons of Quality; yet we think 'em not at all convenient for the Vulgar, because they give 'em extravagant Idea's of practice, and before they have Judgment to byass their Fancies, generally make 'em think themselves some King or Queen, or other: . . . one Fool must be Mazares, t'other Artamen;[2] and so for the Women, no less than Queens or Empresses will serve 'em, the Inconveniences of which are afterwards oftentimes sooner observ'd than remedy'd. Add to this, the softening the Mind by Love, which are the greatest Subject of these sort of Books, and the fooling away so many hours, and days, and years, which might be much better employ'd, and which must be repented of: And upon the whole, we think Young People wou'd do better, either not to read 'em at all, or to use 'em more sparingly than they generally do, when once they set about 'em.

4 From the translator's Preface to *Cassandre*, 1703

Cassandre (1644–50), one of the most widely-known of the heroic romances, was by Gauthier de Costes de la Calprenède (1614–63), who also wrote *Cléopâtre* (1647–56) and *Pharamond* (1661–70). *Cassandre* was twice translated into English between 1652 and 1703; *Cléopâtre* made its appearance in England as *Hymen's Praeludia: or, Love's Masterpiece* (1652–9), and *Pharamond* was translated on two occasions (1662 and 1677).

A Preface to this Work, might well have been spared; yet complying with Custom, I shall only tell you, if what has been acceptable to the greatest part of *Europe*, and still continues its admirable Beauty and Lustre, deck'd in the rich Ornaments of an elegant Stile and sweetness of Language, coming very near to that of the Original, can yet be so successful as to please an Age pretending to be more refined than those of the former, I cannot but suppose I may without any scruple of those doubts and fears (that cause some Works of this nature to come abroad with a kind of a trembling, at the uncertain expectation of the Censure that will pass upon them in the various opinions of the World as to their Merit or Dis-esteem) present you with the Fam'd History of *Cassandra*, faithfully rendred into *English*, from the most correct Copy, that ever yet appear'd in the refined *French*; the Author of which (for the admirable Characters he has given of Vertue in its sublimest notions, as also an unshaken Fidelity and Constancy in what is or ought to be term'd the Essentials of Love, attended with un-blemished Honour in its superlative degree, concentered in illustrious persons of either Sex) has already engrossed to himself a Reputation and Esteem, fixed so high on the Pyramid of deserved Fame, that Prejudice is unable to reach it, and even the eyes of Envy grow weak and dazl'd in her fruitlesly raising them, to tarnish what shines so far above her Sphere.

I might make a long Encomium (and that very justly) on this so much celebrated Work, and tell the Reader, amongst many other admirable things, that it is a perfect pattern of virtuous Love and truly merited Honour, going about frivolously to illustrate what in no part has any occasion of Commendation to set it of. The Esteem it has already gained loudly speaks its due praises, and even those very few who may as yet remain ignorant of that, cannot long be so, if they dare but trust their Eyes or Ears with what will so powerly move upon their Minds and upon their Affections, that they will be insensibly carried away to pursue it to the end, and no doubt mingle some Tears with those of the unfortunate Ladies and valliant Heroes, whose virtuous and whose glorious Lives take up all the space of these many pages; or in a failure of it, their hearts must needs be obdurate beyond what is really Compassion, Good Nature, or, (as our Ladies term it,) Complacency. I am not vain in telling you, I have seen many Books of the Original blotted in a manner all over with tears, falling, no doubt, from those bright eyes that have traced the passionately moving lines that are to be found in this Translation. From the more tender-hearted they flowed without all peradventure spontaneously, by a natural Inclination to pity the afflicted, and where they meet with any thing of flinty, they perhaps mollified it by degrees, and at last forced that pearly dew to drop in spite of resistance, and pay an unvoluntary tribute to so many suffering Virtues, and to the misfortunes of the most worthy and greatest persons that former Ages could boast of. I must own indeed that to illustrate this Work, and to render it the more pleasingly ornamental, there is something of the Author's rich Conceits interwoven with the truth of those Histories, on which it is primarily grounded, which (like Roses and Jessamine intertwining with an over-spreading fragrancy and beauty to make some curious Bower) render it the more charming and delightful.

I think I need only tell you farther, that the design is the best that ever was laid on any History, and that this is so upon *Plutarch* and other Ancient Writers on the Life of *Alexander* the Great, his Victories over *Darius* and the *Persian* Monarchy, with other admirable Adventures; and that the Author was a Noble and Learned *Frenchman* (as well as a Lover) at the time he wrote it; which appears by the many Epistles I find in the Original, full of Love Compliments to his dear and adored *Calista*; who as he says inspired him to write very lively, and so feelingly the passions of others by that of his own: and indeed in the Characters he has given, from the lowest to the highest, I never heard it so much as contradicted, but that he has outdone all those that ever writ before him, or that have since attempted to come up to him. You may indeed, by the way, demand who this *Cassandra* is, that gives a name to the History, and it is but reasonable, for it will take up some time to find her out; yet here I shall only tell you that within a while you shall see her break through a Cloud in all her brightness, and know her to be that incomparable Beauty which put the whole World in admiration to find such perfection in Nature, which so easily could subdue her Conqueror, and captivate the hearts of all that beheld her, and whose Character I fear will be envied by some as much as it will be highly esteemed by others, who are not such Admirers of Beauty for its own particular, as they are Adorers of it when it comes cloathed with Robes of Virtue and Innocency.

Vale.

5 Preface to *The Secret History of Queen Zarah...*, 1705

by MARY DE LA RIVIÈRE MANLEY

Mary de la Rivière Manley (1672–1724), was a dramatist, translator and novelist. *Queen Zarah*...was followed by three publications (1709, 1710 and 1711), which completed the series which is known under the general title of *The New Atlantis*...The principles stated in this preface bear little resemblance to the author's practice; Mrs. Manley was well known in her period as the author of a succession of 'secret histories' and 'scandalous chronicles', with a more or less prominent element of indecency.

The Romances in *France* have for a long Time been the Diversion and Amusement of the whole World; the People both in the City and at Court have given themselves over to this Vice, and all Sorts of People have read these Works with a most surprizing Greediness; but that Fury is very much abated, and they are all fallen off from this Distraction: The *Little Histories* of this Kind[1] have taken place of *Romances*, whose Prodigious Number of Volumes were sufficient to tire and satiate such whose Heads were most fill'd with those Notions.

These little Pieces which have banish'd *Romances* are much more agreeable to the Brisk and Impetuous Humour of the *English*, who have naturally no Taste for long-winded Performances, for they have no sooner begun a Book but they desire to see the End of it: The Prodigious Length of the Ancient *Romances*, the Mixture of so many Extraordinary Adventures, and the great Number of Actors that appear on the Stage, and the Likeness which is so little managed, all which has given a Distaste to Persons of good Sense, and has made Romances so much cry'd down, as we find 'em at present. The Authors of Historical Novels,[2] who have found out this Fault, have run into the same Error, because they take for the Foundation of their History no more than one Principal Event, and don't overcharge it with *Episodes*, which would extend it to an Excessive Length; but they are run into another Fault, which I cannot Pardon, that is, to please by Variety the Taste of the Reader, they mix particular Stories with the Principal

History, which seems to me as if they reason'd Ill; in Effect the Curiosity of the Reader is deceiv'd by this Deviation from the Subject, which retards the Pleasure he wou'd have in seeing the End of an Event; it relishes of a Secret Displeasure in the Author, which makes him soon lose Sight of those Persons with whom he began to be in Love; besides the vast Number of Actors who have such different Interests, embarresses his Memory, and causes some Confusion in his Brain, because 'tis necessary for the Imagination to labour to recal the several Interests and Characters of the Persons spoken of, and by which they have interrupted the *History*.

For the Reader's better Understanding, we ought not to chuse too Ancient Accidents, nor unknown Heroes, which are fought for in a Barbarous Countrey, and too far distant in Time, for we care little for what was done a Thousand Years ago among the *Tartars* or *Ayssines*.[3]

The Names of Persons ought to have a Sweetness in them, for a Barbarous Name disturbs the Imagination;[4] as the Historian describes the Heroes to his Fancy, so he ought to give them Qualities which affect the Reader, and which fixes him to his Fortune; but he ought with great Care to observe the Probability of Truth, which consists in saying nothing but what may Morally be believed.

For there are Truths that are not always probable; as for Example, 'tis an allowed Truth in the *Roman History* that *Nero* put his Mother to Death, but 'tis a Thing against all Reason and Probability that a Son shou'd embrue his Hand in the Blood of his own Mother; it is also no less probable that a Single Captain shou'd at the Head of a Bridge stop a whole Army, although 'tis probable that a small Number of Soldiers might stop, in Defiles, Prodigious Armies, because the Situation of the Place favours the Design, and renders them almost Equal. He that writes a True History ought to place the Accidents as they Naturally happen, without endeavouring to sweeten them for to procure a greater Credit, because he is not obliged to answer for their Probability; but he that composes a History to his Fancy, gives his Heroes what Characters he pleases, and places the Accidents as he thinks fit, without believing he shall be contradicted by other Historians, therefore he is obliged to Write nothing that is improbable; 'tis nevertheless allowable that an Historian shows the Elevation of his *Genius*, when advancing Improbable Actions, he gives them Colours and Appearances capable of Perswading.

One of the Things an Author ought first of all to take Care of, is to keep up to the Characters of the Persons he introduces. The Authors of *Romances* give Extraordinary Virtues to their Heroins, exempted from all the Weakness of Humane Nature, and much above the Infirmities of their Sex; 'tis Necessary they shou'd be Virtuous or Vicious to Merit the Esteem or Disesteem of the Reader; but their Virtue ou[gh]t to be spared, and their Vices exposed to every Trial: It wou'd in no wife be probable that a Young Woman fondly beloved by a Man of great Merit, and for whom she had a Reciprocal Tenderness, finding her self at all Times alone with him in Places which favour'd their Loves, cou'd always resist his Addresses; there are too Nice Occasions; and an Author wou'd not enough observe good Sense, if he therein exposed his Heroins; 'tis a Fault which Authors of *Romances* commit in every Page; they would blind the Reader with this Miracle, but 'tis necessary the Miracle should be feisable,[5] to make an Impression in the Brain of Reasonable Persons; the Characters are better managed in the Historical Novels, which are writ now-a-days; they are not fill'd with great Adventures, and extraordinary Accidents, for the most simple Action may engage the Reader by the Circumstances that attend it; it enters into all the Motions and Disquiets of the Actor, when they have well express'd to him the Character. If he be Jealous, the Look of a Person he Loves, a Mouse, a turn of the Head, or the least complaisance to a Rival, throws him into the greatest Agitations, which the Readers perceive by a Counter-blow; if he be very Vertuous, and falls into a Mischance by Accident, they Pity him and Commiserate his Misfortunes; for Fear and Pity in Romance as well as Tragedies are the Two Instruments which move the Passion; for we in some Manner put our selves in the Room of those we see in Danger; the Part we take therein, and the fear of falling into the like Misfortunes, causes us to interest our selves more in their Adventures, because that those sort of Accidents may happen to all the World; and it touches so much the more, because they are the common Effects of Nature.

The Heroes in the Ancient *Romances* have nothing in them that is Natural; all is unlimited in their Character; all their Advantages have Something Prodigious, and all their Actions Something that's Marvellous; in short, they are not Men: A single Prince attact by a great Number of Enemies, is so far from giving way to the Croud, that he does Incredible Feats of Valour, beats them, puts them to flight, delivers all the Prisoners, and kills an infinite Number of People, to deserve the Title of a Hero. A Reader who has any Sense does not take part with these Fabulous Adventures, or at least is but slightly touch'd with them, because they are not natural, and therefore cannot be believ'd. The Heroes of the Modern Romances are better Characteriz'd, they give them Passions, Vertues or Vices, which resemble Humanity; thus all the World will find themselves represented in these Descriptions, which ought to be exact, and mark'd by Tracts which express clearly the Character of the Hero, to the end we may not be deceived, and may presently know our predominant Quality, which ought to give the Spirit all the Motion and Action of our Lives; 'tis that which inspires the Reader with Curiosity, and a certain impatient Desire to see the End of the Accidents, the reading of which causes an Exquisite Pleasure when they are Nicely handled; the Motion of the Heart gives yet more, but the Author ought to have an Extraordinary Penetration to distinguish them well, and not to lose himself in this Labyrinth. Most Authors are contented to describe Men in in general, they represent them Covetous, Courageous and Ambitious, without entering into the Particulars, and without specifying the Character of their Covetousness, Valour or Ambition; they don't perceive Nice Distinctions, which those who know it Remark in the Passions; in Effect, the Nature, Humour and Juncture, give New Postures to Vices; the Turn of the Mind, Motion of the Heart, Affection and Interests, alter the very Nature of the Passions, which are different in all Men; the Genius of the Author marvellously appears when he Nicely discovers those Differences, and exposes to the Reader's Sight those almost unperceivable Jealousies which escape the Sight of most Authors, because they have not an exact Notion of the Turnings and Motions of Humane Understanding; and they know nothing but the gross Passions, from whence they make but general Descriptions.

He that Writes either a True or False History, ought immediately to take Notice of the Time and Sense where those Accidents happen'd, that the Reader may not remain long in Suspence; he ought also in few Words describe the Person who bears the most Considerable Part in his Story to engage the Reader; 'tis a Thing that little conduces to the raising the Merit of a Heroe, to Praise him by the Beauty of his Face; this is mean and trivial, Detail discourages Persons of good Taste; 'tis the Qualities of the Soul which ought to render him acceptable; and there are those Qualities likewise that ought to be discourag'd in the Principle Character of a Heroe, for there are Actors of a Second Rank, who serve only to bind the Intrigue, and they ought not to be compar'd with those of the First Order, nor be given Qualities that may cause them to be equally Esteem'd; 'tis not by Extravagant

Expressions, nor Repeated Praises, that the Reader's Esteem is acquired to the Character of the Heroe's, their Actions ought to plead for them; 'tis by that they are made known, and describe themselves; altho' they ought to have some Extraordinary Qualities, they ought not all to have 'em in an equal degree; 'tis impossible they shou'd not have some Imperfections, seeing they are Men, but their Imperfections ought not to destroy the Character that is attributed to them; if we describe them Brave, Liberal and Generous, we ought not to attribute to them Baseness or Cowardice, because that their Actions wou'd otherwise bely their Character, and the Predominant Virtues of the Heroes: 'Tis no Argument that *Salust*,[6] though so Happy in the Description of Men, in the Description of *Cataline* does not in some manner describe him Covetous also; for he says this Ambitious Man spent his own Means profusely, and raged after the Goods of another with an Extream Greediness, but these Two Motions which seem contrary were inspired by the same Wit; these were the Effects of the Unbounded Ambition of *Cataline*, and the desire he had to Rise by the help of his Creatures on the Ruins of the *Roman* Republick; so vast a Project cou'd not be Executed by very great Sums of Money, which obliged *Cataline* to make all Sorts of Efforts to get it from all Parts.

Every Historian ought to be extreamly uninterested; he ought neither to Praise nor Blame those he speaks of; he ought to be contented with Exposing the Actions, leaving an entire Liberty to the Reader to judge as he pleases, without taking any care not to blame his Heroes, or make their Apology; he is no judge of the Merit of his Heroes, his Business is to represent them in the same Form as they are, and describe their Sentiments, Manners and Conduct; it deviates in some manner from his Character, and that perfect uninterestedness, when he adds to the Names of those he introduces Epithets either to Blame or Praise them; there are but few Historians who exactly follow this Rule, and who maintain this Difference, from which they cannot deviate without rendring themselves guilty of Partiality.

Although there ought to be a great Genius required to Write a History perfectly, it is nevertheless not requisite that a Historian shou'd always make use of all his Wit, nor that he shou'd strain himself, in Nice and Lively Reflexions; 'tis a Fault which is reproach'd with some Justice to *Cornelius Tacitus*,[7] who is not contented to recount the Feats, but employs the most refin'd Reflexions of Policy to find out the secret Reasons and hidden Causes of Accidents, there is nevertheless a distinction to be made between the Character of the Historian and the Heroe, for if it be the Heroe that speaks, then he ought to express himself Ingeniously, without affecting any Nicety of Points or Syllogisms, because he speaks without any Preparation; but when the Author speaks of his Chief, he may use a more Nice Language, and chuse his Terms for the better expressing his Designs; Moral Reflexions, Maxims and Sentences are more proper in Discourses for Instructions than in Historical Novels, whose chief End is to please; and if we find in them some Instructions, it proceeds rather from their Descriptions than their Precepts.

An Acute Historian ought to observe the same Method at the Ending as at the Beginning of his Story, for he may at first expose Maxims relating but a few Feats, but when the End draws nigher, the Curiosity of the Reader is augmented, and he finds in him a Secret Impatience of desiring to see the Discovery of the Action; an Historian that amuses himself by Moralizing or Describing, discourages an Impatient Reader, who is in haste to see the End of Intrigues; he ought also to use a quite different Sort of Stile in the main Part of the Work, than in Conversations, which ought to be writ after an easie and free Manner: Fine Expressions and Elegant Turns agree little to the Stile of Conversation, whose Principal Ornament consists in the Plainness, Simplicity, Free and Sincere Air, which is much to be preferr'd before a great Exactness: We see frequent Examples in Ancient Authors of a Sort of Conversation which seems to clash with Reason; for 'tis not Natural for a Man to entertain himself, for we only speak that we may communicate our Thoughts to others; besides, 'tis hard to comprehend how an Author that relates Word for Word, the like Conversation cou'd be instructed to repeal them with so much Exactness; these Sort of Conversations are much more Impertinent when they run upon strange Subjects, which are not indispensibly allied to the Story handled: If the Conversations are long they indispensibly tire, because they drive from our Sight those People to whom we are engaged, and interrupt the Sequel of the Story.

'Tis an indispensible Necessity to end a Story to satisfie the Disquiets of the Reader, who is engag'd to the Fortunes of those People whose Adventures are described to him; 'tis depriving him of a most delicate Pleasure, when he is hindred from seeing the Event of an Intrigue, which has caused some Emotion in him, whose Discovery he expects, be it either Happy or Unhappy; the chief End of History is to instruct and inspire into Men the Love of Vertue, and Abhorrence of Vice, by the Examples propos'd to them; therefore the Conclusion of a

Story ought to have some Tract of Morality which may engage Virtue; those People who have a more refin'd Vertue are not always the most Happy; but yet their Misfortunes excite their Readers Pity, and affects them; although Vice be not always punish'd yet 'tis describ'd with Reasons which shew its Deformity, and make it enough known to be worthy of nothing but Chastisements.

6 John Dennis: (a) from the *Essay on the Genius and Writings of Shakespeare*, 1712; (b) from *Remarks upon Cato*, 1713

John Dennis (1657–1734), author of several tragedies, one of which was satirized by Pope (*Essay on Criticism*, III, 585–8), with whom he conducted a controversy, also wrote *The Advancement and Reformation of Poetry* (1701) and *The Growth of Criticism in Poetry* (1704).

Joseph Addison's *Cato* was produced in 1713.

(a)—[. . . . .]
We find that a Romance entertains the generality of Mankind with more Satisfaction than History, if they read only to be entertain'd; but if they read History thro' Pride or Ambition, they bring their Passions along with them, and that alters the case. Nothing is more plain than that even in an Historical Relation some Parts of it, and some Events, please more than others. And therefore a Man of Judgment, who sees why they do so, may in forming a Fable, and disposing an Action, please more than an Historian can do. For the just Fiction of a Fable moves us more than an Historical Relation can do, for the two following Reasons: First, by reason of the Communication and mutual Dependence of its Parts. For if Passion springs from Motion, then the Obstruction of that Motion or a counter Motion must obstruct and check the Passion: And therefore an Historian and a Writer of Historical Plays passing from Events of one nature to Events of another nature without a due Preparation, must of necessity stifle and confound one Passion by another. The second Reason why the Fiction of a Fable pleases us more, than an Historical Relation can do, is, because in an Historical Relation we seldom are acquainted with the true Causes of Events, whereas in a feign'd Action which is duly constituted, that is, which has a just beginning, those Causes always appear. For 'tis observable, that both in a Poetical Fiction and an Historical Relation, those Events are the most entertaining, the most surprizing, and the most wonderful, in which Providence most plainly appears. And 'tis for this Reason that the Author of a just Fable, must please more than

the Writer of an Historical Relation. The Good must never fail to prosper, and the Bad must be always punish'd: Otherwise the Incidents, and particularly the Catastrophe which is the grand Incident, are liable to be imputed rather to Chance, than to Almighty Conduct and to Sovereign Justice.

[. . . . .]

(*b*)—[. . . . .]

But setting aside for a Moment the Rules of the *Drama*, which are the Rules of exact Reason, there is not with all its Improbability so much as any thing in this Tragedy[1] of that Art and Contrivance, which is to be found in an entertaining Romance or agreeble Novel; that Art and Contrivance, by which their Authors excite our Curiosities, and cause those eager Longings in their Readers to know the Events of things, those Longings, which by their pleasing Agitations, at once disturb and delight the Mind, and cause the prime Satisfaction of all those Readers who read only to be delighted. Instead of that this Author has found out the Secret, to make his Tragedy highly improbable, without making it wonderful, and to make some Parts of it highly incredible, without being in the least entertaining.

[. . . . .]

7 From the Preface to *The Lover's Secretary: or, the Adventures of Lindamira, A Lady of Quality*, 1713

According to W. H. McBurney's *A Check List of English Prose Fiction 1700–1739* (1960), this novel was first published in 1702. I have not seen what appears to be the only extant copy of this edition. Both the edition mentioned by McBurney and the 1713 edition, the Preface to which is reproduced below, have as part of their title, 'Revised and Corrected by Mr. Tho. Brown'. Presumably this was Thomas Brown (1663–1704), wit, satirist and translator, who was partly responsible for the English version of the works of Scarron (1700).

[In view of the fact that 'Foreign Amours and Scenes beyond the sea' have been recently so popular . . .
. . .]'Tis presum'd, that Domestick Intrigues, manag'd according to the Humours of the Town, and the natural Temper of the Inhabitants of this our Island, will be at least equally grateful. But above all, the weight of Truth, and the importance of the Matter of Fact, ought to over-balance the feign'd Adventures of a fabulous Knight-Errantry.
    [. . . . .]

8 *The History of Romances, An Enquiry into their Original; Instructions for composing them; An Account of the most Eminent Authors; With Characters and Curious Observations upon the Best Performances of that Kind,* 1715

The History of Romances ... was translated by Stephen Lewis from the French of Pierre Daniel Huet (1630–1721), Bishop of Avranches, scholar and controversialist, who also wrote *Censura Philosophiae Cartesianae* (1689), *Carmina Latina et Graeca* (1700) and *Histoire du commerce et de la Navigation des anciens* (1716). Huet's essay was originally entitled *Sur l'origine des Romans* (1670) and was addressed to Jean Regnault de Segrais (1624–1701), himself a writer of fiction, who published *Divertissements de la Princesse Auréliane* (1656–7) and *Bérénice* (1648–51). The essay was used as a preface by Samuel Croxall for his *Select Collection of Novels and Romances* (1720); see below, No. 13.

THE PREFACE

There is not any Speculation, which affords a more agreeable Pleasure to the Mind, than that of beholding from what Obscure and Mean Beginnings, the most Polite and Entertaining Arts have risen to be the Admiration and Delight of Mankind. To pursue them up to the most Abstruse Fountains, and then to view by what Steps they arise to Perfection; does not only excite an Amazement at their increase; but an Impatient Desire of Inventing some New Subject, to be improv'd and advanc'd by Posterity.

The first Occasion of Introducing *Romance* into the World, was, without Dispute, to mollify the Rigour of Precepts, by the Allurements of Example. Where the Mind can't be subdued into Virtue, by Reason and Philosophy; nothing can influence it more, than to present to it the Success and Felicity, which Crowns the Pursuit of what's Great and Honourable. As the *Poet* very elegantly alludes to *Homer*;

> *Qui quid fit pulchrum, quid turpe, quid utile, quid non*
> *Planius & melius, Chrysippo & Crantore dicit.*[1]

And since in all Ages there were very few real Instances, fit to be proposed for Exact Patterns of Imitation; the *Ingenious Fabulist* was forced to supply them out of his own Invention.

Hence it appears, that the Original of *Romance* is very Ancient; since this Way of Promoting Virtue has been received in the Earliest Ages; as is evident from the first Records of Mankind. And as it stands very remote from Modern Ages; so, That it is found out, must be an High Satisfaction to the Curious in Antiquity.

Upon this Account, They are very much indebted to the Labour and Penetration of *Huetius*; who has, with the greatest Accuracy and Judgment, traced the Subject he undertook to Illustrate, till he found it in its Infancy, involved in the Umbrage of *Fable*, and perplexed in the Folds of *Mystery* and *Riddle*.

This Task was enjoin'd Him (He informs us,) by his Acquaintance and Friend, Monsieur *Segrais*; a Gentleman very intimately versed in all Polite Learning; and admirably well qualified, to Discern and Judge, upon the Subject of *Romances*; since He had discover'd himself to be a Compleat Master in the Art, by several inimitable Productions of that Nature, which he published in the Language of his Country: A Country, Famous for all Sorts of Delightful Amusement, and producing Men of the Quickest Apprehension, and Strong Propensity to the Advancement of Letters; as appears from the Labours of the Learned of that Nation; among whom, *Huetius* has the Honour not to be the Lowest in Esteem.

This Modest *Encomium* may possibly be thought Profuse, upon the Author of so invaluable a Treatise as the following; but,

> *In tenui labor; at tenuis non gloria; si quem.*
> *Numina læva sinunt, auditque vocatus Apollo.*
>
> VIRG.[2]

And, in my Opinion, the Man who acquits himself well of the Province he undertakes, (tho' of small Importance) deserves as much, as He who has been more Fortunate in the Choice of a Subject for his Application.

Without doubt, *Huetius* was sensible of this; otherwise he would have bestowed his Time to a better Account, since He had before approv'd himself very well to the World, by his Ingenious Performances in Divinity, and other Learning. And I dare assert, that none of his Labours have contributed more to his Reputation, than his Accurate Disquisition into the *Original* of *Romances*.

For if it has not improved, It has certainly enlarg'd his Fame; because It is Recommended to the World, in Two of the most Extensive Languages Known in it; I mean, *Latin* and *French*: So that I have no great Reason to fear its being well received in *English*: Especially since *Romance* has of late convey'd it self very far into the Esteem of this Nation, and is become the Principal Diversion of the Retirement of People of all Conditions.

And (tho' we have been hitherto, for the most part, supply'd with Translations from the *French*) it is to be hoped, that we *won't* any longer subsist upon *Reverse*; but that some *English Genius* will *dare* to Naturalize *Romance* into our Soil;[3] which (I don't doubt) it will agree with, as well as that of a Neighbouring Country; since we are acknowledg'd to be very Ingenious, in Improving Foreign Inventions.

To promote this Design, the Reader will find in the following Treatise, the Best Instructions for Composing *Romances*, with all Necessary Dispositions for the Perfection of the *Art*. And because the only Way to a *Right Judgment* upon our own, is to Compare them with the *Performances* of other Men; Our Author has, with Great Perspicuity and Clearness, illustrated the Beauties, and pointed out the Deficiencies, of the Best Productions of this Kind; and, according to the Direction of the Poet,

——miscuit utile dulci.
HOR. [4]

I have no more to add, by way of *Preface*; but to hope the *Original* has not suffer'd, by Translation into *English*: If it has; This, I presume, is not the first Case, where a Good Design has aton'd for some slight Imperfections in the Prosecution of it.

ORIGINAL OF ROMANCES

Sir, our Curiosity and Desire to be inform'd of *The Original of Romances*, is both Reasonable and Natural, since you Excel in the Art of Composing them. I wish I may discover the same Perfection in the History I now send you of 'em.

At present my Books are not with me, and my Thoughts are taken up with Matters of a very different Nature. I am satisfy'd of the Labour and Difficulty of such an Attempt, since 'tis neither *Provence*, nor *Spain*, as some are of Opinion, that we shall find to have given Birth to this agreeable Amusement: We must in the Pursuit of it, enquire into the remotest Countries, and derive our Account from the most Latent Part of Antiquity. However, I must gratify your Request, since our continu'd and strict Friendship gives you a Right to demand, and divests me of the Power to deny you any Thing.

The Name of *Romance* was formerly extended not only to Prose but Verse; *Giraldi* and *Pigra*, in their Treatises *de Romanzi*,[5] scarce mention any other, and lay down the *Bayardos* and *Arioste*[6] for Instances of their Opinion. But the Custom of this Age prevails to the contrary; so that we esteen nothing to be properly *Romance* but Fictions of Love Adventures, disposed into an Elegant Style in Prose, for the Delight and Instruction of the Reader.

I call them Fictions, to discriminate them from True Histories; and I add, of Love Adventures, because Love ought to be the Principal Subject of *Romance*. It is required to be in Prose by the Humour of the Times. It must be compos'd with Art and Elegance, lest it should appear to be a rude undigested Mass, without Order or Beauty.

The principal End of *Romance*, or at least what ought to be so, and is chiefly to be regarded by the Author, is the Instruction of the Reader; before whom he must present Virtue successful, and Vice in Disgrace; but because the Mind of Man naturally hates to be inform'd, and (by the Influence of Self-Conceit) resists Instruction; 'tis to be deceived by the Blandishments of Pleasure; and the Rigor of Precept is to be subdued by the Allurements of Example. Thus we regulate our own Defects, and at the same Time condemn them in others.

Thus it appears, That the Entertainment of the Reader, which the Ingenious Romancer seems chiefly to design, is subordinate to his Principal Aim, which is the Instruction of the Mind, and Correction of Manners; and the Beauty of a *Romance* stands or falls according to its Attention to this Definition and End.

'Tis with an Account of this Sort that I shall endeavour to entertain you, and I hope your Curiosity extends no farther.

I shall not therefore in this Place take *Romances* in Verse, much less *Epic Poems*, which beside the Difference of their Style, are compos'd of very different Essentials which distinguish them from *Romances*: Tho' in several Respects there is a great Relation between them; and according to *Aristotle* (who informs us, That 'tis Ficton rather than Verse which makes a Poet) a Writer of *Romance* may be reckon'd among the Poets.[7] *Petronius* tells us, That Poems are to move in a great Circumference by the Ministry of the Gods, and Expressions vast and audacious;[8] so that First, They may be looked upon as Oracles throughout, from a Spirit full of Fury, and then for a faithful and exact Narration.

Romances preserve a much greater Simplicity, and are not so exalted, nor have the same Figures in Invention and Expression.

Poems have more of the sublime, though they are not always confined to Probability. *Romances* have more of Probability, though they don't advance so far toward the Sublime.

Poems are more regular and correct in the Frame of their Contrivance, and receive less Addition from Events and Episodes than *Romances*, which are capable of these Accessions, because their Style is not so elevated, and they don't so far distend the Intellect, so that they give it leave to admit a greater Number of different Ideas.

In short, *Poems* make some Military Act, or Politic Conduct, their Theme, and only descant upon Love at Pleasure; whereas *Romances*, on the contrary, have Love for their Principal Subject, and don't concern themselves in War or Politicks, but by Accident. I speak of Regular *Romances*, for those in Old *French*, *Spanish*, and *Italian*, have generally more of the Soldier than Gallant.

This induced *Giraldi* to conceive, That the Name *Romance* was derived from a *Greek* Word, signifying *Force* and *Strength*, since the Performances in that kind made it their Business to Illustrate and Display the Valour and Atchievements of the *Palladines*;[9] but *Giraldi* was mistaken in this, as you'll find hereafter.

Neither would I here be understood to comprehend Histories which are observed to contain many Falsities; such is that of *Herodotus* (which, by the Way, is not so Guilty in this Respect as some imagine): The Navigation of *Hanno*, the Life of *Apollonius* wrote by *Philostratus*, and many others.[10]

These Works are true in the Main, and false in some Parts. *Romances*, on the contrary, are false in the Gross, and true in some Particulars. These contain Truth mingled with Falshood; those Falshood irradiated by some Inspersion of Truth; I mean, that Falshood is so Predominant in *Romance*, that it may be altogether False in Whole and every Particular.

Aristotle informs us, That that Tragedy whose Argument is known, and extracted from History, is the most Perfect, because it arises nearer to Verisimility than that whose Subject is New and Fictitious.[11] However, this he does not condemn, because tho' the Plot of the Former be taken from History, yet the Generality of the Spectators may be Ignorant of it, and therefore this Sort can't fail to give Diversion to the Company. The same may be apply'd to *Romances*, with this Restraint, that a total Fiction of the Argument is more allowable in *Romances*, where the Actors are of indifferent Quality, (such are the Comic) than in Heroic Performances, where Princes and Conquerors are the Characters, and where the Adventures are Memorable and Illustrious; because it can't be probable that great Transactions and Events lie hid to the World, and neglected by Historians; and Probability, which is not always observ'd in History, is essential to a *Romance*.

I exclude that sort of History which is False throughout the whole Narration, but was invented through the Deficiency of true Accounts and Information; such are the imaginary Originals of most Nations, especially those which are Barbarous. Of this kind are the Histories so palpably forged by the Monk *Annius Viterbensis*, which deserve the Indignation and Contempt of the Learned World.[12]

There's the same difference between *Romances*, and these sort of Works, as between those, who by innocent Artifice Disguize themselves in Masquerade for their own Pleasure, and the Diversion of others, and those who assume the Name and Person of the Dead, or absent, or possess themselves of their Estates, by the Colour of a Resemblance to them.

Lastly, I shall exclude Fables from my Subject, for *Romance* is a Fiction of Things which may, but never have happen'd; whereas the Matter of Fables is what never has, nor ever will be perform'd.

[. . . . .][13]

Thus *Spain* and *Italy* received from us an Art, which was the Effect of our Ignorance and Barbarity, and which the Politeness of the *Persians*, *Ionians*, and *Greeks* had produced. As Necessity engages us, in a Dearth of Bread, to sustain our Bodies with Herbs and Roots; so when the Knowledge of Truth, which is the Proper and Natural Aliment of the Mind, begins to fail, we have Recourse to Falshood, which is the Imitation of Truth. As in Plenty we refuse Bread, and our ordinary Viands, for Ragousts; so our Minds, when acquainted with the Truth, forsake the Study and Speculation of it, to be entertained with its Image, which is Fiction. This Imitation, according to *Aristotle*, is often more agreeable than the Original itself;[14] so that two oppositely different Paths, which are Ignorance and Learning, Rudeness and Politeness, do often conduct us to the same End; which is, an Application to Fictions, Fables, and Romances. Hence it is, that the most Barbarous Nations are taken with Romantic Inventions, as well as the most Refined. The Originals of all the Savages of *America*, and particularly those of *Peru*, are nothing but Fables; no more are those of the *Goths*, which they wrote in their Ancient *Runic* Characters, upon great Stones; the Remains of which I my self have seen in *Denmark*. And if any Thing were left us of the Works, which the *Bards* among the Ancient *Gauls* composed, to eternize the Memory of their Nation, I don't question but we should find them enriched with Abundance of Fictions.

This Inclination to Fables, which is common to all Men, is not the Result of Reason, Imitation, or Custom. 'Tis Natural to them, and has its Seat in the very Frame and Disposition of their Soul. For the Desire of Knowledge is particular to Man, and distinguishes him from Beasts no less than his Reason. Nay we may observe in other Creatures some Rude Impressions of this; whereas the Desire of Understanding is Peculiar to Us only.

The Reason of this, according to my Opinion, is; because the Faculties of the Soul are of too Vast an Extent, to be supplied by the Present Objects, so that 'tis obliged to have recourse to what's past, and to come, in Truth and in Fictions, in Imaginary Spaces and Impossibilities, for Objects to exert it self upon. The Objects of Sense fill the Desires of the Soul of Brutes, who have no farther Concern; so that we can't discover in them these restless Emotions, which continually actuate the Mind of Man, and carry it into the Pursuit of a recent Information, to proportion (if possible) the Object to the Faculty; and enjoy a Pleasure, resembling that which we perceive in the Appeasing a Violent Hunger, and Extinguishing a Corroding Thirst. This is that which *Plato* intends, in the Marriage of *Dorus* and *Penia*, (in which Terms he would express Riches and Poverty,) which produces exquisite Pleasure.[15] The Object is signified by Riches, which are not so but in Use and Intention; otherwise they are Unfruitful, and afford no Delight. The Faculty is intended by Poverty; which is sterile, and always attended by Inquietude, while 'tis separated from Riches; whereas its Union with them, supplies the Highest Satisfaction. The Case is the same with our Souls: Poverty, the same with Ignorance, is Natural to it; it sighs continually after Science, which is its Riches; and when 'tis possess'd of this Enjoyment, it feels the greatest Pleasure. But this Pleasure is not always equal; it often is the Purchase of much Labour and Difficulty: As when the Soul applies it self to Intricate Speculations, and Occult Sciences, the Matter whereof is not present to our Senses; where the Imagination, which acts with Facility, has a Less Part in the Pursuit than the Understanding, whose Operations are more Vehement and Intense: And because Labour is naturally tedious, the Soul is not carried to Hard and Spinous[16] Learning, unless in Prospect of some Advantage, or Hopes of some remote Amusement, or else by Necessity. But the Knowledge which attracts and delights it most, is that which is acquired without Pain, and where the Imagination alone acts on Subjects which fall under our Sense, ravish our Passions, and are great Movers in all the Affairs of Life. Such are Romances, which require no great Intention or Dispense of Mind, to understand them. No long Reasonings are exacted; the Memory is not overburthened: Nothing is demanded, but Fancy and Imagination. They move our Passions; but 'tis on purpose to sooth and calm them again: They excite neither Fear nor Compassion; unless it be to display to us the Pleasure of seeing those we were afraid, or concern'd for, out of the Reach of Danger or Distress. In short, all our Emotions there find themselves agreeably provoked and appeased.

'Tis hence, that those who act more by Reason than Passion, and labour more with their Imagination than Understanding, are affected by them; tho' these other are touched by them too, but after another manner. These are touched by the Beauties of Art, which amuse the Understanding; but the former, Ignorant and Simple, are sensible of no more than what strikes upon the Imagination, and stirs their Passions. They love the Fiction, and enquire no farther. Now Fictions being nothing but Narrations, True in Appearance, and False in Reality; the Minds of the Simple, who discern only the Disguise, are pleased and highly satisfied with this Shew of Truth. But those who penetrate farther, and see into the Solid, are easily disgusted with the Falsity: So that the First love Falshood, because 'tis concealed under an Appearance of Truth; the Latter are distasted with the Image of Truth, because of the Real Forgery which is couched under it; unless it be varnished with Ingenuity, Subtilty, and Instruction, and recommends it self by the Excellency of Invention and Art. St. *Augustin* makes this Observation somewhere; 'That these Falsities which carry a Signification, and suggest an Hidden Meaning, are not Lies, but the Figures of Truth; which the most Wise and Holy Persons, and even our *Saviour* himself, have used upon Honourable and Pious Occasions.'[17]

Since then 'tis true, that Lies commonly flow from Ignorance, and the Grossness of our Intellect; and that this Inundation of the *Barbarians*, who issued from the *North*, spread over all *Europe*, and plunged it into such profound Ignorance, as it could not clear it self from, within the Space of Two Ages; is it not then probable, that this Ignorance caused the same Effect in *Europe*, which it had produced every where besides? And is it not vain to enquire for that in Chance, which we find in Nature? There is then no Reason to contend, but that *French*, *German*, and *English* Romances, and all the Fables of the *North*, are the Fruits of those Countries, and not imported from Abroad: That they never had other Originals than the Histories stuffed with Falsities, and made in Obscure Ignorant Times, when there was neither Industry nor Curiosity to discover the Truth of Things, nor Art to describe it, if 'twas found: That these Histories have been well received by the Unpolished and Half barbarous People; and that the Historians thereupon took upon them the Liberty to present them with what was purely forged, which were the Romances.

'Tis a common Opinion, that Histories have formerly been called by this Title, which is since applied only to Fictions; which is an Irrefragable Testimony that the one proceeded from the other.

Romances, [saith *Pigna*] according to the Common Opinion in *France*, were the *Annals*: And because the History of the War, which was published successively, had that Name; some afterwards who neglected the Truth, (howsoever Fabulous they were) gave their Writings the same Name.[18]

Strabo, in a Passage I have already alledged,[19] saith, That the Histories of the *Medes*, *Persians*, and *Syrians*, have deserved but little Credit; since those who wrote them, when they saw the Inventers of Fables in great Esteem, believed they might Establish Reputation, by writing Fables in the Form of Histories, which were the same with Romances. Whence we may conclude, that Romances had (in all Probability) the same Original with us, which they formerly had with other People.

But to return to the *Troubadours*, or *Trouverres*, (for so they called their Poets) of *Provence*, who were the Princes of Romancing in *France*. Their Mystery was so generally approved of, that all the Counties of *France* had Persons of that Profession.

The Eleventh Age produced a Matchless Number of them, both in Prose and Verse. Many of their Works are preserved, in Spite of the Envy of Time. Of this Number were the Romances of *Garin le Loheran*, of *Tristram*, *Lancelot*, *Du Lake*, *St. Greal*, *Merlin*, *Arthur*, *Perceval*, *Peneforest*, and of most of those 127 Poets who lived before the Year 1300, who have received the Censure of the President *Fauchet*.[20]

I shall not undertake to represent them in a Catalogue; nor examine whether the *Amadis de Gaul* were originally from *Spain*, *Flanders*, or *France*; and whether the Romance of *Tiel Ulespiegel* be a Translation from the *German*; or in what Language the Romance of the *Seven Wise Men of* Greece was first written; or that of *Dolopathos*, which some say was extracted from the Parables of *Sandaber* the *Indian*. Some say 'tis to be found in *Greek* in some Libraries; which has furnished the Matter of an *Italian* Book call'd *Erastus*, (and of many of *Boccace* his Novels, as the same *Fauchet* has remarked) which was written in *Latin* by *John Morck*, of the Abby *de Hauteselne*, whereof Ancient Copies are to be seen; and translated into *French* by the Clerk *Hubert*, about the End of the Twelfth Age, and into *High Dutch* about Three Hundred Years afterwards; and an Hundred Years after that, from *High Dutch* into *Latin* again, by a Learned Hand, who changed the Names of it, and was ignorant that the *Dutch* had come from the *Latin*.[21]

It shall suffice if I tell you, that all these Works which Ignorance has given Birth to, carried along with them the Marks of their Original, and were no other than a Complication of Fictions, grossly cast together in the greatest Confusion, and infinitely short of the Excellent Degree of Art and Elegance, to which the *French* Nation is now arrived in Romances. 'Tis truly a Subject of Admiration, that we, who have yielded to others the Bays for *Epic* Poetry, and History, have nevertheless advanced these to so high a Perfection, that the Best of theirs are not Equal to the Meanest of ours.

We owe (I believe) this Advantage to the Refinement and Politeness of our Gallantry; which proceeds, in my Opinion, from the great Liberty which the Men of *France* allow to the Ladies. They are in a manner Recluses in *Italy* and *Spain*; and separated from Men by so many Obstacles, that they are scarce to be seen, and not to be spoken with at all. Hence the Men have neglected the Art of Engaging the Tender Sex, because the Occasions of it are so rare. All the Study and Business there, is to surmount the Difficulties of Access; when this is effected, they make Use of the Time, without amusing themselves with Forms. But in *France*, the Ladies go at large upon their Parole; and being under no Custody but that of their own Heart, erect it into a Fort, more strong and secure than all the Keys, Grates, and Vigilance of the *Douegnas*.[22] The Men are obliged to make a Regular and Formal

Assault against this Fort, to employ so much Industry and Address to reduce it, that they have formed it into an Art scarce known to other Nations.

'Tis this Art which distinguishes the *French* from other Romances, and renders the Reading of them so Delicious, that they cause more Profitable Studies to be neglected.

The Ladies were first taken with this Lure: They made Romances their Study; and have despised the Ancient Fable and History so far, that they now no longer understand those Works, from which they received their greatest Embellishments: And lest they should blush at this Ignorance, which they find themselves so often guilty of; they perceive they had better disapprove what they don't know, than take the Pains to learn it.

The Men, in Complaisance, have imitated them; condemned what they disliked, and call that Pedantry, which made an Essential Part of Politeness, even in *Malherbe's* Time.[23] The Poets, and other *French* Writers who succeeded, have been constrained to submit to this Arbitration; and many of them, observing that the Knowledge of Antiquity would be of no Advantage to them, have ceased to study what they durst not practise: Thus a very Good Cause has produced an Ill Effect; and the Beauty of our Romances has drawn upon them the Contempt of Good Letters, and consequently Ignorance.

I don't, for all this, pretend to condemn the Reading of them. The Best Things in the World are attended with their Inconveniences; Romances too may have much worse than Ignorance. I know what they are accused for: They exhaust our Devotion, and inspire us with Irregular Passions, and corrupt our Manners. All this may be, and sometimes does happen. But what can't Evil and Degenerated Minds make an Ill Use of? Weak Souls are contagious to themselves, and make Poyson of every Thing. Histories must be forbidden, which relate so many Pernicious Examples; and the Fable must undergo the same Fate; for there Crimes are authorized by the Practice of the Gods.

A Marble Statue, which was adored by the Publick Devotion of the *Heathens*, incited the Passion, Brutality, and Despair of a Young Man.[24]

Cherea, in *Terence*, fortifies himself in a Criminal Design, at the Sight of a Picture of *Jupiter*, which drew the Reverence of all other Spectators.[25]

Little Regard was had to Sobriety of Manners, in most Part of the *Greek* and Old *French* Romances, by Reason of the Vice of the Times in which they were composed. Even the *Astrea*,[26] and some others which have followed, are Licentious. But the Modern Romances (I speak of the Good ones) are so far from this Fault, that you'll scarce find an Expression, or Word, which may shock Chaste Ears, or one single Action which may give Offence to Modesty.

If any one object; That Love is treated of in a Manner so Soft and Insinuating, that the Bait of this Dangerous Passion invades too easily the Tender Hearts: I answer, That it is so far from being Dangerous, that it is in some Respects Necessary, that the Young People of the World should be acquainted with it; that they may stop their Ears to that which is Criminal, and be better fortified against its Artifices; and know their Conduct, in that which has an Honest and Sacred End. This is so true, that Experience lays before us, that such as are least acquainted with Love, are the most unguarded to its Assaults, that the most Ignorant are the soonest decoyed. Add to this, that Nothing so much refines and polishes Wit; Nothing conduces so much to the Forming and Advancing it to the Approbation of the World, as the Reading of Romances. These are the Dumb Tutors, which succeed those of the College, and teach us how to Live and Speak by a more Persuasive and Instructive Method than their's; who deserve the Complement [*sic*] of *Horace* upon the *Iliad*, 'That it teaches Morality more effectually, than the Precepts of the most Able Philosophers.[27]

Monsieur *D'Urfee* was the first who retrieved them from Barbarity, and reduced them to Rules, in his Incomparable *Astrea*, The most Ingenious and Polite Work which has appeared in this Kind, and which Eclipsed the Glory which *Greece*, *Italy* and *Spain*, had acquired. However, he has not discouraged those who come after him to undertake what he has performed. He has not so far engrossed the Public Admiration, but that some are still left for the many Excellent Romances which displayed themselves in *France* since His.

None can, without Amazement, read those which a Maid, as Illustrious in her Modesty, as her Merit, has published under a Borrowed Name;[28] depriving her self so Generously of that Glory which was her Due, and not seeking for a Reward, but in her Virtue; as if while She took so much Trouble for the Honour of our Nation, She would spare that Shame to Our Sex. But Time has done her that Justice, which She denied her self; and has informed us, that the *Illustrious Bassa*, *Grand Cyrus*, and *Clælia*, are the Performances of Madam *de Scudery*: That the Art of making Romances, which might defend it self against Scrupulous Censures, not only by the Commendations which the Patriarch *Photius* gives it,[29] but by the great Examples of those who have applied themselves to it, might justify it self by Her's: That that which has been improved by Philosophers, as *Apuleius*, and *Athenagoras*; by a *Roman Prætor*, as *Sisenna*; by a *Consul*, as *Petronius*; by a Pretender to the Empire, as *Clodius Albinus*; by a Priest, as *Theodorus Prodromus*; by Bishops, as *Heliodorus*, and *Achilles Tatius*; by a Pope, as *Pius Secundus*, who wrote the Loves of *Euryalus* and *Lucretia*; by a Saint, as *John Damascenus*;[30] might have the Honour to be attended to by a Wife and Virtuous Maid.

For your Part, Sir, since 'tis true, as I have demonstrated, and *Plutarch* assures us, that one of the Greatest Charms which can affect the Soul of Man, is the Connexion of a Fable, well Invented, and well Related;[31] what Success may you not presume upon from *Zayde*, where the Adventures are so New and Touching, and the Narration so Just and Polite?[32]

I could wish, for the Concern I have for that Great Prince which Heaven has placed over us,[33] that we had a History of his Wonderful Reign, wrote in a Style so Noble, and with the same Accurateness and Discernment. The Virtues which conduct his Reign are so Noble, and the Fortune which attends them so Surprizing, that Posterity would doubt whether it were an History, or a Romance.

9 Preface to *Robinson Crusoe*, 1719

by DANIEL DEFOE

If ever the Story of any private Man's Adventures in the World were worth making Publick, and were acceptable when Publish'd, the Editor of this Account thinks this will be so.

The Wonders of this Man's Life exceed all that (he thinks) is to be found extant; the Life of one Man being scarce capable of a greater Variety.

The Story is told with Modesty, with Seriousness, and with a religious Application of Events to the Uses to which wise Men always apply them (*viz*) to the Instruction of others by this Example, and to justify and honour the Wisdom of Providence in all the Variety of our Cirumstances, let them happen how they will.

The Editor believes the thing to be a just History of Fact; neither is there any Appearance of Fiction in it: And however thinks, because all such things are dispatch'd, that the Improvement of it, as well to the Diversion, as to the Instruction of the Reader, will be the same; and as such, he thinks, without farther Compliment to the World, he does them a great Service in the Publication.

10 From *An Epistle to Daniel Defoe...*, 1719

by CHARLES GILDON

Charles Gildon (1665–1724), dramatist and critic, also wrote *The Lives and Characters of the English Dramatick Poets* (1710), *The Complete Art of Poetry* (1718), and *The Laws of Poetry ... explained and illustrated* (1721). This pamphlet was not published until after the appearance of Defoe's *Farther Adventures ...* (1719), but the earlier part of it was written immediately after the publication of *Robinson Crusoe*, as Gildon informs us in his *Postscript*; see below, No. 12.

Mr. *F——e,*

I have perus'd your pleasant Story of *Robinson Crusoe*; and if the Faults of it had extended no farther than the frequent Solecisms, Looseness and Incorrectness of Stile, Improbabilities, and sometimes Impossibilities, I had not given you the Trouble of this Epistle. But when I found that you were not content with the many Absurdities of your Tale, but seem'd to discover a Design, which proves you as bad an *Englishman* as a Christian, I could not but take Notice in this publick Manner of what you had written; especially, when I perceiv'd that you threaten'd us with more of the same Nature, if this met with that Success which you hop'd for, and which the Town has been pleas'd to give it. If by this I can prevent a new Accession of Impieties and Superstition to those which the Work under our Consideration has furnish'd us with, I shall not think my Labour lost.

I am far from being an Enemy to the Writers of Fables, since I know very well that this Manner of Writing is not only very Ancient, but very useful, I might say sacred, since it has been made use of by the inspir'd Writers themselves; but then to render any Fable worthy of being receiv'd into the Number of those which are truly valuable, it must naturally produce in its Event some useful Moral, either express'd or understood; but this of *Robinson Crusoe*, you plainly inculcate, is design'd against a publick Good. I think there can be no Man so ignorant as not to know that our Navigation produces both our

Safety and our Riches, and that whoever therefore shall endeavour to discourage this, is so far a profest Enemy of his Country's Prosperity and Safety; but the Author of *Robinson Crusoe*, not only in the Beginning, but in many Places of the Book, employs all the Force of his little Rhetoric to dissuade and deter all People from going to Sea, especially all Mothers of Children who may be capable of that Service, from venturing them to so much Hazard and so much Wickedness, as he represents the Seafaring Life liable to. But whatever M[r]. F——e may think of the Matter, I dare believe that there are few Men who consider justly, that would think the Profession of a *Yorkshire* Attorney more innocent and beneficial to Mankind than that of a Seaman, or would judge that *Robinson Crusoe* was so very criminal in rejecting the former, and chusing the latter, as to provoke the Divine Providence to raise two Storms, and in the last of them to destroy so many Ships and Men, purely to deter him from the Course of Life, to which at last he was to owe so ample a Reward of all his Labours and Fatigues, as the End of this very Book plainly tells us he met with.

I know you will reply, that it was his Disobedience to his Parents, for which he was punish'd in all the Misfortunes he met with, and that you frequently remind us of the Conviction of his Conscience in this Particular thro' the whole Course of his Life. I would by no Means be thought to encourage Disobedience to Parents; but the honouring our Father and Mother does not include a Duty of blindly submitting to all their Commands, whether good or bad, rational or irrational, to the entire excluding of all Manner of free Agency from the Children, which would in effect be to make the Children of Freemen absolute Slaves, and give the Parent a Power even beyond that of a Sovereign, to whom both Parents and Children are subject. Tho' the Authority therefore of Parents be great, it cannot extend to the Suppression of our Obedience to Reason, Law and Religion; and when a Child obeys these, tho' contrary to his Parents Command, he is not to be esteem'd disobedient or culpable. To apply this to the Case in Hand, *Robinson Crusoe* was above eighteen Years of Age when he left his Father's House, and this after a long Deliberation and Struggle with that secret Impulse to a Seafaring Life, to which Impulse you so often recommend a blind Obedience, whether grounded on Reason or not, and would perswade us that it proceeds from the secret Inspiration either of Providence, or some good Spirit; but here *Robinson* had a great many Reasons to urge and justify himself; for notwithstanding the wise Harangue of the Father to the Son of the great Advantages of a middle

State of Life; yet I cannot find that he himself thought that what he was to leave his Son would be sufficient to support him in that middle State, on which he had made so tedious an Encomium; for he propos'd to put him out either to some Trade, or to an Attorney. But first, as to a Trade, either he propos'd to put him to a beneficial Trade, or to one that was not so; if to a beneficial Trade, then he departed from his own Principle of a Mediocrity; if to a Trade that was not so, his Design was extreamly foolish, since the Cares and Solicitudes of that mean Profession might prove, and would in probability be as great, if not greater, than those of a more beneficial Employment; and this, indeed, would be contrary to the Design and Aim of all People who put their Children to Trades, since they always propose and hope, that the Trades to which they put them will in the end make them Rich and Prosperous. If this was his Father's Design in putting him to a Trade, he acted directly against the Principle he laid down, of being contented with what they had; if it was not his Design, he acted confessedly without Reason, and therefore could not reasonably desire an implicit Obedience to his Will: But if instead of a Trade he design'd his Son for an Attorney, a Conscientious Youth might well scruple to obey him in that particular. You have given him the Education of a Free-School, besides House Learning, as you are pleas'd to call it, which I confess I do not understand, it being a Term I never met with before in all my Reading and Conversation; but by a Free-School Education till eighteen Years of Age, he must have been perfect in all the Classicks, and fit for the University; and his Conversation with those Books might well inspire him with Notions abhorrent of a Profession in which there was nothing generous, and I am afraid very little just. But because you have said it, we will suppose that *Robinson Crusoe* was not deter'd from being an Attorney by any of these more noble Considerations, but by a pure rambling Fancy, which render'd him incapable of taking up any Profession that was more confin'd than that of a Seafaring Person; yet, how could he imagine that he should raise his Fortune by going to Sea in the Manner that he went? that is, indeed, as a common Seaman, contrary to his Friends Inclination, or any Provision made by himself to turn and improve by his Navigation; but this Difficulty vanishes, when we remember what you tell us from his own Mouth, that he never was in the right in his Life. Omitting, therefore, the Oddness of his running away at so well grown an Age, tho' he had not done it in his more early and giddy Years, we'll proceed: He is now set out, arriv'd at *Hull,* and got on

Board a Ship, without so much as ever saying one Word to the Master of her, who we must suppose never saw him for about three Weeks, till, after his Ship was cast away, he met him in *Yarmouth*, and was there inform'd by his Son, who, and what he was; tho' presently after he had heard this, he asks him, who, and what he was, as if he had known nothing of the Matter; and plainly tells him that his Ship was cast away upon his Account, making his Case and that of *Jonas* the same, who was actually in Disobedience to the positive Command and Order of God himself. But you, indeed, every where are pleas'd to make very free with the Holy Scriptures, which you quote as fluently, as the Devil once did, and much to the same End; that is, to make a Lie go down for Truth. But more of this hereafter. Well, the Master of the Ship having now understood who and what he was, makes this fine Speech to him: *And, young Man*, said he, *depend upon it, if you do not go back, wherever you go, you will meet with nothing but Disasters and Disappointments, till your Father's Words are fulfill'd upon you.*[1] Here he makes the Master of the Ship a Prophet, as well as he had done his Father, which I should as little suspect him to be, considering the wicked Character you give of all Seamen, as that a profest Seaman should make a Speech, and urge the Storms for a Motive against any one's going to Sea. But I must not dwell too long upon mere Absurdities, I shall therefore take no Notice of *Robinson's* swooning away at the Noise of a Gun, tho' he knew not for what end the Gun was discharg'd; yet I cannot pass in Silence his Coining of Providences; that is, of his making Providence raise a Storm, cast away some Ships, and damage many more, meerly to fright him from going to Sea. If this be not a bold Impiety, I know not what is, and an Impiety for which I can see very little ground; for why should he imagine that the Storm was sent to hinder him from going to Sea, more than any other that were in it, and suffer'd more by it? Nor, indeed, can I see any reason why your *Crusoe* should think it any more a Crime in him to go to Sea than in a hundred and fifty thousand more, who constantly use the Sea in these Nations, besides ten times that Number in all the Nations of the World who do the same. If Storms are sent by Providence to deter Men from Navigation, I may reasonably suppose, that there is not one of all that vast Number I have mention'd, to whom Providence has not sent the same Warning. At this absurd Way of Arguing, most of the Communication and Traffick of Nations would soon be at an end, and Islanders especially would be entirely cut off from the rest of the World; and if your Doctrine prevail'd, none would venture upon Salt Water, but such as cared not for the Safety either of Body or Soul, both which you all along endeavour to perswade us are more in danger there than any where else. But sure, dear Sir, you have neither consider'd the Wickedness, nor the Hazards of the Land; for if you had, you would find that it was morally impossible that the Seamen, at least, while on Shipboard, could be guilty of the tenth part of the Crimes which abound every where on Shore. For the Seaman, however wicked he may be in his Will, has not the Power in his floating Castle to reduce that Wickedness to Action; and to conclude that he is so wicked in Will, requires some better Proof than you have been pleas'd any where to give us. It is plain, that the Seafaring Men are generally (for here we speak only of Generals, and not of Particulars) generally, I say, are more free, open, disinterested, and less tricking and designing than those who never go to Sea; and tho' you are pleas'd often to mention the Wickedness of *Crusoe*, whom, being a Creature of your own, you might have made as wicked as you pleas'd: This very *Crusoe*, I say, does not appear to be guilty of any heinous Crimes; and it would be very hard to perswade us to believe, that a Man, who seems in all Things else innocent enough, should be so very abandon'd in Impiety, as never to pray and acknowledge the overuling Providence of God in all the Transactions of this World; and by consequence in all that did or could happen to him. But after all, if you will needs have him this impious Person; for he is a Creature of your making, and not of God's; you have given him *Manners*, as the Critics call it, quite out of Nature, and no ways necessary to your *Fable*. But more of this hereafter.

We must now attend Monsieur *Crusoe* from *Yarmouth* to *London*, where he arrives with what small remainder of his *Yarmouth* Collection he had left; and tho' a Stranger in this great City, the next thing we hear of him, is, that he abounds in fine Cloaths and Money, being able to put on Board the *Guinea* Man a Venture of forty Pounds, which how he comes by the Lord knows. He tells us, indeed, some time after, that he got this Money of his Friends; but it is not very probable, at least it is not very common, for People that have Money, to trust it to a young Fellow who had run from his Father, and was likewise under Age. This I say is not common; nay, I believe, never did happen to any Body in his Circumstances, but to *Robinson Crusoe*, and may well be put into the Number of the Miracles of his Life: Well, we'll suppose, with *Robinson* himself, that his Father secretly encourag'd his Friends to supply him; yet certainly his Father would have been very cautious of letting him be entrusted with Money entirely to manage it himself, since he had given him no Reason to imagine that his Prudence would dispose of it to the best Advantage; and, indeed, it was very plain that he did not, since he laid it out in fine Cloaths, and keeping Company with such People, from whom he could propose to derive very little Benefit: And, I believe, he is the first young Gentleman that ever thought, that to see the World by Travel, was to go to *Guinea* amongst the barbarous *Negroes*. Well, let that pass, *Crusoe* has found a Master of a Vessel according to his own Heart, and so embarks both his Cargo and himself with him for *Guinea*, makes a prosperous Voyage, his forty Pounds having produc'd about three hundred; two of which he puts into a Female Friend's Hand, and with the third sets out for a second Voyage to the *African* Shore, but is taken by a *Turkish* Rover and carried into *Sallee*; where, after he had remain'd in Bondage above two Years, he makes his escape by throwing his Master's Kinsman into the Sea, and carrying off his Master's Boat, a kind of Long-Boat, and his Boy *Xury*; and in this small Vessel goes above a thousand Miles thro' various Hazards and Adventures, to which I have nothing to say. All that I shall remark, is, that you seem very fond of all Occasions of throwing in needless Absurdities to make the Truth of your Story still the more doubted. What occasion else had you to make *Xury* speak broken *English*, when he never convers'd with any *English* but *Robinson Crusoe*? so that it had been more natural to have made *Robinson* speak broken *Arabick*, which Language he must be forc'd in some Measure to learn; whereas *Xury* had no Motive in the World to study so much *English* as he makes him speak; but this is a Peccadillo and not worth dwelling upon. Well then, we are now to suppose *Robinson Crusoe* and *Xury* got as far almost as *Cape de Verd*, when a *Portuguese* Ship takes them up and carries them to *Brasil*; where, with the Money he had rais'd by the Sale of his *Boat*, his *Skins*, and his *Boy*, he settles himself as a Planter, and accordingly turns Papist in Thankfulness to Heaven for his great Deliverance; and, indeed, he always retains some Spice of the Superstition of that Religion, in that vain Faith, which he not only himself puts in *secret Hints*, as he calls them, but earnestly recommends to all others. Well, having fix'd his Plantation, he sets out upon new Adventures, as Super-Cargo to a *Portuguese* Ship, bound to the Coast of *Guinea* to buy Slaves; and tho' he afterwards proves so scrupulous about falling upon the Cannibals or Men-Eaters, yet he neither then nor afterwards found any check of Conscience in that infamous Trade of buying and selling of Men for Slaves;

else one would have expected him to have attributed his *Shipwreck* to this very Cause.

He sets out from *Brasil*, is taken in a Storm, and at last cast away upon an uninhabited Island in the Mouth of the River *Oroonoque*; where he only escapes, all the rest being drown'd. But here I can't omit one Observation of his, which is, that the Waves buried him twenty or thirty Foot in their own Body; I would fain know by what Art *Robinson* could distinguish between five Foot, and twenty five or thirty. Well, be that as it will, your Friend *Robinson* is now got on Shore, tho' bruised in Body and troubled in Mind; and had, indeed, been in a very pitiful Condition, had not you the next Day sent the Ship on Shore after him; I mean, so near the Shore, that *Robinson* could easily get on Board her, and furnish himself with all Necessaries which his solitary Mansion requir'd; that is, with Tools, Powder, Guns, Cutlasses, Bullets, and other Shot, and Lead to make more, as well as Cloaths, Linnen and Woollen; besides so large a Cargo of Rum, that it lasted him, unconsum'd, above eight and twenty Years. Tho' I should have wonder'd how three *English* Bibles came on Board a *Portuguese* Ship, had he not told us, that they had come to him in a Cargo from *England*; yet I must still wonder, why *Robinson* should put three on Board for his Voyage to *Guinea*, when one was likely to be more than he would make use of, if we may believe his own Account of the little regard he had to any Religion. But it was necessary that he should have a Bible, to furnish you with the Means of Burlesquing the Sacred Writ, in the tedious Reflections you design'd to put into his Mouth; of which by and by.

[. . . . .[2]]

11 Preface to *The Farther Adventures of Robinson Crusoe*, 1719

by DANIEL DEFOE

The Farther Adventures . . . was published on August 20, 1719, only 117 days after *Robinson Crusoe* itself. In spite of this rapidity, however, an abridgement had already appeared, so that Defoe was able to expostulate with those responsible in the Preface to his continuation. The fourth edition of *Robinson Crusoe* contained the following note to its title-page:

> The Pretended Abridgement of this Book, clandestinely Printed for *T. Cox* at the *Amsterdam* Coffee-House, consists only of some scatter'd Passages incoherently tacked together; wherein the Author's Sense throughout is wholly mistaken, the Matters of Fact misrepresented, and the Moral Reflections misapplied. It is hop'd the Publick will not give Encouragement to so base a Practice, the Proprietor intending to Prosecute the Venders according to Law. [Quoted from the Shakespeare Head edition (1927).]

The Success the former Part of this Work has met with in the World, has yet been no other than is acknowledg'd to be due to the surprising Variety of the Subject, and to the agreeable Manner of the Performance.

All the Endeavours of envious People to reproach it with being a Romance, to search it for Errors in Geography, Inconsistency in the Relation, and Contradictions in the Fact, have proved abortive, and as impotent as malicious.

The just Application of every Incident, the religious and useful Inferences drawn from every Part, are so many Testimonies to the good Design of making it publick, and must legitimate all the Part that may be call'd Invention, or Parable in the Story.

The Second Part, if the Editor's Opinion may pass, is (contrary to the Usage of Second Parts), every Way as entertaining as the First, contains as strange and surprising Incidents, and as great a Variety of them; nor is the Application less serious, or suitable; and doubtless will, to the sober, as well as ingenious Reader, be every way as profitable and diverting; and this makes the abridging this Work, as scandalous, as it is knavish and ridiculous; seeing, while to shorten the Book, that they may seem to reduce the Value, they strip it of all those Reflections, as well religious as moral, which are not only the greatest Beautys of the Work, but are calculated for the infinite Advantage of the Reader.

By this they leave the Work naked of its brightest Ornaments; and if they would, at the same Time pretend, that the Author has supply'd the Story out of his Invention, they take from it the Improvement, which alone recommends that Invention to wise and good Men,

The Injury these Men do the Proprietor of this Work, is a Practice all honest Men abhor; and he believes he may challenge them to shew the Difference between that and Robbing on the Highway, or Breaking open a House.

If they can't shew any Difference in the Crime, they will find it hard to shew why there should be any Difference in the Punishment: And he will answer for it, that nothing shall be wanting on his Part, to do them Justice.

12 From the *Postscript* to *An Epistle to Daniel Defoe . . .*, 1719

by CHARLES GILDON

POSTSCRIPT

Having just run thro' the first Volume and clos'd my Letter, I was told that the second Volume was at last come out. I was too much tir'd with the Badness of the Road in my first Journey, to venture upon another the same Way, without resting to recover my Patience, of which I was to have sufficient use in my passing thro' the second Part. I am afraid that *Robinson Crusoe* reserv'd so much *Opium* for his own Use, when he dispos'd of the rest to the Merchant of *Japan*, that he has scarce been thoroughly awake ever since; and has communicated that somniferous Quality of the Drug to his Writing thro' the whole second Part, which every where prepares you for Sleep; to avoid a Lethargy therefore, I shall not dwell upon it, and its perpetual Succession of Absurdities, but only touch upon some few, which may serve for Samples of the whole. I cannot, however, omit taking particular Notice of the Editor's Preface, because it is not only written by the same Hand, but also very singular in its kind: You begin with a Boast of the Success of your Book, and which you say deserves that Success by its Merits, that is, *The surprising Variety of the Subject, and the agreeable Manner of the Performance.* It's well you tell us so yourself, the judicious Reader else must have been puzzel'd to find out the Mystery of its Success. For first, as to the Variety of the Subject, it will be a hard Matter to make that good, since it's spread out into at least five and twenty Sheets, clog'd with Moral Reflections, as you are pleas'd to call them, every where insipid and aukward, and in many Places of no manner of Relation to the Occasion on which they are deliver'd, besides being much larger than necessary, and frequently impious and prophane; and always canting are the Reflections which you are pleas'd to call religious and useful, and *the brightest Ornaments of your Book*, tho' in reality they were put in by you to swell the Bulk of your Treatise up to a five Shilling Book; whereas, the Want of Variety in your Subject would never have made it reach to half the Price; nay, as it is, you have been forc'd to give us the same Reflections over and over again, as well as repeat the same Fact afterwards in a Journal, which you had told us before in a plain Narration. So *agreeable is the Manner of your Performance*! which is render'd more so by the excessive Sterility of your Expression, being forc'd perpetually to say the same Things in the very self same Words four or five times over in one Page; which puts me in Mind of what *Hudibras* says,

> Would it not make one strange
> That some Mens Fancies should ne'er change,
> But always make them do and say
> The self same Things, the self same Way?[1]

Another agreeable Thing in the Performance is, that every Page is full of *Solecisms* or false Grammar. However, this may be, for ought I know, a very agreeable Performance to most of your Buyers.

Your next Triumph is, that the Reproaches of your Book as a Romance, and as being guilty of bad Geography, Contradictions, and the like, *have prov'd Abortive* (I suppose you mean ineffectual) *and as impotent as malicious*; but here, as well as in other Places, you are guilty of a great Abuse of Words: For first, they have not been impotent, since all but the very *Canaille* are satisfied by them of the Worthlessness of the Performance; nor can the exposing the Weakness and Folly of any assuming and ignorant Scribbler be properly call'd malicious; they who malign eminent Worth, may, indeed, deserve such a Name; but what hath been said of, or done against such an incoherent Piece as *Robinson Crusoe*, can at worst be only call'd Indignation; and that was what the eminent Satirist was not asham'd to own, as the Motive and Support of his Verses.

Si Natura negat facit Indignatio versum.[2]

And thus I may say of my present Letter to you; that if want of Genius forbid my Writing at all, that Defect is largely supplied by Indignation, not Malice or Envy; for Folly and Ignorance can never produce them. However, I find that these Endeavours you seem to contemn as impotent, have yet had so great a Force upon yourself, as to make you more than tacitly confess, that your Book is nothing but a Romance. You say, indeed, *The just Application of every Incident, the religious and useful Inferences drawn from every Part, are so many Testimonies to the good Design of making it Publick, and must Legitimate all the Part that may be called Invention or Parable in the Story*. But when it is plain that there are no true, useful or just Inferences drawn from any of the Incidents; when Religion has so little to do in any Part of these Inferences; when it is evident that what you call Religion, is only to mislead the Minds of Men to reject the Dictates of Reason, and embrace in its Room a meer superstitious Fear of I know not what *Instinct* from unbodied Spirits; when you impiously prophane the very Name of Providence, by allotting to it either contradictory Offices, or an unjust Partiality: I think we may justly say, that the Design of the Publication of this Book was not sufficient to justify and make Truth of what you allow to be Fiction and Fable; what you mean by *Legitimating, Invention* and *Parable,* I know not; unless you would have us think, that the Manner of your telling a Lie will make it a Truth.[3] One may say a great deal in Answer to what you urge against the Abridgment of your Book, but it is too absurd to dwell upon, and against the Practice of all Ages and all Nations: What think you, honest *D——n,* of the *History of Justin?* was not that an Abridgment of *Trogus Pompeius,* whose long History of the World is lost, and the Abridgement of *Justin* remains to this Day? nor can I find that ever he was stigmatiz'd for it with a Crime as bad as Robbing on the Highway.[4] What think you of *Darius Tibertus,* a Modern *Italian,* who abridg'd the Lives of *Plutarch* in the *Latin* Tongue? what do you suppose of the Abridgment of the Voluminous History of *Guarini?* what of the *Latin* Abridgment of *Pliny?* what think you of the great *Fontinel?* (for I think I may call him great, after what Sir *William Temple* has said of him) he tells you himself, in his Preface to his *History of Oracles,* that this Book is but an Abridgment of *van Dale,* who writ a prolix Treatise upon that Subject.[5] But not to dwell upon Foreigners, we have a hundred Instances in our own Tongue of the like Practice, in many of which Booksellers of undoubted Probity have been concern'd; indeed, there is this to be said, that most of these Abridgments have been of books of a real intrinsick Value; but yours might for me have continu'd unabridg'd, and still retain'd all its *brightest Ornaments,* as you call them; but if the omitting of those be the only Fault of the Abridgment, I can't but think his Work more valuable than the Original, nor do I see that he has done your Proprietor any damage, since he has left to your larger Volume all those Beauties you are so fond of, and may, indeed, be said to be only an Advertiser of them to those that have them not. If he has preserv'd the Fable entire, the Judicious will not want your clumsy and tedious Reflections to recommend it; for, indeed, by what you say, you seem not to understand the very Nature of a Fable, which is a sort of Writing which has always been esteem'd by the wisest and best of Men to be of great use to the Intruction of Mankind; but then this Use and Instruction should naturally and plainly arise from the Fable itself, in an evident and useful Moral, either exprest or understood; but this is too large a Subject to go thro', and to shew that by the Rules of Art you have not attain'd any one End or Aim of a Writer of Fables in the Tale that you have given us. I shall therefore proceed to those few Remarks, which I have made in a cursory reading of your second Part.

The first Thing I remark, is, that you are at your Dreams again Page 3d and 4th; for most of the Religion of your Book consists in Dreams. The next Thing I shall just hint at, is what you say about the three Pirate Sailors in the same Page—*So if I had hang'd them all, I had been much in the right, and should have been justifiable both by the Laws of God and Man*, the contrary of which Assertion is directly true, *viz*. That if you had hang'd them all, you had been guilty of downright Murther by all the Laws of God and Man; for pray, sweet Sir, what Authority had *Robinson Crusoe* so much as to fine, or inflict any Punishment upon any Man?

Some Follies, I find, are like some Distempers, catching: Thus, Madam *Crusoe*, by conversing with her wise Husband, extravagantly fancies his fantastick Whimsies to be the Impulse of Divine Providence, *ibid*.

Against the next Edition of your Book, profound *Da——l*, I wish you would take the Pains to explain the following Piece of Nonsense, so far as to make it intelligible; for I can meet with no Body, no, not the most skill'd in the abstruser Sciences, that can so much as guess what you would be at. I transcribe them for your serious Consideration, *Nothing can be a greater Demonstration of a future State, and of the Existence of an invisible World, than the Concurrence of second Causes with the Ideas of Things, which we form in our Minds, perfectly reserv'd and not communicated to any in the World*, Page 10; and in Page 12, he is making it a resisting of Providence, if he did not go a rambling at about sixty five Years of Age. I only note this *en passant*, to remind you of what noble Offices you assign to the Divine Providence, by attributing to the Impulse of that all Things that are irrational; a very pious Notion of the eternal Divine Wisdom! I shall only observe on that odd Account, given Page 20, of the extravagant Joy of the *French* that were sav'd by *Crusoe*, when their Ship was burnt, that they were certainly a Ship-load of extreme Cowards or Madmen; for nothing but the

Extremity of Cowardice or Lunacy could ever produce so general a Distraction. It is confess'd, that unexpected Deliverances will have strange Effects upon some very few particular People, but then this Deliverance must be very sudden and very unexpected; but this is not the Case here; for all the Time the Ship was burning, *Crusoe* discharg'd Guns to let them know that Relief was at Hand; and all the Night after, when the Flame of the burnt Ship was extinguish'd by the Sea, the same *Crusoe* set out Lights upon his Ship, and frequently discharg'd Guns to direct the Boats loaded with the Crew of the burnt Ship towards their Safety, which they found could not be far off; and towards which, by this Means, they might every Minute make some approach; so that Hope was not gone, no not for one Minute, which makes all those extravagant Effects of Joy utterly improbable; nay, I may say, impossible.

I shall pass *Friday's* speaking broken *English* twelve Years after he had been with his Master, and almost as unintelligibly, as after he had been with him but twelve Days; nor shall I stop long upon the *Spaniards* Prognosticating Humour, from Dreams and unaccountable Whimsies, because the *Spaniard* seems to have learnt this by dwelling so long in *Crusoe's* Habitation; for he has the same Notion of secret Correspondence betwixt unbodied and embodied Spirits, which *Crusoe* every where avows. But, dear *Da——l*, you have forgot yourself, you make a *Spaniard* speak here, the most bigotted of all Papists; and therefore it had been more natural for him to have attributed this secret Intelligence to Saint *Jago*, or the Blessed *Virgin*, or even to his Angel Guardian: But, indeed, you frequently forget the Religion of your Speaker, and make the *Spaniard* in your first Part quote Scripture Instances, which he could never be suppos'd to have read in all his Life, or ever heard mention'd. But to go on, for I will say nothing of the Savages Landing in the Night to make their Feast; for they are your Savages, and you may make them go where and when you please, and for what you please. I shall pass, therefore, on to *Crusoe's* Learned Discourse with the *French Popish Priest* in Page 146, &c. which has, indeed, as gross Marks of Falshood and inartificial Fiction, as any thing in your Book:

[. . . . .]

13 Preface to *A Select Collection of Novels*, 1720

by SAMUEL CROXALL

Samuel Croxall (d. 1752) dramatist, compiler and hack-writer, also wrote *The Fair Circassian. A Dramatic Performance* . . . (1720), *Scripture Politics* (1735), and produced a popular translation of *The Fables of Aesop* . . . (1722). The *Select Collection* included a number of miscellaneous pieces, both separate publications and *novella* abstracted from longer works by Segrais, Cervantes, Le Sage, Mme. de Lafayette, César de Saint-Réal (see below, No. 24), Paul Scarron and Mateo Aleman. In Volume I, immediately after the Preface, Croxall printed Huet's *Essai sur l'origine des Romans* (see above, No. 8).

The Origine of Romances and Novels is so amply, so pertinently, so perspicuously display'd, in a Treatise written expressly on this Subject, which is prefixt to the following *Collection*,[1] that it might well supersede the Necessity of any other Preface; did not the great Abuse of Novels (as no good thing in the World escapes being perverted)[2] require a few Words to be premis'd, for the removing of such Prejudices as that Abuse has occasion'd against all Performances of this Kind.

Had not the original Design of these Imitations of History been to instil the Noblest Sentiments after the most Agreeable Manner, which is always the surest; and were not the Grand Moral of them, the Rewarding of Honour and Virtue, and the Punishing of Dishonour and Vice: A Person of no less unspotted a Reputation, than universal Learning, as Monsieur *Huet* the Bishop of *Avranches* in *France*, wou'd never have been at the Pains to write the History of such Works, much less wou'd he recommend the perusing of them, under any Restriction whatever. Referring the Reader therefore to his justly admir'd Treatise, we shall only say, that the main Conditions he requires, namely Instruction and Entertainment, are the reigning Perfections of this Collection; wherein the utmost Care has been taken, that no Novel shou'd have a

Place, which cou'd possibly offend the Gravity of the Aged, or the Modesty of the Young; and that did not inspire Disinterestedness, Generosity, Fidelity, Constancy, with the like Virtues; which, if steddily pursu'd, wou'd procure to both Sexes that Happiness, for which they all so ardently Wish, but of which they generally miss by sordid Avarice, or giddy Ambition.

When it was laid down as a Maxim, that agreeable Entertainment shou'd be one principal End of Romances, this is not merely understood of the surprising Events, or the artful Texture of the Story, but likewise of the Language and Expressions: Wherefore the Publisher being fully appris'd of the Nature of his Undertaking, and observing how wretchedly some of these Novels have been formerly translated into *English*, did not only get them done over again by complete Masters both of the Subject and the two Languages; but likewise took Care to have the others, which had never been attempted, to be translated by as able Hands, all of 'em being Men of Letters: So that, in every Respect we have mention'd, it may be said, without the least Appearance of Presumption, that so Choice a Collection as this has not hitherto appear'd in this Kingdom.

14 Preface to *Colonel Jack*, 1722

by DANIEL DEFOE

Prefaces are so customary before Books of this Nature, to introduce them into the World by a Display of their Excellencies, that it might be thought too presuming to send this Performance abroad, without some such Preliminary. And yet I may venture to say it needs this good office as little as any that has ever gone before it. The pleasant and delightful Part speaks for itself; the useful and instructive is so large, and has such a Tendency to improve the Mind, and rectify the Manners, that it would employ a Volume, large as itself, to particularize the Instructions that may be drawn from it.

Here's Room for just and copious Observations, on the Blessing, and Advantages of a sober and well-govern'd Education, and the Ruin of so many Thousands of all Ranks in this Nation, for want of it here; also we may see how much publick Schools and Charities might be improved to prevent the Destruction of so many unhappy Children, as, in this Town, are every Year bred up for the Executioner.

The miserable Condition of multitudes of Youth, many of whose natural Tempers are docible, and would lead them to learn the best Things rather than the worst, is truly deplorable, and is abundantly seen in the History of this Man's Childhood; where, though Cirumstances form'd him by Necessity to be a Thief, surprizing Rectitude of Principles remain'd with him, and made him early abhor the worst Part of his Trade, and at length to forsake the whole of it. Had he come into the World with the Advantage of a virtuous Education, and been instructed how to improve the generous Principles he had in him, what a Figure might he not have made, either as a Man, or a Christian.

The various Turns of his Fortune, in different Scenes of Life, make a delightful Field for the Reader to wander in; a Garden where he may gather wholesome and Medicinal Fruits, none noxious or poisonous; where he will see Virtue, and the Ways of Wisdom, every where applauded, honour'd, encourag'd, and rewarded; Vice and Extravagance attended with Sorrow, and every kind of Infelicity; and at last, Sin and Shame going together, the Offender meeting with Reproach, and Contempt, and the Crimes with Detestation and Punishment.

Every vicious Reader will here be encouraged to a Change, and it will appear that the best and only good End of an impious mispent Life is Repentance; that in this, there is Comfort, Peace, and often Times Hope, that the Penitent shall be received like the Prodigal, *and his latter End be better than his Beginning.*

A book founded on so useful a Plan, calculated to answer such valuable Purposes as have been Specified, can require no Apology: Nor is it of any Concern to the Reader, whether it be an exact historical Relation of real Facts, or whether the Hero of it intended to present us, at least in part, with a moral Romance: On either Supposition it is equally Serviceable for the Discouragement of Vice, and the Recommendation of Virtue.

15 Preface to *Moll Flanders*, 1722

by DANIEL DEFOE

The World is so taken up of late with Novels and Romances, that it will be hard for a private History to be taken for Genuine, where the Names and other Circumstances of the Person are concealed; and on this Account we must be content to leave the Reader to pass his own Opinion upon the ensuing Sheets, and take it just as he pleases.

The Author is here supposed to be writing her own History, and in the very beginning of her Account she gives the Reasons why she thinks fit to conceal her true Name, after which there is no Occasion to say any more about that.

It is true that the original of this Story is put into new Words, and the stile of the famous Lady we here speak of, is a little alter'd, particularly she is made to tell her own tale in modester Words than she told it at first; the Copy which came first to Hand, having been written in Language more like one still in *Newgate*, than one grown Penitent and Humble, as she afterwards pretends to be.

The pen employ'd in finishing her Story, and making it what you now see it to be, has had no little Difficulty to put it into a Dress fit to be seen, and to make it speak Language fit to be read: When a Woman debauched from her Youth, nay, even being the Offspring of Debauchery and Vice, comes to give an Account of all her vicious Practices, and even to descend to the particular Occasions and Circumstances, by which she first became wicked, and of all the progressions of Crime, which she run through in Threescore Years, an Author must be hard put to it to wrap it up so clean, as not to give room, especially for vicious Readers, to turn it to his Disadvantage.

All possible Care however has been taken to give no lew'd Ideas, no immodest turns in the new dressing up this Story, No, not to the worst part of her Expressions; to this Purpose some of the vicious part of her Life, which could not be modestly told, is quite left out, and several other Parts are very much shortened; what is left 'tis hoped will not offend the chastest Reader, or the modestest Hearer; and as the best use is to be made even of the worst Story, the Moral 'tis hoped will keep the Reader serious, even where the Story might incline him to be otherwise: To give the History of a wicked Life repented of, necessarily requires that the wicked part should be made as wicked as the real History of it will bear; to illustrate and give a Beauty to the Penitent part, which is certainly the best and brightest, if related with equal Spirit and Life.

It is suggested there cannot be the same Life, the same Brightness and Beauty in relating the penitent Part, as is in the criminal Part: If there is any Truth in that Suggestion, I must be allow'd to say, 'tis because there is not the same taste and relish in the Reading; and indeed it is too true that the difference lies not in the real worth of the Subject so much as in the Gust and Palate of the Reader.

But as this Work is chiefly recommended to those who know how to read it, and how to make the good Uses of it, which the Story all along recommends to them; so it is to be hop'd that such Readers will be much more pleas'd with the Moral, than the Fable, with the Application than with the Relation, and with the end of the Writer than with the Life of the Person written of.

There is in this Story abundance of delightful Incidents, and all of them usefully apply'd. There is an agreeable turn Artfully given them in the relating, that naturally Instructs the Reader, either one way, or another. The first part of her lew'd Life with the young gentleman at *Colchester*, has so many happy turns given it to expose the Crime, and warn all whose Circumstances are adapted to it, of the ruinous End of such things, and the foolish, Thoughtless, and abhor'd Conduct of both the parties, that it abundantly attones for all the lively Description she gives of her Folly and Wickedness.

The Repentance of her Lover at the *Bath*,[1] and how brought by the just alarm of his Fit of Sickness to abandon her; the just Caution given there against even the lawful Intimacies of the dearest Friends, and how unable they are to preserve the most solemn Resolutions of Virtue without divine Assistance; these are Parts, which to a just Discernment will appear to have more real Beauty in them, than all the amorous Chain of Story, which introduces it.

In a Word, as the whole Relation is carefully garbled[2] of all the Levity and Looseness that was in it: So it is applied, and with the utmost care to vertuous and religious Uses. None can without being guilty of manifest Injustice, cast any Reproach upon it, or upon our Design in publishing it.

The Advocates for the Stage, have in all Ages made this the great Argument to perswade People that their Plays are useful, and that they ought to be allow'd in the most civiliz'd, and in the most religious Government; namely, that they are apply'd to vertuous Purposes, and that by the most lively Representations, they fail not to recommend Virtue, and generous Principles, and to discourage and expose all sorts of Vice and Corruption of Manners; and were it true that they did so, and that they constantly adhered to that Rule, as the Test of their acting on the *Theatre*, much might be said in their Favour.

Throughout the infinite variety of this Book, this Fundamental is most strictly adhered to; there is not a wicked Action in any part of it, but is first or last rendered Unhappy and Unfortunate; There is not a superlative Villain brought upon the Stage, but either he is brought to an unhappy End, or brought to be a Penitent: There is not an ill thing mention'd but it is condemn'd, even in the Relation, nor a vertuous just thing, but it carries its Praise along with it: What can more exactly answer the Rule laid down, to recommend, even those Representations of things which have so many other just Objections lying against them? Namely, of Example of bad Company, obscene Language, and the like.

Upon this Foundation this Book is recommended to the Reader, as a Work from every part of which something may be learned, and some just and religious Inference is drawn by which the Reader will have something of Instruction, if he pleases to make use of it.

All the Exploits of this Lady of Fame, in her Depredations upon Mankind stand as so many warnings to honest People to beware of 'em, intimating to 'em by what Methods innocent People are drawn in, plundered, and rob'd, and by Consequence how to avoid them. Her robing a little Child, dress'd fine by the Vanity of the Mother, to go to the Dancing School, is a good Memento to such People hereafter; as is likewise her picking the Gold-Watch from the young Ladies side in the *Park*.

Her getting a parcel from a hairbrain'd Wench at the Coaches in *St. John's-street*; her Booty at the Fire, and also at *Harwich*; all give us excellent Warning in such Cases to be more present to ourselves in sudden Surprises of every Sort.

Her application to a sober Life, and industrious management at last in *Virginia*, with her Transported Spouse, is a Story fruitful of Instruction, to all the unfortunate Creatures who are oblig'd to seek their Re-establishment abroad; whether by the Misery of Transportation, or other Disaster; letting them know that Diligence and Application have their due encouragement, even in the remotest part of the World, and that no Case can be so low, so despicable, or so empty of Prospect, but that an unwearied Industry will go a great way to deliver us from it, will in time raise the meanest Creature to appear again in the World, and give him a new Cast for his Life.

These are a few of the serious Inferences which we are led by the Hand to in this Book, and these are fully sufficient to Justify any Man in recommending it to the World, and much more to Justify the Publication of it.

There are two of the most beautiful Parts still behind, which this Story gives some Idea of, and lets us into the Parts of them, but they are either of them too long to be brought into the same Volume; and indeed are, *as I may call them*, whole Volumes of themselves, *viz*, 1. The Life of her Governess, as she calls her, who had run thro', it seems in a few Years all the eminent degrees of a Gentlewoman, a Whore, and a Bawd; a Midwife, and a Midwife keeper, as they are call'd; a Pawnbroker, a Child-taker, a Receiver of Thieves, and of stolen Goods; and in a Word, herself a Thief, a breeder up of Thieves, and the like, and yet at last a Penitent.

The second is the Life of her Transported Husband, a Highway-man; who it seems liv'd a twelve Years' Life of successful Villany upon the Road, and even at last came off so well as to be a Voluntier Transport, not a Convict; and in whose Life there is an incredible Variety.

But as I said, these are things too long to bring in here, so neither can I make a Promise of their coming out by themselves.

We cannot say indeed, that this History is carried on quite to the End of the Life of this famous *Moll Flanders*, for no Body can write their own Life to the full End of it, unless they can write it after they are dead: but her Husband's Life being written by a third Hand, gives a full Account of them both, how long they lived together in that Country, and how they came both to *England* again, after about eight Years, in which time they were grown very Rich, and where she liv'd it seems, to be very old; but was not so extraordinary a Penitent, as she was at first; it seems only that indeed she always spoke with abhorrence of her former Life, and of every Part of it.

In her last Scene at *Maryland* and *Virginia*, many pleasant things happen'd, which makes that part of her Life very agreeable, but they are not told with the same Elegancy as those accounted for by herself; so it is still to the more Advantage that we break off here.

16 From the Dedication of *Lasselia; or the Self Abandon'd. A Novel*, 1723

by ELIZA HAYWOOD

Eliza Haywood (1693–1756) was a dramatist, essayist and writer of numerous novels and other pieces of prose fiction. She left her husband in 1721 and began writing for the stage. Among her many works are: *Love in Excess: or, the Fatal Enquiry* (1719–20); *British Recluse: or, Secret History of Cleomira, Suppos'd Dead* (1722); *Idalia: or, The Unfortunate Mistress* (1723); and the long novels, *Betsy Thoughtless* (1751) and *The History of Jemmy and Jenny Jessamy* (1753). Other works are referred to below, Nos. 18, 19 and 21.

[. . . . .]

My Design in writing this little *Novel* (as well as those I have formerly publish'd) being only to remind the unthinking Part of the World, how dangerous it is to give way to Passion, will, I hope, excuse the too great Warmth, which may perhaps, appear in some particular Pages; for without the *Expression* being invigorated in some measure proportionate to the *Subject*, 'twou'd be impossible for a Reader to be sensible how far it touches him, or how probable it is that he is falling into those Inadvertencies which the Examples I relate wou'd caution him to avoid.

I take the liberty of mentioning this to your Lordship, to clear my self of that Aspersion which some of my own Sex have been unkind enough to throw upon me, that 'I seem to endeavour to *divert* more than *improve* the Minds of my Readers'. Now, as I take it, the Aim of every Person, who pretends to write (tho' in the most insignificant and ludicrous way) ought to tend at least to a good *Moral* Use; I shou'd be sorry to have my Intentions judg'd to be the very reverse of what they are in Reality. How far I have been able to *succeed* in my Desires of infusing those Cautions, too necessary to a Number, I will not pretend to determine: but where I have had the Misfortune to *fail*, must impute it either to the obstinacy of those I wou'd persuade, or to my own Deficiency in that very Thing which they are pleased to say I too much abound in—a true Description of Nature.

[. . . . .]

17 Preface to *Roxana, or the Fortunate Mistress*, 1724

by DANIEL DEFOE

The History of this *Beautiful Lady* is to speak for itself: If it is not as Beautiful as the Lady herself is reported to be; if it is not as diverting as the Reader can desire, and much more than he can reasonably expect; and if all the most diverting Parts of it are not adapted to the Instruction and Improvement of the Reader, the *Relator says*, it must be from the Defect of his Performance; dressing up the Story in worse Cloaths than the *Lady*, whose Words he speaks, prepar'd it for the World.

He takes the Liberty to say, That this Story differs from most of the Modern Performances of this Kind, tho' some of them have met with a very good Reception in the World: *I say*, It differs from them in this Great and Essential Article, *Namely*, That the Foundation of This is laid in Truth of Fact; and so the Work is not a Story but a History.

The Scene is laid so near the Place where the Main Part of it was transacted, that it was necessary to conceal Names and Persons; lest what cannot be yet entirely forgot in that Part of the Town shou'd be remember'd, and the Facts trac'd back too plainly, by the many People yet living, who wou'd know the Persons by the Particulars.

It is not always necessary that the Names of Persons shou'd be discover'd, though the History may be many Ways useful; and if we shou'd be always oblig'd to name the Persons or not to relate the Story, the Consequence might be only this, That many a pleasant and delightful History wou'd be Buried in the Dark, and the World be depriv'd both of the Pleasure and the Profit of it.

The *Writer* says, He was particularly acquainted with this Lady's First Husband, the Brewer, and with his Father; and also with his Bad Circumstances; and knows that first Part of the Story to be Truth.

This may, he hopes, be a Pledge for the Credit of the rest, tho' the Latter Part of her History lay Abroad, and cou'd not so well be vouch'd as the First; yet, as she has told it herself, we have the less Reason to question the truth of that Part also.

In the Manners he has told the Story, it is evident she does not insist upon her Justification in any one Part of it; much less does she recommend her Conduct, or indeed any Part of it, except her Repentance, to our Imitation: On the contrary, she makes frequent Excursions in a just censuring and condemning her own Practice: How often does she reproach herself in the most passionate Manner; and guide us to just Reflections in the like Cases?

It is true She met with unexpected Success in all her wicked Courses; but even in the highest Elevations of her Prosperity she makes frequent Acknowledgments, That the Pleasure of her Wickedness was not worth the Repentance; and that all the Satisfaction she had, all the Joy in the View of her Prosperity, no, nor all the Wealth she rowl'd in; the Gaiety of her Appearance; the Equipages, and the Honours, she was attended with, cou'd quiet her Mind, abate the Reproaches of her Conscience, or procure her an Hour's Sleep, when just Reflections kept her waking.

The Noble Inferences that are drawn from this one Part, are worth all the rest of the Story; and abundantly justify (as they are the profess'd Design of) the Publication.

If there are any Parts in her Story which being oblig'd to relate a wicked Action, seem to describe it too plainly, the *Writer* says, all imaginable Care has been taken to keep clear of Indecencies and immodest Expressions; and 'tis hop'd you will find nothing to prompt a vicious Mind, but everywhere much to discourage and expose it.

Scenes of Crime, can scarce be represented in such a Manner but some may make a Criminal Use of them; but when Vice is painted in its Low-priz'd Colours, 'tis not to make People in love with it, but to expose it; and if the Reader makes a wrong Use of the Figures, the Wickedness is his own.

In the mean-time the Advantages of the present Work are so great, and the Virtuous Reader has room for so much Improvement, that we make no Question, the Story, however meanly told, will find a Passage to his best Hours, and be read both with Profit and Delight.

18 From *The Tea-Table, or a Conversation between some Polite Persons of both sexes at a Lady's Visiting Day*, 1725

by ELIZA HAYWOOD

The passage reproduced below follows the reading of a *novella* by one of the group of characters mentioned in the title. The setting of the tale is itself an interesting comment on the way in which such works must have been disseminated—especially in the early part of the eighteenth century.

[. . . . .]
I thank you, my Dear! (said AMIANA, perceiving she had done) in the behalf of the Company, since I dare swear there are none here who have not thought themselves well entertain'd.———But notwithstanding the Pains you have taken to oblige us, and that there are some lively Strokes of Passion in the Story, I cannot help saying that I think the Character of CELEMENA faulty.———She yields, in my Opinion, with too much Ease, to create that Pity for her Misfortunes, which otherwise they cou'd not fail of exciting.———I wou'd have all Women have a better Excuse for such an Excess of Passion, than meerly the agreeable Person of a Man.———If there were no Measures to be taken to secure ones self of his Affection, there are certainly to discover if he has Wit, Honour, and Good-nature; and she that can love where these encourage not, her Expectations receive an Impression which from the very first can promise nothing but Misery and Contempt. But you forget, Madam, answer'd PHILETUS, that if the Ladies always made use of their Penetration, and chose for their Favourites only such as were worthy of them, there wou'd be no such thing as Woes in *Love*; to be possess'd of that Passion wou'd be the highest Felicity a Mortal cou'd arrive at, and to devote ones whole Soul to it rather a *Merit* than the contrary. PHILETUS is beyond all dispute in the right, added DORINTHUS; Pity wou'd be a Passion which the equally loving, equally deserving Pair, would have no need of.———Mournful MELPOMENE wou'd cease to be invok'd.———*Complaints* no more

wou'd be the *Muses* Theme.——*Panegyrick* wou'd be the sole Business of the *Poet's* Quill.——*Satyr* grow out of Fashion, and all the Histories for *Novels* lost. I cannot own the Justice of what you say, reply'd AMIANA; there are doubtless many Misfortunes to be found in Love, even where both Parties are perfectly sincere, which may afford Theme enough to gratify an Author's Genius, and if I were of Counsel with the Writers of such Books, I shou'd advise 'em to chuse only such ——For, methinks, to read of Villany so gross, so monstrous as that we have just now heard in the Character of BERALDUS, gives too great a Shock to the Soul, and poysons the rest of the Entertainment. But yet sometimes 'tis necessary, said BRILLIANTE, to be reminded that there have been Men so base; our Sex is of it self so weak, especially when we suffer what little share of Reason we have to be debilitated by Passion, that we stand in need of all the Helps we can procure, to defend us from becoming the Victim of our own Softness. I am so far of your Mind, Madam, answer'd DORINTHUS, that these kind of Stories are of great use to persuade the Ladies to make use of that Penetration which AMIANA just now recommended. I wou'd have Beauty the Reward of Merit, not fall the Prey of Villany and Deceit; and if a Woman, when she reads of such a Fate as CELEMENA's, will but give her self leave to reflect how very possible it is that the Man she is most inclin'd to favour, may be a BERALDUS, it will certainly make her inspect into his Behaviour with a Care and Watchfulness which cannot fail of discovering the *True* Affection from the *Counterfeit*. In my Mind, therefore, rejoyn'd PHILETUS, these kind of Writings are not so trifling as by many People they are thought.——Nor are they design'd, as some imagine, for *Amusement* only, but *Instruction* also, most of them containing Morals, which if well observed would be of no small Service to those that read 'em.——Certainly if the Passions are well represented, and the Frailties to which Humane Nature is incident, and cannot avoid falling into, of one kind or another, it cannot fail to rouze the sleeping Conscience of the guilty Reader to a just Remorse for what is *past*, and an Endeavour at last of Amendment for the *future*.——Those who wou'd, perhaps, be impatient of Reproof when given them by a Parent, a Guardian, or a Friend, listen calmly to it when instill'd this way.——Tho' the Follies we find expos'd are our own, we hear of them without Anger, because related in the Character of another, and reap all the Benefit of the Admonition, without the Shame of having receiv'd it.——But, methinks, pursued he, there is little occasion of Defence for writing of *Novels*, the very Authority of those great Names which adorn the Title-Pages of some large Volumes of them, is a sufficient Recommendation; and we cannot believe that the celebrated Madam D'Anois, Monsieurs Bandell, Scudery, Segrais, Bonaventure Des Perriers,[1] and many other learned Writers, would have been at the Expence of so much Time and Pains, only for the Pleasure of inventing a Fiction, or relating a Tale.————No, they had other Views.——They had an Eye to the Humours of the Age they liv'd in, and knew that Morals, meerly as Morals, wou'd obtain but slight Regard: to inspire Notions, therefore, which are necessary to reform the Manners, they found it most proper to cloath Instruction with Delight.————And 'tis most certain that when Precepts are convey'd this way, they steal themselves into the Soul, and work the wish'd Effect, almost insensibly, to the Person who receives them.————We become virtuous ere we are aware, and by admiring the great Examples which in the Narrative appear so amiable, are led to an Endeavour of imitating them.

He was about to add something more; but was prevented by the coming in of a Lady in a new Suit of Cloaths.————Her Appearance put an End to the Conversation we were upon, and it turn'd immediately on Dress.

[. . . . .[2]]

19 Preface to *The Fair Hebrew: or, a True, but Secret History of Two Jewish Ladies, who lately resided in London*, 1729

by ELIZA HAYWOOD

There are so many Things, meerly the effect of Invention, which have been published, of late, under the Title of SECRET HISTORIES, that, to distinguish this, I am obliged to inform my Reader, that I have not inserted one Incident which was not related to me by a Person nearly concerned in the Family of that unfortunate Gentleman, who had no other Consideration in the Choice of a *Wife*, than to gratify a present Passion for the Enjoyment of her Beauty.

I found something so particular in the Story, and so much Room for the most useful and moral Reflections to be drawn from it, that I thought I should be guilty of an Injury to the Publick in concealing it. If among all who shall read the following Sheets, any one Person may reap so much Advantage as to avoid the Misfortunes the SUBJECT of them fell into by his Inadvertency, and giving a Loose to Passion; the Little Pains I have been at will be infinitely recompenc'd.

20 From the Preface to *The Finish'd Rake; or Gallantry in Perfection: being the Genuine and Entertaining Adventures of a Young Gentleman of Fortune*, 1733

The author of this work is not known.

It is customary for Persons, whose Actions have made some Noise in the World, to have their Lives transmitted down to Posterity; and that by those who are wholly unqualified for such an Undertaking, being generally such as have been altogether unacquainted with the People whose Histories they pretend to write, only through common Report, and consequently must take all their Accounts upon Trust. To avoid the like Fate after my Decease, I thought proper, with my own Hand, to throw together the most remarkable Transactions of my Life, tho' no Man living has a greater Aversion to Scribbling than myself.

I had besides this another Vuew in so doing, which is, that as my Adventures have been very uncommon, and most of them have carried their own Punishment along with them, they may serve as a Warning to deter other People from following my Example; lest they should meet with the same Misfortunes, and be made sensible, like me, to their Cost, that the best that can be expected from a dissolute Life, is a *broken Constitution*, and an *incumber'd Estate*, not to mention a *lost Character*, and *perpetual Remorse*, if they have the good Fortune to escape *utter Ruin*.

[. . . . .]

21 From the Preface to *The Disguis'd Prince: or, the Beautiful Parisian. A True History...*, 1733

by ELIZA HAYWOOD

This novel was translated from the French of Jean de Préchac, who entitled it *L'Illustre Parisienne, histoire galante et véritable* (1679). Haywood's translation first appeared in 1728; the passage reproduced below is taken from the second edition.

Those who undertake to write Romances, are always careful to give a high Extraction to their *Heroes* and *Heroines*; because it is certain we are apt to take a greater Interest in the Destiny of a *Prince* than of a *private Person*. We frequently find, however, among those of a middle State, some, who have Souls as elevated, and Sentiments equally noble with those of the most illustrious Birth: Nor do I see any Reason to the contrary; *Nature* confines not her Blessings to the *Great* alone, and where a fine Genius has the Improvements of a liberal Education, it will undoubtedly be the same in one Rank as in another. As the following Sheets, therefore, contain only real Matters of Fact, and have, indeed, something so very surprising in themselves, that they stand not in need of any Embellishments from Fiction: I shall take my *Heroine* such as I find her, and believe the Reader will easily pass by the Meanness of her Birth, in favour of a thousand other good Qualities she was possess'd of.

[. . . . .]

22 Preface to *The Life and entertaining Adventures of Mr. Cleveland, Natural Son of Oliver Cromwell, Written by Himself,* 1734-5

This is the English version of *Le Philosophe anglais ou l'histoire de Mr. Cleveland . . .* (1732-9), by Antoine Francois Prévost d'Exiles (1697-1763). This work was sold in England by N. Prévost, the author's brother, and was presumably translated by himself. Prévost wrote several other novels—*Mémoirs d'un homme de qualité* (1728-31), *Manon Lescaut* (1731, but not published separately until 1733), *Le Doyen de Killerine* (1735-40) —and translated or was involved in the translation of the three novels of Samuel Richardson (1742, 1751 and 1755-8 respectively).

The study of history is so advantageous, and at the same time so delightful, that 'tis no wonder it has been cultivated by the finest spirits in all ages. The history of kingdoms and empires, raises our admiration, by the solemnity, if I may so call it, of the images, and furnishes one of the noblest entertainments. But at the same time that it is so well suited to delight the imagination, it yet is not so apt to touch and affect as the history of private men; the reason of which seems to be, that the personages in the former, are so far above the common level, that we consider ourselves, in some measure, as aliens to them; whereas those who act in a lower sphere, are look'd upon by us as a kind of relatives, from the similitude of conditions; whence we are more intimately mov'd with whatever concerns them.

But as there is a difference between the benefit which may be reap'd from the histories of kingdoms, and those of private persons; so the advantage which may accrue from particular histories themselves is no less considerable. The subjects of some of these are so trifling, and the manner in which they are writ, so unnatural, that they only impose upon the mind, and convey nothing substantial: While those of a superior kind, as they treat of persons whose lives have been remarkable for extraordinary circumstances; so they often serve as an excellent lesson to all who are desirous of avoiding those rocks on which others have split; and of meriting the highest character to which human nature can attain, that of wise men.

That the following piece may justly be rank'd among the latter, will, I believe, be readily granted by all judicious readers. 'Tis the history of a man who was as remarkable for the uninterrupted calamities of his life, as his father for his continual successes. One, who tho' son to a man, that from an obscure condition, broke his way to the throne, and maintain'd himself peaceably in it; was yet expos'd to all the rigours of fortune; and so barbarously us'd by him who gave him birth, that he became one of his most inveterate enemies, and went over to King *Charles II.*

If any man had a perfect knowledge of the world 'tis our author. Brought up, like another *Lemuel*,[1] under a mother's eye, whose vast love for him, made her extremely solicitous to form his mind, and whose large experience, capacity and understanding, enabled her to do it without any foreign assistance; the depravity of his fellow-creatures was strongly inculcated to him, at an age when others amuse themselves with trifles. The solitude he was brought up in; the excellent moral authors which his fond parent put into his hands; and the judicious comment she made upon them, gave a peculiar bent to Mr. *Cleveland's* mind; so that when he came to enter upon the Stage of the world, which he did with the utmost reluctance, it appear'd to him in a quite different light, from what it does to the rest of men.

But as the relation which he gives of his solitude is very extraordinary, and the employments of it instructive and entertaining; so when he leaves it, and comes to associate with mankind, he gives a just and natural description of the diffidence which is almost inseparable from the best and most ingenuous minds; a circumstance, which as it too often depresses them, so it may teach others who labour under any difficulty that way, to set a proper value on their own talents; and not suffer themselves to be over-aw'd by the vain, the ignorant, and the noisy.

The Treachery he afterwards met with, points out to us, that we ought not to repose too great a confidence in any man, till we know him thoroughly; nor suffer our selves to be deluded by a specious appearance of friendship. Hypocrisy, as it is a very odious vice, so it is the most apt to impose upon us; for the mask it puts on, is often so natural, and bears so great a resemblance to virtue, that the most wary sometimes mistake the one for the other.

The passion he had for my lord *Axminster's* daughter, is of the chastest, and at the same time of the most beautiful kind. Struck before he was sensible of it, he has given so lively a picture of the rise and progress of it, that all who have ever been in love, must own it to be vastly tender and natural. The struggles he had with himself when he first knew his distemper, are so delicately describ'd; and the resolution he had hitherto shewn in combating his inclinations, so great, that we may justly say of him with *Adam* in the *Paradise Lost,*

———————————— only weak
Against the Charm of Beauty's powerful Glance.[2]

His going over to king *Charles II* and the particulars he gives of *Oliver's* private history are very curious, and have till now been a secret. Possibly some may doubt the veracity of them, from *Oliver's* specious indifference to the fair sex, and the silence of historians on that head. But whoever considers his deep dissimulation, and the strong reasons he had to conceal his amours, will not wonder at their being known hitherto only to the parties concern'd.

If any one should accuse him of drawing his father's character in too odious colours, he must call to mind the principles he had imbib'd in his infant years, and the inhuman treatment he met with from him. That he agrees in this particular with the most celebrated *English* historians is well known. My lord *Clarendon*, among others, says, 'That he attempted those things which no good man durst have ventur'd on——No man,' (says his lordship,) 'with more wickedness ever attempted any thing, or brought to pass what he desir'd more wickedly.'[3]

An objection may be made to *Oliver's* being mention'd as Speaker of the *House of Commons*; since we don't find any such circumstance in history. This I myself hinted to some persons of distinction, who assur'd me, that they knew by undoubted tradition, that *Oliver* had been nominated to this employment by several members upon a particular view; but that he declined it, from a sense of his incapacity (nothwithstanding his other great talents,) to fill it with honour.

The Reader will very possibly be desirous of knowing how these Papers came into my Hands. To satisfy his curiosity, I am to inform him, that they were given me by Mr. *Cleveland*, the author's son, a person advanced in years, who spent the greatest part of his life in foreign countries, and lives now in *Kingstreet*, *Westminster*. I first got acquainted with him about three years ago at *Montpelier*. His good sense, experience and affability, gave me a very advantageous idea of him; which, with some unexpected favours he afterwards indulg'd me, made me very desirous of cultivating his friendship. After some stay in this city we return'd to *Paris*, where we lodg'd in the same house. There he first shew'd me his father's papers, which gave me so much pleasure and satisfaction, that I was very urgent with him to have them printed, persuaded that they would be a very acceptable present to the public. He told me, that the only objection he had to my proposal, was, the confus'd method in which they were writ; and the difficult task it would be to digest 'em in such a manner, as might make them worthy of appearing in the world; especially as he was engag'd in a tedious law suit, which took up the greatest part of his time. This I obviated by a modest offer of my service, which my good friend accepted; and an ingenious *French* gentleman, who understands the *English* tongue perfectly well, agreeing to share with me in it, we methodiz'd it in the manner in which it is now publish'd, without altering a single circumstance in the whole work. After we had finish'd it, Mr. *Cleveland* was pleas'd to give us the approbation of the whole, and returning to *England* with me, he consented readily to its publication.

Some surprising incidents which we meet with in the following sheets, may perhaps incline some readers to doubt the truth of them. But how many famous authors have been accus'd of writing untruths, which afterwards have been found to be matters of fact? *Pliny*, the naturalist, suffer'd long under this aspersion; and the *Travels* of Sir *John Chardin* were consider'd in the same light by multitudes; till several persons of undoubted credit, who have since visited the same countries, assure us of his veracity.[4] We might extend this observation to numberless instances, if it were necessary.

The things about which Mr. *Cleveland* writes, did not happen so many years ago but that there are persons now living who remember them. That the lord *Axminster* suffer'd under great misfortunes, is well known: Not to mention that our author agrees in a great many particulars with the most authentic historians; a circumstance which adds no little weight to his testimony in general.

The cave of *Rumney-Hole* is well known to be of a prodigious extent. If it should be ask'd, how the several recesses of it came not to be discover'd before, I answer, that possibly no one was ever reduced to the same necessity of hiding himself in it, as the lord *Axminster* and Mr. *Cleveland*; a circumstance which might prompt them to pierce further into it, than any other person had done before. *Camden* speaking of the famous Peak in *Derbyshire*, says, *Sub hoc specus sive subterraneus meatus——magno hiatu patet, multiplicesque recessus habet.*[5] Wockey-Hole, under *Mendip* hills near *Wells* in *Somersetshire*, is a vast cavern, containing spacious apartments, stone walls, labyrinths, &c. The cave near *Ryegate* in *Surrey*, the retreat of the *Barons* in the reign of king *John*, where we still see the hall in which they sat in council, is affirm'd by the inhabitants to have run four miles under ground, and to have been stopt up not long since by the falling in of the earth.

The relation which Mr. *Bridge*, halfbrother to our author, gives of the colony from *Rochel*,[6] which setled near the island of *St. Helena*, is curious and surprising. But are we to wonder that those people conceal'd themselves so carefully from the rest of the world? Harass'd by a dreadful siege, in which they suffer'd the extremes of misery, they well might pant after some *asylum*, there to live in full liberty, and enjoy a freedom of thinking agreable to the dictates of their religion; and having found such a one, what could be more natural than for 'em to wish to live in it for ever, secluded from all commerce with the rest of their fellow creatures?

If notwithstanding what has been said, the reader should still suspect the truth of some particulars, I yet am persuaded he will not think the time spent in the perusal of this work lost; since, besides the agreable turn of the incidents; the many solid and masterly reflections which are scatter'd up and down the work, afford a most useful instruction to all who are desirous of it. *Telemachus* is well known to be a fictitious piece, but what book was ever more entertaining, or abounds with finer precepts for the conduct of life?[7]

As I have been absent some years from my native country, possibly the expression may not, in some few places, be altogether so correct as it ought to have been, for which I must desire the judicious reader's indulgence. In a little time I shall publish two volumes more, which will conclude the work.

23 Introductory material to *Pamela*, 1740

by SAMUEL RICHARDSON

Pamela was written between November 10, 1739, and January 10, 1740, but not published until November 6, 1740. Richardson received several offers of prefaces, but eventually decided to write the Preface himself. The first of the letters reproduced below was written by J. B. de Fréval, a French hack-writer living in London; the second appeared as part of the advertisement for *Pamela* in the *Weekly Miscellany* for October 11, 1740.

PREFACE BY THE EDITOR

If to Divert *and* Entertain, *and at the same time to* Instruct, *and* Improve *the Minds of the* YOUTH *of* both Sexes:

If to inculcate Religion *and* Morality *in so easy and agreeable a manner, as shall render them equally* delightful *and* profitable *to the* younger Class *of Readers, as well as worthy of the Attention of Persons of* maturer *Years and Understandings:*

If to set forth in the most exemplary Lights, the Parental, *the* Filial, *and the* Social *Duties, and that from* low *to* high *Life:*

If to paint VICE *in its proper Colours, to make it* deservedly Odious; *and to set* VIRTUE *in its own amiable Light, to make it* truly Lovely:

If to draw Characters justly, *and to support them* equally:

If to raise a Distress from natural *Causes, and to excite Compassion from* proper *Motives:*

If to teach the Man of Fortune *how to use it; the Man of* Passion *how to subdue it; and the Man of* Intrigue, *how, gracefully, and with Honour to himself, to* reclaim:

If to give practical *Examples, worthy to be followed in the most* critical *and* affecting *Cases, by the* modest *Virgin, the* chaste *Bride, and the* obliging *Wife:*

If to effect all these goods Ends, in so probable, so natural, so lively a manner, as shall engage the Passions of every sensible Reader, and strongly interest them in the edifying Story:

And all without raising a single *Idea throughout the Whole, that shall shock the exactest Purity, even in those tender Instances where the exactest Purity would be most apprehensive:*

If these, (embellished with a great Variety of entertaining Incidents) be laudable or worthy Recommendations of any Work, the Editor of the following Letters, which have their Foundation in Truth *and* Nature, *ventures to assert, that all these desirable Ends are obtained in these Sheets: And as he is therefore confident of the favourable Reception which he boldly bespeaks for this little Work; he thinks any* further Preface or Apology *for it, unnecessary: And the rather for two Reasons,* 1st. *Because he can Appeal from his own Passions, (which have been uncommonly* moved *in perusing these engaging Scenes) to the Passions of* Every one *who shall read them with the least Attention: And, in the next place, because an* Editor *may reasonably be supposed to judge with an Impartiality which is rarely to be met with in an* Author *towards his own Works.*

THE EDITOR.

To the Editor of the Piece inititled, PAMELA; *or,* VIRTUE REWARDED.

Dear SIR,

I have had inexpressible Pleasure in the Perusal of your PAMELA. It intirely answers the Character you give of it in your Preface; nor have you said one Word too much in Commendation of a Piece that has Advantages and Excellencies peculiar to itself. For, besides the beautiful Simplicity of the Style, and a happy Propriety and Clearness of Expression (the Letters being written under the immediate Impression of every Circumstance which occasioned them, and that to those who had a Right to know the fair Writer's most secret Thoughts) the several Passions of the Mind must, of course, be more affectingly described, and Nature may be traced in her undisguised Inclinations with much more Propriety and Exactness, than can possibly be found in a Detail of Actions long past, which are never recollected with the same Affections, Hopes, and Dreads, with which they were felt when they occurred.

This little Book will infallibly be looked upon as the hitherto much-wanted Standard or Pattern for this Kind of Writing. For it abounds with lively Images and Pictures; with Incidents natural, surprising, and perfectly adapted to the Story; with Circumstances interesting to Persons in common Life, as well as to those in exalted Stations. The greatest Regard is everywhere paid in it to Decency, and to every Duty of Life: There is a constant Fitness of the Style to the Persons and Characters described; Pleasure and Instruction here always go hand in hand: Vice and Virtue are set in constant Opposition, and Religion every-where inculcated in its native Beauty and chearful Amiableness; not dressed up in stiff, melancholy, or gloomy Forms, on one hand, nor yet, on the other, debased below its due Dignity and noble Requisites, in Compliment to a too fashionable but depraved Taste. And this I will boldly say, that if its numerous Beauties are added to its excellent Tendency, it will be found worthy a Place, not only in all Families (especially such as have in them young Persons of either Sex) but in the Collections of the most curious and polite Readers. For, as it borrows none of its Excellencies from the romantic Flights of un-natural Fancy, its being founded in Truth and Nature, and built upon Experience, will be a lasting Recommendation to the Discerning and Judicious; while the agreeable Variety of Occurrences and Characters, in which it abounds, will not fail to engage the Attention of the gay and more sprightly Readers.

The moral Reflections and Uses to be drawn from the several Parts of this admirable History, are so happily deduced from a Croud of different Events and Characters, in the Conclusion of the Work, that I shall say the less on that Head. But I think, the Hints you have given me, should also prefatorily be given to the Publick; *viz.* That it will appear from several Things mentioned in the Letters, that the Story must have happened within these Thirty Years past: That you have been obliged to vary some of the Names of Persons, Places, &c. and to disguise a few of the Circumstances, in order to avoid giving Offence to some Persons, who would not chuse to be pointed out too plainly in it; tho' they would be glad it may do the Good so laudably intended by the Publication. And as you have in Confidence submitted to my Opinion some of those Variations, I am much pleased that you have so managed the Matter, as to make no Alteration in the Facts; and, at the same time, have avoided the digressive Prolixity too frequently used on such Occasions.

Little Book, charming PAMELA! face the World, and never doubt of finding Friends and Admirers, not only in thine own Country, but far from Home; where thou mayest give an Example of Purity to the Writers of a neighbouring Nation; which now shall have an Oppor-tunity to receive *English* Bullion in Exchange for its own Dross, which has so long passed current among us in Pieces abounding with all the Levities of its volatile Inhabitants. The reigning Depravity of the Times has yet left Virtue many Votaries. Of their Protection you need not despair. May every head-strong Libertine whose Hands you reach, be reclaimed; and every tempted Virgin who reads you, imitate the Virtue, and meet the Reward of the high-meriting, tho' low-descended, PAMELA. I am, Sir,

Your most Obedient,
and Faithful Servant,
J. B. D. F.

To my worthy Friend, the Editor of PAMELA.

SIR,

I return the Manuscript of *Pamela* by the Bearer, which I have read with a great deal of Pleasure. It is written with that Spirit of Truth and agreeable Simplicity, which, tho' much wanted, is seldom found in those Pieces which are calculated for the Entertainment and Instruction of the Publick. It carries Conviction in every Part of it; and the Incidents are so natural and interesting, that I have gone hand-in-hand, and sympathiz'd with the pretty Heroine in all her Sufferings, and been extremely anxious for her Safety, under the Apprehensions of the bad Consequences which I expected, every Page, would ensue from the laudable Resistance she made. I have interested myself in all her Schemes of Escape; been alternately pleas'd and angry with her in her Restraint; *pleas'd* with the little Machinations and Contrivances she set on foot for her Release, and *angry* for suffering her Fears to defeat them; always lamenting, with a most sensible Concern, the Miscarriages of her Hopes and Projects. In short, the whole is so affecting, that there is no reading it without uncommon Concern and Emotion. Thus far only as to the *Entertainment* it gives.

As to *Instruction* and *Morality*, the Piece is full of both. It shews Virtue in the strongest Light, and renders the Practice of it amiable and lovely. The beautiful Sufferer keeps it ever in her View, without the least Ostentation, or Pride; she has it so strongly implanted in her, that thro' the whole Course of her Sufferings, she does not so much as hesitate once, whether she shall sacrifice it to Liberty and Ambition, or not; but, as if there were no other way to free and save herself, carries on a determin'd Purpose to persevere in her Innocence, and wade with it throughout all Difficulties and Temptations, or perish under them. It is an astonishing Matter, and well worth our most serious Considera-

tion, that a young beautiful Girl, in the low Scene of Life and Circumstance in which Fortune placed her, without the Advantage of a Friend
capable to relieve and protect her, or any other Education than what
occurr'd to her from her own Observation and little Reading, in the
Course of her Attendance on her excellent Mistress and Benefactress,
could, after having a Taste of Ease and Plenty in a higher Sphere of
Life than what she was born and first brought up in, resolve to return
to her primitive Poverty, rather than give up her Innocence. I say, it
is surprising, that a young Person, so circumstanced, could, in Contempt of proffer'd Grandeur on the one side, and in Defiance of Penury
on the other, so happily and prudently conduct herself thro' such a
Series of Perplexities and Troubles, and withstand the alluring Baits,
and almost irresistible Offers of a fine Gentleman, so universally
admired and esteemed, for the Agreeableness of his Person and good
Qualities, among all his Acquaintance; defeat all his Measures with so
much Address, and oblige him, at last, to give over his vain Pursuit,
and sacrifice his Pride and Ambition to Virtue, and become the Protector of that Innocence which he so long and so indefatigably labour'd
to supplant: And all this without ever having entertain'd the least previous Design or Thought for that Purpose: No Art used to inflame
him, no Coquetry practised to tempt or intice him, and no Prudery
or Affectation to tamper with his Passions; but, on the contrary, artless
and unpractised in the Wiles of the World, all her Endeavours, and
even all her Wishes, tended only to render herself as un-amiable as she
could in his Eyes: Tho' at the same time she is so far from having any
Aversion to his Person, that she seems rather prepossess'd in his Favour,
and admires his Excellencies, whilst she condemns his Passion for her.
A glorious Instance of Self-denial! Thus her very Repulses became
Attractions: The more she resisted, the more she charm'd; and the very
means she used to guard her Virtue, the more endanger'd it, by inflaming his Passions: Till, at last, by Perseverance, and a brave and
resolute Defence, the Besieged not only obtain'd a glorious Victory
over the Besieger, but took him Prisoner too.

I am charmed with the beautiful Reflections she makes in the Course
of her Distresses; her Soliloquies and little Reasonings with herself, are
exceeding pretty and entertaining: She pours out all her Soul in them
before her Parents without Disguise; so that one may judge of, nay,
almost see, the inmost Recesses of her Mind. A pure clear Fountain
of Truth and Innocence; a Magazine of Virtue and unblemish'd
Thoughts!

I can't conceive why you should hesitate a Moment as to the Publication of this very natural and uncommon Piece. I could wish to see it out in its own native Simplicity, which will affect and please the Reader beyond all the Strokes of Oratory in the World; for those will but spoil it: and, should you permit such a murdering Hand to be laid upon it, to gloss and tinge it over with superfluous and needless Decorations, which, like too much Drapery in Sculpture and Statuary, will but encumber it; it may disguise the Facts, mar the Reflections, and unnaturalize the Incidents, so as to be lost in a Multiplicity of fine idle Words and Phrases, and reduce our Sterling Substance into an empty Shadow, or rather *frenchify* our *English* Solidity into Froth and Whip-syllabub. No; let us have *Pamela* as *Pamela* wrote it; in her own Words, without Amputation, or Addition. Produce her to us in her neat Country Apparel, such as she appear'd in, on her intended Departure to her Parents; for such best becomes her Innocence, and beautiful Simplicity. Such a Dress will best edify and entertain. The flowing Robes of Oratory may indeed amuse and amaze, but will never strike the Mind with solid Attention.

In short, Sir, a Piece of this Kind is much wanted in the World, which is but too much, as well as too early, debauched by pernicious *Novels*. I know nothing Entertaining of that Kind that one might venture to recommend to the Perusal (much less the Imitation) of the Youth of either Sex: All that I have hitherto read, tends only to corrupt their Principles, mislead their Judgments, and initiate them into Gallantry, and loose Pleasures.

Publish then, this good, this edifying and instructive little Piece for their sakes. The Honour of *Pamela*'s Sex demands *Pamela* at your Hands, to shew the World an Heroine, almost beyond Example, in an unusual Scene of Life, whom no Temptations, or Sufferings, could subdue. It is a fine, and glorious Original, for the Fair to copy out and imitate. Our own Sex, too, require it of you, to free us, in some measure, from the Imputation of being incapable of the Impressions of Virtue and Honour; and to shew the Ladies, that we are not inflexible while they are so.

In short, the Cause of Virtue calls for the Publication of such a Piece as this. Oblige then, Sir, the concurrent Voices of both Sexes, and give us *Pamela* for the Benefit of Mankind: And as I believe its Excellencies cannot be long unknown to the World, and that there will not be a Family without it; so I make no Doubt but every Family that has it, will be much improv'd and better'd by it. 'Twill form the tender Minds of *Youth* for the Reception and Practice of Virtue and Honour; confirm and establish those of *maturer Years* on good and steady Principles; reclaim the Vicious, and mend the Age in general; insomuch that as I doubt not *Pamela* will become the bright Example and Imitation of all the fashionable young Ladies of *Great Britain*; so the truly generous Benefactor and Rewarder of her exemplary Virtue, will be no less admired and imitated among the *Beau Monde* of our own Sex. I am

Your affectionate Friend, &c.

24 From a letter of Philip Dormer Stanhope Earl of Chesterfield (1740–1?)

This letter was originally written in French to Chesterfield's illegitimate son, Philip Stanhope, and was published in *Letters written by . . . Earl of Chesterfield to His Son . . .* (1774), I, Letter III. The translation is taken from this edition, but the letter is dated according to the edition of Bonamy Dobrée, who publishes it between letters dated November 1740 and January 1741 (see *Letters . . .* (1932), II, 435–7).

Thursday night.

MY DEAR CHILD,

You are now reading the *Historical Novel* of *Don Carlos*, written by the Abbé of St. Real.[1] The foundation of it is true; the Abbé has only embellished a little, in order to give it the turn of a Novel; and it is prettily written. *A propos*; I am in doubt whether you know what a Novel is: it is a little gallant history, which must contain a great deal of love, and not exceed one or two small volumes. The subject must be a love affair; the lovers are to meet with many difficulties and obstacles to oppose the accomplishment of their wishes, but at last overcome them all; and the conclusion or catastrophe must leave them happy. A Novel is a kind of abbreviation of a Romance; for a Romance generally consists of twelve volumes, all filled with insipid love non-sense, and most incredible adventures. The subject of a Romance is sometimes a story intirely fictitious, that is to say, quite invented; at other times, a true story, but generally so changed and altered, that one cannot know it. For example: in *Grand Cyrus*, *Clelia*, and *Cleopatra*, three celebrated Romances, there is some true history; but so blended with falsities, and silly love-adventures, that they confuse and corrupt the mind, instead of forming and instructing it. The greatest Heroes of antiquity are there represented in woods and forests, whining insipid love-tales to their inhuman Fair-one, who answers them in the same style. In short, the reading of Romances is a most frivolous occupation, and time merely thrown away. The old Romances, written two or three hundred years ago, such as *Amadis of Gaul, Orlando the Furious*,[2] and others, were stuft with enchantments, magicians, giants, and such sort of impossibilities; whereas the more modern Romances keep within the bounds of possibility but not of probability. For I would just as soon believe, that the great Brutus, who expelled the Tarquins from Rome, was shut up by some magician in an enchanted castle, as imagine that he was making silly verses for the beautiful Clelia, as he is represented in the Romance of that name.

[. . . . .]

25 Introductory material to *Pamela*, 1741

by SAMUEL RICHARDSON

This material was inserted by Richardson in the second edition of *Pamela*, published in February 1741. The first and the third letters were from Richardson's friend and fulsome admirer, Aaron Hill (1685–1750), dramatist and literary discontent. The anonymous letter which Hill deals with was forwarded to Richardson through the bookseller Charles Rivington on November 15, 1740; the novelist acknowledged it in two advertisements, published in the *Daily Gazeteer* for November 20, 1740, and the *London Evening Post* for December 11 and 13, 1740.

The kind Reception which this Piece has met with from the Publick, (a large Impression having been carried off in less than Three Months) deserves not only Acknowledgment, but that some Notice should be taken of the Objections that have hitherto come to hand against a few Passages in it, that so the Work may be rendered as unexceptionable as possible, and, of consequence, the fitter to answer the general Design of it; which is to promote Virtue, and cultivate the Minds of the Youth of both Sexes.

But Difficulties having arisen from the different Opinions of Gentlemen, some of whom applauded the very Things that others found Fault with, it was thought proper to submit the Whole to the Judgment of a Gentleman of the most distinguish'd Taste and Abilities; the Result of which will be seen in the subsequent Pages.

We begin with the following Letter, at the Desire of several Gentlemen, to whom, on a very particular Occasion, it was communicated, and who wish'd to see it prefixed to the New Edition. It was directed,

To the Editor of PAMELA.

Dear Sir,
You have agreeably deceiv'd me into a Surprize, which it will be as hard to express, as the Beauties of PAMELA. Though I open'd this

powerful little Piece with more Expectation than from common Designs, of like Promise, because it came from *your* Hands, for my *Daughters*, yet, who could have dreamt, he should find, under the modest Disguise of a *Novel*, all the *Soul* of Religion, Good-breeding, Discretion, Good-nature, Wit, Fancy, Fine Thought, and Morality?— I have done nothing but read it to others, and hear others again read it, to me, ever since it came into my Hands; and I find I am likely to do nothing else, for I know not how long yet to come: because, if I lay the Book down, it comes after me.—When it has dwelt all Day long upon the Ear, It takes Possession, all Night, of the Fancy.—It has Witchcraft in every Page of it; but it is the Witchcraft of Passion and Meaning. Who is there that will not despise the false, empty *Pomp* of the Poets, when he observes in this little, unpretending, mild Triumph of *Nature*, the whole Force of Invention and Genius, creating new Powers of Emotion, and transplanting *Ideas* of *Pleasure* into that unweeded low Garden the *Heart*, from the dry and sharp *Summit* of *Reason?*

Yet, I confess, there is *One*, in the World, of whom I think with still greater Respect, than of PAMELA: and That is, of the wonderful AUTHOR of PAMELA.—Pray, Who is he, Dear Sir? and where, and how, has he been able to hide, hitherto, such an encircling and all-mastering Spirit? He possesses every Quality that ART could have charm'd by: yet, has lent it to, and conceal'd it in, NATURE.—The Comprehensiveness of his Imagination must be truly prodigious!—It has stretch'd out this diminutive mere *Grain* of *Mustard-seed*, (a poor Girl's little, innocent, Story) into a Resemblance of That *Heaven*, which the Best of Good Books has compar'd it to.[1]—All the Passions are His, in their most close and abstracted Recesses: and by selecting the most delicate, and yet, at the same time, most powerful, of their Springs, thereby to act, wind, and manage, the Heart, He *moves* us, every where, with the Force of a TRAGEDY.

What is there, throughout the *Whole*, that I do not sincerely admire! —I admire, in it, the strong distinguish'd Variety, and picturesque glowing Likeness to *Life*, of the Characters. I know, hear, see, and live among 'em All: and, if I cou'd paint, cou'd return you their *Faces*. I admire, in it, the noble Simplicity, Force, Aptness, and Truth, of so many modest, œconomical, moral, prudential, religious, satirical, and cautionary, *Lessons*; which are introduc'd with such seasonable Dexterity, and with so polish'd and exquisite a Delicacy, of Expression and Sentiment, that I am only apprehensive, for the *Interests* of *Virtue*, lest some of the *finest*, and *most touching*, of those elegant Strokes of Good-breeding, Generosity, and Reflection, shou'd be lost, under the too gross Discernment of an unfeeling Majority of Readers; for whose Coarseness, however, they were kindly design'd, as the most useful and charitable Correctives.

One of the best-judg'd Peculiars, of the Plan, is, that These Instructions being convey'd, as in a Kind of Dramatical Representation, by those beautiful *Scenes*, Her own Letters and Journals, who acts the most moving and suffering *Part*, we feel the Force in a threefold Effect,—from the Motive, the Act, and the Consequence.

But what, above All, I am charm'd with, is the amiable *Good-nature* of the AUTHOR; who, I am convinc'd, has one of the best, and most generous Hearts, of Mankind: because, mis-measuring *other* Minds, by *His Own*, he can draw Every thing, to Perfection, but *Wickedness.*—I became inextricably in *Love* with this delightful Defect of his Malice;—for, I found it owing to an *Excess* in his *Honesty*. Only observe, Sir, with what *virtuous Reluctance* he complies with the Demands of his Story, when he stands in need of some blameable Characters. Tho' his Judgment compels him to mark 'em with disagreeable Colourings, so that they make an odious Appearance at first, He can't forbear, by an unexpected and gradual Decline from Themselves, to soften and transmute all the Horror conceiv'd for their Baseness, till we are arriv'd, through insensible Stages, at an Inclination to forgive it intirely.

I must venture to add, without mincing the matter, what I really believe, of this Book.—It will live on, through Posterity, with such unbounded Extent of Good Consequences, that Twenty Ages to come may be the Better and Wiser, for its Influence. It will steal first, imperceptibly, into the Hearts of the *Young* and the *Tender*: where It will afterwards guide and moderate their Reflections and Resolves, when grown Older. And, so, a gradual moral Sunshine, of un-austere and compassionate *Virtue*, shall break out upon the *World*, from this TRIFLE (for such, I dare answer for the *Author*, His Modesty misguides him to think it).—No Applause therefore can be too *high*, for *such* Merit. And, let me abominate the contemptible *Reserves of mean-spirited Men*, who while they but *hesitate* their Esteem, with Restraint, can be fluent and uncheck'd in their *Envy*.—In an Age so deficient in Goodness, Every such Virtue, as That of this Author, is a salutary *Angel*, in *Sodom*. And *One* who cou'd stoop to conceal, a Delight he receives from the *Worthy*, wou'd be equally capable of submitting to an Approbation of the *Praise* of the *Wicked*.

I was thinking, just now, as I return'd from a *Walk* in the *Snow*, on that *Old Roman Policy*, of Exemptions in Favour of Men, who had given a few, bodily, Children to the Republick.—What superior Distinction ought *our* Country to find (but that *Policy* and *We* are at Variance) for Reward of this *Father*, *of Millions of* MINDS, which are to owe new Formation to the future Effect of his Influence!

Upon the whole, as I never met with so pleasing, so honest, and so truly deserving a Book, I shou'd never have done, if I explain'd All my Reasons for admiring its Author.—If it is not a *Secret*, oblige me so far as to tell me his *Name*: for since I feel him the *Friend* of my Soul, it would be a Kind of Violation to retain him a *Stranger*.—I am not able to thank you enough, for this highly acceptable Present. And, as for my Daughters, They have taken into their Own Hands the Acknowledgment due from their Gratitude. I am,

Dec. 17,   DEAR SIR,
    1740.   *Your*, &c.

Abstract of a second Letter from the same Gentleman

'—No Sentiments which I have here, or in my last, express'd, of the sweet *Pamela*, being more than the bare Truth, which every Man must feel, who lends his Ear to the inchanting Prattler, Why does the Author's Modesty mislead his Judgment, to suspect the Style wants Polishing?—No, Sir, there is an *Ease*, a *natural Air*, a dignify'd *Simplicity*, and measured Fullness, in it, that, resembling Life, outglows it! He has reconciled the *Pleasing* to the *Proper*. The *Thought* is every-where exactly *cloath'd* by the *Expression*: And becomes its Dress as roundly, and as close, as *Pamela* her Country-habit. Remember, tho' she put it on with humble Prospect, of descending to the Level of her Purpose, it *adorn'd* her, with such unpresum'd *Increase* of Loveliness; sat with such neat Propriety of Elegant Neglect about her, that it threw out All her Charms, with tenfold, and resistless Influence.—And so, dear Sir, it will be always found.—When modest Beauty seeks to hide itself by casting off the *Pride* of *Ornament*, it but displays itself without a *Covering*: And so, becoming more distinguished, by its Want of *Drapery*, grows *stronger*, from its *purpos'd Weakness*.'

There were formed by an anonymous Gentleman, the following Objections to some Passages in the Work.

1. That the Style ought to be a little raised, at least so soon as

Pamela knows the Gentleman's Love is honourable, and when his Diffidence is changed to Ease: And from about the fourth Day after Marriage, it should be equal to the Rank she is rais'd to, and charged to fill becomingly.

2. That to avoid the Idea apt to be join'd with the Word '*Squire*, the Gentleman should be styled Sir *James*, or Sir *John*, &c. and Lady *Davers* in a new Edition might procure for him the Title of a Baronet.

3. That if the sacred Name were seldomer repeated, it would be better; for that the Wise Man's Advice is, *Be not righteous over-much*.

4. That the Penance which *Pamela* suffers from Lady *Davers* might be shorten'd: That she is too timorous after owning her Marriage to that Lady, and ought to have a little more Spirit, and get away sooner out at the Window, or call her own Servants to protect, and carry her to her Husband's Appointment.

5. That Females are too apt to be struck with Images of Beauty; and that the Passage where the Gentleman is said to span the Waist of *Pamela* with his Hand, is enough to ruin a Nation of Women by Tight-lacing.

6. That the Word *naughty* had better be changed to some other, a *Bad, Faulty, Wicked, Vile, Abominable, Scandalous*: Which in most Places would give an Emphasis, for which recourse must otherwise be had to the innocent Simplicity of the Writer; an Idea not necessary to the Moral of the Story, nor of Advantage to the Character of the Heroine.

7. That the Words, *Foolish Thing that I am*, had better be *Foolish that I am*. The same Gentleman observes by way of *Postscript*, that Jokes are often more severe, and do more Mischief, than more solid Objections; and would have one or two Passages alter'd, to avoid giving Occasion for the Supposition of a double Entendre, particularly in two Places which he mentions.

He is pleased to take notice of several other Things of less Moment, some of which are merely typographical; and very kindly expresses, on the Whole, a high Opinion of the Performance, and thinks it may do a great deal of Good: For all which, as well as for his Objections, the Editor gives him very sincere Thanks.

Others are of Opinion, That the Scenes in many Places, in the Beginning especially, are too low; and that the Passions of Lady Davers, *in particular, are carried too high, and above Nature.*

And others have intimated, That Pamela *ought, for Example sake, to have discharg'd Mrs.* Jewkes *from her Service.*

These are the most material Objections that have come to hand, all which

*are considered in the following Extracts from some of the most beautiful Letters
that have been written in any Language:*

'The Gentleman's Advice, not to alter *Pamela* at all, was both friendly,
and solidly just. I run in, with full Sail to his Anchorage, that the low
Scenes are no more out of Nature, than the high Passions of proud
Lady *Davers*. Out of Nature, do they say? 'Tis my Astonishment how
Men of Letters can read with such absent Attention! They are so far
from *Out of Nature*, They are absolute *Nature herself*! or, if they must
be confess'd her *Resemblance*; they are *such* a Resemblance, at least, as
our *true Face* gives our *Face* in the *Looking-glass*.

'I wonder indeed, what it is, that the Gentlemen, who talk of *Low*
Scenes, wou'd desire should be understood by the Epithet?—Nothing,
properly speaking, is *low*, that suits well with the Place it is rais'd to.—
The Passions of Nature are the same, in the *Lord*, and his *Coachman*.
All, that makes them seem different consists in the *Degrees*, in the
Means, and the *Air*, whereto or wherewith they indulge 'em. If, in
painting Distinctions like these, (which arise but from the Forms of
Men's Manners, drawn from *Birth*, *Education*, and *Custom*) a Writer
falls short of his Characters, there his Scene is a low one, indeed, whatever high Fortune it flatter'd. But, to imagine that Persons of Rank are
above a Concern for what is thought, felt, or acted, by others, of their
Species, between whom and themselves is *no Difference*, except such as
was owing to Accident, is to reduce Human Nature to a Lowness,—*too
low* for the *Truth* of her *Frailty*.—

'In *Pamela*, in particular, we owe All to her *Lowness*. It is to the
docile Effects of this Lowness of *that amiable Girl*, in her birth, her
Condition, her Hopes, and her Vanities, in every thing, in short, but
her *Virtue*,—that her Readers are indebted, for the moral *Reward*, of
that *Virtue*. And if we are to look for the *Low* among the Rest of the
Servants, less lovely tho' they are, than a *Pamela*, there is something
however, so glowingly painted, in the Lines whereby the Author has
mark'd their Distinctions—Something, so movingly forceful, in the
Grief at their *Parting*, and *Joy* at the happy *Return*,—Something so
finely, at once, and so strongly and feelingly, *varied*, even in the smallest
and least promising, little Family Incidents! that I need only appeal
from the *Heads*, to the *Hearts* of the Objectors themselves, whether
these are *low* Scenes to be censur'd?

'And as for the opposite Extreme they wou'd quarrel with, the
high-passion'd, and un-tam'd Lady *Davers*,—I cou'd direct 'em to a

Dozen or two of *Quality Originals*, from whom (with Exception perhaps of her *Wit*) one wou'd swear the Author had taken her Copy.—
What a Sum might these Objectors ensure, to be paid, by the *Husbands*
and *Sons*, of such termagant, hermaphrodite Minds, upon their making
due Proof, that they were no longer to be found, in the Kingdom!

'I know, you are too just to imagine me capable of giving any other
Opinion than my best-weigh'd and true one. But, because it is fit you
should have *Reasons*, in Support of a Judgment that can neither deserve
nor expect an implicit Reception, I will run over the Anonymous
Letter I herewith return you; and note with what Lightness even Men
of *good-natur'd* Intention fall into *Mistakes*, by Neglect in too hasty
Perusals, which their Benevolence wou'd take Pleasure in blushing at,
when they discover their Weakness, in a cooler Revisal.

'The Writer of this Letter is for having the Style *rais'd*, after *Pamela*'s
Advance in her Fortune. But surely, This was hasty Advice: because,
as the Letters are writ to her Parents, it wou'd have look'd like forgetting, and, in some sort, insulting, the Lowliness of their inferior
Condition, to have assum'd a new Air in her Language, in Place of
retaining a steady Humility. But here, it must not be pass'd unobserv'd,
that in her Reports of Conversations that follow'd her Marriage, she
does, aptly and beautifully, heighten her Style, and her Phrases; still
returning however to her decent Simplicity, in her Addresses to her
Father and Mother.

'I am against giving a Gentleman (who has ennobled himself, by
reforming his Vices, and rewarding the Worth of the *Friendless*) the
unnecessary new Toy of a *Title*. It is all strong in Nature, as it stands in
the Letters: and I don't see how Greatness, from Titles, can add Likeness or Power, to the Passions. So complete a Resemblance of *Truth*
stands in need of no borrow'd Pretensions.

'The Only of this Writer's Objections, which, I think, carries
Weight, is That, which advises some little *Contraction* of the Prayers,
and Appeals to the Deity. I say *little* Contraction: for they are nobly
and sincerely pathetic. And I say it only in Fear, lest, if fansied too long,
by the fashionably *Averse* to the Subject, Minds, which most want the
purpos'd Impression, might hazard the *Loss* of its *Benefit*, by passing over
those pious Reflections, which, if shorter, would catch their Attention.

'Certainly, the Gentleman's Objection against the Persecution that
Pamela suffers from Lady *Davers*, in respect to the Relation this Mad-
woman bears to the *Brother*, is the rashest of All his Advices! And when
he thinks she ought rather to have assum'd the Protection of her

Servants, he seems unaware of the probable *Consequence*; where there was a Puppy, of Quality, in the Case, who had, even without Provocation, drawn his Sword on the poor passive PAMELA. Far from bearing a Thought of exciting an abler Resentment, to the Danger of a Quarrel with so worthless a Coxcomb, how charmingly natural, apprehensive, and generous, is her Silence (during the Recital she makes of her Sufferings) with regard to his *masculine* Part of the Insult! as also her Prevention of Mrs. *Jewkes*'s less delicate Bluntness, when she was beginning to complain of the whelp Lord's Impertinence!

'If I were not afraid of a *Pun*, I shou'd tell the anonymous Letter-writer, that he made a too *tight-laced* Objection, where he quarrels with the spann'd Waist of *Pamela*. What, in the Name of Unshapeliness! cou'd he find, to complain of, in a beautiful Girl of Sixteen, who was born *out of Germany*, and had not, yet, reach'd ungraspable *Roundness*!— These are wonderful Sinkings from Purpose, where a Man is considering such mental, and passionate Beauties, as this Gentleman profess'd to be touch'd by!

'But, when he goes on, to object against the Word *naughty*, (as apply'd in the Phrase *naughty Master*) I grow mortified, in Fear for our human Sufficiency, compar'd with our Aptness to blunder! For, here, 'tis plain, this Director of Another's Discernment is quite blind, Himself, to an Elegance, one wou'd have thought it *impossible* not to be struck by?—Faulty, wicked, abominable, scandalous, (which are the angry Adjectives, he prefers to that sweet one) wou'd have carried Marks of her Rage, not Affliction—whereas *naughty* contains, in One single significant Petulance, twenty thousand inexpressible Delicacies! It insinuates, at once, all the beautiful Struggle, between her Contempt of his Purpose, and tender Regard for his Person; her Gratitude to Himself and his Family; her Recollection of his superior Condition.— There is in the elegant Choice of this half-kind, half-peevish, *Word*, a never-enough to be prais'd speaking Picture of the Conflict betwixt her Disdain, and her Reverence! See, Sir, the Reason I had, for apprehending some Danger that the refin'd Generosity in many of the most charming of the Sentiments wou'd be *lost*, upon the too coarse Conception of some, for whose Use the Author intended them.

'It is the same Case again, in *foolish Thing that I am!* which this nice, un-nice, Gentleman wou'd advise you to change, into *foolish that I am!* He does not seem to have tasted the pretty Contempt of Herself, the submissive *Diminutive*, so distant from Vanity, yet allay'd by the gentle Reluctance in Self-condemnation;—and the other fine Touches

of Nature which wou'd All have been lost, in the grave, sober Sound
of his *Dutch Emendation*.

'As to his Paragraph in *Postscript*, I shall say the less of it, because the
Gentleman's own good Sense seems to confess, by the Place he has
chosen to rank it in, that it ought to be turn'd out of Doors, as too
dirty for the rest of his Letter.—In the Occasions he is pleas'd to discover
for *Jokes*, I either find not, that he has any Signification at all, or such
vulgar, coarse-tasted Allusions to loose low-life Idioms, that *not* to
understand what he means, is both the cleanliest, and prudentest Way
of confuting him.

'And now, Sir, you will easily gather how far I am from thinking
it needful to change any thing in *Pamela*. I would not scratch such a
beautiful Face, for the *Indies*!

'You can hardly imagine how it charms me to hear of a Second
Edition already! but the News of still new upon new ones, will be
found no Subject of Wonder. As 'tis sure, that no Family is without
Sisters, or Brothers, or Daughters, or Sons, who can *read*; or wants
Fathers, or Mothers, or Friends, who can *think*; so equally certain it is,
that the Train to a Parcel of Powder does not run on with more natural
Tendency, till it sets the whole Heap in a Blaze, than that *Pamela*,
inchanting from Family to Family, will overspread all the Hearts of
the Kingdom.

'As to the Objection of those warm Friends to *Honesty*, who are for
having *Pamela* dismiss Mrs. *Jewkes*; there is not One, among All these
benevolent Complainers, who wou'd not discern himself to have been,
laudably, in the *wrong*, were he only to be ask'd this plain Question—
Whether a Step, both ill-judg'd, and undutiful, had not been the
Reverse of a PAMELA's Character?—Two or three times over, Mr. *B*—
had inform'd her, that Mrs. *Jewkes* and Himself having been equally
involv'd in *One Guilt*, she just forgive, or condemn, *Both together*.
After this, it grew manifest *Duty* not to treat her with Marks of
Resentment.—And, as here was a visible Necessity to appear not
desirous of turning her away, so, in point of mere *Moral* Regard to the
bad Woman Herself, it was nobler, to retain her, with a Prospect of
correcting, in Time, her loose Habit of thinking, than, by casting her off,
to the licentious Results of her Temper, abandon her to Temptations and
Danger, which a Virtue like PAMELA's cou'd not wish her expos'd to.'

*The Manner in which this admirable Gentleman gives his Opinion of the
Piece, and runs thro' the principal Characters, is so masterly, that the Readers*

of Pamela *will be charm'd by it, tho' they should suppose, that his inimitable Benevolence has overvalu'd the Piece itself.*

'Inspir'd, without doubt, by some Skill, more than human, and comprehending in an humble, and seemingly artless, Narration, a Force that can tear up the Heartstrings, this Author has prepar'd an enamouring *Philtre* for the Mind, which will excite such a *Passion* for Virtue, as scarce to leave it in the Power of the *Will* to neglect her.

'*Longinus*, I remember, distinguishing by what Marks we may know the *Sublime*, says, it is chiefly from an Effect that will follow the Reading it: a delightfully-adhering Idea, that clings fast to the Memory; and from which it is difficult for a Man to disengage his Attention.²— If *this* is a Proof of the *Sublime*, there was never *Sublimity* so lastingly felt, as in PAMELA!

'Not the Charmer's own prattling Idea stuck so close to the Heart of her Master, as the Incidents of her Story to the Thoughts of a Reader.— The Author transports, and transforms, with a Power more extensive than *Horace* requires, in his POET!—³

'Mr. *B*—, and the Turns of his Passions—and the Softness, yet Strength, of their amiable Object—after having given us the most masterly Image of Nature, that ever was painted! take Possession of, and *dwell in*, the Memory.

'And there, too, broods the kind and the credulous Parson WILLIAMS's *Dove*, (without *serpentine* Mixture) hatching *Pity* and *Affection*, for an Honesty so sincere, and so silly!⁴

'There too, take their Places All the *lower* Supports of this beautiful Fabrick.—

'I am sometimes transform'd into plain Goodman ANDREWS, and sometimes the good Woman, his Wife.

'As for old Mr. LONGMAN, and JONATHAN, the Butler, they are sure of me both, in their Turns.

'Now and-then, I am COLBRAND the *Swiss*: but, as *broad* as *I stride*, in that Character, I can never escape Mrs. JEWKES: who often keeps me awake in the Night—

'Till the Ghost of Lady DAVERS, drawing open the Curtains, scares the *Scarer*, of me, and of PAMELA!—

'And, then, I take Shelter with poor penitent JOHN, and the rest of the *Men* and the *Maids*, of all whom I may say, with compassionate *Marcia*,

'——*The Youths* DIVIDE *their Reader.*'⁵

And this fine Writer adds:

'I am glad I made War, in my last, upon the Notion of altering the Style: for, having read it twice over since then, (and to Audiences, where the *Tears* were applausively eloquent) I could hardly, here and there, find a Place, where one Word *can* be chang'd for a better. There are some indeed, where 'twere *possible* to leave out a few, without making a Breach in the Building. But, in short, the Author has put so bewitching a Mixture together, of the *Rais'd* with the *Natural*, and the *Soft* with the *Strong* and the *Eloquent*—that never Sentiments were finer, and fuller of Life! never any were utter'd so sweetly!—Even in what relates to the pious and frequent Addresses to God, I now retract (on these two last Revisals) the Consent I half gave, on a *former*, to the anonymous Writer's Proposal, who advis'd the Author to *shorten* those Beauties.—Whoever considers his *Pamela* with a View to find Matter for Censure, is in the Condition of a passionate Lover, who breaks in upon his Mistress, without Fear or Wit, with Intent to accuse her, and quarrel—He came to her with Pique in his Purpose; but his *Heart* is too hard for his *Malice*—and he goes away more enslav'd, for complaining.'

The following delightful Story, so admirably related, will give great Pleasure to the Reader; and we take the Liberty of inserting it, for that very Reason.

'What a never-to-be satisfied *Length* has this Subject always the Power of attracting me into! And yet, before I have done, I must by your means tell the Author a *Story*, which a Judge not so skilful in Nature as he is, might be in Danger perhaps of mistaking, for a trifling and silly one. I expect it shou'd give him the clearest Conviction, in a Case he is subjected to question.

'We have a lively little Boy in the Family, about seven Years old— but, alas for him, poor Child! quite unfriended; and born to no Prospect. He is the Son of an honest, poor Soldier, by a Wife, grave, unmeaning, and innocent. Yet the Boy, (see the Power of connubial *Simplicity*) is so pretty, so genteel, and gay-spirited, that we have made him, and design'd him, our *own*, ever since he could totter, and waddle. The wanton Rogue is half Air: and every Motion he acts by has a Spring, like *Pamela's* when she threw down the Card-table. All this Quickness, however, is temper'd by a good-natur'd Modesty: so that the wildest of his Flights are thought rather diverting than troublesome. He is an hourly Foundation for Laughter, from the Top of the House to the Parlours: and, to borrow an Attribute from the Reverend Mr. *Peters*, (tho' without any Note of his Musick) *plays a very good* FIDDLE in the Family.[6] I have told you the History of this *Tom-tit* of a Prater, because, ever since my first reading of PAMELA, he puts in for a Right to be *one* of her Hearers; and, having got half her Sayings by heart, talks in no other Language but hers: and, what really surprises, and has charm'd me into a *certain* Fore-taste of her Influence, he is, at once, become fond of his Book; which (before) he cou'd never be brought to attend to—that *he may read* PAMELA, he says, *without stopping*. The first Discovery we made of this Power over so unripe and unfix'd an Attention, was, one Evening, when I was reading her Reflections at the *Pond* to some Company. The little rampant Intruder, being kept out by the Extent of the Circle, had crept under my Chair, and was sitting before me, on the Carpet, with his Head almost touching the Book, and his Face bowing down toward the Fire.—He had sat for some time in this Posture, with a Stillness, that made us conclude him asleep: when, on a sudden, we heard a Succession of heart-heaving Sobs; which while he strove to conceal from our Notice, his little Sides swell'd, as if they wou'd burst, with the throbbing Restraint of his Sorrow. I turn'd his innocent Face, to look toward me; but his Eyes were quite lost, in his *Tears*: which running down from his Cheeks in free Currents, had form'd two sincere little Fountains, on that Part of the Carpet he hung over. All the Ladies in Company were ready to devour him with Kisses: and he has, since, become doubly a Favourite —and is perhaps the youngest of *Pamela*'s *Converts*.'

The same incomparable Writer has favour'd us with an Objection, that is more material than any we have mention'd; which cannot be better stated nor answer'd, than in his own beautiful Words; viz.

'An Objection is come into my Thoughts, which I should be glad the Author would think proper to obviate in the Front of the Second Edition.

'There are Mothers, or Grandmothers, in all Families of affluent Fortune, who, tho' they may have none of Lady *Davers*'s *Insolence*, will be apt to feel one of her *Fears*,—that the Example of a Gentleman so amiable as Mr. *B—* may be follow'd, by the *Jackies, their Sons*, with too blind and unreflecting a Readiness. Nor does the Answer of that Gentleman to his Sister's Reproach come quite up to the Point they will rest on. For, tho' indeed it is true, all the World wou'd acquit the best Gentleman in it, if he married such a Waiting-maid as *Pamela*, yet, there is an ill-discerning Partiality, in Passion, that will overthrow all the Force of that Argument: because *every belov'd Maid will be* PAMELA, in a Judgment obscur'd by her Influence.

'And, since the Ground of this Fear will *seem* solid, I don't know how to be easy, till it is shewn (nor ought it to be left to the Author's Modesty) that they who consider his Design in that Light will be found but short-sighted Observers.

'Request it of him then to suffer it to be told them, that not a limited, but general, Excitement to Virtue was the first and great End to his story: And that this Excitement must have been deficient, and very imperfectly offer'd, if he had not look'd quite *as low as he cou'd* for his Example: because if there had been any Degree or Condition, more remote from the Prospect than that which he had chosen to work on, that Degree might have seem'd out of Reach of the Hope, which it was his generous Purpose to encourage.—And, so, he was under an evident *Necessity* to find such a Jewel in a *Cottage*: and expos'd, too, as she was, to the severest Distresses of Fortune, with Parents unable to support their own Lives, but from the daily hard Product of *Labour*.

'Nor wou'd it have been sufficient to have plac'd her thus *low* and *distressful*, if he had not also suppos'd her a *Servant*: and that too in some elegant Family; for if she had always remain'd a Fellow-cottager with her Father, it must have carried an Air of Romantick Improbability to account for her polite Education.

'If she had *wanted* those Improvements, which she found means to acquire in her *Service*, it wou'd have been very unlikely, that she shou'd have succeeded so well; and had destroy'd *one* great *Use* of the Story, to have allow'd such uncommon Felicity to the Effect of mere *personal Beauty*.—And it had not been *judicious* to have represented her as educated in a superior Condition of Life with the proper Accomplishments, before she became reduc'd by Misfortunes, and so not a Servant, but rather an Orphan under hopeless Distresses—because Opportunities which had made it no Wonder how she came to be so winningly qualified, wou'd have lessen'd her Merit in being so. And besides, where had then been the purpos'd Excitement of Persons in PAMELA'S Condition of Life, by an Emulation of her Sweetness, Humility, Modesty, Patience, and Industry, to attain some faint Hope of arriving, in time, within View of *her* Happiness?—And what a delightful Reformation shou'd we see, in all Families, where the Vanity of their *Maids* took no Turn toward Ambition to *please*, but by such innocent Measures, as PAMELA's!

'As it is clear, the, the Author was under a Necessity to suppose her a *Servant*, he is not to be accountable for mistaken Impressions, which the Charms he has given her may happen to make, on wrong Heads, or weak Hearts, tho' in Favour of Maids the Reverse of her Likeness.

'What is it then (they may say) that the Lowness, and Distance of *Pamela's* Condition from the Gentleman's who married her, proposes to teach the *Gay World*, and the *Fortunate*?—*It is this*—By Comparison with that infinite Remoteness of her Condition from the Reward which her Virtue procur'd her, one great *Proof* is deriv'd, (which is Part of the *Moral* of PAMELA) that Advantages from *Birth*, and Distinction of *Fortune*, have no Power at all, when consider'd against those from *Behaviour*, and Temper of *Mind*: because where the *Last* are *not added* all the *First* will be boasted in vain. Whereas she who possesses the Last finds *no Want* of the First, in her Influence.

In *that* Light alone let the Ladies of *Rank* look at PAMELA.—Such an alarming Reflection as that will, at the same time that it raises the Hope and Ambition of the *Humble*, correct and mortify the Disdain of the *Proud*. For it will compel them to observe, and acknowledge, that 'tis the Turn of their *Mind*, not the Claims of their *Quality*, by which (and which only) Womens [*sic*] Charms can be lasting: And that, while the *haughty Expectations*, inseparable from an elevated Rank, serve but to multiply its Complaints and Afflictions, the Condescensions of *accomplish'd Humility*, attracting Pity, Affection, and Reverence, secure an hourly Increase of Felicity.—So that the *moral Meaning* of PAMELA's Good-fortune, far from tempting young Gentlemen to marry *such* Maids as are found in their Families, is, by teaching Maids *to deserve to be Mistresses*, to stir up Mistresses *to support their Distinction*.'

We shall only add, That it was intended to prefix two neat Frontispieces *to this Edition, (and to present them to the Purchasers of the first) and one was actually finished for that Purpose; but there not being Time for the other, from the Demand for the new Impression; and the Engraving Part of that which was done (tho' no Expense was spared) having fallen very short of the Spirit of the Passages they were intended to represent, the Proprietors were advised to lay them aside.*[7] *And were the rather induced to do so, from the following Observations of a most ingenious Gentleman, in a Letter to the Editor.* 'I am so jealous, *says he*, in Behalf of our *inward* Idea of PAMELA's *Person*, that I dread *any* figur'd Pretence to Resemblance. For it will be pity to look at an *Air*, and imagine it *Hers*, that does not carry some such elegant Perfection of Amiableness, as will be sure to find place in the *Fancy*.'

26 Preface to Volume I of *Clarissa Harlowe*, 1747

by SAMUEL RICHARDSON

This Preface appeared in Volume I of *Clarissa*, which was published in December 1747, though the title-page has 1748.

The following History is given in a Series of Letters, written principally in a double, yet separate, Correspondence;

Between Two young Ladies of Virtue and Honour, bearing an inviolable Friendship for each other, and writing upon the most interesting Subjects: And

Between Two Gentlemen of free Lives; one of them glorying in his Talents for Stratagem and Invention, and communicating to the other, in Confidence, all the secret Purposes of an intriguing Head, and resolute Heart.

But it is not amiss to premise, for the sake of such as may apprehend Hurt to the Morals of Youth from the more freely-written Letters, That the Gentlemen, tho' professed Libertines as to the Fair Sex, and making it one of their wicked Maxims, to keep no Faith with any of the Individuals of it who throw themselves into their Power, are not, however, either Infidels or Scoffers: Nor yet such as think themselves freed from the Observance of those other moral Obligations, which bind Man to Man.

On the contrary, it will be found, in the Progress of the Collection, that they very often make such Reflections upon each other, and each upon himself, and upon his Actions, as reasonable Beings, who disbelieve not a future State of Rewards and Punishments (and who one day propose to reform) must sometimes make:—One of them actually reforming, and antidoting the Poison which some might otherwise apprehend would be spread by the gayer Pen, and lighter Heart, of the other.

And yet that other, (altho' in unbosoming himself to a *select Friend*, he discover Wickedness enough to intitle him to general Hatred) preserves a Decency, as well in his Images, as in his Language, which is not always to be found in the Works of some of the most celebrated modern Writers, whose Subjects and Characters have less warranted the Liberties they have taken.

Length will be naturally expected, not only from what has been said, but from the following Considerations:

That the Letters on both Sides are written while the Hearts of the Writers must be supposed to be wholly engaged in their Subjects: The Events at the Time generally dubious:—So that they abound, not only with critical Situations; but with what may be called *instantaneous* Descriptions and Reflections; which may be brought home to the Breast of the youthful Reader:—As also, with affecting Conversations; many of them written in the Dialogue or Dramatic Way.

To which may be added, that the Collection contains not only the History of the excellent Person whose Name it bears, but includes The Lives, Characters, and Catastrophes, of several others, either principally or incidentally concerned in the Story.

But yet the Editor (to whom it was referred to publish the Whole in such a Way as he should think would be most acceptable to the Public) was so diffident in relation to this Article of *Length*, that he thought proper to submit the Letters to the Perusal of several judicious Friends; whose Opinion he desired of what might be best spared.

One Gentleman, in particular, of whose Knowledge, Judgment, and Experience, as well as Candor, the Editor has the highest Opinion, advised him to give a Narrative Turn to the Letters; and to publish only what concerned the principal Heroine;—striking off the collateral Incidents, and all that related to the Second Characters; tho' he allowed the Parts which would have been by this means excluded, to be both instructive and entertaining. But being extremely fond of the affecting Story, he was desirous to have everything parted with, which he thought retarded its Progress.

This Advice was not relished by other Gentlemen. They insisted, that the Story could not be reduced to a Dramatic Unity, nor thrown into the Narrative Way, without divesting it of its Warmth; and of a great Part of its Efficacy; as very few of the Reflections and Observations, which they looked upon as the most useful Part of the Collection, would, then, find a Place.

They were of Opinion, That in all Works of This, and of the Dramatic Kind, STORY, or AMUSEMENT, should be considered as little more than the *Vehicle* to the more necessary INSTRUCTION: That many of the Scenes would be render'd languid, were they to be made less busy:

And that the Whole would be thereby deprived of that Variety, which is deemed the Soul of a Feast, whether *mensal* or mental.

They were also of Opinion, That the Parts and Characters, which must be omitted, if this Advice were followed, were some of the most natural in the whole Collection: And no less instructive; especially to *Youth*. Which might be a Consideration perhaps overlooked by a Gentleman of the Adviser's great Knowledge and Experience: For, as they observed, there is a Period in human Life, in which, youthful Activity ceasing, and Hope contenting itself to peep out of its own domestic Wicket upon bounded Prospects, the half-tired Mind aims a little more than *Amusement*.—And with Reason; for what, in the *instructive* Way, can appear either *new* or *needful* to one who has happily got over those dangerous Situations which call for Advice and Cautions, and who has fill'd up his Measures of Knowledge to the Top?

Others, likewise gave *their* Opinions. But no Two being of the same Mind, as to the Parts which could be omitted, it was resolved to present to the World, the Two First Volumes, by way of Specimen; and to be determined with regard to the rest by the Reception those should meet with.

If that be favourable, Two others may soon follow; the whole Collection being ready for the Press: That is to say, If it be not found necessary to abstract or omit some of the Letters, in order to reduce the Bulk of the Whole.

Thus much in general. But it may not be amiss to add, in particular, that in the great Variety of Subjects which this Collection contains, it is one of the principal Views of the Publication,

To caution Parents against the *undue* Exertion of their natural Authority over their Children, in the great Article of Marriage:

And Children against preferring a Man of Pleasure to a Man of Probity, upon that dangerous, but too commonly received Notion, *That a Reformed Rake makes the best Husband.*

But as the Characters will not all appear in the Two First Volumes, it has been thought advisable, in order to give the Reader some further Idea of Them, and of the Work, to prefix
A brief Account of the principal Characters
throughout the Whole.[1]

27 Preface to *Roderick Random*, 1748

by TOBIAS SMOLLETT

Of all kinds of satire, there is none so entertaining and universally improving, as that which is introduced, as it were, occasionally in the course of an interesting story, which brings every incident home to life; and, by representing familiar scenes in an uncommon and amusing point of view, invests them with all the graces of novelty, while nature is appealed to in every particular.

The reader gratifies his curiosity in pursuing the adventures of a person in whose favour he is prepossessed; he espouses his cause, he sympathizes with him in distress, his indignation is heated against the authors of his calamity; the humane passions are inflamed; the contrast between dejected virtue and insulting vice appears with greater aggravation; and every impression having a double force on the imagination, the memory retains the circumstance, and the heart improves by the example. The attention is not tired with a bare catalogue of characters, but agreeably diverted with all the variety of invention; and the vicissitudes of life appear in their peculiar circumstances, opening an ample field for wit and humour.

Romance, no doubt, owes its origin to ignorance, vanity, and superstition. In the dark ages of the world, when a man had rendered himself famous for wisdom or valour, his family and adherents availed themselves of his superior qualities, magnified his virtues, and represented his character and person as sacred and supernatural. The vulgar easily swallowed the bait, implored his protection, and yielded the tribute of homage and praise even to adoration; his exploits were handed down to posterity with a thousand exaggerations; they were repeated as incitements to virtue; divine honours were paid, and altars erected, to his memory, for the encouragement of those who attempted to imitate his example; and hence arose the heathen mythology, which is no other than a collection of extravagant romances. As learning advanced, and genius received cultivation, these stories were embellished with the graces of poetry: that they might the better recommend themselves to the attention, they were sung in public, at festivals, for the instruction and delight of the audience; and rehearsed before battle, as incentives to deeds of glory. Thus tragedy and the epic muse were born, and, in the progress of taste, arrived at perfection. It is no wonder that the ancients could not relish a fable in prose, after they had seen so many remarkable events celebrated in verse by their best poets; we therefore find no romance among them, during the era of their excellence, unless the *Cyropaedia* of Xenophon may be so called, and it was not till arts and sciences began to revive, after the irruption of the barbarians into Europe, that any thing of this kind appeared. But when the minds of men were debauched, by the imposition of priestcraft, to the most absurd pitch of credulity, the authors of romance arose, and, losing sight of probability, filled their performances with the most monstrous hyperboles. If they could not equal the poets in point of genius, they were resolved to excel them in fiction, and apply to the wonder rather than the judgment of their readers. Accordingly, they brought necromancy to their aid, and, instead of supporting the character of their heroes by dignity of sentiment and practice, distinguished them by their bodily strength, activity, and extravagance of behaviour. Although nothing could be more ludicrous and unnatural than the figures they drew, they did not want patrons and admirers; and the world actually began to be infected with the spirit of knight errantry, when Cervantes, by an inimitable piece of ridicule, reformed the taste of mankind, representing chivalry in the right point of view, and converting romance to purposes far more useful and entertaining, by making it assume the sock, and point out the follies of ordinary life.

The same method has been practised by other Spanish and French authors, and by none more successfully than by Monsieur Le Sage, who, in his *Adventures of Gil Blas*, has described the knavery and foibles of life with infinite humour and sagacity.[1] The following sheets I have modelled on his plan, taking the liberty, however, to differ from him in the execution, where I thought his particular situations were uncommon and extravagant, or peculiar to the country in which the scene is laid. The disgraces of Gil Blas are, for the most part, such as rather excite mirth than compassion; he himself laughs at them; and his transitions from distress to happiness, or at least ease, are so sudden, that neither the reader has time to pity him, nor himself to be acquainted with affliction. This conduct, in my opinion, not only deviates from probability, but prevents that generous indignation which ought to animate the reader against the sordid and vicious disposition of the world.

I have attempted to represent modest merit struggling with every difficulty to which a friendless orphan is exposed from his own want of experience, as well as from the selfishness, envy, malice, and base indifference of mankind. To secure a favourable prepossession, I have allowed him the advantage of birth and education, which, in the series of his misfortunes, will, I hope, engage the ingenuous more warmly in his behalf; and, though I foresee that some people will be offended at the mean scenes in which he is involved, I persuade myself the judicious will not only perceive the necessity of describing those situations to which he must of course be confined, in his low estate, but also find entertainment in viewing those parts of his life, where the humours and passions are undisguised by affectation, ceremony, or education, and the whimsical peculiarities of disposition appear as Nature has implanted them. But I believe I need not trouble myself in vindicating a practice authorized by the best writers in this way, some of whom I have already named.

Every intelligent reader will, at first sight, perceive I have not deviated from Nature in the facts, which are all true in the main, although the circumstances are altered and disguised, to avoid personal satire.

It now remains to give my reasons for making the chief personage of this work a North Briton; which are chiefly these:—I could, at a small expence, bestow on him such education as I thought the dignity of his birth and character required, which could not possibly be obtained in England by such slender means as the nature of my plan would afford. In the next place, I could represent simplicity of manners, in a remote part of the kingdom, with more propriety than in any other place near the capital; and, lastly, the disposition of the Scots, addicted to travelling, justifies my conduct in deriving an adventurer from that country.

That the delicate reader may not be offended at the unmeaning oaths which proceed from the mouths of some persons in these memoirs, I beg leave to premise, that I imagined nothing could more effectually expose the absurdity of such miserable expletives, than a natural and verbal representation of the discourse in which they occur.

28 Preface to Volume III of *Clarissa Harlowe*, 1748

by WILLIAM WARBURTON

William Warburton (1698–1779), Bishop of Gloucester from 1759, was best known for *The Alliance between Church and State* (1736), *The Divine Legation of Moses* (1737–41) and his editions of Shakespeare (1747) and Pope (1751). Richardson had solicited this Preface from Warburton for the first edition of Volumes III and IV of *Clarissa* (April, 1748), and seems to have felt obliged to publish it in spite of his dislike for it. He dropped Warburton's Preface as soon as he could (see below, No. 38, and R. S. Crane, 'Richardson Warburton and French Fiction', *M.L.R.*, XVII (1922), 17–23).

THE EDITOR *to the* READER

If it may be thought reasonable to criticize the Public Taste, in what are generally supposed to be Works of mere Amusement; or modest to direct its Judgment, in what is offered for its Entertainment; I would beg leave to introduce the following Sheets with a few cursory Remarks, that may lead the common Reader into some tolerable conception of the nature of this Work, and the design of its Author.

The close connexion which every Individual has with all that relates to MAN in general, strongly inclines us to turn our observation upon human affairs, preferably to other attentions, and impatiently to wait the progress and issue of them. But, as the course of human actions is too slow to gratify our inquisitive curiosity, observant men very easily contrived to satisfy its rapidity, by the invention of *History*. Which, by recording the principal circumstances of past facts, and laying them close together, in a continued narration, kept the mind from languishing, and gave constant exercise to its reflections.

But as it commonly happens, that in all indulgent refinements on our satisfactions, the Procurers to our pleasures run into excess; so it happened here. Strict matters of fact, how delicately soever dressed up, soon grew too simple and insipid to a taste stimulated by the Luxury of Art: They wanted something of more poignancy to quicken and enforce a jaded appetite. Hence the original of the first barbarous *Romances*, abounding with this false provocative of uncommon, extraordinary, and miraculous Adventures.

But satiety, in things unnatural, soon brings on disgust. And the Reader, at length, began to see, that too eager a pursuit after *Adventures* had drawn him from what first engaged his attention, MAN *and his Ways*, into the Fairy Walks of Monsters and Chimeras. And now those who had run farthest after these delusions, were the first that recovered themselves. For the next Species of Fiction, which took its name from its *novelty*, was of *Spanish* invention. These presented us with something of Humanity; but of Humanity in a stiff unnatural state. For, as every thing before was conducted by *Inchantment*; so now all was managed by *Intrigue*. And tho' it had indeed a kind of *Life*, it had yet, as in its infancy, nothing of *Manners*. On which account, those, who could not penetrate into the ill constitution of its plan, yet grew disgusted at the dryness of the Conduct, and want of ease in the Catastrophe.

The avoiding these defects gave rise to the *Heroical Romances* of the *French*; in which some celebrated Story of antiquity was so stained and polluted by modern fable and invention, as was just enough to shew, that the contrivers of them neither knew how to lye, nor speak truth. In these voluminous extravagances, *Love* and *Honour* supplied the place of *Life* and *Manners*. But the over-refinement of Platonic sentiments always sinks into the dross and feces of that Passion. For in attempting a more natural representation of it, in the little amatory Novels, which succeeded these heavier Volumes tho' the Writers avoided the dryness of the Spanish Intrigue, and the extravagance of the French Heroism, yet, by too natural a representation of their Subject, they opened the door to a worse evil than a corruption of *Taste*; and that was, A corruption of *Heart*.

At length, this great People (to whom, it must be owned, all Science has been infinitely indebted) hit upon the true Secret, by which alone a deviation from strict fact, in the commerce of Man, could be really entertaining to an improved mind, or useful to promote that Improvement. And this was by a faithful and chaste copy of real *Life and Manners*: In which some of their late Writers have greatly excelled.

It was on this sensible Plan, that the Author of the following Sheets attempted to please, in an Essay, which had the good fortune to meet with success: That encouragement engaged him in the present Design: In which his sole object being *Human Nature*, he thought himself at liberty to draw a Picture of it in that light which would shew it with most strength of Expression; tho' at the expence of what such as read merely for Amusement, may fancy can be ill-spared, the more artificial composition of a story in one continued Narrative.

He has therefore told his Tale in a Series of Letters, supposed to be written by the Parties concerned, as the circumstances related, passed. For this juncture afforded him the only natural opportunity that could be had, of representing with any grace those lively and delicate impressions which *Things present* are known to make upon the minds of those affected by them. And he apprehends, that, in the study of Human Nature, the knowlege of those apprehensions leads us farther into the recesses of the Human Mind, than the colder and more general reflections suited to a continued and more contracted Narrative.

This is the nature and purport of his Attempt. Which, perhaps, may not be so well or generally understood. For if the Reader seeks here for Strange Tales, Love Stories, Heroical Adventures, or, in short, for anything but a *Faithful Picture of Nature* in *Private Life*, he had better be told beforehand the likelihood of his being disappointed. But if he can find Use or Entertainment, either *Directions for his Conduct*, or *Employment for his Pity*, in a HISTORY of LIFE and MANNERS, where, as in the World itself, we find Vice, for a time, triumphant, and Virtue in distress, an idle hour or two, we hope, may not be unprofitably lost.

29 From a letter of Elizabeth Carter, June 20, 1749

Elizabeth Carter (1717–1806), the author of the *Ode to Wisdom*, which Richardson appropriated in manuscript for publication in *Clarissa Harlowe*, was a friend of Samuel Johnson and contributed two numbers to the *Rambler* (Nos. 44 and 100), and was known as the translator of Epictetus (1758). Her letter was addressed to Catherine Talbot (1720–70), who also contributed to the *Rambler* (No. 30) and wrote various essays and letters which were published after her death.

[. . . . .]
I am sorry to find you so outrageous about poor Tom Jones; he is no doubt an imperfect, but not a detestable character, with all that honesty, goodnature, and generosity of temper. Though nobody can admire Clarissa more than I do; yet with all our partiality, I am afraid, it must be confessed, that Fielding's book is the most natural representation of what passes in the world, and of the bizarreries which arise from the mixture of good and bad which makes up the composition of most folks. Richardson has no doubt a very good hand at painting excellence, but there is a strange awkwardness and extravagance in his vicious characters. To be sure, poor man, he had read in a book, or heard some one say, there was such a thing in the world as wickedness, but being totally ignorant in what manner the said wickedness operates upon the human heart, and what checks and restraints it meets with to prevent its ever being perfectly uniform and consistent in any one character, he has drawn such a monster, as I hope never existed in mortal shape, for to the honor of human nature, and the gracious author of it, be it spoken, Clarissa is an infinitely more imitable character, than Lovelace, or the Harlowes.

[. . . . .]

30 From a review of *Tom Jones* (1749), *The London Magazine*, XVIII, February 1749

The London Magazine (1732–85), was founded by a group of booksellers in opposition to the *Gentleman's Magazine* (see below, No. 32), and, although it tended to follow a more liberal policy, was a page-by-page imitation of its rival.

A Book having been lately published, which has given great Amusement, and, we hope, Instruction to the polite Part of the Town, we think ourselves obliged to give our Readers some Account of it

It is intitled, *The History of* TOM JONES, *a Foundling*, by Henry Fielding, Esq;[1] being a novel, or prose epick composition, and calculated to recommend religion and virtue, to shew the bad consequences of indiscretion, and to set several kinds of vice in their most deformed and shocking light. This piece, like all such good compositions, consists of a principal history, and a great many episodes or incidents; all which arise naturally from the subject, and contribute towards carrying on the chief plot or design. Through the whole, the reader's attention is always kept awake by some new surprizing accident, and his curiosity upon the stretch, to discover the effects of that accident; so that after one has begun to read, it is difficult to leave off before having read the whole.

[. . . . .]

Thus ends this pretty novel, with a most just distribution of rewards and punishments, according to the merits of all the persons that had any considerable share in it; but this short abstract can only serve as an incitement to those, that have not yet had the pleasure of reading it; for we had not room for many of the surprizing incidents, or for giving any of them in their beautiful dress.[2]

31   *The Fool, No. 422.* 'A Censure on the present reigning taste for Novels and Romances, and how to cure it', *The London Magazine,* XVIII, May 1749

Hoc fonte derivata clades
In patriam populumque fluxit.
                                HOR.[1]

There is at last a very happy taste sprung up amongst us for *novel* and *romance,* such a one as appeared in *France* when *Richlieu* was forming his schemes for the making his master absolute at home, and shining abroad.[2] It was about this time the most celebrated *novels* made their appearance, and amused the better sort of people into a matchless inattention to what the directors of publick affairs were concerting for the fettering of the people. The follies of the persons of rank very aptly catch the regard of the vulgar, who are ever ready to be led by the examples of those they esteem their betters; nor needs there any other means to make the common people behave sillily, than the observing their superiors descend from their dignity, and very gravely become buffoons.

There is a certain relish for rational pleasures, which the wisest men may condescend to entertain; such as instructive plays well acted, musick finely executed, orations on science, perspective views of improved scenes in nature, painting, poetry, and polite prose essays, where the dignity of humour is not suffered to degenerate into mere farce and idleness, but as in the *Spectators,* where the mind is at once bettered and delighted; but when whims and conundrums run away with the applause of a sensible people, mimick gestures and drollery command their attention, and *a tale of a tub*[3] becomes fashionable reading, we perceive the human spirit lost in the pursuit of a non-entity, and reasonable delight, true glory, and a firm resolution to be free, exchanged for negligence and folly.

When *Cervantes* wrote his famous *romance* of *Don Quixote,* his views were just and noble; it was an attempt to retrieve the natural good sense of his nation, and, by a palatable regimen timely applied, to cool the brains of his countrymen, and to reduce them to the equal standard of reason. The lunacy of the age by degrees evaporated, calm and serene thinking gradually resumed its native seat, and the author's happy success approved his wisdom.

I believe we may say, without partiality to ourselves, that we have naturally as much good sense as our neighbours, and have occasionally shown it; but are at the same time such professed humourists, and are so well satisfied whenever the *ridiculous* gains the ascendant, that no sooner a droll rogue touches that foible, but he commands all our affections. This man may put on a grave face, that woman assume the prude, the clergy may preach, the orator harangue, the essayist write; like poison that has once got possession of the human body, and circulates thro' the vital frame, its powers are only wasted or overcome by the superior opposite qualities in the corporeal disposition, or qualified by lenients, or eradicated by sudorificks. So foolery runs its race, until wasted by the natural inferiority of its own powers, is overcome by cool reflection, or eradicated be [sic] common sense. They who attempt to stop it in its career, may as well think of stemming a flood-tide in the river *Humber,* or of impeding the first emotions of the violence of a heated faction; while it can hold the passions, it will triumph, and as they cool, it gradually resigns its pre-eminence over the mind, passes and is forgot.

I know not of any better way to rectify this casual disorder, than by collecting together all the ridiculous circumstances that have occurred for 30 years past, whether in writing, conversation, or action, whereby the publick have for a time been diverted, and for ever after ashamed of: Such a work well digested, and illustrated with suitable cuts, would probably answer the same end here as *Don Quixote* did in *Spain;* our follies would then stare us so eminently in the face, and the reflection of our own weakness strike us so keenly, as must go a great way towards rooting out this national evil, and at the same time guarding us for the future against such like vicious affections.

I would have this done historically, each reigning folly deduced down regularly in due order of time, and the whole so prettily chained together, as to make it at least as pleasant in the reading, as *Tom Jones,*[4] or any other modern *romance.* I could wish likewise it was executed in the airy stile, the diction light and free, the reflections, if any where necessary, rather humorous than grave, and the whole so happily calculated to make men wiser, as might bring us back to that even state of thinking, which did an honour to our ancestors, and made them revered, dreaded, and applauded, where-ever the *British* name had being. It may be entitled, *A genuine history of* British *wisdom*; or, if it is better liked, *my character* is at the author's service; and, if it will add any thing to the main design, he may furnish it with proper remarks on my wise lucubrations.

32 An account of *Clarissa* and Richardson's reply, *Gentleman's Magazine*, XIX, June and July 1749

The passages reproduced in the *Gentleman's Magazine* were taken from the *Bibliotèque raisonnée*, XLII (1749), 325ff. They were written by Albrecht von Haller (1708–77), Swiss physician and physiologist, Professor of Anatomy and Surgery at the University of Gottingen, poet and writer of philosophical romances. The footnotes provided in the *Gentleman's Magazine* were by Richardson himself.

The *Gentleman's Magazine*, founded in 1731 by the printer Edward Cave (1691–1754), the first periodical of its kind and the first to use the word 'magazine', was immediately successful and became the model of many similar ventures. Cave was a personal friend of Richardson and the magazine was consistently favourable to that writer's work.

As every Englishman *appropriates to himself some degree of the honour paid to his countrymen abroad, it is with the greater pleasure that we insert the following character of Clarissa, from a book lately published at* Amsterdam; *and we hope our readers will share this pleasure with us.*

Clarissa: ou l'Histoire d'une Demoiselle de Qualité, &c.
Clarissa: or, the History of a Young Lady.

The Editor of this celebrated performance is Mr. *S. Robinson*,[1] a bookseller, the suppos'd author of *Pamela*; and with equal reason said to be the author as well as editor of the present work: and it must be confessed that, in this, the public voice has paid an high compliment to his taste and abilities.

Clarissa may be said to be the younger sister and imitater of *Pamela*. The author, however, appears to have drawn great advantages from the criticisms (*profite des critques*) which have been made on the prior work; in particular, he has avoided the tiresome gravity which prevails in the last Vol. of his *Pamela*, and the stile and sentiments rise in proportion as the catastrophe approaches. As there are many more persons introduced in *Clarissa*, the author has drawn and maintained a great number of characters, and enriched this work with a variety that is wanting in *Pamela*. The heroes of his performance being almost all persons of distinction whose minds may be supposed to have received much greater improvements from education than that of a country girl, he has had an opportunity to intersperse, in the course of the work, a great number of reflexions arising from an extensive knowledge of life, and a polite and cultivated taste, which renders it more elegant, and at the same time greatly more useful. Instead of a statue of a lover, who never speaks but by the organs of another, the admirer of *Clarissa* writes himself the greater part of those letters, which are animated with a warmth of expression, and a kind of humorous gaiety, not to be admitted in the correspondence of a lady without indecency.

The interesting descriptions are much more frequent than in *Pamela*; here they succeed each other in an almost uninterrupted series. The reader is allowed no interval of rest; but urged on from one event to another, his curiosity is perpetually both excited and gratified. Very large impressions of this work have been impatiently bought up in *England*, and all the readers whom we know concur in giving it the first rank among romances.

This expression probably may be resented by the *French*, who have written so many, and imagine they have succeeded so well; but perhaps they will acquiesce in our opinion, if the following observations be considered. The most applauded of the *French* romances are generally no more than representations of the illustrious actions of illustrious persons. All the incidents of their private life are suppressed: the heroe only is exhibited, a being, who has neither wants, or manners, or virtues, or vices, in common with the rest of mankind: the qualities with which these heroes are endow'd may be all included either in courage, generosity, or, which is more common, in constancy, and a devotion of their whole lives and fortunes to the service of certain ladies, who, in return, treat them with indifference and contempt. Who can but smile to see *Cyrus*[2] fill *Asia* with his conquests only in the search of his mistress? Indeed, love is so universally predominant in the *French* writings, that they appear to be ignorant of all the virtues except that of loving with ardour and constancy.

It must, however, be confessed that *Marivaux* endeavour'd to bring back his countrymen to nature.[3] His *Marianne* and his *Paisan parvenu* are paintings after life; in these the author speaks less, and his characters more: but this genius could not wholly cure himself of the fashion, nor

131

did he dare to entertain his country with private and domestic occurrences. His *Marianne* speaks like a girl of wit, who loves a kind of general virtue, which consists in preferring her honour to the gratification of her tenderest wishes. But the particulars which constitute a virtuous life are not exhibited; there is no representation of the minutiæ of *Virtue*, no example of *her* conduct to those by whom *she* is surrounded as equals, superiors, or inferiors. *Marianne* is a kind of chronicle, in which some memorable adventures are well described. *Clarissa* is an history, where the events of her life follow each other in an uninterrupted succession. *Marianne* is a young lady of quality, who knows neither the duty of managing or educating children, nor the employments which fill the life of a person of merit; whenever she appears she is loaded with ornament, either to please her benefactress, or her lover. —*Clarissa* is a very different person: she is a lady of quality, who at once knows and fulfils her duty: she mentions, in the most minute and particular manner, her duties towards God (never found in *French* romances) her parents, her relations, her friends, her servants, and herself; the duties peculiar to every hour of a life of perfect virtue are there delineated. The reflexions and remarks which are interspersed in her letters are the result of great knowledge of mankind; yet the whole is within the reach of every capacity, and is calculated to make every reader both the wiser and the better. *Marianne* amuses, *Clarissa* not only amuses, but instructs; and the more effectually, as the writer paints nature, and nature alone.

(*This* French *original coming at a late day, we must defer the judicious remarks on the characters, which follow in an epitome of this history.*)

A critical Account of Clarissa in 7 Volumes. Translated from the French. (*Continued from* [above]).

The method which the author has pursued, in the history of *Clarissa*, is the same as in the life of *Pamela*; both are related in familiar letters, by the parties themselves, at the very time in which the events happened; and this method has given the author great advantages, which he could not have drawn from any other species of narration. The minute particulars of events, the sentiments and conversation of the parties, are, upon this plan, exhibited with all the warmth and spirit that the passion, supposed to be predominant at the very time, could produce, and with all the distinguishing characteristicks, which memory can supply, in a history of recent transactions. Romances in general, and *Marivaux's* among others, are wholly improbable; because they suppose the history to be written after the series of events is closed by the catastrophe; a circumstance, which implies a strength of memory, beyond all example and probability, in the persons concerned, enabling them, at the distance of several years, to relate all the particulars of a transient conversation: Or rather it implies a yet more improbable confidence and familiarity between all these persons and the author. There is, however, one difficulty attending the epistolary method, for it is necessary that all the characters should have an uncommon taste for this kind of correspondence, and that they should suffer no event, nor even a remarkable conversation to pass without immediately committing it to writing; but, for the preservation of these letters, once written, the author has provided with great judgment, so as to render this circumstance highly probable.

We shall now proceed to the history itself, to which we shall add some cursory remarks.

CLARISSA, a young lady of consummate merit, singular beauty, and uncommon delicacy, had refused many offers on account of the defects which she had discovered in the morals of the persons by whom she had been addressed. Among others, a young gentleman, whose name was *Lovelace*, of a noble family, a fine person, and sprightly wit, becomes enamour'd of her; and, by the mistake of an uncle, is introduced, as a suitor, to the elder sister of *Clarissa*, as disagreeable as *Clarissa* is lovely; and his relations having made some advances towards engaging him with this lady, whom he can never love, he has recourse to an artifice to get her to reject his suit, from which he could not otherwise conveniently desist. As his principles are not strictly virtuous, and as he has an extraordinary talent for gratifying his passions, by intrigue and dissimulation, he succeeds, and pursues his design of espousing *Clarissa*, who permits his addresses, with the consent of her parents. Her only brother, who is insolent and avaricious to excess, and has an absolute ascendency over the father, just at this crisis, arrives from his travels; and, as he had conceived an irreconcileable hatred against *Lovelace*, opposes his match with his sister, and, at length, provokes him to a duel, in which the aggressor is wounded and disarm'd.

The family incensed at this event, and prompted by the sister whom *Lovelace* had slighted, forbid him the house. Another suitor, wholly disagreeable to *Clarissa*, is introduced, and supported by her parents, who use her with great and unjust severity, in order to compel her to marry him, which she absolutely refuses.

Clarissa had begun a kind of correspondence with Mr. *Lovelace*, by her mother's consent, which she now continues, partly for prudential reasons, and, perhaps, more by inclination. In the course of this correspondence, and after the intervention of a great variety of scenes, which are finely painted, she is led to give *Lovelace* a private meeting, which, by a new artifice, he causes to terminate in her going off with him, almost in spight of herself; an event which overwhelms her with doubts and terrors, very natural to a young lady in such circumstances. *Lovelace* has no sooner got her into his hands, than he falters in his resolution to marry her, and resolves to attempt to prevail on her to live with him as a mistress, and in spight of frequent intervals of virtue and tenderness, which incline him, from time to time, to do justice to so much merit, his criminal resolution becomes predominant. To carry this design into execution, he finds means to bring the lady into a private brothel, where she lodges some time, without knowing her danger; he talks to her of marriage and of a licence without reserve, to lull suspicion; he wrests from her a confession of her regard for him, and attempts to get admission into her chamber, at midnight, under favour of a fire, which had been contrived, between him and the people of the house, to break out in one of the upper rooms. The virtue of *Clarissa* delivers her from this snare, and on the next day she leaves the house, and escapes to *Hampstead. Lovelace* persues her thither, and by various subtleties and intrigues cuts off all correspondence between *Clarissa* and her friend, whom we shall mention in a proper place. *Clarissa* is then deceiv'd by a new artifice, and carry'd back to the vile house, from whence she had escaped, where opium is given her, and during her insensibility the last outrage is committed on her person. Scenes of the utmost horror succeed the perpetration of this crime. She frustrates a second attempt of *Lovelace*, by being prepared to kill herself if he should persist, and escapes from the house a second time. The abandoned wretch, whose house she quits, discovers the place of her retreat, and causes her to be arrested, under pretence of debts; she is accordingly carry'd to prison, where she suffers a thousand insults from the wretched associates of the vile woman. *Lovelace*, touched with remorse, and a just, but involuntary, reverence for unhappy virtue, sends an old friend and companion of his follies, who was, notwithstanding, less abandoned to vice and dissimulation, to set her at liberty. *Belford*, for that is the name of his friend, accordingly releases her from prison; but the inhumanities she has suffered, particularly the cruel behaviour of her own relations, during her distress, bring on a consumption, of which she dies. *Lovelace* is killed in a duel, by a relation of *Clarissa*, and all the persons, who have been parties in his crime, receive a punishment proportioned to their guilt. All these events happen within the space of 8 months.

The principal characters, next to *Clarissa* and *Lovelace*, are the following:

Miss *Howe*, the intimate friend of *Clarissa*, to whom she addresses her letters. This lady has many good qualities, but they are allay'd by too much fire and impatience, which serve as a foyle to the mild and gentle temper of *Clarissa*.

Mr. *Belford*, the intimate friend of *Lovelace*, and the person who is supposed to have collected and preserved all the letters which compose this work, had been in his youth a debauchee; but was at length reformed, by the amiableness of [*Clarissa's*] virtue, and his own reflexions on the death of many of his friends and relations, whom he had intimately known, and whom he has inimitably described: He becomes the hero of the piece, at the end of the work, and inherits the estate which was intended for *Lovelace*, who was too much abandoned to wickedness; and he merited this good fortune by the generous protection which he afforded *Clarissa*, in the depth of her distress. His stile is natural, less florid than that of *Lovelace*, but full of just reasoning, and he excels in drawing a character.

There are twenty other characters, which are essentially connected with the principal action, and they are all sustained with an exactness, that requires the truest taste, and the most diligent attention. There is not a single person, whose character is not impressed on all his letters, as the bust of a prince is upon all his coins, and a glance is sufficient to distinguish the pen of the virtuous *Norton*, the cruel *Arabella*, the indulgent *John Harlow*, and the rude *Antony*. Even the middle characters are justly painted, which is much more difficult than to give a strong likeness of those which are distinguished by any excess or extream.

The style of *Clarissa* is peculiar to itself; that of *Lovelace* is full of new words, arbitrarily formed in his own manner, which are strongly expressive of his ideas. The style of every letter is excellently adapted to the character of the writer; but there is such a gentility, so easy and natural an elegance preserved in the whole, as would alone render this work valuable. As the greater part of the most interesting scenes are exhibited in dialogue, proper attention must be given to the change of the speakers, the author being, in every sense, above the common way of distinguishing them by putting their names before their respective parts of the conversation.

The pathetic has never been exhibited with equal power, and it is manifest, in a thousand instances, that the most obdurate and insensible tempers have been softened into compassion, and melted into tears, by the death, the sufferings, and the sorrows of *Clarissa*. We have not read any performance, in any language, that so much as approaches to a competition; for here nature is represented with all its circumstances, and nature only can persuade and move. In *Clarissa* we see a virtuous character, in the same station of life with ourselves, suffer with an immovable and unshaken constancy. The misfortunes of an *Ariane* move me not at all, those of a Princess of *Cleves* but faintly.[4] The heroes there are beings too different from myself, and the misfortunes which happen to them, bear no proportion to any that may happen to me. I cannot but know it to be a fable, and the necessary effect of this knowledge is insensibility.

The chief ornament of *Clarissa* is the description; there are some in *Pamela* which are excellent, but those of her younger sister are more frequent, more elevated, and more animated. The death of *Belton* is represented with such circumstances of horror, as cannot but intimidate the most daring profligate. The sufferings of *Clarissa* during her injurious imprisonment, the preparations which she makes for her death, her death itself, her noble defence against the second attempt of *Lovelace*, her sorrows, and even her deliriums, her funeral; all this, is drawn with an animated expression, that strikes, persuades, subdues——Such is the unanimous opinion of all readers, however diversified by taste, disposition, and capacity.

But *Clarissa* is rendered almost inestimable, by those exalted sentiments of piety, virtue, generosity, prudence, and humility, which adorn the person of the heroine, and are inculcated by her discourse and conduct. It is impossible to read the three last volumes without being conscious to a secret elation of mind, a species of delight, equally pure and noble, arising from the contemplation of human nature in the highest perfection to which it can attain by the purest virtue, and the most distinguish'd grace.

But has this *Clarissa*, which we thus extol, no faults? This reflexion frequently arises to the reader, whom a journalist too apparently endeavours to prepossess. There is a degree of malignity in the human breast, and we should be inconsolable when our praise is extorted by admiration,★ but for the pleasure of mingling some criticisms with our eulogium; this raises us nearer to a level with those whom we cannot but commend. But to be serious and impartial, *Clarissa* has faults, at least, with respect to *our manners* and *customs*; for, I will not venture to assert, that they can justly be styled faults by an *English* reader.

I do not mean the faults of which *Clarissa* is guilty, and which bring on her ruin: It is, however, certain, that a lady of her prudence, and purity of mind, should have broke off all correspondence with *Lovelace*, the moment it was forbidden by her mother; for the necessity of continuing it, to prevent ill consequences (1), is apparently no more than a pretence; and a good intention does not justify an evil action.

She is also guilty of another very considerable fault, in consenting to two (2) assignations with a lover, whom she knew to be a rake, and had been forbidden the house by her parents, whom she loved and honoured.

She seems also to take the part of *Lovelace*, against her relations, with too much zeal (3). She ought rather to have heard their accusations, and to have suffer'd herself to be disabused.

Answers *to the* Objections.

★ The *French* author has here furnished us with an excuse for adding some critical annotations, in answer to what he has objected, probably, for want of a second perusal.

(1) The author of *Clarissa* seems to know human nature too well, to attempt to draw a character, however nearly perfect, absolutely so. *Clarissa* has something to blame herself for, at setting out, tho' nothing in intention; and often blames herself for faults, for which every reader, her circumstances and resolutions considered, is willing to acquit her. The generality of readers have thought she bore too much. Her self-blame, and strict impartiality, are a shining part of her character.

(2) Mr *Lovelace* had behav'd so well in an interview into which he had surprised her (*See Vol*. I. *Letter* XXXVI.) that she had no reason to apprehend any ill consequences from these assignations. One of the assignations she revokes, from proper motives; so that she met him but once; and that in hopes to pacify him on the persecution she had taken, contrary to the expectation given him, not to abandon her father's house.

(3) She takes no part with *Lovelace* against her relations, but from the effect of that strict impartiality, which is her almost peculiar grace. She repeatedly offers to give up *Lovelace*, the man she owns she could love, if her friends would not insist upon her marrying the man she hates. Her father, a gloomy and implacable tyrant, both as a husband and a father, made her opposition to his will, in a point so interesting to herself, a crime. She had actually heard what their accusations were, from her more tender and indulgent mother; and *Lovelace* at that time appear'd to her, as he does to the reader, in the light of a persecuted man: And this engaged her generosity in his favour.

She treats Mr. *Solmes* with too much disrespect; she might laudably have refus'd him, in such terms as might leave him no hope, but she ought not to have (4) insulted him.

On the other hand, she shows too scrupulous a delicacy after she has suffered herself to be carry'd off by *Lovelace* (5): It then became expedient for her to marry *Lovelace*, who, more than once, offer'd her his hand, in the involuntary transports of his passion.——A lady, who has once put herself into the power of her lover, is no longer to affect distance, or expect the punctilio's of courtship should be observed.

But, I repeat it, all these petty faults of the heroine are, with respect to the reader, no faults at all. It was necessary that *Clarissa* should be unfortunate, because parents were to be warn'd against forcing the inclinations of their children in marriage, and daughters against trusting themselves with a lover, whom they knew to be a libertine, whatever his profession and their distress. And for the more natural and useful cultivation of these morals, the author has acted judiciously in rendering the indiscretions of a virtuous character productive of its misfortunes, and in giving opportunity of striking reflexions to those who have all the failings, without any of the eminent virtues of *Clarissa*.

It is also certain, that the author has abused the privilege, which he derives from the unbounded liberty of his country: He has dispersed,

Objections answered.

(4) Every reader, it is presumed, who reflects upon *Solmes's* odious qualities, and upon his obstinate adherence to his pretensions on her, against intreaties of hers, so earnest as would have moved any other man, for his own sake, to withdraw them (*See her Letter to him, Vol.* I. pp. 225–227. Edit. II.) will acquit her of this charge. He would *not* be refus'd. She could not but look upon him, as is evident from a conversation, which she overhears between him and her brother and sister, as an implement in their hands to bring about their deep-laid designs against her. An unimpeachable sincerity was another of her amiable qualities. She left no body in doubt of her heart, whether her openness made for or against herself.

(5) *Clarissa* has been accused of over-scrupulousness, when in the power of *Lovelace*, by many of the readers of her story in *England*, as well as by this gentleman. But, whoever reads with attention, *Lovelace's* letters to his friend *Belford*, when he had got her into his power, and considers the artifice which she found he had been guilty of, in order to obtain that power over her, will, perhaps, find reason to acquit a person of her character and delicacy. The author, in his 2d Edition, has endeavoured to obviate this objection, by notes on the places. He there observes, that Mr *Lovelace* never offers her his hand in such a way, that a *Clarissa* could accept of it, but *once*. And her suspension of the day (for it was only a suspension) is then naturally accounted for.

in some parts of his book, the particulars of freedoms taken by *Lovelace*, which exceed the bounds of decency. The infamous house into which the heroine is introduced, and in which she is so grosly abused, makes me fear that *Clarissa*, at least in *France*, will share the same fate with the *Theodore* of *Corneille*.[5] All the libertines of *Paris*, all the ladies of gallantry, who feared nothing in the crime itself, were disgusted with the coarseness of the expression, and the piece, though it was the work of *Pierre Corneille*, was not suffer'd to be play'd out. (6)

It is even a doubt with me, whether probability is preserved in the detestable audacity of *Lovelace*; to carry a lady of quality to a brothel, to confine her a captive there against her will, to give her opium, and to violate her person. Is this possible in a country so jealous of its laws and its liberty? Can it be thought that *Lovelace*, who was not deficient in understanding, and who expected to be a peer of the realm, would expose himself to the persecution of a powerful family, exasperated against him, beyond the possibility of reconciliation? An answer to these questions can only be expected from a native of *England*. (7)

Objections answered

(6) The freedoms here objected to, seem to have been particularized to do justice to the virtue of *Clarissa*. We can hardly think, that even the *French* delicacy can be wounded by the manner in which they are related, even when *Lovelace* is the relator. Whatever *coarseness of expression* the great *Corneille* was guilty of in his *Theodore*, all such seems to be avoided in *Clarissa*. A nice person of the sex may not, moreover, be able to bear those scenes in action, and on the stage, in presence of a thousand witnesses, which she may not think objectible in her closet.

(7) As to the improbability supposed by the ingenious and good natur'd remarker, of carrying a lady of quality to a bad house, &c. we shall leave it to the author to defend this part of his history. Mean time we may observe, from many places of the story, that this house was a place of genteel appearance; that two of the principal women in it were persons of education, ruined by *Lovelace*, and therefore entitled, as he might think, to his consideration; and who maintain'd great outward decency, especially when in the presence of *Clarissa*; who, tho' she liked them not, little imagin'd what they were. The lady was not a captive in the house. She thought herself at liberty (and that upon trial) to go and come as she pleas'd, till things arose so high between them, after the vile outrage, that *Lovelace* must have lost her for ever, if he had suffer'd her to leave him, and was in hopes, by detaining her, to induce her to forgive and marry him. He defied the laws of his country, as too many of his cast do. Mr. *Morden* hints at crimes committed by him at *Florence*, which had made his sudden departure from thence necessary. And in one place *Lovelace* vows revenge upon *Clarissa's* family, altho', for the sake of it, he were to become an exile from his native country for ever; and frequently declares, that all countries are alike to him. Are there not such men in

There is yet another scene which *Belford* has painted in the most offensive colours; a view of the life of common women. It is, indeed, excellently drawn; but can it be exhibited at all, without disgusting a delicate reader? (8)

Is there not something trifling in the incoherences, which *Clarissa* writes in her delirium? in the counterfeit signing of her name by letters cut in wood, in which (by the way) there appears to be some degree of affectation?

Was not *Lovelace* himself too little criminal in the duel that occasioned his death? *Morden* had threatned him, and does not this circumstance too much excuse him, according to the general opinion of the polite world concerning duels? And could he not have been urged to his own destruction by the mere impulse of his irregular appetites? (9)

Let us here quit the subject. There never was a book without fault; at least, in which a fault could not be found, if it was diligently sought. Happy are the authors who, with the editor of *Clarissa*, can captivate nations, and to whom the suffrage of some, who are critics by profession, is not deny'd!

Objections answered

all nations? in all governments? Need we refer to the public executions for crimes the most atrocious?

The author seems to us, to have provided against the main force of this objection of improbability, on this head, by giving early the situation of the house: A back-house within a front one; the lady residing in the latter, as the most elegant, and most retired; the two houses communicating by a long passage, and made secure with doors within, and iron rails without, as if for ornament. A house made convenient, as *Clarissa* afterwards says, for dreadful mischief. The wicked woman of it, is very solicitous for the credit, for the reputation of her house. The lady is deprived of all other refuge, denied all other protection. How is her glory heightened by the difficulties in which she was involved!——Nor does *Lovelace* bring her thither, till he found all his artifices to intangle her virtue ineffectual; and was convinced, that her generosity, her innocence, and other amiable qualities, could not fail, in any other dwelling, to procure her friends and partisans, who would, probably, frustrate his wicked purposes.

(8) The scene which *Belford has painted in the most offensive colours,* to use the remarker's words, is, indeed, a shocking one. It could not be otherwise. It was evidently designed to be so. The question is, Whether such a scene ought to have been at all exhibited? The author seems to be aware, that this objection would be made, by affixing a note to the place, apologizing for it. Be his apology allow'd or not allow'd, satisfactory, let him look to that. There is no question, that the history of *Clarissa* has faults. But we scruple not to say, that most of those above remarked (candid as the remarker certainly is) are not of the number. And this we may observe (which is a peculiar of the work) that the different persons,

writing to each other in this piece with great freedom, point out what the faults of each other are; as *Clarissa* does her own; and that without aiming at palliation.

(9) As to the objection, that *Lovelace* was too little criminal in the duel that occasioned his death; it may be answered, that his punishable crime was not to be the duel, which yet he himself brought on, by effect of his natural courage and impetuosity. The *Thunder*, as is said by Miss *Howe*, *seems to have been for some time rolling towards him* for his accumulated crimes; some of which, perhaps, were other duels; for he tells *Belford*, that he was no unfleshed novice; and that he loved this sport as well as he loved his food. And he fell in the way that was most likely to add to the pangs of his disappointment; confident as he was of victory.

It was, we think, no improper instance of the author's *charity*——shall we call it? that he left some little room for pity to be shewn to *Lovelace*, and for dividing of blame, as to the duel, between him and Col. *Morden*, who, tho' the least apparently faulty of all the men in the piece, was to have something to blame himself for in this affair. And that he *does* blame himself, affords an opportunity to decry the practice of duelling; which the author has not, on other proper occasions, as well as on this, forgotten to censure as such a subject demands.

We shall add, that the author has prefixed to his second edition, a table of contents; which he has so drawn up, that the reader will see, by the distinction of a *different character*, where the answers may be found, in the work itself, to particular passages that had been thought objectible; and which take in some of the above. And this he has had the justice to print separate, for the sake of the purchasers of the first edition.

33 *Rambler*, 4, Saturday, March 31, 1750

by SAMUEL JOHNSON

It was suggested (and the suggestion has been universally accepted), by Alexander Chalmers (1759–1834), editor of the *British Essayists* (1803), that this article was the result of the publication of *Tom Jones* and *Roderick Random* and a desire to defend the theory of fiction held by Richardson. Johnson's friendship for Richardson did not prevent him from an objective assessment of the latter's character (see *Boswell's Life of Johnson* . . ., ed. G. B. Hill and L. F. Powell (1964), II, 49, 174, 175, n. 2), but he thought very highly of the later novels. His comparison between Richardson and Fielding is well known now (see *Boswell's Life* . . ., II, 49, 174, 494–5), and his comment on Richardson in the Introduction to the *Rambler* paper (No. 97), which the novelist gave him was well known at the time:

> The reader is indebted for this day's entertainment to an author from whom the age has received greater favours, who has enlarged the knowledge of human nature, and taught the passions to move at the command of virtue. [No. 97, Tuesday, February 19, 1751.]

Simul et jucunda et idonea discere Vitæ.
HOR.
And join both profit and delight in one.
CREECH.[1]

The works of fiction, with which the present generation seems more particularly delighted, are such as exhibit life in its true state, diversified only by accidents that daily happen in the world, and influenced by passions and qualities which are really to be found in conversing with mankind.

This kind of writing may be termed not improperly the comedy of romance, and is to be conducted nearly by the rules of comic poetry. Its province is to bring about natural events by easy means, and to keep up curiosity without the help of wonder; it is therefore precluded from the machines and expedients of the heroic romance, and can neither employ giants to snatch away a lady from the nuptial rites, nor knights to bring her back from captivity; it can neither bewilder its personages in deserts, nor lodge them in imaginary castles.

I remember a remark made by Scaliger upon Pontanus, that all his writings are filled with the same images; and that if you take from him his lilies and his roses, his satyrs and his dryads, he will have nothing left that can be called poetry.[2] In like manner, almost all the fictions of the last age will vanish, if you deprive them of a hermit and a wood, a battle and a shipwreck.

Why this wild strain of imagination found reception so long, in polite and learned ages, it is not easy to conceive; but we cannot wonder that while readers could be procured, the authors were willing to continue it; for when a man had by practice gained some fluency of language, he had no farther care than to retire to his closet, let loose his invention, and heat his mind with incredibilities; a book was thus produced without fear of criticism, without the toil of study, without knowledge of nature, or acquaintance with life.

The task of our present writers is very different; it requires, together with that learning which is to be gained from books, that experience which can never be attained by solitary diligence, but must arise from general converse and accurate observation of the living world. Their performances have, as Horace expresses it, *plus oneris, quanto veniae minus*, little indulgence, and therefore more difficulty.[3] They are engaged in portraits of which every one knows the original, and can detect any deviation from exactness of resemblance. Other writings are safe, except from the malice of learning, but these are in danger from every common reader; as the slipper ill executed was censured by a shoemaker who happened to stop in his way at the Venus of Apelles.[4]

But the fear of not being approved as just copiers of human manners, is not the most important concern that an author of this sort ought to have before him. These books are written chiefly to the young, the ignorant, and the idle, to whom they serve as lectures of conduct, and introductions into life. They are the entertainment of minds unfurnished with ideas, and therefore easily susceptible of impressions; not fixed by principles, and therefore easily following the current of fancy; not informed by experience, and consequently open to every false suggestion and partial account.

That the highest degree of reverence should be paid to youth, and that nothing indecent should be suffered to approach their eyes or ears; are precepts extorted by sense and virtue from an ancient writer, by no means eminent for chastity of thought.[5] The same kind, though not the same degree of caution, is required in every thing which is laid before them, to secure them from unjust prejudices, perverse opinions and incongruous combinations of images.

In the romances formerly written, every transaction and sentiment was so remote from all that passes among men, that the reader was in very little danger of making any applications to himself; the virtues and crimes were equally beyond his sphere of activity; and he amused himself with heroes and with traitors, deliverers and persecutors, as with beings of another species, whose actions were regulated upon motives of their own, and who had neither faults nor excellences in common with himself.

But when an adventurer is levelled with the rest of the world, and acts in such scenes of the universal drama, as may be the lot of any other man; young spectators fix their eyes upon him with closer attention, and hope, by observing his behaviour and success, to regulate their own practices, when they shall be engaged in the like part.

For this reason these familiar histories may perhaps be made of greater use than the solemnities of professed morality, and convey the knowledge of vice and virtue with more efficacy than axioms and definitions. But if the power of example is so great, as to take possession of the memory by a kind of violence, and produce effects almost without the intervention of the will, care ought to be taken, that when the choice is unrestrained, the best examples only should be exhibited; and that which is likely to operate so strongly, should not be mischievous or uncertain in its effects.

The chief advantage which these fictions have over real life is, that their authors are at liberty, though not to invent, yet to select objects, and to cull from the mass of mankind, those individuals upon which the attention ought most to be employed; as a diamond, though it cannot be made, may be polished by art, and placed in such a situation, as to display that lustre which before was buried among common stones.

It is justly considered as the greatest excellency of art, to imitate nature; but it is necessary to distinguish those parts of nature, which are most proper for imitation: greater care is still required in representing life, which is so often discoloured by passion, or deformed by wickedness. If the world be promiscuously described, I cannot see of what use it can be to read the account; or why it may not be as safe to turn the eye immediately upon mankind as upon a mirror which shews all that presents itself without discrimination.

It is therefore not a sufficient vindication of a character, that it is drawn as it appears, for many characters ought never to be drawn; nor of a narrative, that the train of events is agreeable to observation and experience, for that observation which is called knowledge of the world will be found much more frequently to make men cunning than good. The purpose of these writings is surely not only to shew mankind, but to provide that they may be seen hereafter with less hazard; to teach the means of avoiding the snares which are laid by Treachery for Innocence, without infusing any wish for that superiority with which the betrayer flatters his vanity; to give the power of counteracting fraud, without the temptation to practise it; to initiate youth by mock encounters in the art of necessary defence, and to increase prudence without impairing virtue.

Many writers, for the sake of following nature, so mingle good and bad qualities in their principal personages, that they are both equally conspicuous; and as we accompany them through their adventures with delight, and are led by degrees to interest ourselves in their favour, we lose the abhorrence of their faults, because they do not hinder our pleasure, or, perhaps, regard them with some kindness for being united with so much merit.

There have been men indeed splendidly wicked, whose endowments threw a brightness on their crimes, and whom scarce any villainy made perfectly detestable, because they never could be wholly divested of their excellences; but such have been in all ages the great corrupters of the world, and their resemblance ought no more to be preserved, than the art of murdering without pain.

Some have advanced, without due attention to the consequences of this notion, that certain virtues have their correspondent faults, and therefore that to exhibit either part is to deviate from probability. Thus men are observed by Swift to be 'grateful in the same degree as they are resentful.'[6] This principle, with others of the same kind, supposes man to act from a brute impulse, and pursue a certain degree of inclination, without any choice of the object; for, otherwise, though it should be allowed that gratitude and resentment arise from the same constitution of the passions, it follows not that they will be equally indulged when reason is consulted; yet unless that consequence be admitted, this sagacious maxim becomes an empty sound, without any relation to practice or to life.

Nor is it evident, that even the first motions to these effects are always in the same proportion. For pride, which produces quickness of resentment, will obstruct gratitude, by unwillingness to admit that inferiority which obligation implies; and it is very unlikely, that he who cannot think he receives a favour, will acknowledge or repay it.

It is of the utmost importance to mankind, that positions of this tendency should be laid open and confuted; for while men consider good and evil as springing from the same root, they will spare the one for the sake of the other, and in judging, if not of others at least of themselves, will be apt to estimate their virtues by their vices. To this fatal error all those will contribute, who confound the colours of right and wrong, and instead of helping to settle their boundaries, mix them with so much art, that no common mind is able to disunite them.

In narratives, where historical veracity has no place, I cannot discover why there should not be exhibited the most perfect idea of virtue; of virtue not angelical, nor above probability for what we cannot credit we shall never imitate, but the highest and purest that humanity can reach, which, exercised in such trials as the various revolution of things shall bring upon it, may, by conquering some calamities, and enduring others, teach us what we may hope, and what we can perform. Vice, for vice is necessary to be shewn, should always disgust; nor should the graces of gaiety, or the dignity of courage, be so united with it, as to reconcile it to the mind: wherever it appears, it should raise hatred by the malignity of its practices, and contempt by the meanness of its stratagems: for while it is supported by either parts or spirit, it will be seldom heartily abhorred. The Roman tyrant was content to be hated, if he was but feared;[7] and there are thousands of the readers of romances willing to be thought wicked, if they may be allowed to be wits. It is therefore to be steadily inculcated, that virtue is the highest proof of understanding, and the only solid basis of greatness; and that vice is the natural consequence of narrow thoughts; that it begins in mistake, and ends in ignominy.

34 From a letter of Mrs. Donellan, September 25, 1750

Mrs. Donellan's letter is addressed to Samuel Richardson and the text is taken (like that of all other letters to and from Richardson reproduced below) from Mrs. Barbauld's *Correspondence of Samuel Richardson* (1804). According to Mrs. Barbauld, Mrs. Donellan was '. . . among the most judicious of Richardson's correspondents . . .' who '. . . criticized his work with a friendly freedom' (*Correspondence* . . ., I, cxcviii–cxcix).

Sept. 25. 1750.

SIR,

I have often designed answering your last obliging and entertaining letter, but I don't know how it is, that tho' the country seems the place of leisure, it has its businesses and pleasures, and particularly of the writing sort, as one is (at least I am) from most of my family and friends.

But I don't know whether I am giving the main reason that has hindered me from writing, and whether the difficulties I find in the subject you propose to me, and which you so well represent, have not had the greatest share in my silence.

To think of a man with religion, sense, and agreeableness, is easy, and to say he shall have this and that good quality; but to work these up into a story, to produce these into action—I know nobody who is capable of doing it but Mr. Richardson, and if he declines it, how shall I pretend to encourage him? And yet I wish he would try.

Indeed your health is of so much consequence, that I would by no means have you do any thing that should in the least prejudice it; and as you have a family distress on you, less now than at another time.

I am extremely sorry you should have such impediments, but the misfortune is, those who are fit to write delicately, must think so; those who can form a distress must be able to feel it; and as the mind and body are so united as to influence one another, the delicacy is communicated, and one too often finds softness and tenderness of mind in a body equally remarkable for those qualities. Tom Jones could get drunk, and do all sorts of bad things, in the height of his joy for his uncle's recovery. I dare say Fielding is a robust, strong man.

But to come to the point, of which you desire our opinions; the forming a man who shall unite the virtuous, the amiable, the genteel; to throw him into distresses, and extricate him with virtue and honour; to make him shew courage enough to fight, and yet religion enough to refrain; to love with ardour, and yet admire the beauties of his mistress's mind more than her person—I am afraid of falling into Juba in *Cato*, and Beville in the *Conscious Lovers*.[1] If our hero must fight, let it be before we are acquainted with him; and when once a man has shewn his courage, it will keep him from insult. Suppose the woman he likes engaged in her affections before she knew him, to one of a more modern cast, could we not make our hero shew virtue and honour, and at last, to the credit of my sex, triumph over the man of mode?

I am sensible, 'tis impossible to give a man so delicate a distress as a woman; their different situations will not bear it, nor can he so well complain, or raise so much compassion in others; he cannot possibly shew the sort of noble fortitude Clarissa does, as he cannot be in her sort of distress; so that I am afraid, even the pen of a Richardson will not move us in his, as it has done in her history: but if it makes the man of virtue triumph over the man of fashion, or rather the Christian over the infidel, that is the end proposed.

The epistolary style is yours, 'tis speaking, 'tis painting; but I think there must be a friend to tell some things that man can't tell of himself, for I am very delicate on the subject of self-praise, and think it should be as much avoided as possible; but when the scenes represented are passionate, they must come from the persons concerned, or they lose their spirit. Fine sentiments, and noble actions consequent to them, form the character to the reader without the persons being obliged to point them out themselves, and those I am persuaded you can point to us.

Some faults, your observe, our virtuous man must have, some sallies of passion; the best *man's* character will bear it, tho' a Clarissa's would not.

I will not arrogate any merit to our sex from it, but suppose it arises from custom, education, or what you will, 'tis certain our man must not be an angel. Clarissa's goodness seems, if I may use the expression, *intuitive*. Our man, to make him natural, must have some failings from passion, but must be soon recovered by reason and religion, which will vary the character from hers extremely, and give another sort of turn and spirit to the whole. Lovelace, the more he thought the worse he acted, for his fault was in his heart, and strengthened by a bad education; his thinking raised his passions.

Our man must have so much of the Christian and philosopher, that reflection must always set him right. In short, I think he must have more of Miss Howe than of Clarissa; and you seem to have known, that a Clarissa would not have spirit enough to go thro' the whole, and so formed Miss Howe with a good degree of passion and spirit, and yet she has her merits, which management enlivens the whole.

[. . . . .]

35 From *An Essay on the New Species of Writing founded by Mr. Fielding: with a Word or Two upon the Modern State of Criticism*, 1751

This pamphlet was published by William Owen in February 1751, who one year before had published the hostile *Examen of the History of Tom Jones*; it was published anonymously and the author remains unknown, in spite of several attempts to identify him. The passages reproduced below consist of the whole of the author's Preface and about half the text of the essay.

GENTLE READER,

The new Sect of Biographers (founded by Mr. *Fielding*) is already grown so very numerous from the Success of the Original, that an Attempt of this Kind is in some Measure necessary, to put a Stop to the unbounded Liberties the Historians of this comic Stamp might otherwise indulge themselves: and, if possible, to prevent any from undertaking the Labours of Mr. *Fielding*, without an adequate Genius. Should the following Sheets be of Force enough to hinder the weak, sickly Birth of a *Joe Thompson*, *Charlotte Summers*, or *Peregrine Pickle*,[1] in Embrio; the Town would undoubtedly be glad to exchange the heavy Work of a voluminous Scribler for the more easy Burden of a loose Pamphlet.

The first Critics drew their Rules from the first Professors of the Art they made their Observations on; which were afterwards the settled Standards by which the Worth of their Successors was to be determin'd. In Imitation of so great an Example are the Rules for the future Historians of this kind drawn from the Works of their Original Mr. *Fielding*. But I have even ventur'd to exceed these Limits, which I propos'd to myself on first setting out, and have dar'd to censure very freely some Parts of the Works of their great Original; which had I pursu'd, in remarking on the long Series of his Imitators, my Pamphlet would have insensibly swell'd into an enormous Volume. This Part of my Task may, without Vanity, be said to be perform'd in a more

Gentleman-like Manner than our Author has yet been us'd by any of his Critics. If the Examiner of *Tom Jones*, and the Author of *Bampfylde Moore Carew* may deserve that Name.[2] Think not, Gentle Reader, that the Objection made to those Writers are meant to intimate the pre-eminent Worth of this Performance; which, should it meet with Success in the World might entice the Author to expose himself by some future Pieces. If otherwise, will (more perhaps to his Credit) warn him to take an everlasting Farewell of Authorism.

[. . . . .]

I shall now begin to take a critical Review of these Histories in general, in performing which, if even Mr. *Fielding* himself does not confess that my Proceeding is impartial, I'll be content to send him my Name, that he may punish me *propriâ personâ* in the next humorous Piece he publishes.

Sometime before this new Species of Writing appear'd, the World had been pester'd with Volumes, commonly known by the Name of Romances, or Novels, Tales, &c. fill'd with any thing which the wildest Imagination could suggest. In all these Works, Probability was not required: The more extravagant the Thought, the more exquisite the Entertainment. Diamond Palaces, flying Horses, brazen Towers, &c. were here look'd upon as proper, and in Taste. In short, the most finish'd Piece of this kind, was nothing but Chaos and Incoherency. *France* first gave Birth to this strange Monster, and *England* was proud to import it among the rest of her Neighbour's Follies. A Deluge of Impossibility overflow'd the Press. Nothing was receiv'd with any kind of Applause, that did not appear under the Title of a Romance, or Novel; and Common Sense was kick'd out of Doors to make Room for marvellous Dullness. The Stile in all these Performances was to be equal to the Subject—amazing: And may be call'd with great Propriety, 'Prose run mad.' This obtain'd a long Time. Every Beau was an *Orondates*, and all the Belles were *Statiras*.[3] Not a *Billet-doux* but run in Heroics, or the most common Message deliver'd but in the Sublime. The Disease became epidemical, but there were no Hopes of a Cure, 'till Mr. *Fielding* endeavour'd to show the World, that pure Nature could furnish out as agreeable Entertainment, as those airy non-entical Forms they had long ador'd, and persuaded the Ladies to leave this Extravagance to their *Abigails* with their cast Cloaths. Amongst which Order of People, it has ever since been observ'd to be peculiarly predominant.

His Design of Reformation was noble and public-spirited, but the

Task was not quite so easy to perform, since it requir'd an uncommon Genius. For to tread the old beaten Track would be to no Purpose. Lecture would lose it's Force; and Ridicule would strive in vain to remove it. For tho' it was a Folly, it was a pleasing one: And if Sense could not yield the pretty Creatures greater Pleasure, Dear Nonsense must be ador'd.

Mr. *Fielding* therefore, who sees all the little Movements by which human Nature is actuated, found it necessary to open a new Vein of Humour, and thought the only way to make them lay down *Cassandra*, would be to compile Characters which really existed, equally entertaining with those Chimæras which were beyond Conception. This Thought produced *Joseph Andrews*, which soon became a formidable Rival to the *amazing* Class of Writers; since it was not a mere dry Narrative, but a lively Representative of real Life. For chrystal Palaces and winged Horses, we find homely Cots and ambling Nags; and instead of Impossibility, what we experience every Day.

But as Mr. *Fielding* first introduc'd this new kind of Biography, he restrain'd it with Laws which should ever after be deem'd sacred by all that attempted his Manner; which I here propose to give a brief Account of. The first and grand one of all, (without which, in however regular a Manner the rest is conducted, the whole Performance must be dead and languid) is, that thro' the whole Humour must diffuse itself. But this can by no Means be perform'd without a great Genius, nay, even a particular Sort of one: for tho' Mr. *Bayes* informs us, any Man may commence Poet by his infallible Rules;[4] yet in this Kind of Writing he must be at a Stand without this grand Requisite. But to proceed.

The next Thing to be consider'd, is the Choice of Characters, which tho' striking and particular must be exactly copied from Nature. And who can doubt, when they see the Features of an *Abraham Adams*, or Madam *Slipslop*, faithfully delineated, but that Field will afford an agreeable Variety? Every Word they speak must be entirely consonant to the Notion the Author would have his Readers to entertain of them: And here it may not be amiss to remark the great Analogy there is between these Histories and Dramatic Performances, which Similitude I shall enlarge upon occasionally in the Progress of this Review. In regard to Character, after what I have mention'd as necessary, it would be the greatest Affront on the Reader's Understanding to point out the Comparison.

As this Sort of Writing was intended as a Contrast to those in which the Reader was even to suppose all the Characters ideal, and every Circumstance quite imaginary, 'twas thought necessary, to give it a greater Air of Truth, to entitle it *an History*; and the *Dramatis Personæ* (if I may venture to use the Expression) were christened not with fantastic high-sounding Names, but such as, tho' they sometimes bore some Reference to the Character, had a more modern Termination.

At the same Time Mr. *Fielding* ordain'd, that these Histories should be divided into Books, and these subdivided into Chapters; and also that the first Chapter of every Book was not to continue the Narration, but should consist of any Thing the Author chose to entertain his Readers with. These if I don't forget, Mr. *Fielding* himself has nominated, the several Stages of his History, which he metaphorically calls a Journey, in which he and his Readers are Fellow-Travellers. His particular Success in these preliminary Essays demonstrates (notwithstanding what the Author of *Charlotte Summers* hints on that Head) that these are not the easiest Part of his Task: Which I believe, Mr. *Fielding* somewhere says himself.[5]

The Story should be probable, and the Characters taken from common Life, the Stile should be easy and familiar, but at the same Time sprightly and entertaining; and to enliven it the more, it is sometimes heightened to the Mock-heroic, to ridicule the Bombast and Fustian, which obtain'd so much in the Romances. Of this Kind are his various Descriptions of the Morning, and his diverting Similes occasionally dispers'd thro' the Body of his Work. *Horace* tells us, *dulce est desipere*, but Mr. *Fielding* remember'd he added *in loco*.[6] For which Reason, he always takes care to indulge himself in these Liberties of Stile where the Story is least interesting. The last Book of *Tom Jones* is a convincing Proof, that he can comprize a great Variety of Cirumstances in as small a Compass as any Author whatsoever. Besides these Descriptions, Similes, &c. there are other Licenses of Stile which it would be too tedious to be so minute as to enlarge upon. One Circumstance however, as it is a particular one, I cannot entirely pass over in Silence. Take it then as follows.————An Author of true Humour will consider, that his Book should be entertaining in the smallest Particulars, and afford Amusement

ab ovo
Usque ad mala.[7]

For which Reason Mr. *Addison* prefix'd Mottos to his Spectators, and at the Corner of each Paper added some particular Letter, which he himself imagin'd to be not the least entertaining Part of his Speculations. And nearly for the same End, Mr. *Fielding* thought proper to be facetious in the Titles to the several Chapters of his Histories, to shew the Reader he would not permit the least Occasion to slip which offer'd an Opportunity of amusing him.

As I am fallen on the Subject of the Titles to his Chapters, it will not be improper to consider them more largely, since it will only be mentioning now some Remarks I should be obliged to make by-and-by, which, for the Sake of the Connection, I rather chuse to insert here. And perhaps I may convince the Reader, these little Scraps, if rightly manag'd, conduce more to his Entertainment than he is at first aware of. 'Tis quite opposite to the Custom of the very best Writers in this Way, to give too full an Account of the Contents: it should be just hinted to the Reader something extraordinary is to happen in the seven or eight subsequent Pages, but what that is should be left for them to discover. Monsieur *Le Sage*, in his *Gil Blas*, (one of the best Books of the Kind extant) has always pursu'd this Method: He tells us *Gil Blas* is going to such or such a Place, but does not discover the least of his Adventures there; but he is more particularly cautious when any unexpected Event is to happen. The Title to one of his Chapters of that Kind is—*A Warning not to rely too much upon Prosperity.*—To another—*Chapter the fifth, being just as long as the preceding*: With many others which it is needless to enumerate. Note, 'Tis to be wish'd this Custom had been observ'd by the Author of *Roderick Random*, who tells us in his Preface, his Book is wrote in Imitation of the *Gil Blas* of Monsieur *Le Sage*. But with very little Success in my humble Opinion. As to the Titles of his Chapters, he is particularly tedious in them. This judicious Method of detaining the Reader in an agreeable Suspence, though it is right at all Times, is more particularly necessary when the History is near ended. No Writer has so strictly kept up to this as Mr. *Fielding*, in his *Tom Jones*. We are too well assured of *Gil Blas*'s Prosperity a long Time beforehand, to be surpriz'd at it. But at the Beginning of the last Book of *Tom Jones*, the Reader is apt to think it an equal Chance whether he is to be hanged or married; nor does he undeceive him but by gradual Narration of Facts: And lest the Reader's Curiosity should pry too far into the Truth, what admirable Titles has he invented for his Chapters in order to keep him the longer in the Dark! such as———*In which the History draws near to a Conclusion: In which the History draws nearer to a Conclusion*, &c. &c. which every Body will own conduces greatly to their Entertainment, and a Reader of the least Discernment will perceive how much more Consequence the clever Management of these Scraps prefix'd to each Chapter is of than he at first imagin'd. With how little Judgment has the Author of *Charlotte Summers* conducted this Particular! whose great Fault is Anticipation: That is, forestalling, by too explanatory a Title, the most remarkable Occurrences in his History. This appears even in the Title to his Book, which is, *The History of* Charlotte Summers: *or The* FORTUNATE *Parish Girl*. What Mr. *Addison* says of the Tragedies that conclude happily, may with equal Justice be apply'd here. 'We see without Concern (says he) illustrious People in Distress, when we are sure they will at last be deliver'd from their Misfortunes.'[8] Other Writers content themselves with entitling their Pieces, *The History of a Foundling, of Joseph Andrews, of Gil Blas, Roderick Random*, &c. without informing us as to the Event. As I find myself drawn into an unforeseen Length, I shall only subjoin one Instance from his Chapters, but at the same Time such an one, as will convince the Reader of Mr. *Fielding*'s Excellence in this Particular. The Eighth Chapter of the last Book is perhaps one of the most interesting in the whole History, and I dare say drew Tears from many Readers. For my own Part, I am not asham'd to own I have so much of the 'Milk of human Nature' in me, that I should have been in the greatest Concerns for the Misfortunes of the unhappy Miss *Summers*, if unluckily the Author had not assur'd me before I enter'd on these distressful Scenes, she would certainly be deliver'd from her momentary Afflictions before I had read three Leaves further. To confess the Truth I was vastly angry with him for depriving me of such entertaining Sadness. We hope this Instance will convince all future Writers, that the Pleasure of the Reader is much more exquisite from the Reserve in the Title. These Thoughts upon the Inscriptions to the Chapters were thrown together to shew, that Mr. *Fielding* had another Intention besides making the World laugh in the Lines prefix'd to each Portion of his History. Permit me therefore, gentle Reader, upon the Authority of a Critic, to banish from all Histories above the Rank of those printed in *Blackfryars*, and sold at the small Price of one Penny, to tell us—*As how* Thomas Hickathrift *carried a Stack of Corn*. Or—Thomas Thumb *was swallow'd by a Cow*, in a Title longer than the Chapter itself. After this Exertion of my Power, as a Critic, and dispersing these my Presents to all whom they may concern; let us return whence we digress'd.

No Faculty is so scarcely to be met with, tho' at the same Time there is none more frequently necessary, than that of telling a Story well. This Quality must be possess'd in an eminent Degree by a Writer of this kind. In the Progress of his Work he must adhere pretty closely to the Manners of the Drama, *viz*. In the Beginning the Plan of his Story must be clearly open'd, and the principal Characters should appear; towards the Middle his Plot should thicken, and Affairs be brought to a Crisis; and then be gradually unravell'd to the Reader, 'till the Piece is concluded.

The great Critics take Notice, that Epic Poems may be call'd a kind of narrative Tragedies, since they possess Character, Plot, and every Requisite of them, except the entire Dialogue of which they consist. All the Commentators on *Homer*'s *Iliad* observe the Affinity between that Poem and the Drama; and *Milton* is affirm'd to have originally plann'd his *Paradise lost* on the Model of a sacred Tragedy, after the Manner of his *Sampson Agonistes*[.] Let me be permitted then, who am but a low Critic after their high Example, to observe the same Relation these Performances I am now remarking on bear to Comedy. In one Respect indeed they have the Advantage of Theatrical Pieces. For tho' it is the common Business of both Writers to make as deep Researches into Nature as they can, and cull from that ample Field whatever is to their Purpose, yet the Biographer may ingraft in his Performance many Characters and Circumstances, which tho' they are entirely natural and very probable, often fall below the Dignity of the Stage. Nay it often happens that these very kind of Books I am treating of fall into the Hands [of] a Set of People who are apt to cry out, on the Sight of any Thing that gives a lively Representation of the Manners of the common People,—Oh! that's cursed low, intolerably vulgar, &c. Of this the Introducer of these Pieces was aware, and has taken a great deal of Pains to obviate the Objections of these empty Cavillers: and I believe there are few Persons who have a Taste for Humour who would thank those Gentlemen for striking out the very Passages which are the Characteristics of his Excellencies as an Author—*viz*. His thorough Insight into Low-life. I shall at present take my leave of this Subject, with observing, that as the Romances it was intended to ridicule, were a kind of extravagant Landskape, in which the Painter had represented purling Streams and shady Groves; or brazen Towers, and Mountains of Adamant, just as they were uppermost in his wild Imagination; so this kind of Writing is the Work of a more regular Pencil, and the exact Picture of human Life; and though a Novice in Painting may be more struck with the false Glare of the first, a Connoisseur will be more charm'd with the beautiful Plainness, and exact Similitude of the last.

The many Histories of this kind that lately have been publish'd, which undoubtedly owe their Rise to the extraordinary Success of Mr. *Fielding*'s Pieces, make it more necessary to remark on these Performances.

[. . . . . .⁹]

These Remarks could hardly make a just Claim to that Impartiality, I have all along been so great a Stickler for, was I entirely to pass over in Silence the few Mistakes our Author has been guilty of in the Conduct of his several Performances. But I shall be very little inclin'd to enlarge on so disagreeable a Part of the Critic's Office. First then for *Joseph Andrews*.——We are told, that the chief End of these Pieces is the Extirpation of Vice, and the Promotion of Virtue; to say the Truth, which the general Bent of them always tends to. But we fear this grand Rule has in some Places been too much disregarded. As the Works of Mr. *Fielding* are in every Body's Hands, there ought not to be a Line in them which should cause the modestest Lady a single Blush in the Perusal. This Delicacy of Stile and Sentiment has been quite neglected in some Dialogues between the wanton Lady *Booby* and most innocent *Joseph Andrews*; and more particularly so in one Chapter, which must occur to the Remembrance of every Reader conversant with these Works. We may venture to say this one Chapter has been prejudicial to the young People of both Sexes, and that more Readers have look'd upon the Innocence of *Joseph Andrews* as Stupidity, than the Wantonness of Lady *Booby* as Guilt. Lewdness is too mean a Branch of Humour (if indeed it is a Branch of Humour) for a Man of Mr. *Fielding*'s Sense to have Recourse to: and we hope that he will henceforth leave it to those barren Writers of Comedy who have no other Way of pleasing, but a scandalous Coincidence with the deprav'd Taste of a vicious Audience. The next Objection we shall make to *Joseph Andrews* is a general one, which includes the whole Performance. My Reader will start perhaps at the Thoughts of so extensive an Objection, but I must beg leave to say, that tho' the Narration is conducted with great Spirit, and there are innumerable Strokes of Wit and Nature throughout, it is no small Derogation to the Merit of this Work, that the Story on which it is founded is not sufficiently interesting. The Characters indeed are equally natural and entertaining with those of *Tom Jones*, but the Parts they are allotted engage much less of our Attention. In Dramatic Pieces, where the Story must be stretch'd into Five Acts, there is some Excuse for this Inaction, and Want of Incidents, but in these Performances, where the Length of the Work is left entirely to the Discretion of the Writer, little can be alledg'd in his Defence.

We will here take our Leave of *Joseph Andrews*, and briefly observe what deserves Reproof in Mr. *Fielding*'s last Piece, *viz. Tom Jones*; a Performance which on the whole perhaps is the most lively Book ever publish'd, but our Author has here and there put in his Claim to the Privilege of being dull, which the Critics have indulg'd to the Writers of Books of any Length.

> ——*Opere in longo fas est obrepere somnum.*
> HOR.

> ——Sleep
> O'er Works of Length allowably may creep.
> FRANCIS.[10]

The most glaring Instance of this kind in all this Author's Works is the long unenliven'd Story of [T]*he Man of the Hill*; which makes up so great a Part of a Volume. A Narration which neither interests or entertains the Reader, and is of no more Service than in filling up so many Pages. The Substance of the Story is such as (to make use of Mr. *Shirley*'s Phrase)

> '*almost staggers Credibility.*'[11]

For though I have heard it affirm'd, that there is such a Character as the *Man of the Hill*; yet I believe the Generality of Readers concurr'd with me in thinking it chimerical and unnaturally singular. I am very sorry Mr. *Fielding* should have introduc'd so improbable a Story, because there is no kind of Writing where the Rule of *Horace*, concerning Probability, should so strictly be observed, as in these Works.

> *Ficta voluptatis causâ sint proxima veris;*
> *Nec quodcunque volet, poscat sibi fabula credi.*[12]

Of which be pleas'd, my courteous *English* Reader, to accept the following free Translation.

> The Life-wrought Tale should ne'er advance
> A Line that savours of Romance.

I am now most heartily tired of cavilling, for which Reason I shall take no Notice of the other few Blemishes in the Works of this Author, which may have arose from Heedlessness; or the Frailty of human Nature may have given Birth to. And which are more conspicuous in Writings so lively in general, as Freckles are more remarkable in those of Fair Complexions. Praise is Insolence where the Man that praises dares not discommend: on which Account I trust that our *English Cervantes* will not be offended at the Freedom I have taken in censuring some Parts of his Works. I have all along endeavour'd to act according to the laudable Resolution I took at my first setting out; that is, to proceed without Prejudice, or Partiality, like a candid, honest Critic, who will, (according to *Shakespear* in his *Othello*)

Nothing extenuate,
Nor set down aught in Malice.[13]

The Monthly Review, which ran from 1749 to 1845, was founded
by the bookseller Ralph Griffiths (1720–1803), and remained one
of the most successful and highly respected of the literary
periodicals of the eighteenth and nineteenth centuries. Between
October 1751 and July 1752 Smollett contributed three reviews
to this periodical (four years before the founding of *The Critical
Review*; see below, No. 57), and very probably knew the author
of this review of his novel. This was John Cleland (1709–89),
now notorious as the author of *Memoirs of a Woman of Pleasure*
(i.e. *Fanny Hill*, 1747 or 1748), who also wrote *The Memoirs of
a Coxcomb* (1751) and *Surprises of Love* (1765). Smollett returned
Cleland's favour with a review of the second of these novels (see
The Monthly Review, V, October 1751), which concludes:

> . . . we will, upon the whole, venture to pronounce this work
> one of those few productions, which, though hastily, nay and
> carelessly composed, a discerning reader may peruse to an end,
> without yawning, and even rise from it, with a wish, that the
> entertainment had been prolonged.

Complaints are daily made, not without reason, of the number of
useless books, with which town and country are drenched and surfeited. How many productions do we see continually foisted upon the
publick, under the sanction of deceitful title pages, and against which
we have more cause of complaint than merely from our being drawn
in by *false-tokens*, or on account of the loss of our money and time
bestowed upon them: for to say nothing of those works which carry
their own condemnation with them, (such as lewd or profane subjects,
the spawn of indigence, of profligacy, or of both united) what are so
many worthless frivolous pieces as we constantly see brought out, but
the marks of that declension of wit and taste, which is perhaps more
justly the reproach of the public than the authors who have been
forced to consult, and conform to, its vitiated palate? Serious and useful
works are scarce read, and hardly any thing of morality goes down,

unless ticketed with the label of amusement. Hence that flood of novels, tales, romances, and other monsters of the imagination, which have been either wretchedly translated, or even more unhappily imitated, from the *French*, whose literary levity we have not been ashamed to adopt, and to encourage the propagation of so depraved a taste. But this forced and unnatural transplantation could not long thrive in a country, of which the faculty of thinking, and thinking deeply, was once, and it is to be hoped, has not yet entirely ceased to be, the national characteristic.

The necessity then of borrowing from truth its colour at least, in favour of fiction, a point so justly recommended by *Horace*,[1] and common sense, occured, at length, to some of our writers, who tried the experiment with success. To this new species of writing, the title of *biography*, humorously, and of course not improperly, assumed by the first ingenious author, has been however too lightly continued, since it certainly conveys a false idea. Pictures of fancy are not called portrait-painting, and no body who distinguishes terms will allow the title of *biographer*, which can only mean a writer of real lives, such as *Plutarch*, *Nepos*, &c. to be well applied to the authors of *Tom Jones, Roderick Random, David Simple*, &c.[2] who may be more justly styled comic-romance-writers. This piece of verbal criticism is the less insignificant, as it is owing to the mistake of a writer of great wit and humour, who likewise calls this a *life-writing* age, which may be true too, and yet not applicable to it, on most of the examples he quotes for the grounds of this epithet.[3]

If this *epithet* too is used by way of ridiculing, or exploding this species of writing, (unless when too detestably employed in the service of lewdness and immorality, to deserve no more than being ridiculed) the censure does not seem entirely well warranted. There are perhaps no works of entertainment more susceptible of improvement or public utility, than such as are thus calculated to convey instruction, under the passport of amusement. How many readers may be taught to pursue good, and to avoid evil, to refine their morals, and to detest vice, who are profitably decoyed into the perusal of these writings by the pleasure they expect to be paid with for their attention, who would not care to be dragged through a dry, didactic system of morality; or who would, from a love of truth universally impressed on mankind, despise inventions which do not at least pay truth the homage of imitation? To judge then candidly and impartially of works of this sort, and to fix their standard, their mint may be tried by that short and excellent test, which *Horace*, perhaps the greatest, the wisest wit of any age, suggests to us in that so often quoted expression of *utile dulci*.[4]

If we consider then in general, before we come to particular application, the true use of these writings, it is rather to be concluded that we have so few of them, than that there are too many. For as the matter of them is chiefly taken from nature, from adventures, real or imaginary, but familiar, practical, and probable to be met with in the course of common life, they may serve as pilot's charts, or maps of those parts of the world, which every one may chance to travel through; and in this light they are public benefits. Whereas romances and novels which turn upon characters out of nature, monsters of perfection, feats of chivalry, fairy-enchantments, and the whole train of the marvellous absurd, transport the reader unprofitably into the clouds, where he is sure to find no solid footing, or into those wilds of fancy, which go for ever out of the way of all human paths.

No comparison that affords such variety of just applications, as that of human life to a voyage, can ever disgust by its staleness, or repetition. And where is the traveller who would complain of the number of maps, or journals, designed to point him out his way through the number of different roads that choice or chance may engage him in? The objections That the number may bewilder, or the falsity, or insufficiency may mislead him, are of little or no avail, compared to the utility which may redound from them, since hardly a case occurs in these pieces, in which nature and probability have been consulted, but by its appositeness, or similiarity, at least may afford respectively salutary hints, or instructions. And as to the last objection, it is easily refuted, by remarking, in pursuance of the same metaphor, that it would be vain and ridiculous to condemn the use of maps, or charts, because some are laid down by unskilful or treacherous artists. Something in all productions of this sort must be left to judgment: and if fools have not the gift, and are sometimes, in such reading, hurt by the want of it, such a consideration surely says but little against works, from benefiting by which, only fools are excluded: and even that is a misfortune to which nature has made them as insensible as they are incorrigible.

[. . . . .[5]]

37 From a review of *Amelia* (1751)
The London Magazine, XX, April 1751

[. . . . .]
In this history, we have been obliged, for brevity's sake, to omit several episodes, and many incidents which point out the characters of the several persons introduced; but upon the whole, the story is amusing, the characters kept up, and many reflections which are useful, if the reader will but take notice of them, which in this unthinking age it is to be feared, very few will. However, there are some imperfections, as there are in all human productions. A novel, like an epick poem, shou'd at least have the appearance of truth; and for this reason notorious anachronisms ought to be carefully avoided. In this novel, there is a glaring one; for Gibraltar has not been besieged since the year 1727, consequently, if Mr. Booth was wounded at that siege, and married to his Amelia before it, he could neither be a young man, nor his wife a young handsome lady, when the masquerades began at Ranelagh, which is not above three or four years since. Another imperfection, in our opinion, is, that the author should have taken care to have had Amelia's nose so compleatly cured, and set to rights, after its being *beat all to pieces*, by the help of some eminent surgeon, that not so much as a scar remained, and that she shone forth in all her beauty as much after that accident as before, to the unspeakable sorrow of all her envious rivals.

Both these were owing, we suppose, to the author's hurry of business in administring impartial justice to his majesty's good people; but there is another, and a most unpardonable one, because it seems to be designed, which is his ridicule upon *Liberty*, in the second chapter of his eighth book; and since his catchpole could not tell him what *Liberty*[1] is, we will tell him what it is not, by boldly affirming, that there can be no liberty in a country where there is not a free and independent senate or parliament, chosen by the general and uncorrupted voice of the people. There may be a shadow of *Liberty*, there may be a senate or parliament, there may be annual popular elections, nay, there may be a mild and gentle administration of government: All this they had at Rome under Augustus Cæsar; but in the reign of Augustus Cæsar, the Romans had no more *Liberty*, than they had in the reign of Tiberius, or of Nero.

This the author, as well as every honest man in the kingdom, ought seriously to consider; and as he has in this piece very justly exposed some of the private vices and follies of the present age, we hope, that in his next he will direct his satire against those who have been tempted by their ambition, vanity or avarice, to oppose every new law that could be thought of for preventing bribery and corruption; for if he does not, people will be apt to say, that he and his patrons now do, as the enthusiasts did in the days of Hudibras,

> Compound for sins they are inclin'd to,
> By damning those they have no mind to.[2]

38 From the Preface to *Clarissa Harlowe* 1751

by SAMUEL RICHARDSON

Volumes I and II of *Clarissa* had been published in December 1747, Volumes III and IV in April 1748 (see above, Nos. 26 and 28). Volumes V–VII appeared in December 1748, with a change to smaller type in the course of Volume VI. There was a new edition of the novel in April 1751 (together with one in eight volumes duodecimo, called the third), and another in October 1748 (called the fourth). The Preface reproduced below is that which appeared in the second edition, the first part of which corresponds closely to the first part of the Preface to the first edition, Volume I (see above, No. 26). It will be noticed that in the interval between the original publication of Volume I and the time when this Preface was written Richardson had lost all his earlier hesitancy and doubt about length; his increasing self-confidence is also indicated by his abandonment of Warburton's Preface (see above, No. 28).

[. . . . .]
In the Letters of the two young Ladies, it is presumed will be found not only the highest exercise of a reasonable and *practicable* Friendship, between minds endowed with the noblest principles of Virtue and Religion, but occasionally interspersed, such Delicacy of Sentiments, particularly with regard to the other Sex; such instances of Impartiality, each freely, as a fundamental principle of their friendship, blaming, praising, and setting right the other, as are strongly to be recommended to the observation of the *younger* part (more especially) of the Female Readers.

The principal of these two young Ladies is proposed as an Exemplar to her Sex. Nor is it any objection to her being so, that she is not in all respects a perfect character. It was not only natural, but it was necessary, that she should have some faults, were it only to shew the Reader, how laudably she could mistrust and blame herself, and carry to her own heart, divested of self-partiality, the censure which arose from her own convictions, and that even to the acquittal of those, because revered characters, whom no one else would acquit, and to whose much greater faults her errors were owing, and not to a weak or reproachable heart. As far as is consistent with human frailty, and as far as she could be perfect, considering the people she had to deal with, and those with whom she was inseparably connected, she *is* perfect. To have been impeccable, must have left nothing for the Divine Grace and a Purified State to do, and carried our idea of her from woman to angel. As such is she often esteemed by the man whose *heart* was so corrupt, that he could hardly believe human nature capable of the purity, which, on every trial or temptation, shone out in *hers*.

Besides the four principal persons, several others are introduced, whose Letters are characteristic: And it is presumed that there will be found in some of them, but more especially in those of the chief character among the men, and the second character among the women, such strokes of Gaiety, Fancy, and Humour, as will entertain and divert; and at the same time both warn and instruct.

All the Letters are written while the hearts of the writers must be supposed to be wholly engaged in their subjects (The events at the time generally dubious): So that they abound not only with critical Situations, but with what may be called *instantaneous* Descriptions and Reflections (proper to be brought home to the breast of the youthful Reader); as also with affecting Conversations; many of them written in the dialogue or dramatic way.

'*Much more* lively and affecting, says one of the principal characters (Vol. VII. Let. 22.) must be the Style of those who write in the height of a *present* distress; the mind tortured by the pangs of uncertainty (the Events then hidden in the womb of Fate); *than* the dry, narrative, unanimated Style of a person relating difficulties and dangers surmounted, can be; the relater perfectly at ease; and if himself unmoved by his own Story, not likely greatly to affect the Reader.'

What will be found to be more particularly aimed at in the following Work, is—To warn the Inconsiderate and Thoughtless of the one Sex, against the base arts and designs of specious Contrivers of the other— To caution Parents against the undue exercise of their natural authority over their Children in the great article of Marriage—To warn Children against preferring a Man of Pleasure to a Man of Probity, upon that dangerous but too commonly-received notion, *That a reformed Rake makes the best Husband*—But above all, To investigate the highest and most important Doctrines not only of Morality, but of Christianity, by shewing them thrown into action in the conduct of the *worthy* characters; while the *unworthy*, who set those Doctrines at defiance, are condignly, and, as may be said, consequentially, punished.

From what has been said, considerate Readers will not enter upon the perusal of the Piece before them, as if it were designed *only* to divert and amuse. It will probably be thought tedious to all such as *dip* into it, expecting a *light Novel*, or *transitory Romance*; and look upon Story in it (interesting as that is generally allowed to be) as its *sole end*, rather than as a vehicle to the Instruction.

It is proper to observe, with regard to the *present Edition*, that it has been thought fit to restore many Passages, and several Letters, which were omitted in the former merely for shortening-sake; and which some Friends to the Work thought equally necessary and entertaining. These are distinguished by Dots or inserted Full-points. And will be printed separately, in justice to the Purchasers of the former Editions.

Fault having been found, particularly by elderly Readers, and by some who have weak Eyes, with the Smallness of the Type, on which some Parts of the Three last Volumes were printed (which was done in order to bring the Work, that had extended to an undesirable Length, into as small a Compass as possible) the present Edition is uniformly printed on the larger-sized Letter of the three made use of before. But the doing this, together with the Additions above-mentioned, has unavoidably run the Seven Volumes into Eight.

The Work having been originally published at three different times; and a greater distance than was intended having passed between the first publication and the second; a Preface was thought proper to be affixed to the third and fourth volumes; being the second publication. A very learned and eminent Hand was so kind as to favour the Editor, at his request, with one. But the occasion of inserting it being *temporary*, and the Editor having been left at liberty to do with it as he pleased, it was omitted in the Second Edition, when the whole Work came to be printed together; as was, for the same reason, the Preface to the first Volume;[1] and a short Advertisement to the Reader inserted instead of both. That Advertisement being also temporary, the present Address to the Reader is substituted in its place.

In the Second Edition an ample *Table of Contents* to the *whole* Work was prefixed to the first volume: But that having in some measure anticipated the Catastrophe, and been thought to detain the Reader too long from entering upon the History, it has been judged adviseable to *add* (and that rather than *prefix*) to *each* Volume its *particular* Contents;

which will serve not only as an Index, but as a brief Recapitulation of the most material passages contained in it; and which will enable the Reader to connect in his mind the perused volume with that which follows; and more clearly shew the characters and views of the particular correspondents.

An ingenious Gentleman having made a Collection of many of the Moral and Instructive Sentiments in this History, and presented it to the Editor, he thought the design and usefulness of the Work could not be more strikingly exhibited, than by inserting it (greatly enlarged) at the end of the last volume. The Reader will accordingly find it there, digested under proper Heads, with References to the Pages where each Caution, Aphorism, Reflection, or Observation, is to be found, either wrought into the *practice* of the respective correspondents, or recommended by them as useful *theory* to the Youth of both Sexes.

Different persons, as might be expected, have been of different opinions, in relation to the conduct of the Heroine in particular Situations; and several worthy persons have objected to the general Catastrophe, and other parts of the History. Whatever is thought material of these shall be taken notice of by way of POSTSCRIPT, at the conclusion of the History;[2] for this Work being addressed to the Public as a History of *Life* and *Manners*, those parts of it which are proposed to carry with them the force of an Example, ought to be as unobjectible as is consistent with the *design of the whole*, and with *human nature*.

39 From a letter of Philip Skelton, May 10, 1751

Philip Skelton's letter is addressed to Samuel Richardson, whom he defended in the Irish newspapers during the debate over the piracy of *Sir Charles Grandison*. Skelton was a clergyman in Ireland, author of *Discourses Controversial and Practical* (1754). Mrs. Barbauld said of him: 'Mr. Skelton was a singular character; most singular, perhaps, in his uncommon benevolence' (*Correspondence of Samuel Richardson* (1804), I, cxix).

[. . . . .]
As to your *good man*, I need not bid you christen him; but I would willingly see him as good a Christian, as a fine gentleman can be. I don't mean that the two characters are in the least inconsistent, for I am sure the latter is impossible without the former; but I mean that he should appear on all occasions to act, and suffer, upon Christian principles; that he should fast and pray, but not fast every day, nor pray every hour. The devotional part of Pamela's character was a little too much charged, that of Clarissa somewhat too little, till towards her death. I wish to see the present warm in that respect, but duly tempered; that he may be rather a Christian hero than a saint.

Let him suffer according to the prediction of Plato, and the description of Seneca, in Lactantius,[1] and that greatly, both in respect to the severity of the suffering, and the manner of bearing it. Your good man will be out of nature, if he is not persecuted: nay, he will be no very good man, if the world do not give him this testimony.

Take your characters and incidents from real life, rather than from books, that your work may be new, and not the copy of a copy. Be free with the good or bad now on the stage, but under feigned names and disguises, that the world may feel as it reads.

Above all, consider the bulk of your readers, how grossly attached they are to facts, and adventures, and be sure to enliven the performance with plenty of subordinate events, all conspiring, and leading to the grand event or catastrophe. The main stem of your story may now and then branch into episodes; but take care that every twig grow as naturally out of the tree, and bear as much fruit, as in *Clarissa*.

I hope you intend to give us a bad woman, expensive, imperious, lewd, and at last a drammer. This is a fruitful and a necessary subject, which will strike, and entertain to a miracle. You are so safe already with the sex, that nothing you can say of a bad woman will hinder your being a favourite, especially if now and then, when your she-devil is most a devil, you take occasion to remark how unlike she is to the most beautiful, or modest, or gentle, or polite, part of the creation.

I am far from thinking you will take this freedom of mine ill; yet considering how great a master I am writing to, my affection, which dictates this, can hardly excuse itself to my prudence.

[. . . . .]

40 From a review of *Amelia* (1751), *The Monthly Review*, V, December 1751

This review was by John Cleland; see above, No. 36, headnote.

The ingenious author of this piece is already so well known to the public for his talents in novel-writing, and especially that original turn which he gives to all his works in that way, that it would be superfluous to say any thing more of his literary character.

To give a just idea of this his last production, which, from the choice of his subject, appears to be the boldest stroke that has been yet attempted in this species of writing, will be sufficient.

The author takes up his heroine at the very point at which all his predecessors have dropped their capital personages. It has been heretofore a general practice to conduct the lover and his mistress to the door of matrimony, and there leave them, as if after that ceremony the whole interest in them was at end, and nothing could remain beyond it worthy of exciting or keeping up the curiosity of the reader. Instead of which, Mr. *Fielding*, in defiance of this established custom, has ventured to give the history of two persons already married, but whose adventures, hardships, and distressful situations form a chain of events, in which he has had the art of keeping up the spirit of his narration from falling into that languor and flatness which might be expected from the nature of the subject; for, virtuous and laudable as the tenderness and constancy of a wife to her husband must for ever be considered, these affections are, however, too often esteemed as merely matter of pure duty, and intirely in course; so that he who does not peruse this work, will hardly imagine how the relish of such conjugal endearments, as compose the basis of it, could be quickened enough to become palatable to the reader. The author, however, has interwoven such natural situations, such scenes of trial, taken also from nature, that the attention is for ever kept on the stretch, and one is led on by the attraction of a curiosity artfully provoked, to pursue the *heroine* through all her adventures, and an impatience to know how the married pair will be extricated out of the successive plunges in which they are represented, and in which the writer often successfully presses vice into the service of virtue.

There have been amongst the *French* authors, and even amongst the ladies of that nation, novel-writers, who have given themselves the false air of turning conjugal love into ridicule. One of the most celebrated of them, madam *Villidieu* says expressly, 'that husbands are the last persons on earth one should love,' and in another place, 'That regrets and tears last but a short time when a lady has only the loss of a husband to be grieved for, and that a gallant easily comforts *her*, upon such an occurrence.'[1] Sentiments so loose, and libertine, as these are, might justly indispose the virtuous, and well-minded, to writings which, generally speaking, ran in this vein. But be it said, to the honour of the *English*, and to Mr. *Fielding*, in particular, that he never thought so ill of the public, as to make his court to it at the expence of the sacred duties of morality. Wherever the obligation of painting the corruptions of mankind, and the world, *not as it should be, but as it really exists*, forces him into descriptions in which his actors depart from the paths of virtue and prudence, he is sure to make examples of them, perhaps more salutary, than if he had made them too rigidly adhere to their duty. Their follies and vices are turned so as to become instructions in the issue of them, and which make a far more forcible impression than merely speculative maxims and dry sentences. *Largum iter est per præcepta, breve et efficax per exempla.* Sen., Epist. 6.[2]

By this means too the author imitates nature in inforcing its capital laws; by the attractions of pleasure he puts morality into action; it is alive, and insinuates its greatest truths into the mind, under the colours of amusement and fiction. Readers are, by the magic of this association, made to retain what has at once instructed and diverted them, when they would be apt to forget what has perhaps no more than wearied, or *dulled* them. The chief and capital purport of this work is to inculcate the superiority of virtuous, conjugal, love, to all other joys; to prove that virtue chastens our pleasures, only to augment them; that the paths of vice, are always those of misery, and that virtue, even in distress, is still a happier bargain to its votaries, than vice, attended with all the splendor of fortune. So just, so refined a morality, would alone, with a candid and ingenuous reader, compensate for almost any imperfections in the execution of this work, some parts whereof will doubtless appear, amidst its beauties, to stand in need of an apology: *for example*, where the characters are, however exact copies of nature, chosen in too low, and disgustful a range of it, and rather too often repeated, and too long dwelt upon. The humours of an inn-keeper, an inn-keeper's wife, a gaoler, a highwayman, a bailiff, a street walker, may, no doubt, with great propriety find their place in those novels, of which the matter is taken out of common life; it would even be an absurd affectation to omit them, in compliance to a false delicacy, which calls every thing *low*, that does not relate to a high sphere of life, especially when they present themselves so naturally as in many places of this author's works. But when they occur too often, when the ingredients are not sparingly mixed, they will disgust even those, who, from their distance in rank or circumstance from these subjects, may be curious to have some idea of them, and can only come at it in such descriptions.

[. . . . .]

41 From a letter of Samuel Richardson, February 22, 1752

This letter is addressed to Mrs. Donellan (see above, No. 34).

[. . . . .]
What can I mean, you are pleased to ask, by seeming uncertain whether I shall publish my new work? Have I not, Madam, already obtruded upon the world many volumes; and have I not reason to apprehend that the world will be tired of me if I do? Where will this scribbler stop, will it not be asked? But when no more can be written or published by the same hand, then indulgence will possibly for that very reason be exerted in favour of the new piece. And a defunct author will probably meet with better quarter than a living one; especially as he is known to be a man in business, an obscure man, and one who is guilty of a very great presumption in daring to write at all, or do any thing but print the works of others.

Will I leave you to Captain Booth? Capt. Booth, Madam, has done his own business. Mr. Fielding has over-written himself, or rather *under*-written; and in his own journal seems ashamed of his last piece; and has promised that the same Muse shall write no more for him.[1] The piece, in short, is as dead as if it had been published forty years ago as to sale.

You guess that I have not read *Amelia*. Indeed I have read but the first volume. I had intended to go through with it; but I found the characters and situations so wretchedly low and dirty, that I imagined I could not be interested for any one of them; and to read and not to care what became of the hero and heroine, is a task that I thought I would leave to those who had more leisure than I am blessed with.

Parson Young sat for Fielding's parson Adams,[2] a man he knew, and only made a little more absurd than he is known to be. The best story in the piece, is of himself and his first wife. In his *Tom Jones*, his hero is made a natural child, because his own first wife was such. Tom Jones is Fielding himself, hardened in some places, softened in others. His Lady Bellaston is an infamous woman of his former acquaintance. His

Sophia is again his first wife. Booth, in his last piece, again himself; Amelia, even to her noselessness, is again his first wife. His brawls, his jarrs, his gaols, his spunging-houses, are all drawn from what he has seen and known. As I said (witness also his hamper plot) he has little or no invention: and admirably do you observe, that by several strokes in his *Amelia* he designed to be good, but knew not how, and lost his genius, low humour, in the attempt.

[. . . . .]

42 Dedication to *The History of Pompey the Little*, 1751

by FRANCIS COVENTRY (?)

The Dedication was included in the third edition of this novel (1752), which is now widely attributed to Francis Coventry (d. 1759).

TO
HENRY FIELDING, Esq.;

SIR,

My design being to speak a word or two in behalf of novel-writing, I know not to whom I can address myself with so much propriety as to yourself, who unquestionably stand foremost in this species of composition.

To convey instruction in a pleasant manner, and mix entertainment with it, is certainly a commendable undertaking, perhaps more likely to be attended with success than graver precepts; and even where amusement is the chief thing consulted, there is some little merit in making people laugh, when it is done without giving offence to religion, or virtue, or good manners. If the laugh be not raised at the expence of innocence or decency, good humour bids us indulge it, and we cannot well laugh too often.

Can we help wondering, therefore, at the contempt, with which many people affect to talk of this sort of composition? they seem to think it degrades the dignity of their understandings, to be found with a novel in their hands, and take great pains to let you know that they never read them. They are people of too great importance, it seems, to mispend their time in so idle a manner, and much too wise to be amused.

Now, tho' many reasons may be given for this ridiculous and affected disdain, I believe a very principal one, is the pride and pedantry of learned men, who are willing to monopolize reading to themselves, and therefore fastidiously decry all books that are on a level with common understandings, as empty, trifling and impertinent.

Thus the grave metaphysician for example, who after working night and day perhaps for several years, sends forth at last a profound treatise, where *A.* and *B.* seem to contain some very deep mysterious meaning; grows indignant to think that every little paltry scribbler, who paints only the characters of the age, the manners of the times, and the working of the passions, should presume to equal him in glory.

The politician too, who shakes his head in coffee-houses, and produces, now and then, from his fund of observations, a grave, sober, political pamphlet on the good of the nation; looks down with contempt on all such idle compositions, as lives and romances, which contain no strokes of satire at the ministry, no unmannerly reflections upon *Hanover*, nor any thing concerning the balance of power on the continent. These gentlemen and their readers join all to a man in depreciating works of humour: or if they ever vouchsafe to speak in their praise, the commendation never rises higher than, 'yes, 'tis well enough for such a sort of a thing;' after which the grave observator retires to his news-paper, and there, according to the general estimation, employs his time *to the best advantage*.

But besides these, there is another set, who never read any modern books at all. They, wise men, are so deep in the learned languages, that they can pay no regard to what has been published within these last thousand years. The world is grown old; mens geniuses are degenerated: the writers of this age are too contemptible for their notice, and they have no hopes of any better to succeed them. Yet these gentlemen of profound erudition will contentedly read any trash, that is disguised in a learned language, and the worst ribaldry of *Aristophanes* shall be critiqued and commented on by men, who turn up their noses at *Gulliver* or *Joseph Andrews*.

But if this contempt for books of amusement be carried a little too far, as I suspect it is, even among men of science and learning, what shall be said to some of the greatest triflers of the times, who affect to talk the same language? these surely have no right to express any disdain of what is at least equal to their understandings. Scholars and men of learning have a reason to give; their application to severe studies may have destroyed their relish for works of a lighter cast, and consequently it cannot be expected that they should approve what they do not understand. But as for beaux, rakes, petit-maitres, and fine ladies, whose lives are spent in doing the things which novels record, I do not see why they should be indulged in affecting a contempt of them. People, whose most earnest business is to dress and play at cards, are not so importantly employed, but that they may find leisure now and then to read a novel. Yet these are as forward as any to despise them; and I once heard a very fine lady, condemning some highly finished conversations in one of your works, sir, for this curious reason:— 'because,' said she, ' 'tis such sort of stuff as passes every day between me and my own maid.'

I do not pretend to apply anything here said in behalf of books of amusement, to the following little work, of which I ask your patronage: I am sensible how very imperfect it is in all its parts, and how unworthy to be ranked in that class of writings, which I am now defending. But I desire to be understood in general, or more particularly with an eye to your works, which I take to be master-pieces and complete models in their kind. They are, I think, worthy the attention of the greatest and wisest men, and if any body is ashamed of reading them, or can read them without entertainment and instruction, I heartily pity their understandings.

The late editor of Mr. *Pope*'s works, in a very ingenious note,[1] wherein he traces the progress of romance-writing, justly observes, that this species of composition is now brought to perfection by Mr. *De Marivaux* in *France*, and Mr. *Fielding* in *England*.

I have but one objection to make to this remark, which is, that the name of Mr. *De Marivaux* stands foremost of the two: a superiority I can by no means allow him. Mr. *Marivaux* is indeed a very amiable, elegant, witty, and penetrating writer. The reflections he scatters up and down his *Marianne* are highly judicious, *recherchés*, and infinitely agreeable. But not to mention that he never finishes his works, which greatly disappoints his readers, I think, his *characters* fall infinitely short of those we find in the performances of his *English* contemporary. They are neither so original, so ludic[r]ous, so well distinguished, nor so happily contrasted as your own: and as the characters of a novel principally determine its merit, I must be allowed to esteem my countryman the greater author.

There is another celebrated novel writer, of the same kingdom, now living, who in the choice and diversity of his characters, perhaps exceeds his rival Mr. *Marivaux*, and would deserve greater commendation, if the libertinism of his plans, and too wanton drawings of nature, did not take off from the other merit of his works; tho' at the same time it must be confessed, that his genius and knowledge of mankind are very extensive.[2] But with all due respect for the parts of these two able *Frenchmen*, I will venture to say they have their superior, and whoever has read the works of Mr. *Fielding*, cannot be at a loss to determine who that superior is. Few books of this kind have ever been written with a spirit equal to *Joseph Andrews*, and no story that I know of, was ever invented with more happiness, or conducted with more art and management than that of *Tom Jones*.

43 From *The Female Quixote; or, the Adventures of Arabella,* 1752

by CHARLOTTE LENNOX

Charlotte Lennox (1720–1804), was the friend of Johnson and Goldsmith. The latter wrote the Epilogue to her play, *The Sister,* acted in 1769; the former wrote dedications for several of her works (including *The Female Quixote* . . .), and declared her superior to Mrs. Carter, Hannah More and Fanny Burney (see *Boswell's Life* . . ., IV, 275). Mrs. Lennox also wrote a volume of poems (1747) and several novels: *Harriot Stuart* (1751); *Henrietta* (1758); *Sophia* (1762); *Euphrenia* (1790); *Hermione* (1791); and *The History of Sir George Warrington* (1797). *The Female Quixote* . . . is the history of a young lady's delusion that the world is as it is described in the heroic romances. Immediately before the debate which is reproduced below (from the penultimate chapter), she has cast herself into a river in order to escape a totally imaginary abduction.

CHAP. XI

Being in the Author's Opinion, the best Chapter in this History

The good Divine, who had the Cure of *Arabella*'s Mind greatly at Heart, no sooner perceiv'd that the Health of her Body was almost restor'd, and that he might talk to her without the Fear of any Inconvenience, than he introduc'd the Subject of her throwing herself into the River, which he had before lightly touch'd upon, and still declar'd himself dissatisfy'd with.

Arabella, now more dispos'd to defend this Point than when languishing under the Pressure of Pain and Dejection of Mind, endeavour'd by Arguments founded upon Romantick Heroism, to prove, That it was not only reasonable and just, but also great and glorious, and exactly conformable to the Rules of Heroick Virtue.

[. . . . .]

The Apprehension of any future Evil, Madam, said the Divine, which is called Terror, when the Danger is from natural Causes, and Suspicion, when it proceeds from a moral Agent, must always arise from Comparison.

We can judge of the Future only by the Past, and have therefore only Reason to fear or suspect, when we see the same Causes in Motion which have formerly produc'd Mischief, or the same Measures taken as have before been preparatory to a Crime.

Thus, when the Sailor in certain Latitudes sees the Clouds rise, Experience bids him expect a Storm. When any Monarch levies Armies, his Neighbours prepare to repel an Invasion.

This Power of Prognostication, may, by Reading and Conversation, he extended beyond our own Knowledge: And the great Use of Books, is that of participating without Labour or Hazard the Experience of others.

But upon this Principle how can you find any Reason for your late Fright.

Has it ever been known, that a Lady of your Rank was attack'd with such Intentions, in a Place so publick, without any Preparations made by the Violator for Defence or Escape?

Can it be imagin'd that any Man would so rashly expose himself to Infamy by Failure, and to the Gibbet by Success?

Does there in the Records of the World appear a single Instance of such hopeless Villany?

It is now Time, Sir, said *Arabella*, to answer your Questions, before they are too many to be remembered.

The Dignity of my Birth can very little defend me against an Insult to which the Heiresses of great and powerful Empires, the Daughters of valiant Princes, and the Wives of renowned Monarchs, have been a thousand Times exposed.

The Danger which you think so great, would hardly repel a determin'd Mind; for in Effect, Who would have attempted my Rescue, seeing that no Knight or valiant Cavalier was within View?

What then should have hinder'd him from placing me in a Chariot? Driving it into the pathless Desart? And immuring me in a Castle, among Woods and Mountains? Or hiding me perhaps in the Caverns of a Rock? Or confining me in some Island of an immense Lake?

From all this, Madam, interrupted the Clergyman, he is hinder'd by Impossibility.

He cannot carry you to any of these dreadful Places, because there is no such Castle, Desart, Cavern, or Lake.

You will pardon me, Sir, said *Arabella*, if I recur to your own Principles:

You allow that Experience may be gain'd by Books: And certainly there is no Part of Knowledge in which we are oblig'd to trust them more than in Descriptive Geography.

The most restless Activity in the longest Life, can survey but a small Part of the habitable Globe: And the rest can only be known from the Report of others.

Universal Negatives are seldom safe, and are least to be allow'd when the Disputes are about Objects of Sense; where one Position cannot be inferr'd from another.

That there is a Castle, any Man who has seen it may safely affirm. But you cannot with equal Reason, maintain that there is no Castle, because you have not seen it.

Why should I imagine that the Face of the Earth is alter'd since the Time of those Heroines, who experienc'd so many Changes of uncouth Captivity?

Castles indeed, are the Works of Art; and are therefore subject to Decay. But Lakes, and Caverns, and Desarts, must always remain.

And why, since you call for Instances, should I not dread the Misfortunes which happen'd to the divine *Clelia*, who was carry'd to one of the Isles of the *Thrasymenian* Lake?

Or those which befel the beautiful *Candace*, Queen of *Ethiopia*, whom the Pyrate *Zenedorus* wander'd with on the Seas?

Or the Accidents which imbitter'd the Life of the incomparable *Cleopatra*?

Or the Persecutions which made that of the fair *Elisa* miserable?[1]

Or, in fine, the various Distresses of many other fair and virtuous Princesses: Such as those which happen'd to *Olympia, Bellamira, Parisatis, Berenice, Amalazantha, Agione, Albysinda, Placidia, Arsinoe, Deidamia*, and a thousand others I could mention.[2]

To the Names of many of these illustrious Sufferers I am an absolute Stranger, replied the Doctor.

The rest I faintly remember some Mention of in those contemptible Volumes, with which Children are sometimes injudiciously suffer'd to amuse their Imaginations; but which I little expected to hear quoted by your Ladyship in a serious Discourse.

And though I am very far from catching Occasions of Resentment, yet I think myself at Liberty to observe, That if I merited your Censure for one indelicate Epithet, we have engag'd on very unequal Terms, if I may not likewise complain of such contemptuous Ridicule as you are pleas'd to exercise upon my Opinions by opposing them with the Authority of Scriblers, not only of Fictions, but of senseless Fictions; which at once vitiate the Mind, and pervert the Understanding; and which if they are at any Time read with Safety, owe their Innocence only to their Absurdity.

From these Books, Sir, said *Arabella*, which you condemn with so much Ardour, though you acknowledge yourself little acquainted with them, I have learnt not to recede from the Conditions I have granted, and shall not therefore censure the Licence of your Language, which glances from the Books upon the Readers.

These Books, Sir, thus corrupt, thus absurd, thus dangerous alike to the Intellect and Morals, I have read; and that I hope without Injury to my Judgment, or my Virtue.

The Doctor, whose Vehemence had hinder'd him from discovering all the Consequences of his Position, now found himself entangled, and reply'd in a submissive Tone,

I confess, Madam, my Words imply an Accusation very remote from my Intention.

It has always been the Rule of my Life, not to justify any Words or Actions because they are mine.

I am asham'd of my Negligence, I am sorry for my Warmth, and intreat your Ladyship to pardon a Fault which I hope never to repeat.

The Reparation, Sir, said *Arabella* smiling, over-balances the Offence, and by thus daring to own you have been in the Wrong, you have rais'd in me a much higher Esteem for you.

Yet I will not pardon you, added she, without enjoining you a Penance for the Fault you own you have committed; and this Penance shall be to prove,

First, That these Histories you condemn are Fictions.

Next, That they are absurd.

And Lastly, That they are Criminal.

The Doctor was pleas'd to find a Reconciliation offer'd upon so very easy Terms, with a Person whom he beheld at once with Reverence and Affection, and could not offend without extreme Regret.

He therefore answered with a very chearful Composure:

To prove those Narrative to be Fictions, Madam, is only difficult, because the Position is almost too evident for Proof.

Your Ladyship knows, I suppose to what Authors these Writings are ascrib'd?

To the *French* Wits of the last Century, said *Arabella*.

And at what Distance, Madam, are the Facts related in them from the Age of the Writer?

I was never exact in my Computation, replied *Arabella*; but I think most of the Events happen'd about two thousand Years ago.

How then, Madam, resum'd the Doctor, could these Events be so minutely known to Writers so far remote from the Time in which they happened?

By Records, Monuments, Memoirs, and Histories, answered the Lady.

But by what Accident, then, said the Doctor smiling, did it happen these Records and Monuments were kept universally secret to Mankind till the last Century?

What brought all the Memoirs of the remotest Nations and earliest Ages only to *France*?

Where were they hidden that none could consult them but a few obscure Authors?

And whither are they now vanished again that they can be found no more?

Arabella having sat silent a while, told him, That she found his Questions very difficult to be answer'd; and that though perhaps the Authors themselves could have told whence they borrowed their Materials, she should not at present require any other Evidence of the first Assertion:

But allow'd him to suppose them Fictions, and requir'd now that he should shew them to be absurd.

Your Ladyship, return'd he, has, I find, too much Understanding to struggle against Demonstration, and too much Veracity to deny your Convictions; therefore some of the Arguments by which I intended to shew the Falshood of these Narratives may be now used to prove their Absurdity.

You grant them, Madam, to be Fictions?

Sir, interrupted *Arabella* eagerly, You are again infringing the Laws of Disputation.

You are not to confound a Supposition of which I allow you only the present Use, with an unlimited and irrevocable Concession.

I am too well acquainted with my own Weakness to conclude an Opinion false, merely because I find myself unable to defend it.

But I am in haste to hear the Proof of the other Positions, not only because they may perhaps supply what is deficient in your Evidence of the first, but because I think it of more Importance to detect Corruption than Fiction.

Though indeed Falshood is a Species of Corruption, and what Falshood is more hateful than the Falshood of History.

Since you have drawn me back, Madam, to the first Question, returned the Doctor, Let me know what Arguments your Ladyship can produce for the Veracity of these Books.

That there are many Objections against it, you yourself have allowed, and the highest moral Evidence of Falshood appears when there are many Arguments against an Assertion, and none for it.

Sir, replied *Arabella*, I shall never think that any Narrative, which is not confuted by its own Absurdity, is without one Argument at least on its Side; there is a Love of Truth in the human Mind, if not naturally implanted, so easily obtained from Reason and Experience, that I should expect it universally to prevail where there is no strong Temptation to Deceit; we hate to be deceived, we therefore hate those that deceive us; we desire not to be hated, and therefore know that we are not to deceive. Shew me an equal Motive to Falshood, or confess that every Relation has some Right to Credit.

This may be allowed, Madam, said the Doctor, when we claim to be credited, but that seems not to be the Hope or Intention of these Writers.

Surely Sir, replied *Arabella*, you must mistake their Design; he that writes without Intention to be credited, must write to little Purpose; for what Pleasure or Advantage can arise from Facts that never happened? What Examples can be afforded by the Patience of those who never suffered, or the Chastity of those who were never solicited? The great End of History, is to shew how much human Nature can endure or perform. When we hear a Story in common Life that raises our Wonder or Compassion, the first Confutation stills our Emotions, and however we were touched before, we then chase it from the Memory with Contempt as a Trifle, or with Indignation as an Imposture. Prove, therefore, that the Books which I have hitherto read as Copies of Life, and Models of Conduct, are empty Fictions, and from this Hour I deliver them to Moths and Mould; and from this Time forward consider their Authors as Wretches who cheated me of those Hours I ought to have dedicated to Application and Improvement, and betrayed me to a Waste of those Years in which I might have laid up Knowledge for my future Life.

Shakespear, said the Doctor, calls just Resentment the Child of

Integrity,[3] and therefore I do not wonder, that what Vehemence the Gentleness of your Ladyship's Temper allows, should be exerted upon this Occasion. Yet though I cannot forgive these Authors for having destroyed so much valuable Time, yet I cannot think them intentionally culpable, because I cannot believe they expected to be credited. Truth is not always injured by Fiction. An admirable[4] Writer of our own Time, has found the Way to convey the most solid Instructions, the noblest Sentiments, and the most exalted Piety, in the pleasing Dress of a[5] Novel, and, to use the Words of the greatest Genius in the present Age, 'Has taught the Passions to move at the Command of Virtue.'[6] The Fables of *Æsop*, though never I suppose believed, yet have been long considered as Lectures of moral and domestic Wisdom, so well adapted to the Faculties of Man, that they have been received by all civilized Nations; and the *Arabs* themselves have honoured his Translator with the Appellation of *Locman* the Wise.[7]

The Fables of *Æsop*, said *Arabella*, are among those of which the Absurdity discovers itself, and the Truth is comprised in the Application; but what can be said of those Tales which are told with the solemn Air of historical Truth, and if false convey no instruction?

That they cannot be defended, Madam, said the Doctor, it is my Purpose to prove, and if to evince their Falshood be sufficient to procure their Banishment from your Ladyship's Closet, their Day of Grace is near an End. How is any oral, or written Testimony, confuted or confirmed?

By comparing it, says the Lady, with the Testimony of others, or with the natural Effects and standing Evidence of the Facts related, and sometimes by comparing it with itself.

If then your Ladyship will abide by this last, returned he, and compare these Books with antient Histories, you will not only find innumerable Names, of which no Mention was ever made before, but Persons who lived in different Ages, engaged as the Friends or Rivals of each other. You will perceive that your Authors have parcelled out the World at Discretion, erected Palaces, and established Monarchies wherever the Conveniency of their Narrative required them, and set Kings and Queens over imaginary Nations. Nor have they considered themselves as invested with less Authority over the Works of Nature, than the Institutions of Men; for they have distributed Mountains and Desarts, Gulphs and Rocks, wherever they wanted them, and whenever the Course of their Story required an Expedient, raised a gloomy Forest, or overflowed the Regions with a rapid Stream.

I suppose, said *Arabella*, you have no Intention to deceive me, and since, if what you have asserted be true, the Cause is undefensible, I shall trouble you no longer to argue on this Topic, but desire now to hear why, supposing them Fictions, and intended to be received as Fictions, you censure them as absurd?

The only Excellence of Falshood, answered he, is its Resemblance to Truth; as therefore any Narrative is more liable to be confuted by its Inconsistency with known Facts, it is at a greater Distance from the Perfection of Fiction; for there can be no Difficulty in framing a Tale, if we are left at Liberty to invert all History and Nature for our own Conveniency. When a Crime is to be concealed, it is easy to cover it with an imaginary Wood. When Virtue is to be rewarded, a Nation with a new Name may, without any Expence of Invention, raise her to the Throne. When *Ariosto* was told of the Magnificence of his Palaces, he answered, that the Cost of poetical Architecture was very little; and still less is the Cost of Building without Art, than without Materials. But their historical Failures may be easily passed over, when we consider their physical or philosophical Absurdities; to bring Men together from different Countries does not shock with every inherent or demonstrable Absurdity, and therefore when we read only for Amusement, such Improprieties may be born: But who can forbear to throw away the Story that gives to one Man the Strength of Thousands; that puts Life or Death in a Smile or a Frown; that recounts Labours and Sufferings to which the Powers of Humanity are utterly unequal; that disfigures the whole Appearance of the World, and represents every Thing in a Form different from that which Experience has shewn. It is the Fault of the best Fictions, that they teach young Minds to expect strange Adventures and sudden Vicissitudes, and therefore encourage them often to trust to Chance. A long Life may be passed without a single Occurrence that can cause much Surprize, or produce any unexpected Consequence of great Importance; the Order of the World is so established, that all human Affairs proceed in a regular Method, and very little Opportunity is left for Sallies or Hazards, for Assault or Rescue; but the Brave and the Coward, the Sprightly and the Dull, suffer themselves to be carried alike down the Stream of Custom.

Arabella, who had for some Time listened with a Wish to interrupt him, now took Advantage of a short Pause. I cannot imagine, Sir, said she, that you intend to deceive me, and therefore I am inclined to believe that you are yourself mistaken, and that your Application to Learning has hindered you from that Acquaintance with the World, in which these Authors excelled. I have not long conversed in Public, yet I have found that Life is subject to many Accidents. Do you count my late Escape for nothing? Is it to be numbered among daily and cursory Transactions, that a Woman flies from a Ravisher into a rapid Stream?

You must not, Madam, said the Doctor, urge as an Argument the Fact which is at present the Subject of Dispute.

Arabella blushing at the Absurdity she had been guilty of, and not attempting any Subterfuge or Excuse, the Doctor found himself at Liberty to proceed:

You must not imagine, Madam, continued he, that I intend to arrogate any Superiority, when I observe that your Ladyship must suffer me to decide, in some Measure authoritatively, whether Life is truly described in those Books; the Likeness of a Picture can only be determined by a Knowledge of the Original. You have yet had little Opportunity of knowing the Ways of Mankind, which cannot be learned but from Experience, and of which the highest Understanding, and the lowest, must enter the World in equal Ignorance. I have lived long in a public Character, and have thought it my Duty to study those whom I have undertaken to admonish or instruct. I have never been so rich as to affright Men into Disguise and Concealment, nor so poor as to be kept at a Distance too great for accurate Observation. I therefore presume to tell your Ladyship, with great Confidence, that your Writers have instituted a World of their own, and that nothing is more different from a human Being, than Heroes or Heroines.

I am afraid, Sir, said *Arabella*, that the Difference is not in Favour of the present World.

That, Madam, answered he, your own Penetration will enable you to judge when it shall have made you equally acquainted with both: I have no Desire to determine a Question, the Solution of which will give so little Pleasure to Purity and Benevolence.

The Silence of a Man who loves to praise is a Censure sufficiently severe, said the Lady. May it never happen that you should be unwilling to mention the Name of *Arabella*. I hope wherever Corruption prevails in the World, to live in it with Virtue, or, if I find myself too much endanger'd, to retire from it with Innocence. But if you can say so little in Commendation of Mankind, how will you prove these Histories to be vicious, which if they do not describe real Life, gives us an Idea of a better Race of Beings than now inhabit the World.

It is of little Importance, Madam, replied the Doctor, to decide whether in the real or fictitious Life, most Wickedness is to be found. Books ought to supply an Antidote to Example, and if we retire to a Contemplation of Crimes, and continue in our Closets to inflame our Passions, at what time must we rectify our Words, or purify our Hearts? The immediate Tendency of these Books which your Ladyship must allow me to mention with some Severity, is to give new Fire to the Passions of Revenge and Love; two Passions which, even without such powerful Auxiliaries, it is one of the severest Labours of Reason and Piety to suppress, and which yet must be suppressed if we hope to be approved in the Sight of the only Being whose Approbation can make us happy. I am afraid your Ladyship will think me too serious. I have already learned too much from you, said *Arabella*, to presume to instruct you, yet suffer me to caution you never to dishonour your sacred Office by the Lowliness of Apologies. Then let me again observe, resumed he, that these Books soften the Heart to Love, and harden it to Murder. That they teach Women to exact Vengeance, and Men to execute it; teach Women to expect not only Worship, but the dreadful Worship of human Sacrifices. Every Page of these Volumes is filled with such extravagance of Praise, and expressions of Obedience as one human Being ought not to hear from another; or with Accounts of Battles, in which thousands are slaughtered for no other Purpose than to gain a Smile from the haughty Beauty, who sits a calm Spectatress of the Ruin and Desolation, Bloodshed and Misery, incited by herself.

It is impossible to read these Tales without lessening part of that Humility, which by preserving in us a Sense of our Alliance with all Human Nature, keeps us awake to Tenderness and Sympathy, or without impairing that Compassion which is implanted in us as an Incentive to Acts of Kindness. If there be any preserved by natural Softness, or early Education, from learning Pride and Cruelty, they are yet in danger of being betrayed to the Vanity of Beauty, and taught the Arts of Intrigue.

Love, Madam, is, you know, the Business, the sole Business of Ladies in Romances. *Arabella*'s Blushes now hinder'd him from proceeding as he had intended. I perceive, continued he, that my Arguments begin to be less agreeable to your Ladyship's Delicacy, I shall therefore insist no longer upon false Tenderness of Sentiment, but proceed to those Outrages of the violent Passions, which, though not more dangerous, are more generally hateful.

It is not necessary, Sir, interrupted *Arabella*, that you strengthen by any new Proof a Position which when calmly considered cannot be denied, my Heart yields to the Force of Truth, and I now wonder how the Blaze of Enthusiastic Bravery, could hinder me from remarking with Abhorrence the Crime of deliberate unnecessary Bloodshed.

I begin to perceive that I have hitherto at least trifled away my Time, and fear that I have already made some Approaches to the Crime of encouraging Violence and Revenge. I hope, Madam, said the good Man with Horror in his Looks, that no Life was ever lost by your Incitement. *Arabella* seeing him thus moved, burst into Tears, and could not immediately answer. Is it possible, cried the Doctor, that such Gentleness and Elegance should be stained with Blood? Be not too hasty in your Censure, said *Arabella*, recovering herself, I tremble indeed to think how nearly I have approached the Brink of Murder, when I thought myself only consulting my own Glory; but whatever I suffer, I will never more demand or instigate Vengeance, nor consider my Punctilios as important enough to be ballanced against Life.

The Doctor confirmed her in her new Resolutions, and thinking Solitude was necessary to compose her Spirits after the Fatigue of so long a Conversation, he retired to acquaint Mr. *Glanville* with his Success, who in the Transport of his Joy was almost ready to throw himself at his Feet, to thank him for the Miracle, as he called it, that he had performed.

44 *The Adventurer*, 4, Saturday, November 18, 1752

by JOHN HAWKESWORTH

John Hawkesworth (1715?–73) planned *The Adventurer* in collaboration with Johnson after the decease of the *Rambler* (see above, No. 33), and continued it with the help of Johnson, Dr. Richard Bathurst, Dr. Joseph Warton and Mrs. Chapone until March 4, 1754. The periodical was very successful and gained its conductor the degree of doctor of civil law. Hawkesworth also wrote an Eastern tale, *Almoran and Hamet* (1761; see below, No. 58), very frequently reprinted throughout the eighteenth century, and translated Fénelon's *Télémaque* (1768). He succeeded Johnson as compiler of the Parliamentary reports for the *Gentleman's Magazine*.

Ficta voluptatis causâ sint proxima veris.
HOR.

Fictions to please should wear the face of truth.
ROSC.[1]

No species of writing affords so general entertainment as the relation of events; but all relation of events do not entertain in the same degree.

It is always necessary, that facts should appear to be produced in a regular and connected series, that they should follow in a quick succession, and yet that they should be delivered with discriminating circumstances. If they have not a necessary and apparent connexion, the ideas which they excite obliterate each other, and the mind is tantalized with an imperfect glimpse of innumerable objects that just appear and vanish; if they are too minutely related, they become tiresome; and if divested of all their circumstances, insipid; for who that reads in a table of chronology or an index, that a city was swallowed up by an earthquake, or a kingdom depopulated by a pestilence, finds either his attention engaged, or his curiosity gratified?

Those narratives are most pleasing, which not only excite and gratify curiosity but engage the passions.

History is a relation of the most natural and important events; history, therefore, gratifies curiosity, but it does not often excite either terror or pity; the mind feels not that tenderness for a falling state, which it feels for an injured beauty; nor is it so much alarmed at the migration of barbarians who mark their way with desolation, and fill the world with violence and rapine, as at the fury of a husband, who, deceived into jealousy by false appearances, stabs a faithful and affectionate wife, kneeling at his feet, and pleading to be heard.

Voyages and Travels have nearly the same excellences and the same defects: no passion is strongly excited except wonder; or if we feel any emotion at the danger of the traveller, it is transient and languid, because his character is not rendered sufficiently important; he is rarely discovered to have any excellences but daring curiosity; he is never the object of admiration and seldom of esteem.

Biography would always engage the passions, if it could sufficiently gratify curiosity: but there have been few among the whole human species whose lives would furnish a single adventure; I mean such a complication of circumstances, as hold the mind in an anxious yet pleasing suspense, and gradually unfold in the production of some unforeseen and important event; much less such a series of facts, as will perpetually vary the scene, and gratify the fancy, with new views of life.

But Nature is now exhausted; all her wonders have been accumulated, every recess has been explored, deserts have been traversed, Alps climbed, and the secrets of the deep disclosed; time has been compelled to restore the empires and the heroes of antiquity; all have passed in review; yet fancy requires new gratifications, and curiosity is still unsatisfied.

The resources of Art yet remain: the simple beauties of nature, if they cannot be multiplied, may be compounded, and an infinite variety produced, in which by the union of different graces both may be heightened, and the coalition of different powers may produce a proportionate effect.

The Epic Poem at once gratifies curiosity and moves the passions; the events are various and important; but it is not the fate of a nation, but of the hero in which they terminate, and whatever concerns the hero engages the passions; the dignity of his character, his merit, and his importance, compel us to follow him with reverence and solicitude, to tremble when he is in danger, to weep when he suffers, and to burn when he is wronged; with these vicissitudes of passion every heart attends Ulysses in his wanderings, and Achilles to the field.

Upon this occasion the Old Romance may be considered as a kind of Epic, since it was intended to produce the same effect upon the mind nearly by the same means.

In both these species of writing truth is apparently violated: but though the events are not always produced by probable means, yet the pleasure arising from the story is not much lessened; for fancy is still captivated with variety, and passion has scarce leisure to reflect, that she is agitated with the fate of imaginary beings, and interested in events that never happened.

The Novel, though it bears a nearer resemblance to truth, has yet less power of entertainment; for it is confined within the narrower bounds of probability, the number of incidents is necessarily diminished, and if it deceives us more, it surprises us less. The distress is indeed frequently tender, but the narrative often stands still; the lovers compliment each other in tedious letters and set speeches; trivial circumstances are enumerated with a minute exactness, and the reader is wearied with languid descriptions and impertinent declamations.

But the most extravagant, and yet perhaps the most generally pleasing of all literary performances, are those in which supernatural events are every moment produced by Genii and Fairies: such are the *Arabian Nights' Entertainment*, the Tales of the Countess d'Anois, and many others of the same class. It may be thought strange, that the mind should with pleasure acquiesce in the open violation of the most known and obvious truths; and that relations which contradict all experience, and exhibit a series of events that are not only impossible but ridiculous, should be read by almost every taste and capacity with equal eagerness and delight. But it is not, perhaps, the mere violation of truth or of probability that offends, but such a violation only as perpetually recurs. The mind is satisfied, if every event appears to have an adequate cause; and when the agency of Genii and Fairies is once admitted, no event which is deemed possible to such agents is rejected as incredible or absurd; the action of the story proceeds with regularity, the persons act upon rational principles, and such events take place as may naturally be expected from the interposition of superior intelligence and power: so that though there is not a natural, there is at least a kind of moral probability preserved, and our first concession is abundantly rewarded by the new scenes to which we are admitted, and the unbounded prospect that is thrown open before us.

But though we attend with delight to the achievements of a hero who is transported in a moment over half the globe upon a griffon, and see with admiration a palace or a city vanish upon his breaking a seal or extinguishing a lamp; yet if at his first interview with a mistress, for whose sake he had fought so many battles and passed so many regions, he should salute her with a box on the ear; or if immediately after he had vanquished a giant or a dragon, he should leap into a well or tie himself up to a tree, we should be disappointed and disgusted, the story would be condemned as improbable, unnatural, and absurd, our innate love of truth would be applauded, and we should expatiate on the folly of an attempt to please reasonable beings, by a detail of events which can never be believed, and the intervention of agents which could never have existed.

Dramatic Poetry, especially tragedy, seems to unite all that pleases in each of these species of writing, with a strong resemblance of truth, and a closer imitation of nature: the characters are such as excite attention and solicitude; the action is important, its progress is intricate yet natural, and the catastrophe is sudden and striking; and as we are present to every transaction, the images are more strongly impressed, and the passions more forcibly moved.

From a dramatic poem to those short pieces, which may be contained in such a periodical paper as the *Adventurer*, is a bold transition. And yet such pieces, although formed upon a single incident, if that incident be sufficiently uncommon to gratify curiosity, and sufficiently interesting to engage the passions, may afford an entertainment, which, if it is not lasting, is yet of the highest kind. Of such, therefore, this paper will frequently consist: but it should be remembered, that it is much more difficult and laborious to invent a story, however simple and however short, than to recollect topics of instruction, or to remark the scenes of life as they are shifted before us.

45 From a letter of Philip Skelton, December 28, 1752

This letter is addressed to Samuel Richardson.

Pedego, near Enniskillen,
Dec. 28, 1752.

MY DEAR FRIEND,

I heartily thank you and Dr. Wilson, to whom my best respects, for the information contained in your last. It hath enabled me to oblige a family I greatly regard, and will prevent their involving themselves in fruitless expences.

I am glad to hear your work is what you call long. I am excessively impatient to see it. And shall certainly think it too short, as I did *Clarissa*, although it should run out into seven folios. The world will think so too, if it is sufficiently larded with facts, incidents, adventures, &c. The generality of readers are more taken with the driest narrative of facts, if they are facts of any importance, than with the purest sentiments, and the noblest lessons of morality. Now, though you write above the taste of the many, yet ought it not to be, nay, is it not, your chief design, to benefit the many? But how can you cure their mental maladies, if you do not so wrap up your physic as to make it pass their palates? I know of nothing more unpalatable to most men than morality and religion. They will not go down, if they are not either well peppered and salted with wit, or all alive from end to end with action. Therefore stuff your works with adventures, and wedge in events by way of primings, especially when wit and humour happen to be scarce, as sometimes they will be; for a man cannot have them for calling. They come like the rivers, without calling, or come not at all. But it is no hard matter to invent a story when you please. I am glad you have a bad woman, but sorry she does not shew herself. Is this natural? Did you ever know a bad woman that did not make a figure in her way? No, no; the devil always takes care that his confessors of that sex canonize themselves.

[. . . . .]

46 *The Adventurer*, 16, Saturday, December 30, 1752

by JOHN HAWKESWORTH

Gratior et pulchro veniens in corpore virtus.
VIRG.[1]

More lovely virtue, in a lovely form.

I have observed in a former paper,[2] that the relation of events is a species of writing which affords more general entertainment than any other; and to afford entertainment appears to have been often the principal if not the only design of those to whom events have been related.

It must, indeed, be confessed, that when truths are to be recorded, little is left to the choice of the writer; a few pages of the book of nature or of providence are before him; and if he transcribes with fidelity, he is not to be blamed, if in this fragment good and evil do not appear to be always distributed as reward and punishment.

But it is justly expected of the writer of fiction, who has unbounded liberty to select, to vary and to complicate, that his plan should be complete, that he should principally consider the moral tendency of his work, and that when he relates events he should teach virtue.

The relation of events becomes a moral lecture, when vicious actions produce misery, and vicious characters incur contempt; when the combat of virtue is rewarded with honour, and her sufferings terminate in felicity; but though this method of instruction has been often recommended, yet I think some of its peculiar advantages have been still overlooked, and for that reason not always secured.

Facts are easily comprehended by every understanding: and their dependance and influence upon each other are discovered by those, who would soon be bewildered in a series of logical deductions: they fix that volatility which would break away from ratiocination; and the precept becomes more forcible and striking as it is connected with example. Precept gains only the cold approbation of reason, and compels an assent which judgment frequently yields with reluctance, even when delay is impossible: but by example the passions are roused; we approve, we emulate, and we honour or love; we detest, we despise, and we condemn, as fit objects are successively held up to the mind: the affections are, as it were, drawn out into the field: they learn their exercise in a mock fight, and are trained for the service of virtue.

Facts, as they are most perfectly and easily comprehended, and as they are impressed upon the mind by the passions, are tenaciously remembered, though the terms in which they are delivered are presently forgotten; and for this reason the instruction that results from facts is more easily propagated: many can repeat a story, who would not have understood a declamation; and though the expression will be varied as often as it is told, yet the moral which it was intended to teach will remain the same.

But these advantages have not been always secured by those who have professed 'to make a story the vehicle of instruction,' and to 'surprise levity into knowledge by a show of entertainment;'[3] for instead of including instruction in the events themselves, they have made use of events only to introduce declamation and argument. If the events excite curiosity, all the fine reflections which are said to be interspersed, are passed over; if the events do not excite curiosity, the whole is rejected together, not only with disgust and disappointment, but indignation, as having allured by a false promise, and engaged in a vain pursuit. These pieces, if they are read as a task by those for whose instruction they are intended, can produce none of the effects for which they were written; because the instruction will not be necessarily remembered with the facts; and because the story is so far from recommending the moral, that the moral is detested as interrupting the story. Nor are those who voluntarily read for instruction, less disappointed than those who seek only entertainment; for he that is eager in the pursuit of knowledge, is disgusted when he is stopped by the intervention of a trivial incident or a forced compliment, when a new personage is introduced, or a lover takes occasion to admire the sagacity of a mistress.

But many writers who have avoided this error, and interwoven precept with event, though they intended a moral lecture, have yet defeated their own purpose, by taking from virtue every accidental excellence, and decorating vice with the spoils.

I can think of nothing that could be alleged in defence of this perverse distribution of graces and defects, but a design to shew that virtue alone is sufficient to confer honour upon the lowest character, and that without it nothing can preserve the highest from contempt; and that those excellences which we can acquire by our own efforts, are of more moment than those which are the gift of nature: but in this design, no writer, of whatever abilities, can succeed.

It has been often remarked, though not without wonder, that almost every man is more jealous of his natural than his moral qualities; and resents with more bitterness a satire upon his abilities than his practice: the fact is unquestionably true; and perhaps it will no longer appear strange, if it be considered, that natural defects are of necessity, and moral of choice; the imputation of folly, if it is true, must be suffered without hope, but that of immorality may at any time be obviated by removing the cause.

But whatever be the reason, it appears by the common consent of mankind, that the want of virtue does not incur equal contempt with the want of parts; and that many vices are thought to be rather honourable than infamous, merely because they imply some natural excellence, some superiority which cannot be acquired by those who want it, but to which those who have it believe they can add all that others possess, whenever they shall think fit to make the attempt.

Florio, after having learned the Latin and Greek languages at Westminster, and spent three years at the university, made the tour of Europe, and at his return obtained a place at court. Florio's imagination is sprightly, and his judgment strong: he is well acquainted with every branch of polite literature, and travel has polished the sound scholar into the fine gentleman: his person is graceful, and his manner polite; he is remarkable for the elegance of his dress; and he is thought to dance a minuet, and understand the small sword better than any other man in the kingdom. Among the ladies Florio has made many conquests; and has challenged and killed in a duel an officer, who upbraided him with the breach of a promise of marriage, confirmed by an oath, to a young beauty whom he kept in great splendour as a mistress; his conversation is admired by all who can relish sterling wit and true humour; every private company brightens when he enters, and every public assembly becomes more splendid by his presence: Florio is also liberal to profusion; and is not, therefore, inquisitive about the merit of those upon whom he lavishes his bounty.

Benevolus has also had a liberal education: he learned the languages at Merchant Taylors',[4] and went from thence to the university, where his application was greater than Florio's, but the knowledge that he acquired was less; as his apprehension is slow, and his industry indefatigable, he remembers more than he understands; he has no taste either for poetry or music; mirth never smiled at a sally of his imagination, nor did doubt ever appeal to his judgment: his person, though it is not deformed, is inelegant; his dress is not slovenly, but awkwardly neat; and his manner is rather formal than rude; he is the jest of an assembly, and the aversion of ladies; but he is remarkable for the most uniform virtue and unaffected piety: he is a faithful friend, and a kind master; and so compassionate, that he will not suffer even the snails that eat his fruit to be destroyed; he lays out annually near half his income in gratuities, not to support the idle, but to encourage the industrious; yet there is rather the appearance of parsimony than profusion in his temper; and he is so timorous, that he will turn pale at the report of a musket.

Which of these two characters wouldst thou choose for thy own? whom dost thou most honour, and to whom hast thou paid the tribute of involuntary praise? Thy heart has already answered with spontaneous fidelity in favour of Florio. Florio thou hast not considered as a scoundrel, who by perjury and murder has deserved the pillory and the gibbet; as a wretch who has stooped to the lowest fraud for the vilest purpose; who is continually insnaring the innocent and the weak; who conceals the ruin that he brings by a lie, and the lie by an oath; and who having once already justified a sworn falsehood at the expense of life, is ready again to lie and to kill, with the same aggravation and in the same cause.

Neither didst thou view Benevolus, as having merited the divine eulogium bestowed upon him 'who was faithful over a few things;'[5] as employing life in the diffusion of happiness, with the joy of angels, and in imitation of God.

Surely, if it is true that

Vice to be hated needs but to be seen,
POPE.[6]

she should not be hidden with the ornaments, and disguised in the apparel, which in the general estimation belong to virtue. On the contrary, it should be the principal labour of moral writers, especially of those who would instruct by fiction, the power of which is not less to do evil than good, to remove the bias which inclines the mind rather to prefer natural than moral endowments; and to represent vice with such circumstances of contempt and infamy, that the ideas may constantly recur together. And it should be always remembered, that the fear of immediate contempt is frequently stronger than any other motive: how many have, even in their own opinion, incurred the guilt of blasphemy, rather than the sneer of an infidel, or the ridicule of a club? and how many have rushed not only to the brink of the grave but of hell, to avoid the scorn, with which the foolish and the profligate regard those who have refused a challenge?

Let it, therefore, be the united effort of genius and learning, to deter from guilt by the dread of shame; and let the time past suffice to have saved from contempt, those vices which contempt only can suppress.

47 *The Adventurer,* 18, Saturday, January 6, 1753

by JOHN HAWKESWORTH

Duplex libelli dos est; quòd risum movet,
Et quòd prudenti vitam consilio monet.
PHÆDRUS.[1]

A twofold gift in this my volume lies;
It makes you merry, and it makes you wise.

Among the fictions which have been intended for moral purposes, I think those which are distinguished by the name of Fables, deserve a particular consideration.

A story or tale, in which many different characters are conducted through a great variety of events, may include such a number and diversity of precepts, as, taken together, form almost a complete rule of life: as these events mutually depend upon each other, they will be retained in a series; and, therefore, the remembrance of one precept will almost necessarily produce the remembrance of another, and the whole moral, as it is called, however complicated, will be recollected without labour and without confusion.

In this particular, therefore, the story seems to have the advantage of the fable, which is confined to some single incident: for though a number of distinct fables may include all the topics of moral instruction, caution, and advice, which are contained in a story, yet each must be remembered by a distinct effort of the mind; and they will not recur in a series, because they have no connexion with each other.

The memory of them may, however, be more frequently revived by those incidents in life to which they correspond; and they will, therefore, more readily present themselves, when the lessons which they teach should be practised.

Many, perhaps the greater number of those fables which have been transmitted to us as some of the most valuable remains of the simplicity and wisdom of antiquity, were spoken upon a particular occasion, and then the occasion itself was an index to the intent of the speaker, and fixed the moral of the fable: so, when the Samians were about to put to death a man who had abused a public trust, and plundered the commonwealth, the counsel of Æsop could not be overlooked or mistaken, when he told them, that 'a Fox would not suffer a swarm of flies, which had almost satiated themselves by sucking his blood, to be driven away, because a new swarm might then come, and their hunger drain him of all the blood that remained.'[2]

Those which are intended for general use, and to general use it is perhaps easy to accommodate the rest, are of two kinds: one is addressed to the understanding, and the other to the passions.

Of the preceptive kind is that of the 'Old Man, who, to teach his sons the advantage of unanimity, first directed them to break a number of rods that were bound up together: and when they found it impossible, bade them divide the bundle, and break the rods separately, which they easily effected.' In this fable no passion is excited; the address is to the understanding, and the understanding is immediately convinced.

That of the Old Hound belongs to the other class. When the toothless veteran had seized the stag, and was not able to hold him, he deprecates the resentment of his master, who had raised his arm for the blow, by crying out, 'Ah! do not punish the impotence of age! strike me not, because my will to please thee has survived my power! If thou art offended with what I am, remember what I have been, and forgive me.' Pity is here forcibly excited; and injurious resentment may be repressed, when an instance not equally strong recalls this to the mind.

Fables of the preceptive kind should always include the precept in the event, and the event should be related with such circumstances as render the precept sufficiently evident. As the incident should be simple, the inference should be in the highest degree natural and obvious.

Those that produce their effect upon the passions, should excite them strongly, and always connect them with their proper objects.

I do not remember to have seen any collection, in which these rules have been sufficiently observed; in far the greater number there is a deficiency of circumstance, though there is a redundancy of language; there is, therefore, something to be added, and something to be taken away. Besides that, the peculiar advantages of this method of instruction are given up, by referring the precept to a long discourse, of which the fable is no more than the text, and with which it has so little connexion, that the incident may be perfectly remembered, and the laboured inference totally forgotten. A boy, who is but six years old, will remember a fable after having once heard it, and relate it in words of his own; but it would be the toil of a day to get the terms in which he heard it by heart; and, indeed, he who attempts to supply any deficiency in a fable, by tacking a dissertation to the end of it, appears to me to act just as wisely, as if, instead of clothing a man whom he had found naked, he should place a load upon his shoulders.

When the moral effect of fable had been thus brought to depend, not upon things, but upon words; the arrangement of these words into verse, was thought to be a happy expedient to assist the memory; for in verse words must be remembered in a regular series, or the measure and cadence will not be preserved: the measure and cadence, therefore, discover any confusion or defect, not to the understanding, but to the ear; and shew how the confusion may be regulated, and the defect supplied. The addition of rhyme was another advantage of the same kind; and this advantage was greater, as the rhyme was more frequently repeated. But if the fable is perfect in its kind, this expedient is unnecessary; and much less labour is required to include an evident precept in an incident, than to measure the syllables in which it is related, and place two words of a similar sound at the end of every couplet. Besides, in all verse, however familiar and easy, the words are necessarily thrown out of the order in which they are commonly used; and, therefore, though they will be more easy recollected, the sense which they contain will not be equally perspicuous.

I would not, however, be thought to deny, that verse is at least an ornament to this species of writing; nor to extend my censure to those short stories, which, though they are called fables, are written upon a more extensive plan, and are intended for more improved understandings.

But as fables have been told by some in verse, that they might be more easily remembered; they have been related by others in a barbarous jargon of hackneyed phrases, that they might be more easily understood.

It has been observed of children, that they are longer before they can pronounce perfect sounds, because perfect sounds are not pronounced to them; and that they repeat the gibberish of the nurse, because nothing better has been proposed to them for imitation; and how should the school-boy write English in grammatical purity, when all that he reads, except a foreign language and a literal translation, is written with all the licence of extempore expression, without propriety of idiom, or regularity of combination, and abounds with absurdities that haste only can excuse in a speaker?

The fables of Æsop, for so they are all called, are often first exhibited to youth, as examples of the manner in which their native language is written; they should therefore be pure in the highest degree, though not pompous: and it is surely an affront to understanding to suppose, that any language would become more intelligible by being rendered less perfect.

But the fables that are addressed to the passions, besides the imperfections which they share in common with those that are addressed to the understanding, have others peculiar to themselves: sometimes the passion is not moved with sufficient force, and sometimes it is not connected with a fit object.

When the Fox decoys the poor Goat into a well, in order to leap out from his horns, and leaves him to perish with a witty remark, that 'if his wisdom had been proportioned to his beard, he would not have been so easily overreached,' the goat is not so much the object of pity as contempt; but of contempt, guileless simplicity, caught in the snare of cunning, cannot surely be deemed a proper object. In the fox there appears a superiority which not only preserves him from scorn, but even from indignation: and indeed the general character of Reynard is by no means fit for imitation; though he is frequently the hero of the fable, and his conduct affords the precept for which it is written.

But though I have made a general division of fable into two kinds, there is yet a third, which, as it is addressed both to the understanding and the passions, is consequently more forcible and perfect.

Of this number is that of the Sick Kite, who requested of his mother to petition the gods for his recovery, but was answered, 'Alas! to which of the gods can I sacrifice? for which of their altars hast thou not robbed?' The precept that is here inculcated, is early piety; and the passion that is excited, is terror; the object of which is the despair of him who perceives himself to be dying, and has reason to fear that his very prayer is an abomination.

There are others, which, though they are addressed to the understanding, do yet excite a passion which condemns the precept.

When the melodious complaint of the Nightingale had directed a hungry Hawk to the thorn on which she sung, and he had seiz'd her with his talons, she appealed from his hunger to his mercy: 'I am,' said she, 'little else than voice: and if you devour me, there will be no proportion between my loss and your gain; your hunger will be rather irritated than appeased by so small a morsel, but all my powers of enjoyment will cease for ever; attack, therefore, some larger bird.'—Here the Hawk interrupted her: 'He was not disposed,' he said, 'to controvert what she had advanced; but he was too wise to suffer himself to be persuaded by any argument, to quit a certain for a contingent good.'

Who that reads this fable does not pity the Nightingale, and in his heart condemn the Hawk, whose cruel prudence affords the lesson?

Instruction, in the strong language of eastern metaphor, is called, 'a light to our paths.' The fables of Pagan mythologists may, therefore, be considered as a cluster of stars of the first magnitude, which, though they shine with a distinct influence, may be taken as one constellation: but, like stars, they only break the obscurity of night; they do not diffuse round us the splendours of day: it is by the Sun of Righteousness alone, that we discover completely our duty and our interest, and behold that pattern of Divine perfection which the Christian aspires to imitate, by 'forgiving injuries, and returning good for evil.'

By many of the fables which are still retained in our collections, revenge is encouraged as a principle, and inculcated as a practice. 'The Hare triumphs in the destruction of the Sparrow who had insulted him, and the Thunny, in his last agonies, rejoices at the death of the Dolphin, whose pursuit had driven him upon a rock.' These, if they will not admit of another turn, should without question be omitted; for the mischievous effect of the fable will be remembered as an example that justifies the violence of sudden resentment, and cannot be prevented by a laboured comment, which is never read but as a task, and therefore immediately forgotten.

I think many others may be greatly improved; the practice of virtue may be urged from higher motives, the sentiments may be elevated, and the precepts in general rendered more striking and comprehensive.

I shall conclude this paper with the fable of the Dog and Shadow; which, as it is commonly told, censures no quality but greediness, and only illustrates the trite proverb, 'All covet, all lose.'

'A dog, who was crossing a rivulet with a piece of flesh in his mouth, perceived his shadow in the water, which he mistook for another dog with another piece of flesh. To this he knew he had no right; and yet he could not forbear catching at it; but instead of getting a new prize, he dropped that which he possessed into the water. He saw the smooth surface break into many waves, and the dog whom he had attempted to injure disappear: he perceived at once his loss, his folly, and his fault; and in the anguish of regret cried out, "How righteous and how wise are the gods! since whatever seduces to evil, though but a shadow, becomes the instrument of punishment."'

48 *The World*, 19, Thursday, May 10, 1753

by WILLIAM WHITEHEAD

The World was owned by the bookseller Robert Dodsley and managed by Edward Moore; among its contributors were Horace Walpole and Lord Chesterfield. William Whitehead (1715–85), poet and dramatist, was Poet Laureate from 1757; among his works are the tragedies *The Roman Father* (1750), and *Creusa* (1754), and the comedy *The School for Lovers* (1762). His *Plays and Poems* were collected in 1774.

To MR. FITZ-ADAM[1]

SIR,

The present age is overrun with romances, and yet so strong does the appetite for them continue, that as Otway says on a less delicate occasion,

——every rank fool goes down.[2]

I am not surprised that any sketch of human nature, howsoever imperfect, should attract the attention of the generality of readers. We are easily delighted with pictures of ourselves, and are sometimes apt to fancy a strong likeness where there is not even the least resemblance. Those great masters of every movement of the human mind, Homer and Shakespeare, knew well this propensity of our dispositions. The latter, from the nature of his writings, had more frequent opportunities of opening the most minute avenues of the heart. The former, though his province was more confined, has let no occasion pass of exerting this affecting talent. He has not only contrasted a vast variety of characters, and given all the passions their full play, but even in the stiller parts of his works, the similes and descriptions, every thing is full of human life. It is the Carian woman who stains the ivory;[3] if a torrent descends from the mountains, some cottager trembles at the sound of it; and the fine broken landscape of rocks and woods by moonlight has a shepherd to gaze at and admire it.

But it is not with such painters as these that I am at present concerned.

They drew really from nature; and ages have felt and applauded the truth of their designs. Whereas our modern artists (if we may guess from the motley representations they give us of our species) are so far from having studied the natures of other people, that they seldom seem to have the least acquaintance with themselves.

The writers of heroic romance, or the *Loves of Philodoxus and Urania*,[4] professedly soar *above nature*. They introduce into their descriptions trees, water, air, &c. like common mortals; but then all their rivers are clearer than crystal, and every breeze is impregnated with the spices of Arabia. The manners of their personages seem full as extraordinary to our gross ideas. We are apt to suspect the virtue of two young people who are rapturously in love with each other, and who travel whole years in one another's company; though we are expressly told, that at the close of every evening, when they retire to rest, the hero leans his head against a knotted oak, whilst the heroine seeks the friendly shelter of a distant myrtle. This, I say, seems to us a little unnatural; however, it is not of dangerous example. There can no harm follow if unexperienced persons should endeavour to imitate what may be thought inimitable. Should our virgins arrive but half way towards the chastity of a Parthenia, it will be something gained;[5] and we, who have had learned educations, know the power of early prejudices; some of us having emulated the public spirit, and other obsolete virtues of the old Grecians and Romans, to the age of fifteen or sixteen, some of us later, even to twenty or one-and-twenty.

But peace be to the manes of such authors. They have long enjoyed that elysium which they so frequently described on earth. The present race of romance-writers run universally into a different extreme. They spend the little art they are masters of in weaving into intricacies the more familiar and more comical adventures of a Jack Slap, or a Betty Sallet.[6] These, though they endeavour to copy after a very great original, I choose to call our writers *below nature*; because very few of them have as yet found out their master's peculiar art of writing upon low subjects without writing in a low manner. Romances, judiciously conducted, are a very pleasing way of conveying instruction to all parts of life. But to dwell eternally upon orphan-beggars, and *serving-men of low degree*, is certainly what I have called it, writing *below nature*; and is so far from conveying instruction, that it does not even afford amusement.

The writers *below nature* have one advantage in common with the writers above it, that the originals they would seem to draw from are no where to be found. The heroes and heroines of the former are undoubtedly children of the imagination; and those of the latter, if they are not all of them incapable of *reading* their own adventures, are at least unable to inform us by *writing* whether the representations of them are just, and whether people in their station did ever think or act in the manner they are described to have done. Yet the authors, even in this particular, are not quite so secure as they imagine; for when, towards the end of the third or fourth volume, the He or She of the piece (as is usually the custom) emerges into what they call genteel life, the whole cheat is frequently discovered. From seeing their total ignorance of what they are then describing, we on good grounds conclude that they are equally unacquainted with the inferior parts of life, though we are not able to detect the falsehood. Bath, one should imagine, the easiest place in the world to get a thorough knowledge of: and yet I have observed in books of this kind, several representations of it so excessively erroneous, that they not only shewed the authors to be entirely ignorant of the manners of living there, but of the geography of the town.

But it is not the ignorance of these writers which I would principally complain of; though of that, as a censor, you ought to take notice, and should assure our young men and young women that they may read fifty volumes of this sort of trash, and yet, according to the phrase which is perpetually in their mouths, *know nothing of life*. The thing I chiefly find fault with is their extreme indecency. There are certain vices which the vulgar call fun, and the people of fashion gallantry; but the middle rank, and those of the gentry who continue to go to church, still stigmatize them by the opprobious names of fornication and adultery. These are confessed to be in some measure detrimental to society, even by those who practise them most; at least, they are allowed to be so in all but themselves. This being the case, why should our novel-writers take so much pains to spread these enormities? It is not enough to say in excuse that they write nonsense upon these subjects as well as others; for nonsense itself is dangerous here. The most absurd ballads in the streets, without the least glimmering of meaning, recommend themselves every day both to the great and small vulgar only by obscene expressions. Here, therefore, Mr. Fitz-Adam, you should interpose your authority, and forbid your readers (whom I will suppose to be all persons who can read) even to attempt to open any novel, or romance, unlicensed by you; unless it should happen to be stamped Richardson or Fielding.

Your power should extend likewise to that inundation of obscenity which is daily pouring in from France; and which has too frequently the wit and humour of a Crebillon to support it. The gentlemen, who never read any thing else, will I know be at a loss for amusement, and feel their half-hour of morning hang rather too heavy on their hands. But surely, Mr. Fitz-Adam, when they consider the good of their country (and all of them have that at heart) they will consent to meet a little sooner at the hazard-table, or wile away the tedious interval in studying new chances upon the cards.

If it be said that the heroic romances, which I have recommended for their virtue, are themselves too full of passionate breathings upon some occasions, I allow the charge; but am of opinion that these can do little more harm to the minds of young ladies, than certain books of devotion, which are put into their hands by aunts and grandmothers; the writers of which, from having suffered the softer passions to mix too strongly with their zeal for religion, are now generally known by the name of the *amorous divines.*[7]

I am, Sir, your most humble servant,

I. T.

49 Dedication to *Ferdinand Count Fathom* (1753)

by TOBIAS SMOLLETT

A novel is a large diffused picture, comprehending the characters of life, disposed in different groupes, and exhibited in various attitudes, for the purposes of an uniform plan, and general occurrence, to which every individual figure is subservient. But this plan cannot be executed with propriety, probability, or success, without a principal personage to attract the attention, unite the incidents, unwind the clue of the labyrinth, and at last close the scene, by virtue of his own importance.

Almost all the heroes of this kind who have hitherto succeeded on the English stage, are characters of transcendent worth, conducted through the vicissitudes of fortune, to that goal of happiness which ever ought to be the repose of extraordinary desert.—Yet the same principle by which we rejoice at the remuneration of merit, will teach us to relish the disgrace and discomfiture of vice, which is always an example of extensive use and influence, because it leaves a deep impression of terror upon the minds of those who were not confirmed in the pursuit of morality and virtue, and, while the balance wavers, enables the right scale to preponderate.

In the drama, which is a more limited field of invention, the chief personage is often the object of our detestation and abhorrence; and we are as well pleased to see the wicked schemes of a *Richard* blasted, and the perfidy of a *Maskwell* exposed, as to behold a *Bevil* happy, and an *Edward* victorious.[1]

The impulses of fear, which is the most violent and interesting of all the passions, remain longer than any other upon the memory; and for one that is allured to virtue by the contemplation of that peace and happiness which it bestows, an hundred are deterred from the practice of vice by that infamy and punishment to which it is liable, from the laws and regulations of mankind.

Let me not, therefore, be condemned for having chosen my principal character from the purlieus of treachery and fraud, when I declare my purpose is to set him up as a beacon for the benefit of the inexperienced and unwary, who, from the perusal of these memoirs, may learn to avoid the manifold snares with which they are continually surrounded in the paths of life; while those who hesitate on the brink of iniquity may be terrified from plunging into that irremediable gulf, by surveying the deplorable fate of *Ferdinand Count Fathom*.

That the mind might not be fatigued, nor the imagination disgusted, by a succession of vicious objects, I have endeavoured to refresh the attention with occasional incidents of a different nature; and raised up a virtuous character, in opposition to the adventurer, with a view to amuse the fancy, engage the affection, and form a striking contrast which might heighten the expression, and give a *relief* to the moral of the whole.

If I have not succeeded in my endeavours to unfold the mysteries of fraud, to instruct the ignorant, and entertain the vacant; if I have failed in my attempts to subject folly to ridicule, and vice to indignation; to rouse the spirit of mirth, wake the soul of compassion, and touch the secret springs that move the heart; I have, at least, adorned virtue with honour and applause, branded iniquity with reproach and shame, and carefully avoided every hint or expression which could give umbrage to the most delicate reader: circumstances which (whatever may be my fate with the public) will with you always operate in favour of,

DEAR SIR,

Your very affectionate friend and servant,

THE AUTHOR.

50 From a letter of Johannes Stinstra, December 24, 1753

The letter is addressed to Samuel Richardson. Johannes Stinstra was a Dutch clergyman and controversialist. He translated *Clarissa* into Dutch (1752–5), and was probably involved in the translation of *Sir Charles Grandison* into Dutch (1756–7). According to A. D. McKillop (*Samuel Richardson . . .* (1960), 265), the introductions which Stinstra prefixed to the odd volumes of his translation of *Clarissa* contained some of the best criticism of Richardson produced during the century.

[. . . . .]
Let me tell you, Sir, that I with much delight have read, at different times, and considered your particular and candid narrative.

By the particulars of your being secretary in love matters to several young women, I can perceive that you might come to the full knowledge of the woman's heart, and its deepest recesses: this has enabled you, Sir, to paint with lively colours the most inmost thoughts, deliberations, and affections of a Clarissa, an Anna Howe, a Miss Byron; but by which means you have penetrated into the mysteries of unrighteousness, in the heart of a rake, a libertine, a wanton and sly Lovelace, this continues to me matter of astonishment! nor produce you any thing to deliver me of my wonder. On the contrary, you encrease it by your professions, which I, as the pledges of the truest confidence and friendship, have received. Pardon me, Sir, but I was before of opinion, that you in your Belford had drawn your own picture; that you had seen the world, and loved it; but afterwards escaped out of its inticements. In this case, I should not have been ashamed of corresponding with you; for, am I not a follower of that Saviour, which declared that there was joy in heaven on a repenting sinner? I have formerly conversed with such sinners, especially with one, intimately conversed, who, of a sound judgment and lively wit, having forsaken the follies of his youth, excelled in works of piety and charity; which familiarity has been very useful to me in acquiring my knowledge, whatsoever it may be, of the hearts and characters of men; and peculiarly enabled me to distinguish, with more cognisance, the natural lineaments of a Lovelace. Happy! however, threefold happy are we, my friend, and have abundant reason to thank Heaven, which has favoured us with a virtuous education, and preserved us from the baits of corruption! What an easiness! what a serenity! for a mind striving in the way to eternal happiness!

I am extremely astonished, Sir, by your telling me that you never write by a plan; and when you ended one letter, hardly knew what would be your next. What a happy genius, that can thus prosecute his way through so many mazes and labyrinths, which perplex your common readers, and never deviate, without ever consulting a map!

May I venture yet another remark? Charmingly, most charmingly, paint you the motions and effects of a generous love in the heart of Miss Byron; the object is worthy thereof. But may not this agreeable sensation steal upon the tender bosoms and minds of your readers among the fair sex; melt and soften them; and thus lay open (more than is convenient for the less prudent of that sex) to the allurements of specious lovers? Perhaps it were more proper that this surmise came from your female admirers than from me, a bachelor. I form only those doubts, my dear friend, that you may perceive that I do not read your works with a prepossessed mind, nor blindly praise them; that I read with a searching eye, yet not finding any blemishes, but meeting one or two little bright clouds, which, more accurately viewed, perhaps are a collection of shining stars.

At present I am so overwhelmed with worldly affairs, that I hardly can attend your Clarissa as I wish. Besides, I am bound, by promise to the public, that I should more amply than I before have done, defend the rights of liberty of conscience and religion; from which task I am drawn by the charms of your lovely Clarissa; but which I think myself under obligation to resume, as soon as I shall have ended my attendance on the Christian heroine.

[. . . . .]

51 *The World*, 79, Thursday, July 4, 1754

by RICHARD BERENGER

Richard Berenger (d. 1782), besides his work in *The World*, seems only to have produced two translations, *A New System of Horsemanship* (1754), from the French, and *The History and Art of Horsemanship* (1771), from Xenophon, with some original writing.

To Mr. Fitz-Adam

SIR,

You cannot do a greater service to the world, than by promoting the real happiness of the best part of it, the fair sex; for whose sake I beg you will publish the following animadversions upon an error in education, which the good sense of the present age, with all its attachments to nature, has not totally eradicated. The error I mean is putting romances into the hands of young ladies; which being a sort of writing that abounds in characters no where to be found, can, at best, be but a useless employment, even supposing the readers of them to have neither relish nor understanding for superior concerns. But as this is by no means the case, and as the happiness of mankind is deeply interested in the sentiments and conduct of the ladies, why do we contribute to the filling their heads with fancies, which render them incapable either of enjoying or communicating that happiness? Why do we suffer those hearts, which ought to be appropriated to the various affections of social life, to be alienated by the mere creatures of the imagination? In short, why do we suffer those who were born for the purpose of living in society with men endued with passions and frailties like their own, to be bred up in daily expectation of living *out* of it with such men as never have existed? Believe me, Mr. Fitz-Adam (as much as the age of nature as this is thought to be), I know several unmarried ladies, who in all probability had been long ago good wives and good mothers, if their imaginations had not been early perverted with the chimerical ideas of romantic love, and themselves cheated out of the charities (as Milton calls them),[1] and all the real blessings of those relations, by the hopes of that ideal happiness, which is no where to be found but in romances.

It is a principle with such ladies, that it matters not if the qualities they ascribe to the heroes of these books be real or imaginary: upon which principle, a footman may as well be the hero as his master; for nothing, it seems, is necessary to dub him such, but the magic power of a lady's fancy, which creates chimeras much faster than nature can produce realities.

Surely, Mr. Fitz-Adam, this doctrine of ideal happiness is calculated for the meridian of Bedlam, and ought never to be received beyond the limits of Moorfields.[2] For if we should admit that the monarch in his cell is as happy as the monarch on his throne, while both their objects are ambition; yet the happiness of society must depend only on the reasonableness of individuals. A father is by this pernicious doctrine frequently robbed of the comfort he expected in his child; a daughter is deprived of the protection and support she might otherwise have claimed from her father; and society is interrupted in forming its general system of happiness, which those relations should contribute to establish.

These, Mr. Fitz-Adam, are almost the necessary consequences of reading romances: and as human nature is apt to be more influenced by example than precept, I shall beg leave to enforce the truth of what I have advanced by the following history.

Clarinda was the only child of a wealthy merchant, who placed all his happiness in the expectations of her merit and the rewards of it. Nature had encouraged him in that expectation, by giving her a very liberal portion of her favours; and he determined to improve it by every means which the fondness of a parent could suggest to him. But, unfortunately for Clarinda, her father's good intentions were not guided by a judgment equally good: for it happened to her, as it too often does in the education of young women, that his endeavours were rather directed to grace her person, than to adorn her mind: and whatever qualifications he might wish the latter to possess, he seemed solicitous only of such as might recommend the former. Dress, dancing, and music, were the whole of her accomplishments: and they so immoderately softened the natural effeminacy of her mind, that she contracted an aversion to every kind of reading, which did not represent the same softness of manners. Every hour which was not appropriated to one of these accomplishments, was spent in the ensnaring practice of reading novels and romances; of which *Clelia* was her favourite, and the hero of it continually in her head.

Whilst Clarinda was thus accomplishing herself, the father was studying to reward the merits of his daughter with a husband suitable to her rank and fortune. Nor was he unsuccessful in his care: for Theodore, the son of a neighbouring gentleman in the country, was chosen for this honour. But though all who knew him declared him to be worthy of it, unhappily for Clarinda, she alone thought otherwise. For notwithstanding he loved her with a sincerity hardly to be equalled, yet as he did not approach her in heroics, nor first break his passion to her in shady groves, he was not the hero she expected: he neither bowed gracefully, moved majestically, nor sighed pathetically, enough to charm a heart which doted on romantic grimace: in short, he was not the hero which *Clelia* had impressed on Clarinda's imagination. But, what was still more unfortunate, Theodore's *valet de chambre* was completely so. That happy hero was a Frenchman, who to an imagination little less romantic than Clarinda's, had added all the fantastic levity of his country; which happening first to discover itself in those very shades where she used to meditate on the hero of *Clelia*, so captivated her heart with Monsieur Antoine the valet, that her imagination instantly annihilated every circumstance of his rank and fortune, and added every enchanting accomplishment to his mind and person.

There is no resisting the impetuosity of romantic love. Like enthusiasm, it breaks through all the restraints of nature and custom, and enables, as well as animates its votaries, to execute all its extravagant suggestions. A passion of this sublime original could have none of those difficulties in discovering itself to its subject, which are apt to oppose the rash wills of vulgar mortals: and therefore it was not long before Clarinda gave Antonio (for so she chose to soften the unharmonious name of Antoine) to understand, that love, like death, levelled all distinctions of birth and fortune, and introduced the lowest and highest into Elysium together.

Antonio, who had been almost as conversant with romances as Clarinda, received the first intimations of the lady's passion for him with a transport that had less surprise than joy in it; and from the first discovery of it, there arose an intercourse between them, which entirely defeated the pretensions of Theodore, and confirmed Clarinda's passion for his valet.

But as much a hero as Antonio appeared to be both to Clarinda and himself during the first part of this tender intercourse, in the progress of it he discovered that he wanted one principal ingredient in the the composition of that ideal character: he had not courage enough to be a martyr. For though he doted on Clarinda's person whilst her fortune was annexed to it, yet he could not bring himself to starve with an angel: and this he soon perceived must be his fate, if he possessed the one without the other. Such a disappointment from a hero to a Dido, or to any woman who expected a natural gratification of her passion, would have excited resentment and aversion. This would have been nature, which romantic love has no knowledge of: it never changes any of those ideas with which it first captivates a fantastic heart: therefore Clarinda, though she most pathetically lamented her disappointment in Antonio, yet charged it all upon her stars, and accused only them and the gods of cruelty. Her father at the same time declared his resolution to disinherit her, if she persisted in her folly: and the more effectually to prevent it, he bribed Antonio to leave England; which so inflamed Clarinda's passion (who considered him as banished on her account) that she made a solemn vow never to marry any other man.

To conclude; the consequence of this vow was, that the father settled an annuity on his daughter, and entailed his estate on his next kindred. This annuity she still lives to enjoy; and in the fifty-fifth year of her age prefers the visionary happiness of reading *Clelia* and thinking on her Antonio, to the real blessings of those social relations, which in all probability she had enjoyed through life, if she had never been a reader of romances. I am, &c.

52 A letter written in the character of Lien Chi Altangi, 1760

by OLIVER GOLDSMITH

Goldsmith's letter was part of a series purporting to be written by a Chinese philosopher resident in London. The series appeared first in Newbery's *Public Ledger* (mostly during the course of 1760), and was later republished in book form under the title of *The Citizen of the World* (1762). This letter, No. LIII, first appeared on June 30, 1760.

From Lien Chi Altangi, to Fum Hoam, first president of the Ceremonial Academy at Pekin, in China.

How often have we admired the eloquence of Europe! That strength of thinking, that delicacy of imagination, even beyond the efforts of the Chinese themselves. How were we enraptured with those bold figures which sent every sentiment with force to the heart. How have we spent whole days together in learning those arts by which European writers got within the passions, and led the reader as if by enchantment.

But though we have learned most of the rhetorical figures of the last age, yet there seems to be one or two of great use here, which have not yet travelled to China. The figures I mean are called *Bawdy* and *Pertness*; none are more fashionable; none so sure of admirers; they are of such a nature, that the merest blockhead, by a proper use of them, shall have the reputation of a wit; they lie level to the meanest capacities, and address those passions which all have, or would be ashamed to disown.

It has been observed, and I believe with some truth, that it is very difficult for a dunce to obtain the reputation of a wit; yet by the assistance of the figure *Baudy*, this may be easily effected, and a bawdy blockhead often passes for a fellow of smart parts and pretensions. Every object in nature helps the jokes forward, without scarce any effort of the imagination. If a lady stands, something very good may be said upon that, if she happens to fall, with the help of a little fashionable Pruriency, there are forty sly things ready on the occasion. But a prurient jest has always been found to give most pleasure to a few very old gentlemen, who being in some measure dead to other sensations, feel the force of the allusion with double violence on the organs of risibility.

An author who writes in this manner is generally sure therefore of having the very old and the impotent among his admirers; for these he may properly be said to write, and from these he ought to expect his reward, his works being often a very proper succedaneum to cantharides, or an assa fœtida pill.[1] His pen should be considered in the same light as the squirt of an apothecary, both being directed to the same generous end.

But though this manner of writing be perfectly adapted to the taste of gentlemen and ladies of fashion here, yet still it deserves greater praise in being equally suited to the most vulgar apprehensions. The very ladies and gentlemen of Benin, or Cafraria, are in this respect tolerably polite, and might relish a prurient joke of this kind with critical propriety; probably too with higher gust, as they wear neither breeches nor petticoats to intercept the application.

It is certain I never could have expected the ladies here, biassed as they are by education, capable at once of bravely throwing off their prejudices, and not only applauding books in which this figure makes the only merit, but even adopting it in their own conversation. Yet so it is, the pretty innocents now carry those books openly in their hands, which formerly were hid under the cushion; they now lisp their double meanings with so much grace, and talk over the raptures they bestow with such little reserve, that I am sometimes reminded of a custom among the entertainers in China, who think it a piece of necessary breeding to whet the appetites of their guests, by letting them smell dinner in the kitchen before it is served up to table.

The veneration we have for many things, entirely proceeds from their being carefully concealed. Were the idolatrous Tartar permitted to lift the veil which keeps his idol from view, it might be a certain method to cure his future superstition; with what a noble spirit of freedom therefore must that writer be possessed, who bravely paints things as they are, who lifts the veil of modesty, who displays the most hidden recesses of the temple, and shews the erring people that the object of their vows is either perhaps a mouse, or a monkey.

However, though this figure be at present so much in fashion; though the professors of it are so much caressed by the great, those perfect judges of literary excellence; yet it is confessed to be only a revival of what was once fashionable here before. There was a time, when by this very manner of writing, the gentle Tom. Durfey, as I read in English authors, acquired his great reputation, and became the favourite of a King.[2] The works of this original genius, tho' they never travelled abroad to China, and scarce have reach'd posterity at home, were once found upon every fashionable toilet, and made the subject of polite, I mean very polite conversation. *'Has your Grace seen Mr. Durfey's last new thing, the Oylet Hole.[3] A most facetious piece?' 'Sure, my Lord, all the world must have seen it; Durfey is certainly the most comical creature alive. It is impossible to read his things and live. Was there ever any thing so natural and pretty, as when the Squire and Bridget meet in the cellar. And then the difficulties they both find in broaching the beer barrel, are so arch and so ingenious, we have certainly nothing of this kind in the language.'* In this manner they spoke then, and in this manner they speak now; for though the successor of Durfey does not excel him in wit, the world must confess he out-does him in obscenity.

There are several very dull fellows, who, by a few mechanical helps, sometimes learn to become extremely brilliant and pleasing; with a little dexterity in the management of the eye-brows, fingers, and nose. By imitating a cat, a sow and pigs; by a loud laugh, and a slap on the shoulder, the most ignorant are furnished out for conversation. But the writer finds it impossible to throw his winks, his shrugs, or his attitudes upon paper; he may borrow some assistance indeed, by printing his face at the title page; but without wit to pass for a man of ingenuity, no other mechanical help but downright obscenity will suffice. By speaking to some peculiar sensations, we are always sure of exciting laughter; for the jest does not lie in the writer, but in the subject.

But Bawdry is often helped on by another figure, called Pertness: and few indeed are found to excell in one that are not possessed of the other.

As in common conversation, the best way to make the audience laugh, is by first laughing yourself; so in writing, the properest manner is to shew an attempt at humour, which will pass upon most for humour in reality. To effect this, readers must be treated with the most perfect familiarity: in one page the author is to make them a low bow, and in the next to pull them by the nose: he must talk in riddles, and then send them to bed in order to dream for the solution. He must speak of himself and his chapters, and his manner, and what he would be at, and his own importance, and his mother's importance with the most unpitying prolixity, now and then testifying his contempt for all but himself, smiling without a jest, and without wit possessing vivacity.

Adieu.

53 Dialogue XXVIII from *Dialogues of the Dead*, 1760

by ELIZABETH MONTAGU

Dialogues purporting to be written from the other world were originated by Lucian of Samosata and had several times appeared in English before 1760. The volume from which this dialogue is taken was published under the name of George Lyttleton (1709–1773), First Baron Lyttleton, but four of them were contributed by Elizabeth Montagu (1720–1800). Mrs. Montagu also wrote an *Essay on the Writings and Genius of Shakespeare* (1769) and won the admiration of Johnson, who said of her: 'Sir, Mrs. Montagu does not make a trade of her wit; but Mrs. Montagu is a very extraordinary woman: she has a constant stream of conversation, and it is always impregnated; it always has meaning' (see *Boswell's Life* . . ., IV, 275).

PLUTARCH—CHARON—And a modern BOOKSELLER

CHARON

Here is a fellow who is very unwilling to land in our territories. He says, he is rich, has a great deal of business in the other world, and must needs return to it: he is so troublesome and obstreperous, I know not what to do with him. Take him under your care therefore, good Plutarch; you will easily awe him into order and decency, by the superiority an author has over a bookseller.

BOOKSELLER

Am I got into a world so absolutely the reverse of that I left, that here *authors* domineer over *booksellers*? Dear Charon, let me go back, and I will pay any price for my passage. But, if I must stay, leave me not with any of those who are styled *classical authors*. As to you, Plutarch, I have a particular animosity against you, for having almost occasioned my ruin. When I first set up shop, understanding but little of business, I unadvisedly bought an edition of your *lives*; a pack of old Greeks and

Romans, which cost me a great sum of money. I could never get off above twenty setts of them. I sold a few to the Universities, and some to Eaton and Westminster; for it is reckoned a pretty book for boys and under-graduates; but, unless a man has the luck to light on a pedant, he shall not sell a sett of them in twenty years.

PLUTARCH

From the merit of the subjects, I had hoped another reception for my works. I will own indeed, that I am not always perfectly accurate in every circumstance, nor do I give so exact and circumstantial a detail of the actions of my heroes, as may be expected from a biographer who has confined himself to one or two characters. A zeal to preserve the memory of great men, and to extend the influence of such noble examples, made me undertake more than I could accomplish in the first degree of perfection: but surely the characters of my illustrious men are not so imperfectly sketched, that they will not stand forth to all ages as patterns of virtue, and incitements to glory. My reflections are allowed to be deep and sagacious; and what can be more useful to a reader than a wise man's judgement on a great man's conduct? In my writings, you will find no rash censures, no undeserved encomiums, no mean compliance with popular opinions, no vain ostentation of critical skill, nor any affected *finesse*. In my parallels, which used to be admired as pieces of excellent judgement, I compare with perfect impartiality one great man with another, and each with the rule of justice. If indeed latter ages have produced greater men and better writers, my heroes and my works ought to give place to them. As the world has now the advantage of much better rules of morality than the unassisted reason of poor Pagans could form, I do not wonder that those vices, which appeared to us as mere blemishes in great characters, should seem most horrid deformities in the purer eyes of the present age: a delicacy I do not blame, but admire and commend. And I must censure you for endeavouring, if you could publish better examples, to obtrude on your countrymen such as were defective. I rejoice at the preference which they give to perfect and unallayed virtue; and as I shall ever retain an high veneration for the illustrious men of every age, I should be glad you would give me some account of those persons, who, in wisdom, justice, valour, patriotism, have eclipsed my Solon, Numa, Camillus,[1] and other boasts of Greece or Rome.

BOOKSELLER

Why, master Plutarch, you are talking Greek indeed. That work which repaired the loss I sustained by the costly edition of your books, was, *The lives of the Highwaymen*: but I should never have grown rich, if it had not been by publishing *the lives of men that never lived*. You must know; that though in all times it was possible to have a great deal of learning and very little wisdom, yet it is only by a modern improvement in the art of writing, that a man may read all his life, and have no learning or knowledge at all; which begins to be an advantage of the greatest importance. There is as natural a war between your men of science and fools, as between the cranes and the pigmies of old. Most of our young men having deserted to the fools, the party of the learned is near being beaten out of the field; and I hope in a little while they will not dare to peep out of their forts and fastnesses at Oxford and Cambridge. There let them stay and study old musty moralists, till one fall in love with the Greek, another with the Roman virtue: but our men of the world should read our new books, which teach them to have no virtue at all. No book is fit for a gentleman's reading, which is not void of facts and of doctrines, that he may not grow a pedant in his morals or conversation. I look upon history (I mean real history) to be one of the worst kinds of study. Whatever has happened may happen again; and a well-bred man may unwarily mention a parallel instance he had met with in history, and be betrayed into the aukwardness of introducing into his discourse a Greek, a Roman, or even a Gothick name. But when a gentleman has spent his time in reading adventures that never occurred, exploits that never were atchieved, and events that not only never did, but never can happen, it is impossible that in life or in discourse he should ever apply them. *A secret history*,[2] in which there is *no secret* and *no history*, cannot tempt Indiscretion to blab, or Vanity to quote; and by this means modern conversation flows gentle and easy, unincumbered with matter, and unburthened of instruction. As the present studies throw no weight or gravity into discourse and manners, the women are not afraid to read our books, which not only dispose to gallantry and coquetry, but give rules for them. Caesar's *Commentaries* and the account of Xenophon's expedition are not more studied by military commanders, than our novels are by the fair: to a different purpose indeed; for their military maxims teach to conquer, ours to yield; those inflame the vain and idle love of glory, these inculcate a noble contempt of reputation. The women have greater obligations to our writers than the men. By the commerce of the world, men might learn much of what they get from books; but the poor women, who in their early youth are confined and restrained, if it were not for the friendly assistance of books, would remain long in an insipid purity of mind, with a discouraging reserve of behaviour.

PLUTARCH

As to your men who have quitted the study of virtue for the study of vice, useful truth for absurd fancy, and real history for monstrous fiction, I have neither regard nor compassion for them: but I am concerned for the women who are betrayed into these dangerous studies; and I wish for their sakes I had expatiated more on the character of Lucretia and some other heroines.[3]

BOOKSELLER

I tell you, our women do not read in order to live or to die like Lucretia. If you would inform us, that a *billet-doux* was found in her cabinet after her death, or give an hint as if Tarquin really saw her in the arms of a slave; and that she killed herself, not to suffer the shame of a discovery; such anecdotes would sell very well. Or if, even by tradition, but better still if *by papers in the Portian family*, you could shew some probability that Portia died of *dram-drinking*;[4] you would oblige the world very much; for you must know, that, next to new-invented characters, we are fond of new lights upon ancient characters; I mean, such lights as shew a reputed honest man to have been a concealed knave; an illustrious hero a pitiful coward, &c. Nay, we are so fond of these kinds of information, as to be pleased sometimes to see a character cleared from a vice or crime it has been charged with, provided the person concerned be actually dead. But in this case, the evidence must be authentick, and amount to a demonstration: in the other, a detection is not necessary; a slight suspicion will do, if it concerns a really good and great character.

PLUTARCH

I am the more surprized at what you say of the taste of your contemporaries, as I met with a Frenchman,[5] who assured me that less than

225

a century ago he had written a much-admired life of Cyrus under the name of Artamenes, in which he ascribed to him far greater actions than those recorded of him by Xenophon and Herodotus; and that many of the great heroes of history had been treated in the same manner; that empires were gained and battles decided by the valour of a single man, imagination bestowing what nature has denied, and the system of human affairs rendered impossible.

BOOKSELLER

I assure you, these books were very useful to the authors and their booksellers: and for whose benefit besides should a man write? These romances were very fashionable, and had a great sale: they fell in luckily with the humour of the age.

PLUTARCH

Monsieur Scuderi tells me, they were written in the times of vigour and spirit, in the evening of the gallant days of chivalry, which, though then declining, had left in the hearts of men a warm glow of courage and heroism; and they were to be called to books, as to battle, by the sound of the trumpet: he says too, that, if writers had not accommodated themselves to the prejudices of the age, and written of bloody battles and desperate encounters, their works would have been esteemed too effeminate an amusement for gentlemen. Histories of chivalry, instead of enervating, tend to invigorate the mind, and endeavour to raise human nature above the condition which is naturally prescribed to it; but as strict justice, patriot motives, prudent counsels, and a dispassionate choice of what upon the whole is fittest and best, do not direct these heroes of romance, they cannot serve for instruction and example, like the great characters of true history. It has ever been my opinion, that only the clear and steady light of truth can guide men to virtue, and that the lesson which is *impracticable* must be *unuseful*. Whoever shall design to regulate his conduct by these visionary characters will be in the condition of superstitious people, who chuse rather to act by intimations they receive in the dreams of the night, than by the sober counsels of morning meditation. Yet, I confess, it has been the practice of many nations to incite men to *virtue* by relating the deeds of *fabulous heroes*; but surely it is the custom only of yours to incite them to *vice* by the history of *fabulous scoundrels*. Men of fine imagination have soared into the regions of fancy to bring back Astrea: you go thither in search of Pandora[6]—O disgrace to letters! O shame to the Muses!

BOOKSELLER

You express great indignation at our present race of writers; but, believe me, the fault lies chiefly on the side of the readers. As Monsieur Scuderi observed to you, authors must comply with the manners and disposition of those who are to read them. There must be a certain sympathy between the book and the reader, to create a good liking. Would you present a modern fine gentleman, who is negligently lolling in an easy chair, with the *labours of Hercules* for his recreation? or make him climb the Alps with Hannibal, when he is expiring with the fatigue of last night's ball? Our readers must be amused, flattered, soothed; such adventures must be offered to them as they would like to have a share in.

PLUTARCH

It should be the first object of writers, to correct the vices and follies of the age. I will allow as much compliance with the mode of the times as will make truth and good morals agreeable. Your love of fictitious characters might be turned to good purpose, if those presented to the publick were to be formed on the rules of religion and morality. It must be confessed, that history, being employed only about illustrious persons, publick events, and celebrated actions, does not supply us with such instances of domestick merit as one could wish: our heroes are great in the field and the senate, and act well in great scenes on the theatre of the world: but the idea of a man, who in the silent retired path of life never deviates into vice, who considers no spectator but *the omniscient Being,* and solicits no applause but *his* approbation, is the noblest model that can be exhibited to mankind, and would be of the most general use. Examples of domestick virtue would be more particularly useful to women than those of great heroines. The virtues of women are blasted by the breath of publick fame, as flowers that grow on an eminence are faded by the sun and wind, which expand them. But true female praise, like the musick of the spheres, arises from a gentle, a constant, and an equal progress in the path marked out for them by their great Creator; and, like the heavenly harmony, it is not adapted to the gross ear of mortals, but is reserved for the delight of higher beings, by whose wise laws they were ordained to give a silent light, and shed a mild benignant influence on the world.

BOOKSELLER

We have had some English and French writers who aimed at what you suggest. In the supposed character of Clarissa, (said a clergyman to me a few days before I left the world) one finds the dignity of heroism tempered by the meekness and humility of religion, a perfect purity of mind, and sanctity of manners: in that of Sir Charles Grandison, a noble pattern of every private virtue, with sentiments so exalted as to render him equal to every publick duty.

PLUTARCH

Are both these characters by the same author?

BOOKSELLER

Ay, master Plutarch; and what will surprize you more, this author has *printed* for me.

PLUTARCH

By what you say, it is pity he should *print* any work but *his own*. Are there no other authors who write in this manner?

BOOKSELLER

Yes, we have another writer of these imaginary histories; one who has not long since descended to these regions: his name is Fielding; and his works, as I have heard the best judges say, have a true spirit of comedy, and an exact representation of nature, with fine moral touches. He has not indeed given lessons of pure and consummate virtue; but he has exposed vice and meanness with all the powers of ridicule: and we have some other good wits, who have exerted their talents to the purposes you approve. Monsieur de Marivaux and some other French writers have also proceeded much upon the same plan, with a spirit and elegance which give their works no mean rank among the *belles lettres*. I will own that, when there is wit and entertainment enough in a book to make it sell, it is not the worse for good morals.

228

CHARON

I think, Plutarch, you have made this gentleman a little more humble; and now I will carry him the rest of his journey. But he is too frivolous an animal to present to wise Minos. I wish Mercury were here; he would damn him for his dulness. I have a good mind to carry him to the Danaïdes,[7] and leave him to pour water into their vessels, which, like his late readers, are destined to eternal emptiness. Or shall I chain him to the rock, side to side by Prometheus, not for having attempted to steal celestial fire, in order to animate human forms, but for having endeavoured to extinguish that which Jupiter had imparted? or shall we constitute him *friseur* to Tisiphone, and make him curl up her locks with his satires and libels?

PLUTARCH

Minos does not esteem any thing frivolous that affects the morals of mankind; he punishes authors, as guilty of every fault they have countenanced, and every crime they have encouraged; and denounces heavy vengeance for the injuries which virtue or the virtuous have suffered in consequence of their writings.

54 From a review of *The History of Tom Fool* (1760), *The Monthly Review*, XXIII, August 1760

The History of Tom Fool was by George Alexander Stevens (1710–84), actor, who was well known in his own time as the author of the humorous *Lecture Upon Heads* (1764, but not published until 1785), which he recited with great success in England and America. This review was by William Kenrick.

When the famous Turk first appeared in the Hay-market, and not a man in England thought of walking on a slack wire, and ballancing straws, but himself, great were the qualifications both natural and acquired, that were judged necessary to constitute an Equilibrist.[1] Time and experience, however, have rendered this wonderful art familiar to the common Tumblers at Sadler's Wells.

In like manner it is, that the art of taking off characters and manners, in that species of novel-writing introduced by Mr. Fielding, an art which, from his example, was supposed to require the greatest powers of wit, humour, and genius, is now become common to Writers of ordinary capacities: nay, Booksellers are known to have bespoke performances of this kind, and to have had them executed with success.

One should hence be apt to conceive, that the Critics have hitherto thought rather too highly of those talents, which are sufficient to make a man succeed in this art. A tolerable share of sense, and a turn for observation, will carry any one a good way in making just remarks, and pertinent reflections on men and manners; but it requires the peculiar abilities of a genius to give proper and consistent sentiments to his characters, and to throw his materials together into a form that may be admired, for the beauty of its composition, when the characters and incidents have lost their novelty.

In reading a series of rambling adventures and random observations, we may frequently be made to laugh at the drollery of the one, and admire the justness of the other; but, without art in the composition, and consistency in the several characters, the whole can afford only a slight profit, or a transitory amusement, which we shall seldom have an inclination to repeat.

We have been led into this remark by the perusal of several performances of this kind, (and, among the rest, *Tom Fool*) wherein their Authors have displayed no less wit and good sense, than humour and a knowledge of the world: but, with all this, we could never recommend them as literary productions. Works of this nature, indeed, establish their characters with most Readers, from a few prevailing beauties or distinguishing parts, but every one may recollect instances of his having been greatly pleased with such as, if he had been asked, he could not readily have told their merits. Thus the beauty of composition frequently operates insensibly; and in writing, as in painting and sculpture, we are often captivated with the whole piece, without being struck with the particular beauty of any of its parts.

The generality of our modern novel-readers will hardly enter into the spirit of this criticism; the writings even of Mr. Fielding himself, being generally more admired for the beauties of character and stile, than for their plan and conduct. But set character, humour, sentiment, and language out of the question, and see what a difference there is in point of composition, between a *Tom Fool* and a *Tom Jones*!

55 From a letter written in the character of Lien Chi Altangi, 1761

by OLIVER GOLDSMITH

This letter was first published in Newbery's *Public Ledger* on Wednesday, October 15, 1760 (see above, No. 52).

[. . . . .]

It was a saying of the ancients, that a man never opens a book without reaping some advantage by it. I say with them, that every book can serve to make us more expert except romances, and these are no better than instruments of debauchery. They are dangerous fictions, where love is the ruling passion.

The most indecent strokes there pass for turns of wit, intrigue and criminal liberties for gallantry and politeness. Assignations, and even villainy, are put in such strong lights, as may inspire, even grown men with the strongest passion; how much more therefore ought the youth of either sex to dread them, whose reason is so weak and whose hearts are so susceptible of passion.

To slip in by a back door, or leap a wall are accomplishments that when handsomely set off enchant a young heart. It is true the plot is commonly wound up by a marriage, concluded with the consent of parents, and adjusted by every ceremony prescribed by law. But as in the body of the work there are many passages that offend good morals, overthrow laudable customs, violate the laws, and destroy the duties most essential to society, virtue is thereby exposed to the most dangerous attacks.

But say some, the authors of these romances have nothing in view, but to represent vice punished and virtue rewarded. Granted. But will the greater number of readers take notice of these punishments and rewards? Are not their minds carried to something else? Can it be imagined that the art with which the author inspires the love of virtue, can overcome that crowd of thoughts which sway them to licentiousness. To be able to inculcate virtue by so leaky a vehicle, the author must be a philosopher of the first rank. But in our age we can find but few first rate philosophers.

Avoid such performances where vice assumes the face of virtue, seek wisdom and knowledge without ever thinking you have found them. A man is wise, while he continues in the pursuit of wisdom; but when he once fancies that he has found the object of his enquiry, he then becomes a fool. Learn to pursue virtue from the man that is blind, who never makes a step without first examining the ground with his staff.

The world is like a vast sea, mankind like a vessel sailing on its tempestuous bosom. Our prudence is its sails, the sciences serve us for oars, good or bad fortune are the favourable or countrary winds, and judgment is the rudder, without this last the vessel is tossed by every billow, and will find shipwreck in every breeze. In a word, obscurity and indigence are the parents of vigilance and œconomy; vigilance and œconomy of riches and honour; riches and honour of pride and luxury; pride and luxury of impurity and idleness, and impurity and idleness again produce indigence and obscurity. Such are the revolutions of life.

Adieu.

56 From a review of *Memoirs of Miss Sidney Bidulph* (1761), *The Critical Review*, XI, March 1761

The Critical Review was founded in 1756 by the Scottish printer, Archibald Hamilton, in opposition to *The Monthly Review*. The journal was edited from 1756 to 1759 by Hamilton's fellow Scot and fellow Tory, Tobias Smollett, later by Dr. Guthries, still later by John Stockdale. The *Memoirs of Miss Sidney Bidulph* was by Frances Sheridan (1724–66), mother of the dramatist R. B. Sheridan, well known for her Eastern tale, *The History of Nourjahad* (1767). She also wrote a comedy, *The Discovery* (1763).

If a copy drawn with the most exquisite skill, and heightened with the nicest touches of art, can be allowed merit equal to a justly admired original, the *Memoirs of Miss Bidulph* may deservedly claim a place in our esteem with the histories of *Clarissa* and *Sir Charles Grandison*. They are characterized by the same elegant fluency of narrative, the same interesting minuteness, inimitable simplicity, delicacy of sentiment, propriety of conduct, and irresistible pathos, which render them indisputably the best models in this species of writing, perhaps the most engaging, persuasive, and difficult of any other. Memoirs written in the epistolary manner, necessarily appear prolix and redundant; to imitate nature more closely, the reader is withheld from the principal events by a thousand little previous formalities, which, though they exert his patience at the time, fully recompense it in the end, by marking the characters more strongly, and introducing a variety of natural circumstances, that cannot fall under the pen of an historian. Slight strokes, and gentle touches, seemingly frivolous and impertinent, have an astonishing effect in strengthening the resemblance of the portraiture. Under correction of the critics, we must profess ourselves admirers of this kind of dramatic writing; where every character speaks in his own person, utters his feelings, and delivers his sentiments warm from the heart. It admits of an infinity of natural moral reflections, which a true biographer cannot, without pedantry and seeking the occasions, introduce. To sustain with propriety all the different personages, to think, to act in their peculiar characters thro' a whole life, checquered with prosperity and adversity, requires a truly dramatic genius. If the writer is not confined to the unities of time and place, he labours under other inconveniencies, from which the strict dramatist is exempted. He supports a character through life, the other only through one particular action; he observes probability in the transactions possibly of half a century, the other only of a day; he must rouse the passions, and engage the attention through a variety of unconnected incidents, the dramatist directs his whole strength only to one object; in a word, the memoir writer must be minute, without being tedious; he must study variety, and yet be perfectly simple and natural; he must extend without enervating his characters, rise gradually to his catastrophe, unfold his design slowly, and, after running a long course, appear vigorous, fresh, and unexhausted. It is sufficient proof of the difficulty of this method of writing, that the ingenious inventive lady, to whom the *Memoirs of Miss Bidulph* are attributed, hath not been able to avoid imitation. Her heroine is a type of Miss Clarissa Harlowe, involved like her in a passion which she cannot gratify consistently with the dictates of filial duty, and rigid female delicacy. Faulkland is a composition of features borrowed from Grandison and Lovelace: possessed of the strict honour, the steadiness and integrity of the former, he sometimes delights in the stratagem of the latter. But the characters will best appear from a sketch of the narrative.

[. . . . .]

Such are the outlines of a performance, all the finer touches of which must necessarily be lost in an analysis, that is here exhibited merely to shew the construction of the fable. All the situations are highly interesting, because the passions are strongly engaged in the fate of characters rendered so eminently amiable, noble, and heroic. The reflections are equally just and natural; some of the characters are new, and all of them admirably sustained. Not a single impropriety of thought or expression occurs in the course of three volumes; but the whole flows easy, chaste, natural, simple, and beyond measure affecting and pathetic. In a word, as we entertain the highest opinion of the genius, delicacy, and good sense of Mrs. S——, we cannot but wish she may continue to exert those talents, so honourable to herself, so useful, so entertaining to society, and particularly so beneficial to the republic of letters.

From a review of *The Life and Opinions of Tristram Shandy, Gentleman,* Volumes III and IV (1761), *The Critical Review,* XI, April 1761

The first two Volumes of *Tristram Shandy* appeared in 1760, the second two in 1761; at first quite well received by the monthly reviewers, it was very fiercely attacked after the publication of Sterne's *Sermons,* when the author's identity became known, and accused of indecency and dullness (see, for example, *The Monthly Review,* XXIV, January 1761 and Appendix to XXI). In opposition to *The Monthly Review,* the *Critical* treated Sterne well.

A man who possesses the faculty of exciting mirth, without exposing himself as the subject of it, is said to have humour, and this humour appears in a thousand different forms, according to the variety of attitudes in which folly is exhibited; but all these attitudes must be in themselves ridiculous: for humour is no more than the power of holding up and displaying the ridiculous side of every object with which it is concerned. Every body has heard of the different species of humour; grave humour and gay humour, genteel humour and low humour, natural humour and extravagant humour, grotesque and buffoonery. Perhaps these two last may be more properly stiled the bastards of humour than the power itself, although they have been acknowledged and adopted by the two arch priests of laughter *Lucian* and *Rabelais.* They deserve to be held illegitimate, because they either desert nature altogether, in their exhibitions, or represent her in a state of distortion. Lucian and Rabelais, in some of their writings, seem to have no moral purpose in view, unless the design of raising laughter may in some cases be thought a moral aim. It must be owned, that there is abundance of just satire in both; but at the same time they abound with extravagances, which have no foundation in nature, or in reason. Lucian, in his invective against a man who called him Prometheus, expresly says, that his writings were no more than figures of clay, set up to amuse the people on a shew day.[1] His *true history,* indeed, the most extravagant of all his works, he tells us he intended as a satire upon the ancient poets and historians, particularly *Ctesias*, who wrote the history of the Indies,[2] and *Jambolus*, author of an history of the Wonders of the Ocean.[3] As for Rabelais, notwithstanding the insinuation in his preface, in which he applies to his own writings the comparison of Alcibiades in Plato, who likens Socrates to the gallypots of druggists or apothecaries, painted on the outside with ridiculous figures, but containing within the most precious balsams:[4] notwithstanding the pains which have been taken by many ingenious commentators, to wrest the words and strain the meaning of Rabelais, in order to prove the whole a political satire on the times in which he wrote, we are of opinion, that the book was intended, as well as written, merely *pour la refection corporelle— al'aise du corps et au profit du rains.*[5] We the rather take notice of Rabelais on this occasion, as we are persuaded that he is the pattern and proto-type of *Tristram Shandy*, notwithstanding the declaration of our modern author, when he exclaims in a transport, 'My dear Rabelais, and my dearer Cervantes!' There is no more resemblance between his manner and that of Cervantes, than there is between the solemnity of a Fop-pington and the grimace of a Jack Pudding.[6] On the other hand, we see in *Tristram Shandy* the most evident traces of Rabelais, in the address, the manner, and colouring, tho' he has generally rejected the extrava-gancies of his plan. We find in both the same sort of apostrophes to the reader, breaking in upon the narrative, not unfrequently with an air of petulant impertinence; the same *sales Plautini*; the *immunda—igno-miniosaq*; *dicta*;[7] the same whimsical digressions; and the same parade of learning. Nay, we will venture to say, that the author now before us, when he recorded the birth of Tristram Shandy, had in his eye *La Nativité du tres-redouté Pantagruel.*——*Et parce qu'en ce propre jour nasquit Pantagruel, son Pére luy imposa tel nom——Car alors que sa mere Badebec l'infantoit, et que les sages femmes attenderent pour le recevoir, isserent premier de son ventre soixante et huis greneties, chacun tirant par le licol un mulet tout charge de sel: aprelequels sortirent neuf dromadaires chargez de iambons et langues de bœuf fumées; sept chameaus chargez d'andeüilles; puis vingt cinq charettes de porreaux, d'aulx, d'oignons et de abots, &c.——Et comme illes caquetoyent de ces menus propos entre elles, voici sortit Pantagruel tout velu, comme un ours, dont dit une d'illes en esprit prophetique, il est né à tout le poil, il fera choses merveilleuses, et sil vit, il aura de luage.*[8] Perhaps it would be no difficult matter to point out a much closer affinity between the works of the French and English author; but we have not leisure to be more particular. Nor will it be necessary to explain the conduct of the performance now before us, as it is no more than a continuation of the first two volumes, which were published last year, and received with such avidity by the public, as boded no good to the sequel; for that avidity was not a natural appetite, but a sort of *fames canina*,[9] that must have ended in *nausea* and *indigestion*. Accordingly all novel readers, from the stale maiden of quality to the snuff-taking chambermaid, devoured the first part with a most voracious swallow, and rejected the last with marks of loathing and aversion. We must not look for the reason of this difference in the medicine, but in the patient to which it was administered. While the two first volumes of *Tristram Shandy* lay half-buried in obscurity, we, the Critical Reviewers, recommended it to the public as a work of humour and ingenuity, and, in return, were publickly reviled with the most dull and indelicate abuse:[10] but neither that ungrateful insult, nor the maukish disgust so generally manifested towards the second part of *Tristram Shandy*, shall warp our judgment or integrity so far, as to join the cry in condemning it as unworthy of the first. One had merit, but was extolled above its value; the other has defects, but is too severely decried. The reader will not expect that we should pretend to give a detail of a work, which seems to have been written without any plan, or any other design than that of shewing the author's wit, humour, and learning, in an unconnected effusion of sentiments and remarks, thrown out indiscriminately as they rose in his imagination. Nevertheless, incoherent and digressive as it is, the book certainly abounds with pertinent observations on life and characters, humourous incidents, poignant ridicule, and marks of taste and erudition. We will venture also to say, that the characters of the father and uncle are interesting and well sustained, and that corporal Trim is an amiable picture of low life.

In the third volume we find the form of an[11] excommunication in Latin, said to be procured out of the leger-book of the church of Rochester, writ by Ernulphus the bishop of that diocese; and so far as we are able to judge, it bears the marks of authenticity.

The last volume is enriched with a tale in the same language, said to be extracted from the decads of *Hafen Slakenbergius*; of which tale it would not be easy to point out the scope and intention, unless we suppose it was an expedient to shew that our author could write good Latin; for, in fact, the pretended Slakenbergius is he himself; and all the merit we can allow the tale is, that the part of it which we have in Latin is written with elegance and propriety.

Having pointed out the beauties of this performance, we cannot, in justice to the public, but take some notice also of its defects. We frequently see the author failing in his endeavours to make the reader laugh; a circumstance which throws him into a very aukward attitude, so as even to excite contempt, like an unfortunate *relator*, who says, 'O! I'll tell you a merry story, gentlemen, that will make you burst your sides with laughing;' and begins with a ha! ha! ha! to recite a very dull narrative, which ends in a general groan of the audience. Most of his apostrophes and digressions are mere tittle-tattle, that species which the French distinguish by the word *caqueter*, fitter for the nursery than the closet. A spirit of petulance, an air of self-conceit, and an affectation of learning, are diffused through the whole performance, which is likewise blameable for some gross expressions, impure ideas, and a general want of decorum. If we thought our opinion could have any weight with a gentleman who seems to stand so high in his own opinion, we would advise him to postpone the history of Tristram's childhood and youth, until the world shall have forgot the misfortune he received in his birth: by that time he may pass for a new man, and once more enjoy that advantage which novelty never fails to have with the public.

58 From a review of *Almoran and Hamet: An Oriental Tale* (1761), *Monthly Review*, XXIV, May 1761

Almoran and Hamet . . . was by John Hawkesworth (see above, No. 44). This review was by Owen Ruffhead.

The Genius of Romance seems to have been long since drooping among us; and has, of late, been generally displayed only for the basest purposes; either to raise the grin of Ideotism by its buffoonry, or stimulate the prurience of Sensuality by its obscenity. Novels, therefore, have circulated chiefly among the giddy and licentious of both sexes, who read, not for the sake of thinking, but for want of thought.

So shameful a prostitution has brought this species of writing into such disrepute, that if the more serious and solid Reader is at any time tempted to cast an eye over the pages of Romance, he almost blushes to confess his curiosity.

Compositions of this kind, nevertheless, when conducted by a Writer of fine talents and elegant taste, may be rendered as beneficial as delectable. They have this peculiar advantage, that, by making a forcible impression on the imagination, they answer the purposes of conviction and persuasion, with the generality of mankind, much better than a direct appeal to the judgment.

Very few are disposed to relish the dry precepts of morality, or to connect a lengthened chain of reasoning; the majority must be entertained with novelty, humoured with fiction, and, as it were, cheated into instruction. Old as the world is, it will not attend to the grave lessons of Wisdom, unless Pleasure introduces the Sage——

> *Le Monde est vieux, dit on. Je le crois: Cependant*
> *Il le faut amuser encore comme un Enfant.*[1]

But, though Romance is, in fact, nothing more than a poetical fiction, in the habit of prose, yet, it ought never to exceed the bounds of probability. The Writer may adorn the Probable, however, with every incident to make it agreeable, and to charm and surprize the

Reader. We must copy Nature, it is true; but Nature in the most perfect and elegant form in which conception can paint her.

It is not requisite, therefore, that his characters should bear resemblance to any known original: It is sufficient that they are aggregates of those qualities which lie scattered among the species. He may draw after a prototype in his own mind, and use his pen as Zeuxis did his pencil, who, when he was about to paint a Venus, did not copy from any single original, but collected the most beautiful women of that time, from whom he drew those parts which were most perfect in each;[2] and then formed an idea of perfection in his own mind, resulting from all those beauties combined.

These principles may be of use to us, in judging of the little volumes before us, which are not, we are afraid, among the number of those of which Mr. Lownds[3] need provide a vast many sets for the accommodation of his fair customers. Here they will find no winding up of Clocks, —no wanton double entendres,—no asterisms [sic] pregnant with gross ideas,—no lambent pupilability.[4]—In short, every thing here is chaste, elegant and moral. The tendency of the work is of the most noble and useful nature, though in the conduct or machinery of it, Probability is sometimes wounded, which never fails to create disgust. But we postpone our remarks for the present, and proceed to the story.

59 From a review of *Eloisa: or, a Series of original Letters collected and published by J. J. Rousseau* (1761), *The Critical Review*, XII, September 1761

This anonymous translation was an extremely rapid piece of work; Rousseau's *La Nouvelle Héloïse* was first published in 1761.

There cannot be a more difficult task than to convey a just idea of a performance, where the elecution, fire, sensibility, refinement, and paradoxical humour of the author, constitute its principal ornaments and blemishes. Rousseau despises the common aids of plot, incident, and contrivance, and effects all his purposes by mere strength of genius and variety of colouring. His attitudes are common, but they are painted with such energy and grace, as cannot fail of striking with all the force of novelty. Like a sculptor who has drawn his materials rough from the quarry, he polishes, and in a manner animates the clumsy marble: even the simple Valesians become in his hands the most amiable people on earth. Such are the characteristics of the new Eloisa, of which we formerly exhibited a sketch, under the title of *Lettres de deux Amans habitans d'une petite ville au pied des Alpes*,[1] and upon which we now venture to extend our criticisms, in compliance with the taste of many of our readers.

Our ingenious author, spirited and masterly in all his productions, has formed his *Eloisa* on the plan of the celebrated *Clarissa*, the favourite work of our late countryman the amiable Mr. Richardson. Every one must acknowledge the resemblance between the distinguishing features of the principal characters. Eloisa is a less perfect Clarissa, Clara a miss Howe, as servent in her friendship, as witty and charming, but less humorous; merely because the Swiss writer is an intire stranger to the talent we express by the word humour. It is, indeed, the highest encomium on Mr. Richardson, that he has been deemed worthy the imitation of a writer of Rousseau's eminence, and that he still remains unrivalled in copying nature, though he may perhaps be greatly excel [sic] in deep reflection, the finer tints that discriminate genius, and certain magic powers peculiar to Rousseau, of conjuring into a single expression the substance of volumes. Of this nature we consider the first letter wrote by St. Preux to Eloisa, in which he discovers his love, situation, and all the consequent scruples and difficulties of his passion. Here by a few lines we are as deeply interested in the fate of the lovers, as if the author had traced the progress of the rising passion through a long correspondence: he has, in fact, advanced as far in his design by a few lines, as Mr. Richardson has done in the three first volumes; and nothing, in our opinion, can more justly distinguish the talents of both authors than this single observation. The English moralist describes a young lady exquisitely delicate, virtuous, beautiful, and religious, but prudent, perhaps, to a degree of coldness, an outcast from her family, persecuted by the rancorous envy of a sister, the brutal resentment of a brother, the inflexible tyranny of a father, reduced to extreme wretchedness by the intrigues of an engaging villain her lover, for whom she entertains a secret passion; and yet refusing, out of punctilio, to bestow her hand upon this lover, equal to her in birth and fortune, the admiration of the female world on account of his person, address, wit and stratagem, and at last falling a sacrifice to filial duty and misplaced delicacy. On the contrary, the Swiss philosopher paints a virgin in the bloom of youth, innocent, amiable, full of sensibility, deeply enamoured of virtue, yet swerving from its dictates, and yielding to the violence of her passions; but reclaimed by the horror of her crime, and her innate purity of sentiment. Her lover too a young man honest and sensible, romanticly fond of virtue, confident of his own strength, and discovering his weakness, reasoning like a Platonist on love, and practising like an Epicurean. The very errors of both are engaging, and we admire them in their fall, because they still bear the prejudice of virtue. The one renders his heroine proof against all the assaults of temptation, thereby proposing a perfect pattern for the imitation of her sex; the other describes her subject to human frailty, lest, by elevating virtue too high, we should be discouraged from attempting to climb the steep ascent: which of the writers hath succeeded best in inculcating instruction we must submit to the different dispositions of their readers; one will be animated with an example, which would throw another into despair. If we may speak our own sentiments, Rousseau hath furnished the more useful instruction, as he hath taught us the means of retrieving the esteem of mankind, after a capital slip on conduct; than which he could not have read a more instructive lesson to the female world, who generally resign over to vice and wretchedness those of their own sex, who have once deviated from the path of virtue, though earnest to redeem their errors, and more valuable members of society than those boasters of their single quality,—their *honour* and unsolicited chastity.

If we take a nearer view of the two admired performances in question, we shall find Rousseau's infinitely more sentimental, animated, refined, and elegant; Richardson's, more natural, interesting, variegated, and dramatic. The one every where appears the easy, the other the masterly writer; Rousseau raises your admiration; Richardson solicits your tears; the former is sometimes obscure; the latter too minute. Every circumstance concurs in disclosing Richardson's design; Rousseau is digressive, but his flights are the extravagations of genius. They may be considered as episodes that delight singly, and distinguish the author a fine essayist as well as an original novellist, by the peculiarity of his manner. Richardson unfolds his characters by a variety of slight touches and circumstances, which appear trivial unless you regard his design; while Rousseau, by a felicity of genius, lays naked the heart at a single stroke, and interests you in the fate of his personages, before you can be said to know them. By a simple motion of his pen, the whole groupe is assembled in the imagination, and engage the attention in proportion as they are connected with Eloisa. However, the impression they make is strong, but it is evanescent; like the fleeting pictures of a dream, they strongly agitate for the time, and are afterwards forgot; while those of Richardson imprint the mind more durably, because the stroke is more frequently reiterated.

We may carry the comparison still farther. Richardson has strong ideas, but they arise by association; those of Rousseau flash like lightning, illuminate every surrounding object, are original, rapid, impetuous, unconnected, and scarce deducible from what preceded, or the subject in question: the former expresses a fine sentiment with an amiable but unadorned and languid simplicity; the other cloaths all his thoughts with dignity and strength, displaying every faculty of the poet, orator, and philosopher, without seeming strained, tumid, or unnatural. His great art consists in concealing his art; in giving all the elegance of a court to the manners of his rural characters, and yet perfectly fitting them to their peculiar circumstances. Virgil hath been said to have dressed his shepherds in silk; it may be alledged of Rousseau, that he has educated his personages in the Lyceum. With Richardson every character appears what we really see it in life; even the drapery is not left to the imagination of the painter. The wit, humour, stratagem, and mischievous invention of Lovelace; the rough boisterous disposition of uncle Anthony; the brutal manners of Mowbray, the humanity and natural good sense of the reclaimed Belford; the honour and soldier-like behaviour of Mordaunt; the shocking catastrophe of the abandoned Mrs. Sinclair; in a word, every circumstance of every person is copied with the utmost accuracy from where it really exists, almost without exaggeration. If Richardson hath described in Lovelace a character which exceeds the powers of Rousseau, it is because that species of humour has no existence in Switzerland. If Rousseau hath painted a cold, insensible, stoical lover in Wolmar, who admires the virtue of his wife, and confides in her honour, even while she is present and alone with the object of her first affection, and the author of her fall, it is because the character is natural enough to the country, however strained it may appear to an Englishman. It may be thought that Rousseau has injured the Christian religion by advancing arguments in defence of deism, which he hath left unanswered, and rendering Wolmar so respectable in his infidelity; we are not going to vindicate the author in this particular. To us it appears, that in all his writings he has considered religion too much as a merely political institution, though in his *Eloisa* he has urged nothing except what was perfectly consonant to the character he describes. We may as justly tax Richardson with drawing an amiable profligate, as blame Rousseau for painting a philosophical, truly moral, and exceedingly respectable deist.

The Swiss philosopher has been hardy enough to describe Eloisa in the married state, yoked to a man whose person she could not love, whose principles were directly opposite to her own, but whose practice strongly engaged her esteem, and rendered her constant in her duty in the most trying situations, even in the company of the amiable person who had innocently seduced her virtue, and engaged her whole heart. Wolmar has the address to attach the lovers to him, and tender them more indifferent to each other, by placing an intire confidence in their honour and natural prejudice in favour of virtue. Here we meet with the finest precepts of conjugal duty, and the most enchanting description of the married state and of rural felicity that was ever penned. Without a single interesting event, we are deeply engaged in every situation, and are equally delighted with the narrative of the historian and the lectures of the philosopher.—But it would exceed our design to remark upon every particular: to those who have not read *Eloisa*, our criticisms will afford little entertainment; to those who have, they may appear so congenial to their own reflections, as to furnish little instruction. We shall therefore close our remarks with observing, that Rousseau's manner of expressing the sublimest sentiments is natural, but it may sometimes be thought too philosophical. Some readers will call this pedantry, others affectation; to us it appears the result of original genius, incapable of speaking or thinking in the common beaten tract. Though we feel all the force of studied elocution, yet a veil is drawn over the author's labour, and we think the sentiment and expression natural to the character. Rousseau alone could make the following expressions appear with propriety in the letter of a young lady to her lover. 'If you had not prohibited me geometry, I should say, that my inquietude increases in a compound ratio of the intervals of time and space; so sensible am I that the pain of absence is encreased by distance,' —'Our souls, if I may use the expression, touch in all points, and we feel an intire coherence; correct me if I speak unphilosophically. Our destiny may part us, but cannot disunite us. Henceforward our pains and pleasures must be mutual; and like the magnets of which I have heard you speak, that have the same motion, though in different places, we should have the same sensations at the two extremities of the world.'[2] These are natural sentiments, expressed in a manner so philosophical, as must appear affected in a young lady, unless we reflect that she is writing to her tutor in philosophy as well as her lover.

60 'On Fictitious History', from *Lectures on Rhetoric and Poetry*, 1762

by HUGH BLAIR

Hugh Blair (1718–1800), Scottish divine and rhetorician, is remembered for the work from which this passage is taken and for his sermons (published between 1777 and 1801); both had considerable influence during the period. As the following passage consists of a complete section in the book, it is published without omission marks before or after it.

There remains to be treated of, another species of composition in prose, which comprehends a very numerous, though, in general, a very insignificant class of writings, known by the name of Romances and Novels. These may, at first view, seem too insignificant, to deserve that any particular notice should be taken of them. But I cannot be of this opinion. Mr. Fletcher of Salton, in one of his Tracts, quotes it as the saying of a wise man, that give him the making of all the ballads of a nation, he would allow any one that pleased to make their laws.[1] The saying was founded on reflection and good sense, and is applicable to the subject now before us. For any kind of writing, how trifling soever in appearance, that obtains a general currency, and especially that early pre-occupies the imagination of the youth of both sexes, must demand particular attention. Its influence is likely to be considerable, both on the morals and taste of a nation.

In fact, fictitious histories might be employed for very useful purposes. They furnish one of the best channels for conveying instruction, for painting human life and manners, for showing the errors into which we are betrayed by our passions, for rendering virtue amiable and vice odious. The effect of well contrived stories, towards accomplishing these purposes, is stronger than any effect that can be produced by simple and naked instruction; and hence we find, that the wisest men in all ages have more or less employed fables and fictions, as the vehicles of knowledge. These have ever been the basis of both epic and dramatic poetry. It is not, therefore, the nature of this sort of writing, considered in itself, but the faulty manner of its execution, that can expose it to any

247

contempt. Lord Bacon takes notice of our taste for fictitious history, as a proof of the greatness and dignity of the human mind. He observes, very ingeniously, that the objects of this world, and the common train of affairs which we behold going on in it, do not fill the mind, nor give it entire satisfaction. We seek for something that shall expand the mind in a greater degree: we seek for more heroic and illustrious deeds, for more diversified and surprising events, for a more splendid order of things, a more regular and just distribution of rewards and punishments than what we find here: because we meet not with these in true history, we have recourse to fictitious. We create worlds according to our fancy, in order to gratify our capacious desires. '*Accomodando*,' says that great philosopher, '*rerum simulachra ad animi desideria, non submittendo animum rebus, quod ratio facet, et historia.*'[2] Let us then, since the subject wants neither dignity nor use, make a few observations on the rise and progress of fictitious history, and the different forms it has assumed in different countries.

In all countries we find its origin very ancient. The genius of the eastern nations, in particular, was from the earliest times much turned towards invention, and the love of fiction. Their divinity, their philosophy, and their politics, were clothed in fables and parables. The Indians, the Persians, and Arabians, were all famous for their tales. The *Arabian Nights' Entertainments* are the production of a romantic invention, but of a rich and amusing imagination; exhibiting a singular and curious display of manners and characters, and beautified with a very humane morality. Among the ancient Greeks, we hear of the Ionian and Milesian Tales; but they have now perished, and, from any account that we have of them, appear to have been of the loose and wanton kind. Some fictitious histories yet remain, that were composed during the decline of the Roman Empire, by Apuleius, Achilles Tatius, and Heliodorus, bishop of Trica, in the 4th century; but none of them are considerable enough to merit particular criticisms.

During the dark ages, this sort of writing assumed a new and very singular form, and for a long while made a great figure in the world. The martial spirit of those nations, among whom the feudal government prevailed; the establishment of single combat, as an allowed method of deciding causes both of justice and honour; the appointment of champions in the cause of women, who could not maintain their own rights by the sword; together with the institution of military tournaments, in which different kingdoms vied with one another, gave rise, in those times, to that marvellous system of chivalry, which is one of the most singular appearances in the history of mankind. Upon this were founded those romances of knight-errantry, which carried an ideal chivalry, to a still more extravagant height than it had risen in fact. There was displayed in them a new and very wonderful sort of world, hardly bearing any resemblance to the world in which we dwell. Not only knights setting forth to redress all manner of wrongs, but in every page, magicians, dragons, and giants, invulnerable men, winged horses, enchanted armour, and enchanted castles; adventures absolutely incredible, yet suited to the gross ignorance of these ages, and to the legends, and superstitious notions concerning magic and necromancy which then prevailed. This merit they had, of being writings of the highly moral and heroic kind. Their knights were patterns, not of courage merely, but of religion, generosity, courtesy, and fidelity; and the heroines were no less distinguished for modesty, delicacy, and the utmost dignity of manners.

These were the first compositions that received the name of Romances. The origin of this name is traced, by Mr. Huet, the learned bishop of Avranche, to the Provencal Troubadoures, a sort of story-tellers and bards in the county of Provence, where there subsisted some remains of literature and poetry.[3] The language which prevailed in that country was a mixture of Latin and Gallic, called the Roman or Romance language; and, as the stories of these Troubadoures were written in that language, hence it is said the name of Romance, which we now apply to all fictitious composition.

The earliest of these romances, is that which goes under the name of Turpin, the archbishop of Rheims, written in the 11th century.[4] The subject is, the achievments of Charlemagne and his Peers, or Paladins, in driving the Saracens out of France and part of Spain; the same subject which Ariosto has taken for his celebrated poem of *Orlando Furioso*, which is truly a Chivalry Romance, as extravagant as any of the rest, but partly heroic, and partly comic, embellished with the highest graces of poetry. The Romance of Turpin was followed by *Amadis de Gaul*, and many more of the same stamp. The crusades both furnished new matter, and increased the spirit for such writings; the Christians against the Saracens made the common ground-work of them; and from the 11th to the 16th century, they continued to bewitch all Europe. In Spain, where the taste for this sort of writing had been most greedily caught, the ingenious Cervantes, in the beginning of the last century, contributed greatly to explode it; and the abolition of tournaments, the prohibition of single combat, the disbelief of magic and enchantments, and the change in general of manners throughout Europe, began to give a new turn to fictitious composition.

Then appeared the *Astræa* of D'urfe, the *grand Cyrus*, the *Clelia* and *Cleopatra* of Mad. Scuderi, the *Arcadia* of Sir Philip Sidney, and other grave and stately compositions in the same style. These may be considered as forming the second stage of romance writing. The heroism and the gallantry, the moral and virtuous turn of the chivalry romance, were still preserved; but the dragons, the necromancers, and the enchanted castles, were banished, and some small resemblance to human nature was introduced. Still, however, there was too much of the marvellous in them to please an age which now aspired to refinement. The characters were discerned to be strained; the style to be swoln; the adventures incredible; the books themselves were voluminous and tedious.

Hence, this sort of composition soon assumed a third form, and from magnificent heroic romance, dwindled down to the familiar novel. These novels, both in France and England, during the age of Louis XIV. and King Charles II. were in general of a trifling nature, without the appearance of moral tendency, or useful instruction. Since that time, however, somewhat better has been attempted, and a degree of reformation introduced into the spirit of novel-writing. Imitations of life and character have been made their principal object. Relations have been professed to be given of the behaviour of persons in particular interesting situations, such as may actually occur in life; by means of which, what is laudable or defective in character and conduct may be pointed out, and placed in an useful light. Upon this Plan, the French have produced some compositions of considerable merit. *Gil Blas*, by Le Sage, is a book full of good sense, and instructive knowledge of the world. The works of Maurivaux [sic], especially his *Marianne*, discover great refinement of thought, great penetration into human nature, and paint with a very delicate pencil, some of the nicest shades and features in the distinction of characters. The *Nouvelle Héloïse* of Rousseau is a production of a very singular kind;[5] in many of the events which are related, improbable and unnatural; in some of the details tedious, and for some of the scenes which are described, justly blameable; but withal, for the power of eloquence, for tenderness of sentiment, for ardour of passion, entitled to rank among the highest productions of fictitious history.

In this kind of writing we are, it must be confessed, in Great Britain, inferior to the French. We neither relate so agreeably, nor draw characters with so much delicacy; yet we are not without some performances which discover the strength of the British genius. No fiction, in any language, was ever better supported than the *Adventures of Robinson Crusoe*.[6] While it is carried on with that appearance of truth and simplicity, which takes a strong hold of the imagination of all readers, it suggests at the same time, very useful instruction; by showing how much the native powers of man may be exerted for surmounting the difficulties of any external situation. Mr. Fielding's Novels are highly distinguished for their humour; a humour which, if not of the most refined and delicate kind, is original and peculiar to himself. The characters which he draws are lively and natural, and marked with the strokes of a bold pencil. The general scope of his stories is favourable to humanity and goodness of heart; and in *Tom Jones*, his greatest work, the artful conduct of the fable, and the subserviency of all the incidents to the winding up of the whole, deserve much praise. The most moral of all our novel writers is Richardson, the author of *Clarissa*, a writer of excellent intentions, and of very considerable capacity and genius; did he not possess the unfortunate talent of spinning out pieces of amusement into an immeasurable length. The trivial performances which daily appear in public under the title of lives, adventures, and histories, by anonymous authors, if they be often innocent, yet are most commonly insipid; and though in the general it ought to be admitted that characteristical novels, formed upon nature and upon life, without extravagance and without licentiousness, might furnish an agreeable and useful entertainment to the mind; yet considering the manner in which these writings, have been, for the most part, conducted, it must also be confessed, that they oftener tend to dissipation and idleness, than to any good purpose. Let us now, therefore, make our retreat from these regions of fiction.

61 From *Essay on Poetry and Music, as they affect the Mind . . .*, 1776

by JAMES BEATTIE

This essay was written in 1762, though not published until 1776 in Beattie's *Essays*. Passage (*a*) occurs in Part I, ch. v, paragraph vi; passage (*b*) is a footnote to Part I, ch. v, paragraph vi.

James Beattie (1735–1803), Professor of Moral Philosophy and Logic in Marischal College and the University of Aberdeen, was well known as the author of a number of poems, including *The Minstrel* (1771 and 1774), and a number of essays published under the title of *Dissertations Moral and Critical* (1783) (see also below, No. 76).

(*a*)

If a work have no determinate end, it has no meaning; and if it have many ends, it will distract by its multiplicity. Unity of design, therefore, belongs in some measure to all compositions, whether in verse or prose. But to some it is more essential than to others; and to none so much as to the higher poetry. In certain kinds of history, there is unity sufficient, if all the events recorded be referred to one person; in others, if to one period of time, or to one people, or even to the inhabitants of one and the same planet. But it is not enough, that the subject of a poetical fable be the exploits of *one person*; for these may be of various and even of opposite sorts and tendencies, and take up longer time, than the nature of poetry can admit:—far less can a regular poem comprehend the affairs of *one period*, or of *one people*:—it must be limited to some *one great action or event*, to the illustration of which all the subordinate events must contribute; and these must be so connected with one another, as well as with the poet's general purpose, that one cannot be changed, transposed, or taken away, without affecting the consistence and stability of the whole. In itself an incident may be interesting, a character well drawn, a description beautiful; and yet, if it disfigure the general plan, or if it obstruct or incumber the main action, instead of helping it forward, a correct artist would consider it as but a gaudy superfluity or splendid deformity; like a piece of scarlet cloth sowed upon a garment of a different colour.[1] Not that all the parts of the fable either are, or can be, equally essential. Many descriptions and thoughts, of little consequence to the plan, may be admitted for the sake of variety; and the poet may, as well as the historian and philosopher, drop his subject for a time, in order to take up an affecting or instructive digression.

The doctrine of poetical digressions and episodes has been largely treated by the critics. I shall only remark, that, in estimating their propriety, three things are to be attended to:—their connection with the fable or subject;—their own peculiar excellence;—and their subserviency to the poet's design.

[. . . . .]

(b)

The difficulty of constructing an Epic or Dramatic fable may appear from the bad success of very great writers who have attempted it. Of Dramatic fables there are indeed several in the world, which may be allowed to have come near perfection. But the beauty of Homer's fable remains unrivalled to this day. Virgil and Tasso have imitated, but not equalled it. That of *Paradise Lost* is artful, and for the most part judicious: I am certain the author could have equalled Homer in this, as he has excelled him in some other respects:—but the nature of his plan would not admit the introduction of so many incidents, as we see in the *Iliad*, co-operating to one determinate end.—Of the Comic Epopee we have two exquisite models in English, I mean the *Amelia* and *Tom Jones* of Fielding. The introductory part of the latter follows indeed the historical arrangement, in a way somewhat resembling the practice of Euripides in his Prologues, or at least as excuseable: but, with this exception, we may venture to say, that both fables would bear to be examined by Aristotle himself, and, if compared with those of Homer, would not greatly suffer in the comparison. This author, to an amazing variety of probable occurrences, and of characters well drawn, well supported, and finely contrasted, has given the most perfect unity, by making them all co-operate to one and the same final purpose. It yields a very pleasing surprise to observe, in the unravelling of his plots, particularly that of *Tom Jones*, how many incidents, to which, because of their apparent minuteness, we had scarce attended as they occurred in the narrative, are found to have been essential to the plot. And what heightens our idea of the poet's art is, that all this is effected by natural means, and human abilities, without any machinery: —while his great master Cervantes is obliged to work a miracle for the cure of Don Quixote.—Can any reason be assigned, why the inimitable Fielding, who was so perfect in Epic fable, should have succeeded so indifferently in Dramatic? Was it owing to the peculiarity of his genius, or of his circumstances? to any thing in the nature of Dramatic writing in general, or of that particular taste in Dramatic Comedy which Congreve and Vanburgh[2] had introduced, and which he was obliged to comply with?

62 From the Introduction to *The Works of Henry Fielding, Esq; with the Life of the Author . . .*, 1762

by ARTHUR MURPHY

The passage reproduced below is taken from Volume I of *The Works . . .*, 77–90. The author, Arthur Murphy (1727–1805), a friend of Fielding, was a dramatist and writer of farces. He produced *The Way to Keep Him* (1760), *Three Weeks after Marriage* (1764), *Zenobia* (1768) and *The Grecian Daughter* (1772). He also wrote *An Essay on the Life and Genius of Samuel Johnson* (1792) and *The Life of David Garrick* (1801).

Amidst these severe exercises of his understanding,[1] and all the laborious duties of his office, his invention could not lie still; but he found leisure to amuse himself, and afterwards the world, with the *History of Tom Jones*. And now we are arrived at the second grand epoch of Mr. Fielding's genius, when all his faculties were in perfect unison, and conspired to produce a complete work. If we consider *Tom Jones* in the same light in which the ablest critics have examined the *Iliad*, the *Æneid*, and the *Paradise Lost*, namely, with a view to the fable, the manners, the sentiments, and the stile, we shall find it standing the test of the severest criticism, and indeed bearing away the envied praise of a complete performance. In the first place, the action has that unity, which is the boast of the great models of composition; it turns upon a single event, attended with many circumstances, and many subordinate incidents, which seem, in the progress of the work, to perplex, to entangle, and to involve the whole in difficulties, and lead on the reader's imagination, with an eagerness of curiosity, through scenes of prodigious variety, till at length the different intricacies and complications of the fable are explained after the same gradual manner in which they had been worked up to a crisis: incident arises out of incident; the seeds of every thing that shoots up, are laid with a judicious hand, and whatever occurs in the latter part of the story, seems naturally to grow out of those passages which preceded; so that, upon the whole, the business with great propriety and probability works itself up into various embarrassments, and then afterwards, by a regular series of events, clears itself from all impediments, and brings itself inevitably to a conclusion; like a river, which, in its progress, foams amongst fragments of rocks, and for a while seems pent up by unsurmountable oppositions; then angrily dashes for a while, then plunges under ground into caverns, and runs a subterraneous course, till at length it breaks out again, meanders round the country, and with a clear placid stream flows gently into the ocean. By this artful management, our author has given us the perfection of fable; which, as the writers upon the subject have justly observed, consists in such obstacles to retard the final issue of the whole, as shall at least, in their consequences, accelerate the catastrophe, and bring it evidently and necessarily to that period only, which, in the nature of things, could arise from it; so that the action could not remain in suspense any longer, but must naturally close and determine itself. It may be proper to add, that no fable whatever affords, in its solution, such artful states of suspence, such beautiful turns of surprise, such unexpected incidents, and such sudden discoveries, sometimes apparently embarrassing, but always promising the catastrophe, and eventually promoting the completion of the whole. *Vida*, the celebrated critic of Italy, has transmitted down to us, in his Art of Poetry, a very beautiful idea of a well-concerted fable, when he represents the reader of it in the situation of a traveller to a distant town, who, when he perceives but a faint shadowy glimmering of its walls, its spires, and its edifices, pursues his journey with more alacrity than when he cannot see any appearances to notify the place to which he is tending, but is obliged to pursue a melancholy and forlorn road through a depth of vallies, without any object to flatter or to raise his expectation.

> Haud aliter, longinqua petit qui fortè viator
> Mænia, si positas altis in collibus arces
> Nunc etiam dubias oculis videt, incipit ultrò
> Lætior ire viam, placidumque urgere laborem,
> Quam cum nusquam ullæ cernuntur quas adit arces,
> Obscurum sed iter tedit convallibus imis.[2]

In the execution of this plan, thus regular and uniform, what a variety of humorous scenes of life, of descriptions, and characters has our author found means to incorporate with the principal action; and this too, without distracting the reader's attention with objects foreign to his subject, or weakening the general interest by a multiplicity of episodical events? Still observing the grand essential rule of unity in the design, I believe, no author has introduced a greater diversity of characters, or displayed them more fully, or in more various attitudes. *Allworthy* is the most amiable picture in the world of a man who does honour to his species: in his own heart he finds constant propensities to the most benevolent and generous actions, and his understanding conducts him with discretion in the performance of whatever his goodness suggests to him. And though it is apparent that the author laboured this portrait *con amore*, and meant to offer it to mankind as a just object of imitation, he has soberly restrained himself within the bounds of probability, nay, it may be said, of strict truth; as in the general opinion, he is supposed to have copied here the features of a worthy character still in being. Nothing can be more entertaining than WESTERN; his rustic manners, his natural undisciplined honesty, his half-enlightened understanding, with the self-pleasing shrewdness which accompanies it, and the biass of his mind to mistaken politicks, are all delineated with precision and fine humour. The sisters of those two gentlemen are aptly introduced, and give rise to many agreeable scenes. *Tom Jones* will at all times be a fine lesson to young men of good tendencies to virtue, who yet suffer the impetuosity of their passions to hurry them away. *Thackwum* and *Square* are excellently opposed to each other; the former is a well drawn picture of a *divine*, who is neglectful of the moral part of his character, and ostentatiously talks of religion and grace; the latter is a strong ridicule of those, who have high ideas of the dignity of our nature, and of the native beauty of virtue, without owning any obligations of conduct from religion. But grace, without practical goodness, and the moral fitness of things, are shewn, with a fine vein of ridicule, to be but weak principles of action. In short, all the characters down to Partridge, and even to a maid or an hostler at an inn, are drawn with truth and humour: and indeed they abound so much, and are so often brought forward in a dramatic manner, that every thing may be said to be here in action; every thing has MANNERS; and the very manners which belong to it in human life. They look, they act, they speak to our imaginations just as they appear to us in the world. The SENTIMENTS which they utter, are peculiarly annexed to their habits, passions, and ideas; which is what poetical propriety requires; and, to the honour of the author, it must be said, that, whenever he addresses us in person, he is always in the interests of virtue and religion, and inspires, in a strain of moral reflection, a true love of goodness, and honour, with a just detestation of imposture, hypocrisy, and all specious pretences to uprightness.

There is, perhaps, no province of the comic muse that requires so great a variety of stile as this kind of description of men and manners, in which Mr. Fielding so much delighted. The laws of the mock-epic, in which this species of writing is properly included demand, that, when trivial things are to be represented with a burlesque air, the language should be raised into a sort of tumor of dignity, that by the contrast between the ideas and the pomp in which they are exhibited, they may appear the more ridiculous to our imaginations. Of our author's talent in this way, there are instances in almost every chapter; and were we to assign a particular example, we should refer to the relation of a battle in the *Homerican stile*. On the other hand, when matters, in appearance, of higher moment, but, in reality, attended with incongruous circumstances, are to be set forth in the garb of ridicule, which they deserve, it is necessary that the language should be proportionably lowered, and that the metaphors and epithets made use of be transferred from things of a meaner nature, that so the false importance of the object described may fall into a gay contempt. The first specimen of this manner that occurs to me is in the *Jonathan Wild*: 'For my own part,' says he, 'I confess I look on this death of hanging to be as proper for a hero as any other; and I solemnly declare, that had Alexander the Great been hanged, it would not in the least have diminished my respect to his memory.'[3] A better example of what is here intended might, no doubt, be chosen, as things of this nature may be found almost every where in *Tom Jones*, or *Joseph Andrews*; but the quotation here made will serve to illustrate, and that is sufficient. The mock-epic has likewise frequent occasion for the gravest irony, for florid description, for the true sublime, for the pathetic, for clear and perspicuous narrative, for poignant satire, and generous panegyrick. For all these different modes of eloquence, Mr. Fielding's genius was most happily versatile, and his power in all of them is so conspicuous, that he may justly be said to have had the rare skill, required by Horace, of giving to each part of his work its true and proper colouring.

——*Servare vices, operumquè colores.*[4]

In this consists the specific quality of fine writing: and thus our author being confessedly eminent in all the great essentials of composition, in fable, character, sentiment, and elocution; and as these could not be all united in so high an assemblage, without a rich invention, a fine imagination, an enlightened judgment, and a lively wit, we may fairly here decide his character, and pronounce him the ENGLISH CERVANTES.

It may be added, that in many parts of the *Tom Jones* we find our author possessed the softer graces of character-painting, and of description; many situations and sentiments are touched with a delicate hand, and throughout the work he seems to feel as much delight in describing the amiable part of human nature, as in his early days he had in exaggerating the strong and harsh features of turpitude and deformity. This circumstance breathes an air of philanthropy through his work, and renders it *an image of truth*, as the Roman orator calls a comedy. And hence it arose, from this *truth of character* which prevails in *Tom Jones*, in conjunction with the other qualities of the writer, above set forth, that the suffrage of the most learned critic[5] of this nation was given to our author, when he says, 'Mons. de Marivaux, in France, and Mr. Fielding in England stand the foremost among those, who have given a faithful and chaste copy of *life and manners*, and by enriching their romance with the best part of the comic art, may be said to have brought it to perfection.'[6] Such a favourable decision from so able a judge, will do honour to Mr. Fielding with posterity; and the excellent genius of the person, with whom he has paralleled him, will reflect the truest praise on the author, who was capable of being his illustrious rival.

Marivaux possessed rare and fine talents; he was an attentive observer of mankind, and the transcripts he made from thence are the *image of truth*. At his reception into the French Academy, he was told in an elegant speech, made by the Archbishop of *Sens*, that the celebrated La Bruyére[7] seemed to be revived in him, and to retrace with his pencil those admirable portraits of men and manners, which formerly unmasked so many characters, and exposed their vanity and affectation. *Marivaux* seems never so happy as when he is reprobating the false pretences of assumed characters: the dissimulation of friends, the policy of the ambitious, the littleness and arrogance of the great, the insolence of wealth, the arts of the courtesan, the impertinence of foppery, the refined foibles of the fair sex, the dissipation of youth, the gravity of false-importance, the subtleties of hypocrisy and exterior religion, together with all the delicacies of real honour, and the sentiments of true virtue, are delineated by him in a lively and striking manner. He was not contented merely to copy their appearances; he went still deeper, and searched for all the internal movements of their passions, with a curiosity that is always penetrating, but sometimes appears over-solicitous, and, as the critic expresses it, *ultrà perfectum trahi*.[8] It is not intended by this to insinuate that he exceeds the bounds of truth; but occasionally he seems to refine, till the traces grow minute and almost imperceptible. He is a painter, who labours his portraits with a careful and a scrupulous hand; he attaches himself to them with affection; knows not when to give over, *nescivit quod benè cessit, relinquere*,[9] but continues touching and retouching, till his *traits* become so delicate, that they at length are without efficacy, and the attention of the connoisseur is tired, before the diligence of the artist is wearied. But this refinement of *Marivaux* is apologized for by the remark of the ethic poet, who observes that this kind of enquiry is

> Like following life thro' insects we dissect;
> We lose it in the moment we detect.[10]

If therefore he sometimes seems over-curious, it is the nature of his subject that allures him, and, in general, he greatly recompenses us for the unwillingness he shews to quit his work, by the valuable illustrations he gives it, and the delicacy with which he marks all the finer features of the mind. His diction, it must not be dissembled, is sometimes, but not often, far-fetched and strained; and it was even objected to him in the speech, already mentioned of the *Archbishop of Sens*, that his choice of words was not always pure and legitimate. Each phrase, and often each word is a sentence; but he was apt to be hazardous and daring in his metaphors, which was observed to him, lest his example and the connivance of the Academy, which sits in a kind of legislative capacity upon works of taste, should occasion a vicious imitation of the particulars in which he was deemed defective. This criticism *Marivaux* has somewhere attempted to answer, by observing that he always writes more like a man than an author, and endeavours to convey his ideas to his readers in the same light they struck his own imagination,[11] which had great fecundity, warmth, and vivacity. The *Paysan Parvenu* seems to be the *Joseph Andrews* of this author, and the *Marianne* his higher work, or his *Tom Jones*. They are both, in a very exquisite degree, amusing and instructive. They are not written, indeed, upon any of the laws of composition promulged by *Aristotle*, and expounded by his followers: his romances begin regularly with the birth and parentage of the principal person, and proceed in a narrative of events, including indeed great variety, and artfully raising and suspending our expectation: they are rather to be called *fictitious biography*, than a comic fable, consisting of a *beginning*, a *middle*, and *end*, where one principal action is offered to the imagination, in its process is involved in difficulties, and rises gradually into tumult and perplexity, till, in a manner unexpected, it works itself clear, and comes, by natural but unforeseen incidents, to a termination.

In this last mentioned particular, *Fielding* boasts a manifest superiority over *Marivaux*. Uniformity amidst variety is justly allowed in all works of invention to be the prime source of beauty, and it is the peculiar excellence of *Tom Jones*. The author, for the most part, is more readily satisfied in his drawings of character than the French writer; the strong specific qualities of his personages he sets forth with a few masterly strokes, but the nicer and more subtle workings of the mind he is not so anxious to investigate; when the passions are agitated, he can give us their conflicts, and their various transitions, but he does not always point out the secret cause that sets them in motion, or in the poet's language, 'the small pebble that stirs the peaceful lake.'[12] Fielding was more attached to the *manners* than to the *heart*: in descriptions of the former he is admirable; in unfolding the latter he is not equal to *Marivaux*. In the management of his story, he piques and awakens curiosity more strongly than his rival of France; when he interests and excites our affections, he sometimes operates more by the force of situation, than by the tender pathetic of sentiment, for which the author of *Marianne* is remarkable; not that it must be imagined that Fielding wanted these qualities; we have already said the reverse of him; but in these particulars *Marivaux* has the preference. In point of stile, he is more unexceptionable than *Marivaux*, the critics never having objected to him that his figures are forced or unnatural; and in humour the praise of pre-eminence is entirely his. *Marivaux* was determined to have an air of originality, and therefore disdained to form himself upon any eminent mode of preceding writers; *Fielding* considered the rules of composition as delivered by the great philosophic critic, and finding that Homer had written a work, intitled *Margites*, which bore the same relation to *comedy*, that the *Iliad* or *Odyssey* does to tragedy, he meditated a plan[13] conformable to the principles of a well-arranged fable. Were the *Margites* still extant, it would perhaps be found to have the same proportion to this work of our author, as the sublime epic has to the *Télémaque* of *Fénelon*. This was a noble vehicle for humorous description; and to ensure his success in it, with great judgment, he fixed his eye upon the stile and manner of *Cervantes*, as *Virgil* had before done in respect to *Homer*. To this excellent model, he added all the advantages he could deduce from *Scarron* and *Swift*; few or no sprinklings of *Rablais* [*sic*] being to be found in him. His own strong discernment of the foibles of mankind, and his quick sense of the ridiculous being thus improved, by a careful attention to the works of the great masters of their art, it is no wonder that he has been able to raise himself to the top of the *comic character*, to be admired by readers with the most lively sensations of mirth, and by novel-writers *with a despair that he should ever be emulated with success.*

Thus we have traced our author in his progress to the time when the vigour of his mind was in its full growth of perfection; from this period it sunk, but by slow degrees, into a decline: *Amelia*, which succeeded *Tom Jones* in about four years,[14] has indeed the marks of genius, but of a genius beginning to fall into its decay. The author's invention in this performance does not appear to have lost its fertility; his judgment too seems as strong as ever; but the warmth of imagination is abated; and in his landskips or his scenes of life, Mr. Fielding is no longer the colourist he was before. The personages of the piece delight too much in narrative, and their characters have not those touches of singularity, those specific differences, which are so beautifully marked in our author's former works: of course the humour, which consists in happy delineations of the caprices and predominant foibles of the human mind, loses here its high flavour and relish. And yet *Amelia* holds the same proportion to *Tom Jones*, that the *Odyssey* of *Homer* bears, in the estimation of *Longinus*, to the *Iliad*.[15] A fine vein of morality runs through the whole; many of the situations are affecting and tender; the sentiments are delicate; and upon the whole, it is the *Odyssey*, the moral and pathetic work of Henry Fielding.

63 The Prefaces to *The Castle of Otranto, A Story*, 1764 and 1765

by HORACE WALPOLE

The first edition of *The Castle of Otranto* was published pseu-
donymously in December 1764 as a translation from the Italian
by Ernulpho Marshall. The second edition followed very quickly
in 1765 and was published under Walpole's own name.

The following work was found in the library of an ancient catholic
family in the north of England. It was printed at Naples, in the black
letter, in the year 1529. How much sooner it was written does not
appear. The principal incidents are such as were believed in the darkest
ages of christianity; but the language and conduct have nothing that
favours of barbarism. The style is the purest Italian. If the story was
written near the time when it is supposed to have happened, it must
have been between 1095, the æra of the first crusade, and 1243, the
date of the last, or not long afterwards. There is no other circumstance
in the work that can lead us to guess at the period in which the scene
is laid: the names of the actors are evidently fictitious, and probably
disguised on purpose: yet the Spanish names of the domestics seem to
indicate that this work was not composed until the establishment of the
Arragonian kings in Naples had made Spanish appellations familiar in
that country. The beauty of the diction, and the zeal of the author,
(moderated however by singular judgment) concur to make me think
that the date of the composition was little antecedent to that of the
impression. Letters were then in their most flourishing state in Italy,
and contributed to dispel the empire of superstition, at that time so
forcibly attacked by the reformers. It is not unlikely that an artful priest
might endeavour to turn their own arms on the innovators; and might
avail himself of his abilities as an author to confirm the populace in their
ancient errors and superstitions. If this was his view, he has certainly
acted with signal address. Such a work as the following would enslave
a hundred vulgar minds beyond half the books of controversy that have
been written from the days of Luther to the present hour.

The solution of the author's motives is however offered as a mere conjecture. Whatever his views were, or whatever effects the execution of them might have, his work can only be laid before the public at present as a matter of entertainment. Even as such, some apology for it is necessary. Miracles, visions, necromancy, dreams, and other preternatural events, are exploded now even from romances. That was not the case when our author wrote; much less when the story itself is supposed to have happened. Belief in every kind of prodigy was so established in those dark ages, that an author would not be faithful to the *manners* of the times who should omit all mention of them. He is not bound to believe them himself, but he must represent his actors as believing them.

If this *air of the miraculous* is excused, the reader will find nothing else unworthy of his perusal. Allow the possibility of the facts, and all the actors comport themselves as persons would do in their situation. There is no bombast, no similies, flowers, digressions, or unnecessary descriptions. Every thing tends directly to the catastrophe. Never is the reader's attention relaxed. The rules of the drama are almost observed throughout the conduct of the piece. The characters are well drawn, and still better maintained. Terror, the author's principal engine, prevents the story from ever languishing; and it is so often contrasted by pity, that the mind is kept up in a constant vicissitude of interesting passions.

Some persons may perhaps think the characters of the domestics too little serious for the general cast of the story; but besides their opposition to the principal personages, the art of the author is very observable in his conduct of the subalterns. They discover many passages essential to the story, which could not well be brought to light but by their *naïveté* and simplicity: in particular, the womanish terror and foibles of Bianca, in the last chapter, conduce essentially towards advancing the catastrophe.

It is natural for a translator to be prejudiced in favour of his adopted work. More impartial readers may not be so much struck with the beauties of this piece as I was. Yet I am not blind to my author's defects. I could wish he had grounded his plan on a more useful moral than this; that *the sins of fathers are visited on their children to the third and fourth generation*. I doubt whether in his time, any more than at present, ambition curbed its appetite of dominion from the dread of so remote a punishment. And yet this moral is weakened by that less direct insinuation, that even such anathema may be diverted by devotion to saint Nicholas. Here the interest of the monk plainly gets the better of the judgment of the author. However, with all its faults, I have no doubt but the English reader will be pleased with a sight of this performance. The piety that reigns throughout, the lessons of virtue that are inculcated, and the rigid purity of the sentiments, exempt this work from the censure to which romances are but too liable. Should it meet with the success I hope for, I may be encouraged to re-print the original Italian, though it will tend to depreciate my own labour. Our language falls far short of the charms of the Italian, both for variety and harmony. The latter is peculiarly excellent for simple narrative. It is difficult in English *to relate* without falling too low or rising too high; a fault obviously occasioned by the little care taken to speak pure language in common conversation. Every Italian or Frenchman of any rank piques himself on speaking his own tongue correctly and with choice. I cannot flatter myself with having done justice to my author in this respect: his style is as elegant as his conduct of the passions is masterly. It is pity that he did not apply his talents to what they were evidently proper for, the theatre.

I will detain the reader no longer but to make one short remark. Though the machinery is invention, and the names of the actors imaginary, I cannot but believe that the groundwork of the story is founded on truth. The scene is undoubtedly laid in some real castle. The author seems frequently, without design, to describe particular parts. *The chamber*, says he, *on the right hand; the door on the left hand; the distance from the chapel to Conrad's apartment*: these and other passages are strong presumptions that the author had some certain building in his eye. Curious persons, who have leisure to employ in such researches, may possibly discover in the Italian writers the foundation on which our author has built. If a catastrophe, at all resembling that which he describes, is believed to have given rise to this work, it will contribute to interest the reader, and will make *The Castle of Otranto* a still more moving story.

★ ★ ★

The favourable manner in which this little piece has been received by the public, calls upon the author to explain the grounds on which he composed it. But before he opens those motives, it is fit that he should ask pardon of his readers for having offered his work to them under the borrowed personage of a translator. As diffidence of his own abilities, and the novelty of the attempt, were his sole inducements to assume that

265

disguise, he flatters himself he shall appear excusable, He resigned his performance to the impartial judgment of the public; determined to let it perish in obscurity, if disapproved; nor meaning to avow such a trifle, unless better judges should pronounce that he might own it without a blush.

It was an attempt to blend the two kinds of romance, the ancient and the modern. In the former all was imagination and improbability: in the latter, nature is always intended to be, and sometimes has been, copied with success. Invention has not been wanting; but the great resources of fancy have been dammed up, by a strict adherence to common life. But if in the latter species Nature has cramped imagination, she did but take her revenge, having been totally excluded from old romances. The actions, sentiments, conversations, of the heroes and heroines of ancient days were as unnatural as the machines employed to put them in motion.

The author of the following pages thought it possible to reconcile the two kinds. Desirous of leaving the powers of fancy at liberty to expatiate through the boundless realms of invention, and thence of creating more interesting situations, he wished to conduct the mortal agents in his drama according to the rules of probability; in short, to make them think, speak and act, as it might be supposed mere men and women would do in extraordinary positions. He had observed, that in all inspired writings, the personages under the dispensation of miracles, and witnesses to the most stupendous phenomena, never lose sight of their human character: whereas in the productions of romantic story, an improbable event never fails to be attended by an absurd dialogue. The actors seem to lose their senses the moment the laws of nature have lost their tone. As the public have applauded the attempt, the author must not say he was entirely unequal to the task he had undertaken: yet if the new route he has struck out shall have paved a road for men of brighter talents, he shall own with pleasure and modesty, that he was sensible the plan was capable of receiving greater embellishments than his imagination or conduct of the passions could bestow on it.

With regard to the deportment of the domestics, on which I have touched in the former preface, I will beg leave to add a few words. The simplicity of their behaviour, almost tending to excite smiles, which at first seem not consonant to the serious cast of the work, appeared to me not only not improper, but was marked designedly in that manner. My rule was nature. However grave, important, or even melancholy, the sensations of princes and heroes may be, they do not stamp the same affections on their domestics: at least the latter do not, or should not be made to express their passions in the same dignified tone. In my humble opinion, the contrast between the sublime of the one, and the *naïveté* of the other, sets the pathetic of the former in a stronger light. The very impatience which a reader feels, while delayed by the coarse pleasantries of vulgar actors from arriving at the knowledge of the important catastrophe he expects, perhaps heightens, certainly proves that he has been artfully interested in, the depending event. But I had higher authority than my own opinion for this conduct. That great master of nature, Shakespeare, was the model I copied. Let me ask if his tragedies of *Hamlet* and *Julius Caesar* would not lose a considerable share of the spirit and wonderful beauties, if the humour of the grave-diggers, the fooleries of Polonius, and the clumsy jests of the Roman citizens were omitted, or vested in heroics? Is not the eloquence of Antony, the nobler and affectedly unaffected oration of Brutus, artificially exalted by the rude bursts of nature from the mouths of their auditors? These touches remind one of the Grecian sculptor, who, to convey the idea of a Colossus within the dimensions of a seal, inserted a little boy measuring his thumb.[1]

No, says Voltaire in his edition of Corneille, this mixture of buffoonery and solemnity is intolerable—Voltaire is a genius[2]—but not of Shakespeare's magnitude. Without recurring to disputable authority, I appeal from Voltaire to himself. I shall not avail myself of his former encomiums on our mighty poet; though the French critic has twice translated the same speech in Hamlet, some years ago in admiration, latterly in derision; and I am sorry to find that his judgment grows weaker, when it ought to be farther matured. But I shall make use of his own words, delivered on the general topic of the theatre, when he was neither thinking to recommend or decry Shakespeare's practice; consequently at a moment when Voltaire was impartial. In the preface to his *Enfant prodigue*, that exquisite piece of which I declare my admiration, and which, should I live twenty years longer, I trust I should never attempt to ridicule, he has these words, speaking of comedy, (but equally applicable to tragedy, if tragedy is, as surely it ought to be, a picture of human life; nor can I conceive why occasional pleasantry ought more to be banished from the tragic scene, than pathetic seriousness from the comic) '*On y voit un melange de serieux et de plaisanterie, de comique et de touchant; souvent même une seule avanture produit tous ces contrastes. Rien n'est si commun qu'une maison dans laquelle un pere gronde, une fille occupée de sa passion pleure; le fils se*

*moque des deux, et quelques parens prennent part differemment à la scene, &c.
Nous n'inferons pas de là que toute comedie doive avoir des scenes de bouffon-
nerie et des scenes attendrissantes: il y a beaucoup de tres bonnes pieces où il
ne regne que de la gayeté; d'autres toutes serieuses; d'autres melangées: d'autres
où l'attendrissement va jusques aux larmes:* il ne faut donner l'exclusion
à aucun genre: *et si l'on me demandoit, quel genre est le meilleur, je
repondrois, celui qui est le mieux traité'.*[3] Surely if a comedy may be *toute
serieuse*, tragedy may now and then, soberly, be indulged in a smile.
Who shall proscribe it? Shall the critic, who in self-defence declares that
no kind ought to be excluded from comedy, give laws to Shakespeare?

I am aware that the preface from whence I have quoted these passages
does not stand in monsieur de Voltaire's name, but in that of his editor;
yet who doubts that the editor and author were the same person? Or
where is the editor, who has so happily possessed himself of his author's
style and brilliant ease of argument? These passages were indubitably
the genuine sentiments of that great writer. In his epistle to Maffei,
prefixed to his *Merope*,[4] he delivers almost the same opinion, though I
doubt with a little irony. I will repeat his words, and then give my
reason for quoting them. After translating a passage in Maffei's *Merope*,
monsieur de Voltaire adds, '*Tous ces traits sont naïfs: tout y est convenable
à ceux que vous introduisez sur la scene, et aux mœurs que vous leur
donnez. Ces familiarités naturelles eussent été, à ce que je crois, bien recues
dans Athenes; mais Paris et notre parterre veulent une autre espece de
simplicité.*'[5] I doubt, I say, whether there is not a grain of sneer in this
and other passages of that epistle; yet the force of truth is not damaged
by being tinged with ridicule. Maffei was to represent a Grecian story:
surely the Athenians were as competent judges of Grecian manners,
and of the propriety of introducing them, as the parterre of Paris. On
the contrary, says Voltaire (and I cannot but admire his reasoning) there
were but ten thousand citizens at Athens, and Paris has near eight
hundred thousand inhabitants, among whom one may reckon thirty
thousand judges of dramatic works.—Indeed!—But allowing so
numerous a tribunal, I believe this is the only instance in which it was
ever pretended that thirty thousand persons, living near two thousand
years after the æra in question, were, upon the mere face of the poll,
declared better judges than the Grecians themselves of what ought to
be the manners of a tragedy written on a Grecian story.

I will not enter into a discussion of the *espece de simplicité*, which the
parterre of Paris demands, nor of the shackles with which *the thirty
thousand judges* have cramped their poetry, the chief merit of which, as

I gather from repeated passages in *The New Commentary* on Corneille,[6] consists in vaulting in spite of those fetters; a merit which, if true, would reduce poetry from the lofty effort of imagination, to a puerile and most contemptible labour—*difficiles nugæ*[7] with a witness! I cannot help however mentioning a couplet, which to my English ears always sounded as the flattest and most trifling instance of circumstantial propriety; but which Voltaire, who has dealt so severely with nine parts in ten of Corneille's works, has singled out to defend in Racine;[8]

> *De son appartement cette porte est prochaine,*
> *Et cette autre conduit dans celui de la reine.*

In English,
> To Cæsar's *closet through this door you come,*
> *And t'other leads to the queen's drawing-room.*

Unhappy Shakespeare! hadst thou made Rosencrans inform his compeer Guildenstern of the ichnography of the palace of Copenhagen, instead of presenting us with a moral dialogue between the prince of Denmark and the grave-digger, the illuminated pit of Paris would have been instructed a *second time* to adore thy talents.

The result of all I have said is to shelter my own daring under the cannon of the brightest genius this country, at least, has produced. I might have pleaded, that having created a new species of romance, I was at liberty to lay down what rules I thought fit for the conduct of it: but I should be more proud of having imitated, however faintly, weakly, and at a distance, so masterly a pattern, than to enjoy the entire merit of invention, unless I could have marked my work with genius as well as with originality. Such as it is, the public have honoured it sufficiently, whatever rank their suffrages allot to it.

From *Dissertation on the Idea of Universal Poetry*, 1766

by RICHARD HURD

Richard Hurd (1720–1808), Bishop of Worcester, also wrote *Critical Dissertations* (1753), a *Commentary* on Horace (1753), *Moral and Political Dialogues* (1759), *Letters on Chivalry and Romance* (1762), and a *Commentary* on Addison (1811, posthumously published). The extremely conservative argument reproduced below (a digression from his main discourse) is in striking contrast to the attitude he showed in *Letters on Chivalry and Romance*, where he attempted a reassessment of romance from a more liberal standpoint and attacked narrowly neo-classic criticism.

These reflexions[1] will afford a proper solution of that question, which has been agitated by the critics, 'Whether a work of fiction and imagination (such as that of the archbishop of Cambray,[2] for instance) conducted, in other respects, according to the rules of the epic poem, but written in prose, may deserve the name of POEM, or not.' For, though it be frivolous indeed to dispute about names, yet from what has been said it appears, that if metre be not incongruous to the nature of an epic composition, and it afford a pleasure which is not to be found in mere prose, metre is, for that reason, essential to this mode of writing; which is only saying in other words, that an epic composition, to give all the pleasure which it is capable of giving, must be written in *verse*.

But, secondly, this conclusion, I think, extends farther than to such works as aspire to the name of *epic*. For instance, what are we to think of those *novels* or *romances*, as they are called, that is, fables constructed on some private and familiar subject, which have been so current, of late, through all Europe? As they propose pleasure for their end, and prosecute it, besides, in the way of *fiction*, though without metrical numbers, and generally, indeed, in harsh and rugged prose, one easily sees what their pretensions are, and under what idea they are ambitious to be received. Yet, as they are wholly destitute of measured sounds (to say nothing of their other numberless defects) they can, at most, be considered but as hasty, imperfect, and abortive poems; whether spawned from the dramatic, or narrative species, it may be hard to say—

> Unfinish'd things, one knows not what to call,
> Their generation's so equivocal.[3]

However, such as they are, these *novelties* have been generally well received: *Some*, for the real merit of their execution; *Others*, for their amusing subjects; *All* of them, for the gratification they afford, or promise at least, to a vitiated, palled, and sickly imagination—that last disease of learned minds, and sure prognostic of expiring Letters. But whatever may be the temporary success of these things (for they vanish as fast as they are produced, and are produced as soon as they are conceived) good sense will acknowledge no work of art but such as is composed according to the laws of its *kind*. These KINDS, as arbitrary things as we account them (for I neither forget nor dispute what our best philosophy teaches concerning *kinds* and *sorts*), have yet so far their foundation in nature and the reason of things, that it will not be allowed us to multiply, or vary them, at pleasure. We may, indeed, mix and confound them, if we will (for there is a sort of literary luxury, which would engross all pleasures at once, even such as are contradictory to each other), or, in our rage for incessant gratification, we may take up with half-formed pleasures, such as come first to hand, and may be administered by any body: But true taste requires chaste, severe, and simple pleasures; and true genius will only be concerned in administering such.

65 From the *Gentleman's Magazine,* XXXVII, December 1767

by T. ROW

The following passage is a letter addressed to Sylvanus Urban, the name under which Edward Cave conducted the *Gentleman's Magazine*. T. Row has not been identified; the surname may be abbreviated.

Mr. URBAN,

It must be a matter of real concern to all considerate minds, to see the youth of both sexes passing so large a part of their time in reading that deluge of familiar romances, which, in this age, our island overflows with. 'Tis not only a most unprofitable way of spending time, but extremely prejudicial to their morals, many a young person being entirely corrupted by the giddy and fantastical notions of love and gallantry, imbibed from thence. There is scarce a month passes, but some worthless book of this kind, in order to catch curiosity by its novelty, appears in the form of two volumes 12mo. price five or six shillings, and they are chiefly the offspring, as I take it, of the managers of the circulating libraries, or their venal authors. Some few of them, indeed, have come from better pens, but the whole together are an horrible mass of hurtful insignificance, and, I suppose, may amount now to above an hundred volumes; I speak at the lowest.

The author of *Polly Honeycomb* made a commendable attempt to stop the progress of this growing evil,[1] and parents might learn, if they pleased, to debar their children the use of such pernicious books, from thence. But young gentlemen and ladies of seventeen, are not always under the command of parents, in regard to their private amusements; something further, therefore, should be tried, and one can think of no method so plausible for restraining the mischief, as by driving these books out of their minds, and out of their way, by turning their thoughts into another channel, and introducing a more harmless, and a more beneficial species of reading. I would propose then, that, for this purpose, some friend of yours should oblige young people with a set of books of the following kinds.

1. Portions of history in general, which should contain the most entertaining and instructive passages from authors of all nations. These should be well chosen, and given in the words of the several writers, to make them the more authentic; and where the narrative happens to be too diffuse for the purpose, it might be abridged, so that the collection should not exceed two or three volumes.

2. Portions of *English* history, which in the like number of volumes, might include all the remarkable stories and revolutions comprized in our history, from the *Norman* conquest to the present time; each story to be taken from that author who has treated it most accurately, and given in his own words as far as conveniently could be done.

3. Portions of natural history. In these volumes scenes equally amusing and instructive should be opened to their juvenile minds, and often with proper and suitable reflections. This part of the work would be extremely easy, in the conduct of it, on account of the numerous productions already extant upon the subject.

The design would extend, in the whole, to about nine volumes; and the chief thing required in the editor, would be a little previous thought and recollection in selecting with judgment the proper passages from the various authors, and prefixing (for that I think should be done) a previous account of the author whence the article or the story is taken; as likewise, in case it should be an historical article, to give a short state of affairs as they then stood in the country where the event to be related happened, together with the character of the principal actors, for the sake of making the article the more intelligible to the reader.

Yours, &c.

T. Row.

66 From the *Gentleman's Magazine*, XL, October 1770

The Characters of Prevot, Le Sage, Richardson, Fielding, and Rousseau. From the French of *La Jolie Femme*; *or, La Femme du Jour*: An entertaining Novel, published at Lyons, 1769. pp. 366. in 12mo.[1]

The *Memoirs of a Man of Quality*,[2] *Cleveland, and the Dean of Coleraine*, [*by the Abbé Prevot*,] present us with a number of strong and interesting situations. If the artifice is not so profound as to deprive us of every idea of fiction, the Author is so ingenious as to oblige us to be accessary to it. All the sentiments which he conveys spring from a heart so fertile, so sensible, so honest, that we listen to him as to a friend who relates to us misfortunes which he has suffered. It is a beautiful river, vast and majestic, which sometimes overflows, but which carries you away with it, and makes you go much farther than you intended. Add, that the charm of good manners breathes through his writings, and that the gloom which prevails there, causes a pleasing melancholy, and not a heart-rending grief. He who has not bathed with tears *Manon Lescaut*[3] ought to forswear every sentimental work.

Sage, the parent of *Gil Blas*, was a half Moliere, and abounds with salt, wit, and gaiety. What rectitude of mind appears in his *Lame Devil*.[4] How do I love that Prelate with his Homilies! What truth, what facility in his pencil? What a model should he be for so many persons, who think themselves Philosophers, yet have only a dry and frigid style! They are not sufficiently acquainted with this amiable and easy Author, who might serve for the pattern of a pure diction, at the same time that his sallies present uncommon fire and graces.

The works of *Richardson* are dear to me; I know none in which genius is more discernible. The illusion is lasting, and complete: What art must he have had to produce it! When I read *Clarissa*, I am of the family of the Harlowes. I am interested for one, I hate another, I am indifferent for a third. By turns, I could embrace and fight with Lovelace. His pride, his gaiety, his drollery charm and amuse me: his genius confounds me, and makes me smile; his wickedness astonishes and enrages me; but at the same time, I admire as much as I detest him; he is the Cromwell[5] of women. I interrupt the unhappy Clarissa, in order to mix my tears with hers: I accost her, as if she was present with me. No Author, I believe, ever metamorphosed himself into his characters so perfectly as Richardson; we forget, we no longer see, the hand which puts so many secret springs in motion; sometimes we are tempted to suspect that the letters were intercepted. If you add to so many perfections those excellent morals diffused through all the work, that soul of virtue and sensibility which animates whatever it touches, you must confess that to exhibit such pictures is to be a benefactor to mankind: Above all, *Grandison* is the book which most inspires virtue, Plutarch and Plato not excepted.

Fielding may justly be styled his rival. No man in the world (without excepting Moliere) was better acquainted with the shades which diversify characters; and he is the Author who has best seized the manners of the people, though it is said that they generally form the nation. A living picture animated with its caprices, its passions, its follies; a true, singular pencil; a simple, lively moral, which naturally results from various scenes; all this insures to Fielding a distinguished place among those Writers whose fertile imagination has drawn Nature as she really is. Less sublime, less pathetic than Richardson, but more chearful, more original,[6] he engages us as much as the other makes us weep. If the one has opened all the treasures of morality, the other, with a wise œconomy, has insinuated it with an imperceptible art into the soul of those who would not receive it. The one paints with large strokes, attracts the heart on every side, and imperiously hurries it away; the other, by varied, chosen, delicate touches, brings smiles on the lips, and tears into the eyes. Indeed he soon dries them; but this transition is so managed as not to be abrupt. His style has the same effect as that ancient music, whose art made the soul pass gently, or, as it were, insensibly, from joy to sorrow; thus producing various and even opposite emotions. In short, Richardson is more grand, more formed on models which will live throughout all ages; the other is more simple, more instructive,[7] and his admirers being less idolatrous, he will have, perhaps, a still greater number of readers.

Rousseau (in his *New Eloise*,) inspires every virtue; the human soul is there seen in all its shapes. For my part, I wish, that as soon as the heart is formed, it might be filled with this moral work. We, the rest of the French, commit faults, as the Author judiciously remarks, through a certain levity which allows our sentiments no depth. All, with us, is superficial; we are more prone to libertinism than to love. This book is certainly the best corrective that can be employed; it seems to detach the soul from mean and earthly passions, to raise it to the pure and sacred transports of real love. How has he drawn it fruitful in virtue, in heroic sacrifices, in pure pleasures! How does he inspire the charm of good manners, and that sensibility which does wonders, and enlivens whatever it surrounds. The Author, I think, has some reason to say that he should not esteem the man, who, after having read, should despise, his work:[8] This is not an effusion of pride; it is the firm conviction which he has that the moral there inculcated may and ought to be useful to his age. I regard this Writer as him who, perhaps, has displayed, in our language, the most genius, and I mean by that word, the art of imprinting on our souls strong, fertile, striking, and new ideas. There are Writers who have the talent of destroying, but who know not how to build. I prefer this Author, who leads me to virtue, who paints it, who makes it amiable to me, who gives me a support, and who, instead of driving me into despair, makes me honour the name of *man*, and teaches me at all times to respect it.

67 From *Something New*, 1772

by AUTOMATHES

The passage reproduced below is Chapter XXVIII, entitled
'Novels'. Automathes was Richard Griffiths (1714?-88), who
also wrote *The Triumvirate*, a novel which he praises from behind
the pseudonym.

But read I must, at any rate, and having, in the last Chapter, taken
leave of learning,[1] I seek in books for amusement, only. I imagined,
therefore, that Novels might fully answer this purpose, as fancy is here
free to indulge its wantonness, unrestrained by the prudery or pedantry
of schools, and unfettered by the methodism of system.

In this species of writing, one might expect to meet with the
world, either as it is, or else as it should be. Here characters might be
assemblaged, in order to be contrasted, or compared. Action is un-
controlled, because the writer is master of his own incidents and events.
Here passions may be refined, pointed to their proper objects, and
produce their warrantable, or admonitory effects.

For in passion are sown the seeds of all our virtues, which bear fruit,
according to their culture. Ambition may be restrained to emulation,
avarice rendered œconomy, extravagance exercised in benevolence,
and courage exerted in the vindication of our honour, or the defence
of our country, only. They are but bad philosophers who mistake
fierceness for spirit, and insensibility for bravery.

But I have been generally most miserably disappointed, in all these
hopeful expectations. These writings have little of character, and less
of moral, among them. Amour is the only subject of all our Novelists.
I wish it was somewhat more refined, than we usually find it to be, for
the sake of my fair readers, at least.

But the love we mostly meet with, in such *Circulating Library books*,
is devoid of *passion*; has more of *sensation*, than *sentiment*, in it. More
desire, than *wish*. Were brutes but suddenly gifted with speech and
reason, they would express their *instinct*, in the very stile of modern
Novelists.

Not that I would not permit a proper scope to passion. I am fond of it, on this side vice. I am far from recommending a stoical apathy, to mankind. I know some called good characters, of this sort, that I detest. Which have all the virtues of *philosophy* in them, but want those of *nature*. Where the merits keep their proud throne in the *mind*, without ever sinking into the *heart*. Maintenon[2] was one of these *ready cut and dry* saints. 'One whose blood was very *snow-broth*.'[3] Such persons may be said, in the University phrase, to be *well read in humanity*; and can discourse of the feelings of the heart, with the same skill, and coolness, as a Fencing master does of *passes*.

In my opinion, Tom Jones, and Charles Carewe,[4] are worth a dozen Sir Charles Grandisons; and I have always preferred Lady Townley, to Lady Grace. The latter, perhaps, might not have erred; but if she had, would probably never have reclaimed. There are some sort of people who are not to be *trusted with frailties*.

Such *virtuosos* in morals may be compared to a tilled soil, in a cold climate, where the fruits sown never ripen; presenting you with the *species*, only, but without the *specifics*, of their several kinds. *The outward and visible sign, but not the inward and Spiritual Grace*, of virtue.

68 From a review of *De l'Homme, et de la Femme, considerés physiquement dans l'état du Marriage* (1772), *The Monthly Review*, XLVIII, July 1773

According to the heading of the review, this book was by 'M. d. L . . ., Chirugien'. The review was by William Woodfall.

[. . . . .]

The second volume opens with a long and zealous chapter on marriage.

The Author then enumerates the several sorts of people who are blameable in respect of their celibacy; and we think that what follows is one of the most striking passages in the whole work.

'After the class of literary men, most of whom avoid marriage, there is a more considerable one, which is seldom thought of, and which is more injurious to population; I mean that class of persons whose ardent imagination excites them to devote all their time to reading. It is probable, says M. Tissot,[1] that of all the causes which have injured the health of women, the principal has been the prodigious multiplication of romances within the last century. From the cradle to the most advanced age, they read with an eagerness which keeps them almost without motion, and without sleep. A young girl, instead of running about and playing, *reads*, perpetually reads; and at twenty, becomes full of vapours, instead of being qualified for the duties of a good wife, or nurse. These causes, which influence the physical, equally influence the moral man. I have known persons of both sexes, whose constitutions would have been robust, weakened gradually by the too strong impressions of impassioned writings. The most tender romances hinder marriages instead of promoting them. A woman, while her heart is warmed by the languors of love, does not seek a *husband*; a HERO must lay his laurels at her feet. The fire of love does not warm her heart; it only *enflames* her *imagination*.'

[. . . . .]

69 Three essays from *Miscellaneous Pieces in Prose and Verse*, 1773

by J. AND A. L. AIKIN

J. and A. L. Aikin were brother and sister. John (1747–1822), doctor of medicine, was author of *Essays on Song-writing* (1772), *An Essay on the Application of Natural History to Poetry* (1777) and *Essays Literary and Miscellaneous* (1811). Anna Laetitia (1743–1825), is better known under her married name of Barbauld; she wrote various poems and miscellaneous essays, edited a collection of the *British Novelists* (1810) and the *Correspondence of Richardson* (1804). To the *British Novelists* (fifty volumes) she prefixed a long essay on the novel which influenced the criticism of Sir Walter Scott. The essays reproduced below (the latter two only in part), are: (*a*) *On Romances, An Imitation;* (*b*) *On the Pleasure Derived from Objects of Terror;* (*c*) *An Enquiry into Those Kinds of Distress which excite Agreeable Sensations.* Of (*a*) Samuel Johnson said that it was the best imitation of his style that had been written, because it, '. . . imitated the sentiment as well as the diction' (see *Boswell's Life . . .,* III, 172). (*b*) was originally followed by a short, unfinished Gothic tale by Mrs. Barbauld, entitled *Sir Bertrand, a Fragment,* which was many times re-printed during the eighteenth century and had great influence on the increase of interest in the Gothic romance.

(*a*)

Of all the multifarious productions which the efforts of superior genius, or the labours of scholastic industry, have crowded upon the world, none are perused with more insatiable avidity, or disseminated with more universal applause, than the narrations of feigned events, descriptions of imaginary scenes, and delineations of ideal characters. The celebrity of other authors is confined within very narrow limits. The Geometrician and Divine, the Antiquary and Critic, however distinguished by uncontested excellence, can only hope to please those whom a conformity of disposition has engaged in similar pursuits; and must be content to be regarded by the rest of the world with the smile of frigid indifference, or the contemptuous sneer of self-sufficient folly. The collector of shells and the anatomist of insects is little inclined to enter into theological disputes: the Divine is not apt to regard with veneration the uncouth diagrams and tedious calculations of the Astronomer: the man whose life has been consumed in adjusting the disputes of lexicographers, or elucidating the learning of antiquity, cannot easily bend his thoughts to recent transactions, or readily interest himself in the unimportant history of his contemporaries: and the Cit, who knows no business but acquiring wealth, and no pleasure but displaying it, has a heart equally shut up to argument and fancy, to the batteries of syllogism, and the arrows of wit. To the writer of fiction alone, every ear is open, and every tongue lavish of applause; curiosity sparkles in every eye, and every bosom is throbbing with concern.

It is however easy to account for this enchantment. To follow the chain of perplexed ratiocination, to view with critical skill the airy architecture of systems, to unravel the web of sophistry, or weigh the merits of opposite hypotheses, requires perspicacity, and presupposes learning. Works of this kind, therefore, are not so well adapted to the generality of readers as familiar and colloquial composition; for few can reason, but all can feel, and many who cannot enter into an argument, may yet listen to a tale. The writer of Romance has even an advantage over those who endeavour to amuse by the play of fancy; who from the fortuitous collision of dissimilar ideas produce the scintillations of wit; or by the vivid glow of poetical imagery delight the imagination with colours of ideal radiance. The attraction of the magnet is only exerted upon similar particles; and to taste the beauties of Homer it is requisite to partake his fire: but every one can relish the author who represents common life, because every one can refer to the originals from whence his ideas were taken. He relates events to which all are liable, and applies to passions which all have felt. The gloom of solitude, the languor of inaction, the corrosions of disappointment, and the toil of thought, induce men to step aside from the rugged road of life, and wander in the fairy land of fiction; where every bank is sprinkled with flowers, and every gale loaded with perfume; where every event introduces a hero, and every cottage is inhabited by a Grace. Invited by these flattering scenes, the student quits the investigation of truth, in which he perhaps meets with no less fallacy, to exhilerate his mind with new ideas, more agreeable, and more easily attained: the busy relax their attention by desultory reading, and smooth the agitation of a ruffled mind with images of peace, tranquility, and pleasure: the idle and the gay relieve the listlessness of leisure, and diversify the round of life by a rapid series of events pregnant with rapture and astonishment; and the pensive solitary fills up the vacuities of his heart by interesting himself in the fortunes of imaginary beings, and forming connections with ideal excellence.

It is, indeed, no ways extraordinary that the mind should be charmed by fancy, and attracted by pleasure; but that we should listen to the groans of misery, and delight to view the exacerbations of complicated anguish, that we should chuse to chill the bosom with imaginary fears, and dim the eyes with fictitious sorrow, seems a kind of paradox of the heart, and only to be credited because it is universally felt. Various are the hypotheses which have been formed to account for the disposition of the mind to riot in this species of intellectual luxury. Some have imagined that we are induced to acquiesce with greater patience in our own lot, by beholding pictures of life tinged with deeper horrors, and loaded with more excruciating calamities; as, to a person suddenly emerging out of a dark room, the faintest glimmering of twilight assumes a lustre from the contrasted gloom. Others, with yet deeper refinement, suppose that we take upon ourselves this burden of adscititious[1] sorrows in order to feast upon the consciousness of our own virtue. We commiserate others (say they) that we may applaud ourselves; and the sigh of compassionate sympathy is always followed by the gratulations of self-complacent esteem. But surely they who would thus reduce the sympathetic emotions of pity to a system of refined selfishness, have but ill attended to the genuine feelings of humanity. It would however exceed the limits of this paper, should I attempt an accurate investigation of these sentiments. But let it be remembered, that we are more attracted by those scenes which interest our passions, or gratify our curiosity, than those which delight our fancy: and so far from being indifferent to the miseries of others, we are, at the time, totally regardless of our own. And let not those, on whom the hand of time has impressed the characters of oracular wisdom, censure with too much acrimony productions which are thus calculated to please the imagination, and interest the heart. They teach us to think, by inuring us to feel: they ventilate the mind by sudden gusts of passion; and prevent the stagnation of thought, by a fresh infusion of dissimilar ideas.

(*b*)

That the exercise of our benevolent feelings, as called forth by the view of human afflictions, should be a source of pleasure, cannot appear wonderful to one who considers that relation between the moral and natural system of man, which has connected a degree of satisfaction with every action or emotion productive of the general welfare. The painful sensation immediately arising from a scene of misery, is so much softened and alleviated by the reflex sense of self-approbation attending virtuous sympathy, that we find, on the whole, a very exquisite and refined pleasure remaining, which makes us desirous of again being witnesses to such scenes, instead of flying from them with disgust and horror. It is obvious how greatly such a provision must conduce to the ends of mutual support and assistance. But the apparent delight with which we dwell upon objects of pure terror, where our moral feelings are not in the least concerned, and no passion seems to be excited but the depressing one of fear, is a paradox of the heart, much more difficult of solution.

The reality of this source of pleasure seems evident from daily observation. The greediness with which the tales of ghosts and goblins, of murders, earthquakes, fires, shipwrecks, and all the most terrible disasters attending human life, are devoured by every ear, must have been generally remarked. Tragedy, the most favourite work of fiction, has taken a full share of those scenes; 'it has supt full with horrors'[1]— and has, perhaps, been more indebted to them for public admiration than to its tender and pathetic parts. The ghost of Hamlet, Macbeth descending into the witches' cave, and the tent scene in *Richard* [*III*], command as forcibly the attention of our souls as the parting of Jaffeir and Belvidera, the fall of Wolsey, or the death of Shore.[2] The inspiration of *terror* was by the antient critics assigned as the peculiar province of tragedy; and the Greek and Roman tragedians have introduce[d] some extraordinary personages for this purpose: not only the shades of the dead, but the furies, and other fabulous inhabitants of the infernal regions. Collins, in his most poetical ode to Fear, has finely enforced this idea.

> Tho' gentle Pity claim her mingled part,
>   Yet all the thunders of the scene are thine.[3]

The old Gothic romance and the Eastern tale, with their genii, giants, enchantments, and transformations, however a refined critic may censure them as absurd and extravagant, will ever retain a most powerful influence on the mind, and interest the reader independently of all peculiarity of taste. Thus the great Milton, who had a strong biass to these wildnesses of the imagination, has with striking effect made the stories 'of forests and enchantments drear',[4] a favourite subject with his *Penseroso*; and had undoubtedly their awakening images strong upon his mind when he breaks out,

> Call up him that left half-told
> The story of Cambuscan bold; &c.[5]

How are we then to account for the pleasure derived from such objects? I have often been led to imagine that there is a deception in these cases; and that the avidity with which we attend is not a proof of our receiving real pleasure. The pain of suspense, and the irresistible desire of satisfying curiosity, when once raised, will account for our eagerness to go quite through an adventure, though we suffer actual pain during the whole course of it. We rather chuse to suffer the smart pang of a violent emotion than the uneasy craving of an unsatisfied desire. That this principle, in many instances, may involuntarily carry us through what we dislike, I am convinced from experience. This is the impulse which renders the poorest and most insipid narrative interesting when once we get fairly into it; and I have frequently felt it with regard to our modern novels, which, if lying on my table, and taken up in an idle hour, have led me through the most tedious and disgusting pages, while, like Pistol eating his leek,[6] I have swallowed and execrated to the end. And it will not only force us through dullness, but through actual torture—through the relation of a Damien's execution,[7] or an inquisitor's act of faith. When children, therefore, listen with pale and mute attention to the frightful stories of apparitions, we are not, perhaps, to imagine that they are in a state of enjoyment, any more than the poor bird which is dropping into the mouth of the rattlesnake—they are chained by the ears, and fascinated by curiosity. This solution, however, does not satisfy me with respect to the well-wrought scenes of artificial terror which are formed by a sublime and vigorous imagination. Here, though we know before-hand what to expect, we enter into them with eagerness, in quest of a pleasure already experienced. This is the pleasure constantly attached to the excitement of surprise from new and wonderful objects. A strange and unexpected event awakens the mind, and keeps it on the stretch; and where the agency of invisible beings is introduced, of 'forms unseen, and mightier far than we',[8] our imagination, darting forth, explores with rapture the new world which is laid open to its view, and rejoices in the expansion of its powers. Passion and fancy co-operating elevate the soul to its highest pitch; and the pain of terror is lost in amazement.

Hence, the more wild, fanciful, and extraordinary are the circumstances of a scene of horror, the more pleasure we receive from it; and where they are too near common nature, though violently borne by curiosity through the adventure, we cannot repeat it or reflect on it, without an over-balance of pain. In the *Arabian nights* are many most striking examples of the terrible joined with the marvellous: the story of Aladdin and the travels of Sinbad are particularly excellent. The *Castle of Otranto* is a very spirited modern attempt upon the same plan of mixed terror, adapted to the model of Gothic romance. The best conceived, and most strongly worked-up scene of mere natural horror that I recollect, is in Smollett's *Ferdinand count Fathom*; where the hero, entertained in a lone house in a forest, finds a corpse just slaughtered in the room where he is sent to sleep, and the door of which is locked upon him.[9] It may be amusing for the reader to compare his feelings upon these, and from thence form his opinion of the justness of my theory. The following fragment, in which both these manners are attempted to be in some degree united, is offered to entertain a solitary winter's evening.

(c)

[. . . . .]
A judicious author will never attempt to raise pity by any thing mean or disgusting. As we have already observed, there must be a degree of complacence mixed with our sorrows to produce an agreeable sympathy; nothing, therefore, must be admitted which destroys the grace and dignity of suffering; the imagination must have an amiable figure to dwell upon; there are circumstances so ludicrous or disgusting, that no character can preserve a proper decorum under them, or appear in an agreeable light. Who can read the following description of Polypheme without finding his compassion entirely destroyed by aversion and loathing?

> ———— His bloody hand
> Snatch'd two unhappy of my martial band,
> And dash'd like dogs against the stony floor,
> The pavement swims with brains and mingled gore;

> Torn limb from limb he spreads his horrid feast,
> And fierce devours it like a mountain beast,
> He sucks the marrow and the blood he drains,
> Nor entrails, flesh, nor solid bone remains.

Or that of Scylla,

> In the wide dungeon she devours her food,
> And the flesh trembles while she churns the blood.[1]

Deformity is always disgusting, and the imagination cannot reconcile it with the idea of a favourite character; therefore the poet and romance-writer are fully justified in giving a larger share of beauty to their principal figures than is usually met with in common life. A late genius indeed, in a whimsical mood, gave us a lady with her nose crushed for the heroine of his story;[2] but the circumstance spoils the picture; and though in the course of the story it is kept a good deal out of sight, whenever it does recur to the imagination we are hurt and disgusted. It was an heroic instance of virtue in the nuns of a certain abbey, who cut off their noses and lips to avoid violation; yet this would make a very bad subject for a poem or a play. Something akin to this is the representation of any thing unnatural; of which kind is the famous story of the Roman charity,[3] and for this reason I cannot but think it an unpleasing subject for either the pen or the pencil.

Poverty, if truly represented, shocks our nicer feelings; therefore whenever it is made use of to awaken our compassion, the rags and dirt, the squalid appearance and mean employments incident to that state must be kept out of sight, and the distress must arise from the idea of depression, and the shock of falling from higher fortunes. We do not pity Belisarius as a poor blind beggar;[4] and a painter would succeed very ill who should sink him to the meanness of that condition. He must let us still discover the conqueror of the Vandals, the general of the imperial armies, or we shall be little interested. Let us look at the picture of the old woman in Otway:

> ———— A wrinkled hag with age grown double,
> Picking dry sticks, and muttering to herself;
> Her eyes with scalding rheum were gall'd and red;
> Cold palsie shook her head; her hands seem'd wither'd;
> And on her crooked shoulder had she wrapt
> The tatter'd remnant of an old strip'd hanging,
> Which serv'd to keep her carcase from the cold;
> So there was nothing of a piece about her.[5]

Here is the extreme of wretchedness, and instead of melting into pity we turn away with aversion. Indeed the author only intended it to strike horror. But how different are the sentiments we feel for the lovely Belvidera![6] We see none of those circumstances which render poverty an unamiable thing. When the goods are seized by an execution, our attention is turned to *the piles of massy plate, and all the antient most domestic ornaments,*[7] which imply grandeur and consequence; or to such instances of their hard fortune as will lead us to pity them as lovers: we are struck and affected with the general face of ruin, but we are not brought near enough to discern the ugliness of its features. Belvidera ruined, Belvidera deprived of friends, without a home, abandoned to the wide world—we can contemplate with all the pleasing sympathy of pity; but had she been represented as really sunk into low life, had we seen her employed in the most servile offices of poverty, our compassion would have given way to contempt and disgust. Indeed, we may observe in real life that poverty is only pitied so long as people can keep themselves from the effects of it. When in common language we say *a miserable object*, we mean an object of distress which, if we relieve, we turn away from at the same time. To make pity pleasing, the object of it must not in any view be disagreeable to the imagination. How admirably has the author of *Clarissa* managed this point? Amidst scenes of suffering which rend the heart, in poverty, in a prison, under the most shocking outrages, the grace and delicacy of her character never suffers even for a moment: there seems to be a charm about her which prevents her receiving a stain from any thing which happens; and Clarissa, abandoned and undone, is the object not only of complacence but veneration.

I would likewise observe, that if an author would have us feel a strong degree of compassion, his characters must not be too perfect. The stern fortitude and inflexible resolution of a Cato[8] may command esteem, but does not excite tenderness; and faultless rectitude of conduct, though no rigour be mixed with it, is of too sublime a nature to inspire compassion. Virtue has a kind of self-sufficiency; it stands upon its own basis, and cannot be injured by any violence. It must therefore be mixed with something of helplessness and imperfection, with an excessive sensibility, or a simplicity bordering upon weakness, before it raises, in any great degree, either tenderness or familiar love. If there be a fault in the masterly performance just now mentioned, it is that the character of Clarissa is so inflexibly right, her passions are under such perfect command, and her prudence is so equal to every occasion, that she seems not to need that sympathy we should bestow upon one of a less elevated character: and perhaps we should feel a livelier emotion of tenderness for Lovelace's Rose-bud, but that the story of Clarissa is so worked up by the strength of colouring and the force of repeated impressions, as to command all our sorrow.

Pity seems too degrading a sentiment to be offered at the shrine of faultless excellence. The sufferings of martyrs are rather beheld with admiration and sympathetic triumph than with tears; and we never feel much for those whom we consider as themselves raised above common feelings.

The last rule I shall insist upon is, that scenes of distress should not be too long continued. All our finer feelings are in a manner momentary, and no art can carry them beyond a certain point, either in intenseness or duration. Constant suffering deadens the heart to tender impressions; as we may observe in sailors, and others who are grown callous by a life of continual hardships. It is therefore highly necessary in a long work to relieve the mind by scenes of pleasure and gaiety: and I cannot think it so absurd a practice as our modern delicacy has represented it, to intermix wit and fancy with the pathetic, provided care be taken not to check the passions while they are flowing. The transition from a pleasurable state of mind to tender sorrow is not so difficult as we imagine. When the mind is opened by gay and agreeable scenes, every impression is felt more sensibly. Persons of a lively temper are much more susceptible of that sudden swell of sensibility which occasions tears, than those of a grave and saturnine cast: for this reason women are more easily moved to weeping than men. Those who have touched the springs of pity with the finest hand have mingled light strokes of pleasantry and mirth in their most pathetic passages. Very different is the conduct of many novel writers, who by plunging us into scenes of distress without end or limit, exhaust the powers, and before the conclusion either render us insensible to every thing, or fix a real sadness upon the mind. The uniform stile of tragedies is one reason why they affect so little. In our old plays all the force of language is reserved for the more interesting parts; and in the scenes of common life there is no attempt to rise above common language: whereas we, by that pompous manner and affected solemnity which we think it necessary to preserve through the whole piece, lose the force of an elevated or passionate expression where the occasion really suggests it.

Having thus considered the manner in which fictitious distress must be managed to render it pleasing, let us reflect a little upon the moral tendency of such representations. Much has been said in favour of them, and they are generally thought to improve the tender and humane feelings; but this, I own, appears to me very dubious. That they exercise sensibility is true, but sensibility does not increase with exercise. By the constitution of our frame our habits increase, our emotions decrease, by repeated acts; and thus a wise provision is made, that as our compassion grows weaker, its place should be supplied by habitual benevolence. But in these writings our sensibility is strongly called forth without any possibility of exerting itself in virtuous action, and those emotions, which we shall never feel again with equal force, are wasted without advantage. Nothing is more dangerous than to let virtuous impressions of any kind pass through the mind without producing their proper effect. The awakenings of remorse, virtuous shame and indignation, the glow of moral approbation, if they do not lead to action, grow less and less vivid every time they recur, till at length the mind grows absolutely callous. The being affected with a pathetic story is undoubtedly a sign of an amiable disposition, but perhaps no means of increasing it. On the contrary, young people, by a course of this kind of reading, often acquire something of that apathy and indifference which the experience of real life would have given them, without its advantages.

Another reason why plays and romances do not improve our humanity is, that they lead us to require a certain elegance of manners and delicacy of virtue which is not often found with poverty, ignorance, and meanness. The objects of pity in romance are as different from those in real life as our husbandmen from the shepherds of Arcadia; and a girl who will sit weeping the whole night at the delicate distresses of a lady Charlotte or lady Julia, shall be little moved at the complaint of her neighbour, who, in a homely phrase and vulgar accent, laments to her that she is not able to get bread for her family. Romance-writers likewise make great misfortunes so familiar to our ears, that we have hardly any pity to spare for the common accidents of life: but we ought to remember, that misery has a claim to relief, however we may be disgusted with its appearance; and that we must not fancy ourselves charitable, when we are only pleasing our imagination.

It would perhaps be better, if our romances were more like those of the old stamp, which tended to raise human nature, and inspire a certain grace and dignity of manners of which we have hardly the idea. The high notions of honour, the wild and fanciful spirit of adventure and romantic love, elevated the mind; our novels tend to depress and enfeeble it. Yet there is a species of this kind of writing which must ever afford an exquisite pleasure to persons of taste and sensibility; where noble sentiments are mixed with well fancied incidents, pathetic touches with dignity and grace, and invention with chaste correctness. Such will ever interest our sweetest passions. I shall conclude this paper with the following tale.[9]

[. . . . .]

70 From Volume III of *The Origin and Progress of Language*, 1776

by JAMES BURNETT, LORD MONBODDO

James Burnett, Lord Monboddo (1714–99), published *The Origin and Progress of Language* in six separate volumes, from 1773 to 1792. The work is remembered because it contains some striking anticipations of later theory concerning evolution and Indo-European, but it might be better known for its incidental but highly intelligent comments on literature. The passages reproduced below are as follows: (*a*) Volume III, Part II, Book IV, chapter x, 'Of the two kinds of composition, figured with respect to the sense, *viz*. by imitation of characters . . .'; (*b*) Volume III, Part II, Book IV, chapter x, 'Wherein are discussed three general characteristics of style—the simple, the highly ornamented and the middle; (*c*) Volume III, Part II, Book IV, chapter xvi, 'Of a fourth general character of style, the sublime . . .'. Volume III was published in 1776.

(*a*)

There is lately sprung up among us a species of narrative poem, representing likewise the characters of common life. It has the same relation to comedy that the epic has to tragedy, and differs from the epic in the same respect that comedy differs from tragedy; that is, in the actions and characters, both which are much nobler in the epic than in it. It is therefore, I think, a legitimate kind of poem; and, accordingly, we are told, Homer wrote one of that kind, called *Margites*, of which some lines are preserved. The reason why I mention it is, that we have, in English, a *poem* of that kind, (for so I will call it) which has more of character in it than any work, antient or modern, that I know. The work I mean is, the *History of Tom Jones*, by Henry Fielding, which, as it has more personages brought into the story than any thing of the poetic kind I have ever seen; so all those personages have characters peculiar to them, in so much, that there is not even an host or an hostess upon the road, hardly a servant, who is not distinguished in that way; in short, I never saw any thing that was so much animated, and, as I may say, *all alive* with characters and manners, as the *History of Tom Jones*.

[. . . . .]

(b)

To distinguish this style from the low and the vulgar, is a matter of pretty nice judgment; for that is the extreme which it borders upon; and we see from Terence's prologue to the *Phormio*, that his pieces were said, by his adversaries, to be written *tenui oratione et scriptura levi*, that is, in a style too simple, and too little raised. But not only the learned critic, but even a man of good natural taste, will perceive the difference. And, however easy it may seem to imitate such a style, any one who tries it will find, that it is true what Horace says,

> *Sudet multum, frustraque laboret*
> *Ausus idem.*[1]

And, indeed, take the style of Terence altogether, the expression of characters and manners in it, as well as the elegance and wonderful simplicity, I do not know but it is more difficult to imitate than even the style of Homer.

The author, in English, that has excelled the most in this style is Dr. Swift, in his *Gulliver's Travels*; of which the narrative is wonderfully plain and simple, minute likewise, and circumstantial, so much, as to be disgusting to a reader without taste or judgment, and the character of an English sailor is finely kept up in it. In short, it has every virtue belonging to this style; and I will venture to say, that those monstrous lies so narrated, have more the air of probability than many a true story unskilfully told. And, accordingly, I have been informed, that they imposed upon many when they were first published. The voyage to Lilliput, in my judgment, is the finest of them all, especially in what relates to the politics of that kingdom, and the state of parties there. The debate in the King's council, concerning Gulliver, is a master-piece; and the original papers it contains, of which he says he was so lucky as to get copies, give it an air of probability that is really wonderful. When we add to all this, the hidden satire which it contains, and the grave ridicule that runs through the whole of it, the most exquisite of all ridicule, I think I do not go too far when I pronounce it the most perfect work of the kind, antient or modern, that is to be found. For, as to Lucian's true history, which is the only antient work of the kind that has come down to us, it has nothing to recommend it, except the imitation of the grave style of the antient historians, such as Herodotus; but it wants the satire and exquisite ridicule that is to be found in the Dean's work.

This plain style is not, as I have observed elsewhere, much used in our prose compositions, and is altogether out of fashion in our verse. But it was not so in the days of Milton, as I have already shewn, by examples from him, and shall shew, by examples from others of our antient poets, when I come to speak of the style of poetry.

(c)

But what shews evidently that the matter is principal in the sublime character of style is this, that, if the matter be low and trivial, and, at the same time, the sentiments heroic with language suitable, then it becomes a species of writing altogether different, and indeed opposite, and which, accordingly, bears the name of *mock-heroic*, or *burlesque*. Of this kind we have an antient poem, by some given to Homer, but, probably, the work of a sophist of later times; I mean the battle of the frogs and mice, in which we have ascribed to those little contemptible animals the sentiments and actions of the heroes of the *Iliad* and *Odyssey*; and the ridicule of the pompous language of tragedy, by making it too pompous, or what we call bombast, was frequent among the poets of the old comedy at Athens.

In modern times, there are many works of this kind, both in prose and verse; but the best of them all, in my judgment, is the *Dunciad* of Mr. Pope, in which, to the ridicule of the mock-heroic, is joined the keenest satire. And though, I believe, most scholars who understand the original are of opinion, that he has not translated Homer well; yet every body, I imagine, will admit that, in the *Dunciad*, he has parodied Virgil exceedingly well; but of this I have said enough elsewhere.[1]

Mr. Fielding, in his comic narrative poem, the history of *Tom Jones*, has mixed with his narrative a good deal of the mock-heroic; and, particularly, there is a description of a squabble in a country church-yard wholly in that style.[2] It is, indeed, an excellent parody of Homer's battles, and is highly ridiculous; but, in my opinion, it is not proper for such a work: *First*, because it is too great a change of style, greater than any work of a legitimate kind, which I think Fielding's is, will admit, from the simple and familiar to the heroic or mock-heroic. It is no better than a patch; and, though it be a shining one, no regular work ought to have any at all. For Horace has very properly given it as a mark of a work irregular, and of ill texture, the having such purple clouts as he calls them;

Late qui splendeat unus et alter
Assuiter pannus.[3]

Ars. Poet.

Secondly, because it destroys the probability of the narrative, which ought to be carefully studied in all works, that, like Mr. Fielding's, are imitations of real life and manners, and which, accordingly, has been very much laboured by that author. It is for the probability of the narrative chiefly that I have so much commended *Gulliver's Travels*. Now, I appeal to every reader, whether such a description in those *Travels*, as that of the battle in the church-yard, would not have intirely destroyed the credibility of them, and prevented their imposing upon any body, as it is said they did at first. This, therefore, I cannot help thinking a blemish, in a work which has otherwise a great deal of merit, and which I should have thought perfect of the kind, if it had not been for this, and another fault that I find to it, namely, the author's appearing too much in it himself, who had nothing to do in it at all.★ By this the reader will understand that I mean his reflections, with which he begins his books, and sometimes his chapters.

And so much for the mock-heroic, or burlesque, which I call a fifth general character of style. ·

[. . . . .]

★ The fable of this piece is, I think, an extraordinary effort both of genius and art; for, though it be very complex, taking in as great a variety of matter as, I believe, any heroic fable, it is so simple as to be easily enough comprehended in one view. And it has this peculiar excellency, that every incident of the almost infinite variety which the author has contrived to introduce into it, contributes, some way or other, to bring on the catastrophe, which is so artfully wrought up, and brought about by a change of fortune, so sudden and surprising, that it gives the reader all the pleasure of a well written tragedy or comedy. And, therefore, as I hold the invention and composition of the fable to be the chief beauty of every poem, I must be of opinion, that Mr. Fielding was one of the greatest poetical geniuses of his age; nor do I think that his work has hitherto met with the praise that it deserves.

71 Preface to *Liberal Opinions*, V, 'In which is continued the History of Benignus . . .', 1777

by SAMUEL JACKSON PRATT

Samuel Pratt (1749–1814) wrote under the pseudonym of Courtney Melmoth. He published several novels and miscellaneous works: *The Tears of Genius* (1774); *The Progress of Poetry* (1775); *Emma Corbett* (1780); *Humanity or the Rights of Nature* (1788); *Family Secrets* (1797; see below, No. 100); and translated *The Sorrows of Werter* in 1809.

The History of Benignus is, in these volumes, brought to such a period as sufficiently enforces the *moral* intended to be deduced from it. The laws of romance, novel, and comedy, might require a different catastrophe: for in those, it is too often the custom, (at *all events*, even though many are brought in, as it were, by *the head and shoulders*) to croud the last scene with persons married or murdered, to the novel reader's satisfaction. But the laws of *narrative* ought to be less rigid, and, I flatter myself, the reader will forgive my adhering, upon this occasion, to *human nature*, even though I verge against the formalities of literary custom.—

The former portions of the work contain many of those dialogues, conversation-pieces, and characters, which fell, necessarily, in the way of our emigrating author in his romantic ramble after *happiness*.

But now, as he advances farther into society, a greater variety of *events* and *opinions*, (some serious, some whimsical, according to the particular temper, mind, and manner of the speaker) present themselves: to which have been generally added, the adventurer's reflections, upon peculiar scenes, as they figured before him.

In the progress of these delineations, the great DESIGN of the Work, hath never been lost sight of: on the contrary, every volume, as it may be noted by the discerning reader, carries the intended illustration nearer to the heart and understanding; till the result of the *whole*, it is hoped, appears to be in full lustre, *what* the author himself, feelingly asserts, it *should* be.

'Unhappy['] (says our disappointed adventurer, in the 110th chapter
of the volumes now offered) [']is he, who, in the days of his youth,
traverses this intricate world, without a guide; and of all other preposterous passions, the most preposterous is *that*, which induces an
orphan of fortune to trust himself to mankind, with neither experience
to direct, prudence to advise, nor œconomy to regulate. Let no man
who is new to the active scenes of a city, ever venture again into a
metropolis, unattended: let no man indulge his inclinations for *travelling*, without first considering that if he is miserable at home, he must
tread warily indeed, if he does not *increase* that misery abroad. Let no
man rush into the tumults of life without a virtuous monitor: in a word,
let every *Telemachus* tremble at the conduct, which is not first sanctified
by the approbation of a *Mentor*!'[1]

This apostrophe hath been *variously* exemplified in the course of the
History; in which, it appears to have been, not the *least* effort of the
author, to analize the real characters of men, to display the strange and
ridiculous inconsistences of human opinion respecting HAPPINESS; and,
(after all this shew off of folly, delusion, and absurdity, under their
characteristic disguises) to fix, by predominant arguments, the *highest*
degree of that happiness, in the practice of Virtue, and in the precepts
of Christianity.

Both the editor and the author have, already, entered a caveat
against being accountable for the vice or depravity of any of the
characters. Who ever thought of charging Shakespeare with immorality,
for having drawn an Jago; Fielding, a Blifil; or Richardson, a Lovelace?

It is certain that, in these closing volumes, some reprehensible
characters, will offer themselves; and, perhaps, some scenes that certain
editors might have rejected. But, I am persuaded, those writers, who
only employ themselves in drawing pictures of Virtue, do her but *half*
justice. The real gem is set off by the foil; the charms of beauty are
heightened by deformity: in like manner the lustre of *virtue* derives
greater brilliancy from being opposed to the squallid appearances of
vice. If the maxim of the poet be indeed true: if,

> Vice is a monster of so frightful mein
> As, to be hated, needs but to be *seen*.[2]

it follows, that to *pourtray* that monster, and to place the portrait, (by
way of *contrast*) near the picture of Virtue, is the most commendable
task in which a moral painter, either serious or comic, can engage.

Aye, (it may be said) but if this monster is so disguised by false colouring, and so tricked out by the hand of the painter, as to attract us under the form of a cherub, and is thereby able to 'make the worse, appear the better reason',[3] may not the danger be excessive? To this I answer, that in the world,—in *real* life—infinite are the dangers produced by this polished, and Belial-like hypocrisy: but, it has been the constant care of this History, to make every contrast *conspicuous*: thus the irregular bounty of BENIGNUS is opposed to the rational sympathy of *Greaves*: the coarseness of the *Grocer*, is held in contrast to the delicacy of *Blewett*: the openness of *Benjamin*, to the artifice of his uncle: the polish of *Draper*, to the queerness of *Green*: the purity of conjugal love, in *Sudberry*, to the illicit engagements of *Benignus*, with *Lucy* and *Blake's* wife; the system of the Freethinker, with the system of the Lady who speaks in the FRAGMENT that will be found in the present volumes.

Thus, even the *careless* reader, may detect the cloven foot, as he goes along; and distinguisheth the painted devil, which, (arrayed only in the ornaments of native innocence) in despite of those plausible affectations that are assumed to make him prosper in society, come to merited shame at last.

Here then the editor thinks it necessary to terminate the History, and to take leave both of his author and the public.

72 From the Preface to *The Old English Baron*, 1778

by CLARA REEVE

As Clara Reeve (1729–1807), explains below, the above title was appended to this novel only in the second edition; the novel first appeared (without this Preface) under the title of *The Champion of Virtue, a Gothic Story*, in 1777. This was not Clara Reeve's first work; she preceded this novel with her translation of John Barclay's Latin romance, *Argenis*, under the title of *The Phoenix* (1772), and followed it with *The Two Mentors* . . . (1783), *The Exiles* . . . (1788) and *The School for Widows* (1791). Clara Reeve also published a work which is of considerable interest for criticism of the novel in the eighteenth century—*The Progress of Romance, Through Times, Countries and Manners; with Remarks on the good and bad effects of it* . . . (1785). There are several reasons why this work is not represented in the present collection: it is cast in the form of a series of conversations between three people and would be difficult to represent by selection; it is not strikingly original in the quality or manner of its critical judgments; and, finally, it has been separately published by the Facsimile Text Society (1930) in an edition which is generally available.

As this Story is of a species which, tho' not new, is out of the common track, it has been thought necessary to point out some circumstances to the reader, which will elucidate the design, and, it is hoped, will induce him to form a favourable, as well as a right judgment of the work before him.

This Story is the literary offspring of the *Castle of Otranto*, written upon the same plan, with a design to unite the most attractive and interesting circumstances of the ancient Romance and modern Novel, at the same time it assumes a character and manner of its own, that differs from both; it is distinguished by the appellation of a Gothic Story, being a picture of Gothic times and manners. Fictitious Stories have been the delight of all times and all countries, by oral tradition in barbarous, by writing in more civilized ones; and altho' some persons of wit and learning have condemned them indiscriminately, I would venture to affirm, that even those who so much affect to despise them under one form, will receive and embrace them under another.

Thus, for instance, a man shall admire and almost adore the Epic poems of the Ancients, and yet despise and execrate the ancient Romances, which are only Epics in prose.

History represents human nature as it is in real life:—alas, too often a melancholy retrospect!—Romance displays only the amiable side of the picture; it shews the pleasing features, and throws a veil over the blemishes: Mankind are naturally pleased with what gratifies their vanity; and vanity, like all other passions of the human heart, may be rendered subservient to good and useful purposes.

I confess that it may be abused, and become an instrument to corrupt the manners and morals of mankind; so may poetry, so may plays, so may every kind of composition; but that will prove nothing more than the old saying lately revived by the philosophers the most in fashion, 'that every earthly thing has two handles.'

The business of Romance is, first, to excite the attention; and, secondly, to direct it to some useful, or at least innocent, end; Happy the writer who attains both these points, like Richardson! and not unfortunate, or undeserving praise, he who gains only the latter, and furnishes out an entertainment for the reader!

Having, in some degree, opened my design, I beg leave to conduct my reader back again, till he comes within view of the *Castle of Otranto*; a work which, as already has been observed, is an attempt to unite the various merits and graces of the ancient Romance and modern Novel. To attain this end, there is required a sufficient degree of the marvellous, to excite the attention; enough of the manners of real life, to give an air of probability to the work; and enough of the pathetic, to engage the heart in its behalf.

The book we have mentioned is excellent in the two last points, but has a redundancy in the first; the opening excites the attention very strongly; the conduct of the story is artful and judicious; the characters are admirably drawn and supported; the diction polished and elegant; yet, with all these brilliant advantages, it palls upon the mind (though it does not upon the ear); and the reason is obvious, the machinery is so violent, that it destroys the effect it is intended to excite. Had the story been kept within the utmost *verge* of probability, the effect had been preserved, without losing the least circumstance that excites or detains the attention.

For instance; we can conceive, and allow of, the appearance of a ghost; we can even dispense with an enchanted sword and helmet; but then they must keep within certain limits of credibility: A sword so large as to require an hundred men to lift it; a helmet that by its own weight forces a passage through a court-yard into an arched vault, big enough for a man to go through; a picture that walks out of its frame; a skeleton ghost in a hermit's cowl:—When your expectation is wound up to the highest pitch, these circumstances take it down with a witness, destroy the work of imagination, and, instead of attention, excite laughter. I was both surprised and vexed to find the enchantment dissolved, which I wished might continue to the end of the book; and several of its readers have confessed the same disappointment to me: The beauties are so numerous, that we cannot bear the defects, but want it to be perfect in all respects.

In the course of my observations upon this singular book, it seemed to me that it was possible to compose a work upon the same plan, wherein these defects might be avoided; and the *keeping*, as in *painting*, might be preserved.

But then I began to fear it might happen to me as to certain translators, and imitators of Shakespeare; the unities may be preserved, while the spirit is evaporated. However, I ventured to attempt it; I read the beginning to a circle of friends of approved judgment, and by their approbation was encouraged to proceed, and to finish it.

By the advice of the same friends I printed the first Edition in the country, where it circulated chiefly, very few copies being sent to London, and being thus encouraged, I have determined to offer a second Edition to that public which has so often rewarded the efforts of those, who have endeavoured to contribute to its entertainment.

The work has lately undergone a revision and correction, the former Edition being very incorrect; and by the earnest solicitation of several friends, for whose judgment I have the greatest deference, I have consented to a change of the title from the *Champion of Virtue* to the *Old English Baron*:—as that character is thought to be the principal one in the story.

[. . . . .]

73 Preface to *Evelina, Or, A Young Lady's Entrance into the World*, 1778

by FRANCES BURNEY

Frances Burney (1752–1840) published only one novel other than *Evelina* . . . under her maiden name—*Cecilia, or Memoirs of an Heiress* (1782). She published her two later novels—*Camilla: Or, a Picture of Youth* (1796) and *The Wanderer: Or, Female Difficulties* (1814)—under her married name of D'Arblay. *Evelina* was enthusiastically received by Burney's contemporaries (including the Johnson circle and the Court of George III), and was widely read for forty years after its publication; *Cecilia* and *Camilla* are referred to in Jane Austen's famous outburst against common cant about novel-reading (*Northanger Abbey*, 1818, chapter v), but the later novels represent a progressive deterioration of the writer's talent.

In the republic of letters, there is no member of such inferior rank, or who is so much disdained by his brethren of the quill, as the humble Novelist; nor is his fate less hard in the world at large, since, among the whole class of writers, perhaps not one can be named of which the votaries are more numerous but less respectable.

Yet, while in the annals of those few of our predecessors, to whom this species of writing is indebted for being saved from contempt, and rescued from depravity, we can trace such names as Rousseau, Johnson,[1] Marivaux, Fielding, Richardson, and Smollett, no man need blush at starting from the same post, though many, nay most men, may sigh at finding themselves distanced.

The following letters are presented to the public—for such, by novel writers, novel readers will be called,—with a very singular mixture of timidity and confidence, resulting from the peculiar situation of the editor; who, though trembling for their success from a consciousness of their imperfections, yet fears not being involved in their disgrace, while happily wrapped up in a mantle of impenetrable obscurity.

To draw characters from nature, though not from life, and to mark the manners of the times, is the attempted plan of the following letters.

For this purpose, a young female, educated in the most secluded retirement, makes, at the age of seventeen, her first appearance upon the great and busy stage of life; with a virtuous mind, a cultivated understanding, and a feeling heart, her ignorance of the forms, and inexperience in the manners, of the world, occasion all the little incidents which this volume records, and which form the natural progression of the life of a young woman of obscure birth, but conspicuous beauty, for the first six months after her ENTRANCE INTO THE WORLD.

Perhaps were it possible to effect the total extirpation of novels, our young ladies in general, and boarding-school damsels in particular, might profit by their annihilation; but since the distemper they have spread seems incurable, since their contagion bids defiance to the medicine of advice or reprehension, and since they are found to baffle all the mental art of physic, save what is prescribed by the slow regimen of Time, and bitter diet of Experience, surely all attempts to contribute to the number of those which may be read, if not with advantage, at least without injury, ought rather to be encouraged than contemned.

Let me, therefore, prepare for disappointment those who, in the perusal of these sheets, entertain the gentle expectation of being transported to the fantastic regions of Romance, where Fiction is coloured by all the gay tints of luxurious Imagination, where Reason is an outcast, and where the sublimity of the Marvellous, rejects all aid from sober Probability. The heroine of these memoirs, young, artless, and inexperienced, is

No faultless Monster, that the world ne'er saw,[2]

but the offspring of Nature, and of Nature in her simplest attire.

In all the Arts, the value of copies can only be proportioned to the scarceness of originals; among sculptors and painters, a fine statue, or a beautiful picture, of some great master, may deservedly employ the imitative talents of younger and inferior artists, that their appropriation to one spot, may not wholly prevent the more general expansion of their excellence; but, among authors, the reverse is the case, since the noblest productions of literature are almost equally attainable with the meanest. In books, therefore, imitation cannot be shunned too sedulously; for the very perfection of a model which is frequently seen, serves but more forcibly to mark the inferiority of a copy.

To avoid what is common, without adopting what is unnatural, must limit the ambition of the vulgar herd of authors; however zealous, therefore, my veneration of the great writers I have mentioned, however I may feel myself enlightened by the knowledge of Johnson, charmed with the eloquence of Rousseau, softened by the pathetic powers of Richardson, and exhilarated by the wit of Fielding, and humour of Smollett; I yet presume not to attempt pursuing the same ground which they have tracked; whence, though they may have cleared the weeds, they have also culled the flowers, and though they have rendered the path plain, they have left it barren.

The candour of my readers, I have not the impertinence to doubt, and to their indulgence, I am sensible I have no claim; I have, therefore, only to entreat, that my own words may not pronounce my condemnation, and that what I have here ventured to say in regard to imitation, may be understood, as it is meant, in a general sense, and not be imputed to an opinion of my own originality, which I have not the vanity, the folly, or the blindness, to entertain.

Whatever may be the fate of these letters, the editor is satisfied they will meet with justice; and commits them to the press, though hopeless of fame, yet not regardless of censure.

74 'On Novel Reading', No. XIV, *Essays Moral and Literary*, 1778

by VICESSIMUS KNOX

The Reverend Vicessimus Knox (1752–1821), master of Tonbridge School, a studious imitator of Johnson's style, also published *Elegant Extracts* (1789) (see also below, No. 83).

If it be true, that the present age is more corrupt than the preceding, the great multiplication of Novels has probably contributed to its degeneracy. Fifty years ago there was scarcely a Novel in the kingdom. Romances, indeed, abounded; but they, it is supposed, were rather favourable to virtue. Their pictures of human nature were not exact, but they were flattering resemblances. By exhibiting patterns of perfection, they stimulated emulation to aim at it. They led the fancy through a beautiful wilderness of delights: and they filled the heart with pure, manly, bold, and liberal sentiments.

Those books also, which were written with a view to ridicule the more absurd romantic writers, are themselves most pleasing romances, and may be read without injury to the morals. Such is the immortal work of Cervantes. Perhaps the safest books of entertainment for young people are those of decent humour, which excite a laugh, and leave the heart little affected.

Books are more read in youth than in the advanced periods of life; but there are few perfectly well adapted to the young mind. They should be entertaining, or they will not be attended to. They should not be profound, or they will not be understood. Entertaining books there are in great numbers; but they were not written solely for young people, and are therefore too unguarded in many of their representations. They do not pay that reverence which Juvenal asserts to be due to the puerile age.[1]

That Richardson's Novels are written with the purest intentions of promoting virtue, none can deny. But in the accomplishment of this purpose scenes are laid open, which it would be safer to conceal, and sentiments excited, which it would be more advantageous to early virtue not to admit. Dangers and temptations are pointed out; but many of them are dangers which seldom occur, and temptations by which few in comparison are assaulted. It is to be feared, the moral view is rarely regarded by youthful and inexperienced readers, who naturally pay the chief attention to the lively description of love, and its effects; and who, while they read, eagerly wish to be actors in the scenes which they admire.

The cultivated genius of Fielding entitles him to a high rank among the classics. His works exhibit a series of pictures drawn with all the descriptive fidelity of a Hogarth. They are highly entertaining, and will always be read with pleasure; but they likewise disclose scenes, which may corrupt a mind unseasoned by experience.

Smollet undoubtedly possessed great merit. He would, however, have been more generally read among the polite and refined, if his humour had been less coarse. His *Peregrine Pickle* has, I am convinced, done much mischief; as all books must do, in which wicked characters are painted in captivating colours. And it is advisable to defer the perusal of his works, till the judgment is mature.

The writings of such men do, however, display the beauties of that genius, which allures and rewards the attention of the discreet reader. But the memoirs, private histories, and curious anecdotes, imported from our neighbouring land of libertinism, have seldom any thing to recommend them to perusal but their profligacy. Yet even these, adorned with specious titles, and a pert vivacity of language, have found their way to the circulating libraries, and are often obtruded on the attention at an early age.

The English Press has teemed with similar original productions. That coarse taste, which was introduced in the reign of Charles the Second, was greedily adopted by the juvenile reader. At an inflammatory age, the fuel of licentious ideas will always find a ready reception. The sentimental manner seems of late to have supplanted it. But it is matter of doubt, whether even this manner is not equally dangerous. It has given an amiable name to vice, and has obliquely excused the extra-vagance of the passions, by representing them as the effect of lovely sensibility. The least refined affections of humanity have lost their indelicate nature, in the ideas of many, when dignified by the epithet of sentimental; and transgressions forbidden by the laws of God and man have been absurdly palliated, as proceeding from an excess of those finer feelings, which vanity has arrogated to itself as elegant and amiable distinctions. A softened appellation has given a degree of gracefulness to moral deformity.

The languishing and affectedly sentimental compositions formed on the pattern of Sterne, or of other less original Novelists, not only tend to give the mind a degree of weakness, which renders it unable to resist the slightest impulse of libidinous passion, but also indirectly insinuate, that the attempt is unnatural. What then remains to support the feeble efforts of remaining virtue, but the absence of temptation?

Such books, however pernicious their tendency, are the most easily attained. The prudence of their publishers suggests the expediency of making them conveniently portable. Every corner of the kingdom is abundantly supplied with them. In vain is youth secluded from the corruptions of the living world. Books are commonly allowed them with little restriction, as innocent amusements: yet these often pollute the heart in the recesses of the closet, inflame the passions at a distance from temptation, and teach all the malignity of vice in solitude.

There is another evil arising from a too early attention to Novels. They fix attention so deeply, and afford so lively a pleasure, that the mind, once accustomed to them, cannot submit to the painful task of serious study. Authentic history becomes insipid. The reserved graces of the chaste matron Truth pass unobserved amidst the gaudy and painted decorations of fiction. The boy who can procure a variety of books like *Gil Blas*, and the *Devil upon Two Sticks*, will no longer think his Livy, his Sallust, his Homer, or his Virgil pleasing. He will not study old Lilly, while he can read *Pamela* and *Tom Jones*, and a thousand inferior and more dangerous novels.[2]

When the judgment is ripened by reflection, and the morals out of danger, every well-written book will claim attention. The man of application may always find agreeable refreshment, after severer study, in the amusing pages of a Fielding; but the fungous production of the common Novel-wright will be too insignificant to attract his notice.

The extreme insipidity of some of our later Novels, it might have been supposed, would have prevented their reception. But insipid minds find in them entertainment congenial to their nature. And, indeed, the futility of the modern Novel almost precludes its power of causing any other mischief, than the consumption of time that might be more usefully employed.

If, however, Novels are to be prohibited, in what, it will be asked, can the young mind employ itself during the hours of necessary leisure? To this it may be answered, that when the sweetened poison is removed, plain and wholesome food will always be relished. The growing mind will crave nourishment, and will gladly seek it in true histories, written in a pleasing and easy style, on purpose for its use. Voyages and travels, when not obscured by scientific observations, are always delightful to youthful curiosity. From interesting narratives, like those of *Telemachus*, and *Robinson Crusoe*, a mind not vitiated by a taste for licentious Novels will derive a very sensible pleasure. Let the boy's library consist of such books as Rollin's *History*,[3] Plutarch's *Lives*, and the *Spectators*; and, together with the improvement of his morals and understanding, which he must derive from reading them, he will have it in his power to spend his vacant time in such mental amusements as are truly and permanently delightful.

75 Preface to *The Sorrows of Werter; A German Story, founded on Fact*, 1779

This is the Preface to the first English translation of Goethe's novel; later versions followed in 1784, 1786 and 1789; the translation in this case, by R. Graves, was from the French version of Count F. W. K. von Schmettau.

Those who expect a Novel will be disappointed in this work, which contains few characters and few events; and the design of which is to exhibit a picture of that disordered state of mind, too common in our own country. It is drawn by the masterly hand of Mr. Goethé, and is perhaps little more than the relation of a fact which happened within his knowledge. It went through several editions in German, and soon made its way into France. About two years since the English translator met with it; and being struck with the uncommon genius and originality of the thoughts, and the energy with which they are expressed, translated some of the letters from the French; and led on by the beauty of the work, which increased in proportion as it was attended to, the whole was insensibly finished, and as no translation from the German has hitherto appeared, it is now offered to the Public.

Among the number of pamphlets which this little work gave occasion to, there were not lacking some which censured it; and Mr. Goethé has been called the apologist of Suicide, by those who, not distinguishing the Author from the Work, very absurdly ascribed to him the erroneous sentiments which he has given to his principal Character,—a method of criticism which would equally affect all the epic and tragic writers that ever existed.

Werter appears to have been strongly impressed with sentiments of religion; and it is not to be wondered at, that in his state of mind they should take an irregular form, and sometimes border upon extravagance. A few expressions which had thus appeared, have been omitted by the French, and a few more by the English translator, as they might possibly give offense in a work of this nature.

76 From *On Fable and Romance*, 1783

by JAMES BEATTIE

The essay in which the passages reproduced below occur was published in *Dissertations Moral and Critical* (1783). For Beattie see above, No. 61, headnote.

The love of Truth is natural to man; and adherence to it, his indispensable duty. But to frame a fabulous narrative, for the purpose of instruction or of harmless amusement, is no breach of veracity, unless one were to obtrude it on the world for truth. The fabulist and the novel-writer deceive nobody; because, though they study to make their inventions probable, they do not even pretend that they are true: at least, what they may pretend in this way is considered only as words of course, to which nobody pays any regard. Fabulous narrative has accordingly been common in all ages of the world, and practised by teachers of the most respectable character.

It is owing, no doubt, to the weakness of human nature, that fable should ever have been found a necessary, or a convenient, vehicle for truth. But we must take human nature as it is: and, if a rude multitude cannot readily comprehend a moral or political doctrine, which they need to be instructed in, it may be as allowable, to illustrate that doctrine by a fable, in order to make them attend, and understand it, as it is for a physician to strengthen a weak stomach with cordials, in order to prepare it for the business of digestion. Such was the design of Jotham's parable of the trees chusing a king, in the ninth chapter of the book of *Judges*: and such that famous apologue, of a contention between the parts of the human body, by which Menenius Agrippa satisfied the people of Rome, that the welfare of the state depended on the union and good agreement of the several members of it. In fact, the common people are not well qualified for argument. A short and pithy proverb, which is easily remembered; or little tales, that appeal as it were to their senses, weigh more with them than demonstration.

We need not wonder, then, to find, that, in antient times, moral precepts were often delivered in the way of proverb or aphorism, and enforced and exemplified by fictitious narrative. Of those fables that are ascribed to Esop, some are no doubt modern, but others bear the stamp of antiquity. And nothing can be better contrived, than many of them are, for the purpose of impressing moral truth upon the memory, as well as the understanding. The disappointment, that frequently attends an excessive desire of accumulation, is finely exemplified in the fable of the dog and his shadow; and the ruinous and ridiculous nature of ambition is with equal energy illustrated in that of the frog and the ox. These little allegories we are apt to undervalue, because we learned them at school; but they are not for that reason the less valuable. We ought to prize them as monuments of antient wisdom, which have long contributed to the amusement and instruction of mankind, and are entitled to applause, on account of the propriety of the invention.

The Greek apologues ascribed to Esop, and the Latin ones of Phedrus, are masterpieces in this way of writing; and have hardly been equalled by the best of our modern fabulists. They are (at least many of them are, for some are trifling) remarkable for the simplicity of the style; and for the attention, which their authors have generally given, to the nature of the animals, and other things, that are introduced as agents and speakers. For in most of the modern fables, invented by Gay, La Fontaine, L'Estrange, Poggio,[1] and others, the contrivance is less natural; and the language, though simple, is quaint, and full of witticism. That a dog should snap at the shadow of a dog, and by so doing lose the piece of flesh that was in his own mouth, is suitable to the character of the animal, and is indeed a very probable story: but that an elephant should converse with a bookseller about Greek authors, or a hare intreat a calf to carry her off on his back, and save her from the hounds, is a fiction wherein no regard is had to the nature of things. In this, as in the higher, sorts of fable, it is right to adhere, as much as may be, to probability. Brute animals, and vegetables too, may be allowed to speak and think: this indulgence is granted, from the necessity of the case; for, without it, their adventures could neither improve nor entertain us: but, with this exception, nature should not be violated; nor the properties of one animal or vegetable ascribed to a different one. Frogs have been seen inflated with air, at least, if not with pride; dogs may swim rivers; a man might take a frozen viper into his bosom, and be bit to death for his imprudence; a fox might play with a tragedian's headpiece; a lamb and a wolf might drink of the same brook, and the former lose his life on the occasion: but who ever heard of an elephant reading Greek, or a hare riding on the back of a calf?

The wisdom of antiquity was not satisfied with conveying short lessons of morality in these apologues, or little tales. The poets entered upon a more extensive field of fable; in order to convey a more refined species of instruction, and to please by a more exquisite invention, and a higher probability. But I confine myself at present to prose fable.

One of the first specimens of Fabulous History, that appeared in these western parts of the world, is the *Cyropedia* of Xenophon. This work, however, we are not to consider as of the nature of Romance; for the outlines of the story are true. But the author takes the liberty to feign many incidents; that he may set in a variety of lights the character of Cyrus, whom he meant to exhibit as the model of a great and good prince. The work is very elegant and entertaining, and abounds in moral, political, and military knowledge. It is, nevertheless, to be regretted, that we have no certain rule for distinguishing what is historical in it, from what is fabulous. The history of Cyrus the Great, the founder of the Persian empire, who has the honour to be mentioned by name in the Old Testament, is surely worth knowing. Yet we are much in the dark in regard to it. The account given of him by Herodotus differs greatly from Xenophon's; and in many instances we know not which to prefer. It is observable however, that Xenophon's description of the manner in which Cyrus took Babylon, by turning aside the course of the Euphrates, and entering, through the empty channel, under the walls of the city, agrees very well with several intimations of that event, which we find in the prophecies of Isaiah, Jeremiah, and Daniel.

Allegorical Fables were not unknown in the days of Xenophon. The Table, or Picture, of Cebes the Theban was written about this time; as well as the Story of Hercules conversing with Virtue and Vice and preferring the honours promised by the former to the pleasures offered by the latter.[2] Cebes's Picture of human life excels in accuracy of description, justness of allegory, and a sweet simplicity of style. The fable of Hercules, as originally written by Prodicus, is lost, and seems not to have been extant in the time of Cicero;[3] but Xenophon gives a full and elegant abstract of it, in the beginning of his second book of *Memorabilia*.

Excepting some Allegorical fables scattered up and down in Plato, I do not recollect, among the Classick productions of Greece and Rome, any other remarkable specimen of prose fable: for the heathen mythology, though full of allegories, I am not to touch upon in this place, on account of its connection with poetry; and because my chief purpose is, to inquire into the origin and nature of the Modern Romance.

But, first, it may be proper to observe, that the Oriental nations have long been famous for fabulous narrative. The indolence peculiar to the genial climates of Asia, and the luxurious life which the kings and other great men, of those countries, lead in their seraglios, have made them seek for this sort of amusement, and set a high value upon it. When an Eastern prince happens to be idle, as he commonly is, and at a loss for expedients to kill the time, he commands his Grand Visir, or his favourite, to tell him stories. Being ignorant, and consequently credulous; having no passion for moral improvement, and little knowledge of nature; he does not desire, that they should be probable, or of an instructive tendency: it is enough if they be astonishing. And hence it is, no doubt, that those oriental tales are so extravagant. Every thing is carried on by inchantment and prodigy; by fairies, genii, and demons, and wooden horses, which, on turning a peg, fly through the air with inconceivable swiftness.

Another thing remarkable in these eastern tales, is, that their authors expatiate, with peculiar delight, in the description of magnificence; rich robes, gaudy furniture, sumptuous entertainments, and palaces shining in gold, or sparkling with diamonds. This too is conformable to the character and circumstances of the people. Their great men, whose taste has never been improved by studying the *simplicity* of nature and art, pique themselves chiefly on the *splendour* of their equipage, and the vast quantities of gold, jewels, and curious things, which they can heap together in their repositories.

The greatest, indeed the only, collection that I am acquainted with, of Oriental fables, is the *Thousand and one tales*, commonly called *The Arabian Nights Entertainment*. This book, as we have it, is the work of Mons. Galland of the French Academy, who is said to have translated it from the Arabick original.[4] But whether the tales be really Arabick, or invented by Mons. Galland, I have never been able to learn with certainty. If they be Oriental, they are translated with unwarrantable latitude; for the whole tenor of the style is in the French mode: and the Caliph of Bagdat, and the Emperor of China, are addressed in the same terms of ceremony, which are usual at the court of France. But this, though in my opinion it takes away from the value of the book, because I wish to see Eastern manners in an Eastern tale, is no proof, that the whole work is by M. Galland: for the French are so devoted to their own ceremonies, that they cannot endure any other; and seldom fail to season their translations, even of the gravest and most antient authors, with the fashionable forms of Parisian civility.

As the *Arabian Nights Entertainment* is a book which most young people in this country are acquainted with, I need not draw any character of it, or remark that it exactly answers the account already given of Oriental fable. There is in it great luxury of description, without any elegance; and great variety of invention, but nothing that elevates the mind, or touches the heart. All is wonderful and incredible; and the astonishment of the reader is more aimed at, than his improvement either in morality, or in the knowledge of nature. Two things, however, there are, which deserve commendation, and may entitle it to one perusal. It conveys a pretty just idea of the government, and of some of the customs, of those eastern nations; and there is somewhere in it a story of a barber and his six brothers, that contains many good strokes of satire and comick description.[5] I may add, that the character of the Caliph Haroun Alraschid is well drawn; and that the story of forty thieves destroyed by a slave is interesting, and artfully conducted. The voyages of Sindbad claim attention: they were certainly attended to, by the author of *Gulliver's Travels*.

Tales in imitation of the Oriental have oft been attempted by English, and other European, authors: who, together with the figurative style, and wild invention of the Asiaticks, (which, being extravagant, are easily imitated) endeavour also to paint the customs and manners of that people. They give us good store of gold and jewels; and eunuchs, slaves, and necromancers in abundance: their personages are all Mahometan, or Pagan, and subject to the despotick government of Caliphs, Visirs, Bashaws, and Emperors; they drink sherbet, rest on sophas, and ride on dromedaries. We have Chinese Tales, Tartarian Tales, Persian Tales, and Mogul Tales; not to mention the Tales of the Fairies and Genii; some of which I read in my younger days: but, as they have left no trace in the memory, I cannot now give any account of them.

In the *Spectator*, *Rambler*, and *Adventurer*, there are many fables in the eastern manner; most of them very pleasing, and of a moral tendency. *Rasselas*, by Johnson, and *Almoran and Hamet*, by Hawkesworth, are celebrated performances in this way. The former is admirable in description, and in that exquisite strain of sublime morality by which the writings of this great and good man are so eminently distinguished: —of the latter, the style is rhetorical and solemn, and the sentiments are in general good, but the plan is obscure, and so contrived as to infuse perplexing notions of the Divine Providence; a subject, which the elegant writer seems to have considered very superficially, and very confusedly.[6]—Addison excels in this sort of fable. His vision of Mirzah, in the second volume of the *Spectator*, is the finest piece of the kind I have ever seen; uniting the utmost propriety of invention with a simplicity and melody of language, that melts the heart, while it charms and soothes the imagination.

Modern Prose Fable (if we omit those sorts of it that have been already hinted at) may be divided into two kinds; which, for the sake of distinction, I shall call the ALLEGORICAL and the POETICAL. The Allegorical part of modern prose fable may be subdivided into two species, the *Historical*, and the *Moral*; and the Poetical part I shall also subdivide into two sorts, the *Serious*, and the *Comick*. Thus the Prose Fable of the moderns may be distributed into four species; whereof I shall speak in their order. 1. The Historical Allegory; 2. The Moral Allegory; 3. The Poetical and Serious Fable; 4. The Poetical and Comick Fable. These two last I comprehend under the general term ROMANCE.

I. The FABULOUS HISTORICAL ALLEGORY exhibits real history disguised by feigned names, and embellished with fictitious adventures. This sort of fable may also be subdivided into the *Serious* and the *Comick*.

1. Of the former, the best specimen I know is the *Argenis*; written in Latin, about the beginning of the last century, by John Barclay a Scotchman: and supposed to contain an allegorical account of the Civil wars of France during the reign of Henry the third. I have read only part of the work: and what I read I never took the trouble to decypher, by means of the key which in some editions is subjoined to it, or to compare the fictitious adventures of Meleander and Lycogenes with the real adventures that are alluded to. I therefore am not qualified to criticize the performance: but can freely recommend it, as in some places very entertaining, as abounding in lively description, and remarkable for the most part, though not uniformly, for the elegance of the language.

2. We have a *Comick* specimen of the Historical Allegory, in the *History of John Bull*; a pamphlet written by the learned and witty Dr. Arbuthnot, and commonly printed among the works of Swift. It was published in Queen Anne's time;[7] and intended as a satire on the Duke of Marlborough, and the rest of the whig ministry, who were averse to the treaty of peace that was soon after concluded at Utrecht. The war, which the Queen carried on against the French and Spaniards, is

described under the form of a law-suit, that John Bull, or England, is said to have been engaged in with some litigious neighbours. A candid account of facts is not to be expected in an allegorical tale, written with the express design to make a party ridiculous. The work, however, has been much read, and frequently imitated. It is full of low humour, which in this piece the author affected; but which he could have avoided if he had thought proper; as he undoubtedly possessed more wit and learning, as well as virtue, than any other writer of his time, Addison excepted. In *John Bull*, great things are represented as mean; the style is consequently burlesque, and the phraseology, and most of the allusions, are taken from low life. There is a key printed, in the late editions, at the foot of each page, to mark the coincidence of the fable with the history of that period.

II. The second species of modern fabulous prose I distinguished by the name of the *Moral Allegory*. Moral and Religious Allegories were frequent in Europe about two hundred and fifty years ago. Almost all the Dramatick exhibitions of that time were of this character. In them, not only human virtues and vices personified, but also angels both good and evil, and beings more exalted than angels, were introduced, acting and speaking, as persons of the drama. Those plays, however, notwithstanding their incongruity, were written for the most part with the laudable design of exemplifying religious or moral truth; and hence were called Moralities. The publick exhibition of them in England ceased about the time of Shakspeare, or in the end of the sixteenth century: but several of the English Moralities are extant, and may be seen in some late collections of Old Plays. In Spain and Italy they continued longer in fashion. When Milton was on his travels, he happened to witness a representation of this kind, written by one Andrieno, and call *Original Sin*;[8] from which, rude as it was, he is said to have formed the first draught of the plan of *Paradise Lost*.

Those were poetical allegories: but I confine myself to such as are in prose, and assume something of the historical form.—John Bunyan, an unlettered, but ingenious man, of the last century, was much given to this way of writing. His chief work is the *Pilgrim's Progress*; wherein the commencement, procedure, and completion of the Christian life, are represented allegorically, under the similitude of a journey. Few books have gone through so many editions, in so short a time, as the *Pilgrim's Progress*. It has been read by people of all ranks and capacities. The learned have not thought it below their notice: and among the vulgar it is an universal favourite. I grant, the style is rude, and even indelicate sometimes; that the invention is frequently extravagant; and that in more than one place it tends to convey erroneous notions in theology. But the tale is amusing, though the dialogue be often low: and some of the allegories are well contrived, and prove the author to have possessed powers of invention, which, if they had been refined by learning, might have produced something very noble. This work has been imitated, but with little success. The learned Bishop Patrick wrote the *Parable of the Pilgrim*: but I am not satisfied, that he borrowed the hint, as it is generally thought he did, from John Bunyan. There is no resemblance in the plan; nor does the Bishop speak a word of the *Pilgrim's Progress*, which I think he would have done, if he had seen it. Besides, Bunyan's fable is full of incident: Patrick's is dry, didactick, verbose, and exceedingly barren in the invention.[9]

Gulliver's Travels are a sort of allegory; but rather Satirical and Political, than Moral. The work is in every body's hands; and has been criticized by many eminent writers. As far as the satire is levelled at human pride and folly; at the abuses of human learning; at the absurdity of speculative projectors; at those criminal or blundering expedients in policy, which we are apt to overlook, or even to applaud, because custom has made them familiar; so far the author deserves our warmest approbation, and his satire will be allowed to be perfectly just, as well as exquisitely severe. His fable is well conducted, and, for the most part, consistent with itself, and connected with probable circumstances. He personates a sea-faring man; and with wonderful propriety supports the plainness and simplicity of the character. And this gives to the whole narrative an air of truth; which forms an entertaining contraste, when we compare it with the wildness of the fiction. The style too deserves particular notice. It is not free from inaccuracy: but, as a model of easy and graceful simplicity, it has not been exceeded by any thing in our language; and well deserves to be studied by every person, who wishes to write pure English.—These, I think, are the chief merits of this celebrated work; which has been more read, than any other publication of the present century. Gulliver has something in him to hit every taste. The statesman, the philosopher, and the critick, will admire his keenness of satire, energy of description, and vivacity of language: the vulgar, and even children, who cannot enter into these refinements, will find their account in the story, and be highly amused with it.

But I must not be understood to praise the whole indiscriminately. The last of the four voyages, though the author has exerted himself in it to the utmost, is an absurd, and an abominable fiction. It is absurd:

because, in presenting us with rational beasts, and irrational men, it proceeds upon a direct contradiction to the most obvious laws of nature, without deriving any support from either the dreams of the credulous, or the prejudices of the ignorant. And it is abominable: because it abounds in filthy and indecent images; because the general tenor of the satire is exaggerated into absolute falsehood; and because there must be something of an irreligious tendency in a work, which, like this, ascribes the perfection of reason, and of happiness, to a race of beings, who are said to be destitute of every religious idea.—But, what is yet worse, if any thing can be worse, this tale represents human nature itself as the object of contempt and abhorrence. Let the ridicule of wit be pointed at the follies, and let the scourge of satire be brandished at the crimes, of mankind: all this is both pardonable, and praise-worthy; because it may be done with a good intention, and produce good effects. But when a writer endeavours to make us dislike and despise, every one his neighbour, and be dissatisfied with that Providence, who has made us what we are, and whose dispensations towards the human race are so peculiarly, and so divinely beneficent; such a writer, in so doing, proves himself the enemy, not of man only, but of goodness itself; and his work can never be allowed to be innocent, till impiety, malevolence, and misery, cease to be evils.

The Tale of a Tub, at least the narrative part of it, is another Allegorical fable, by the same masterly hand; and, like the former, supplies no little matter, both of admiration, and of blame. As a piece of humourous writing, it is unequalled. It was the author's first performance, and is, in the opinion of many, his best. The style may be less correct, than that of some of his latter works; but in no other part of his writings has he displayed so rich a fund of wit, humour, and ironical satire, as in the *Tale of a Tub*. The subject is Religion: but the allegory, under which he typifies the Reformation, is too mean for an argument of so great dignity; and tends to produce, in the mind of the reader, some very disagreeable associations, of the most solemn truths with ludicrous ideas. Professed wits may say what they please; and the fashion, as well as the laugh, may be for a time on their side: but it is a dangerous thing, and the sign of an intemperate mind, to acquire a habit of making every thing matter of merriment and sarcasm. We dare not take such liberty with our neighbour, as to represent whatever he does or says in a ridiculous light; and yet some men (I wish I could not say, clergymen) think themselves privileged to take liberties of this sort with the most awful, and most benign dispensations of Providence.

That this author has repeatedly done so, in the work before us, and elsewhere, is too plain to require proof.[10] The compliments he pays the Church of England I allow to be very well founded, as well as part of the satire, which he levels at the Church of Rome; though I wish he had expressed both the one and the other with a little more decency of language. But, as to his abuse of the Presbyterians, whom he represents as more absurd and frantick, than perhaps any rational beings ever were since the world began, every person of sense and candour, whether Presbyterian or not, will acknowledge it, if he know any thing of their history, to be founded in gross misrepresentation. There are other faults in this work, besides those already specified; many vile images, and obscene allusions; such as no well-bred man could read, or endure to hear read, in polite company.

III. I come now to the second species of modern prose fable, to which I gave the appellation of *Poetical*, to distinguish it from the former *Allegorical* species. In reading the *Allegorical Prose Fable*, we attend not only to the fictitious events that occur in the narrative, but also to those real events that are typefied by the allegory: whereas in the *poetical prose fable* we attend only to the events that are before us. Thus, in the *Tale of a Tub*, I not only mind what is related of three brothers, Peter, Martin, and Jack, but also keep it constantly in view, that those three brothers are by the author meant to be the representatives of the Romish, English, and Presbyterian churches: whereas when I read *Robinson Crusoe*, or *Tom Jones*, I attend singly to the narrative; and no *key* is necessary to make me comprehend the author's meaning.

Considering this as the chief part of my subject, I dispatched the former parts as briefly as I could, that I might have the more time to employ upon it. The rise and progress of the MODERN ROMANCE, or POETICAL PROSE FABLE, is connected with many topicks of importance, which would throw (if fully illustrated) great light upon the history and politicks, the manners, and the literature, of these latter ages.— Observe, that I call this sort of fable *poetical*, from the nature of the invention; and *prose*, because it is not in verse. Prose and Verse are opposite, but Prose and Poetry may be consistent. *Tom Jones*, and *Telemachus*, are epick, or narrative poems, though written in prose; the one Comick, the other Serious and Heroick.

[. . . . .]

But the final extirpation of chivalry and all its chimeras was now approaching. What laws and force could not accomplish, was brought about by the humour and satire of one writer. This was the illustrious

Miguel de Cervantes Saavedra. He was born at Madrid in the year
one thousand five hundred and forty-nine. He seems to have had every
advantage of education, and to have been a master in polite learning.
But in other respects fortune was not very indulgent. He served many
years in the armies of Spain, in no higher station, than that of a private
soldier. In that capacity he fought at the battle of Lepanto, under Don
John of Austria, and had the misfortune, or, as he rather thought, the
honour, to lose his left hand. Being now disqualified for military
service, he commenced author; and wrote many Dramatick pieces,
which were acted with applause on the Spanish theatre, and acquired
him both money and reputation. But want of economy and unbounded
generosity dissipated the former: and he was actually confined in
prison for debt, when he composed the first part of *The History of Don
Quixote*; a work, which every body admires for its humour; but which
ought also to be considered as a most useful performance, that brought
about a great revolution in the manners and literature of Europe, by
banishing the wild dreams of chivalry, and reviving a taste for the
simplicity of nature. In this view, the publication of *Don Quixote* forms
an important era in the history of mankind.

Don Quixote is represented as a man, whom it is impossible not to
esteem for his cultivated understanding, and the goodness of his heart:
but who, by poring night and day upon the old romances, had impaired
his reason to such a degree, as to mistake them for history, and form the
design of going through the world, in the character, and with the
accoutrements, of a knight errant. His distempered fancy takes the most
common occurrences for adventures similiar to those he had read in
his books of chivalry. And thus, the extravagance of those books being
placed, as it were, in the same groupe with the appearances of nature and
the real business of life, the hideous disproportion of the former becomes so glaring by the contrast, that the most inattentive observer
cannot fail to be struck with it. The person, the pretensions, and the
exploits, of the errant knight, are held up to view in a thousand
ridiculous attitudes. In a word, the humour and satire are irresistable;
and their effects were instantaneous.

This work no sooner appeared, than chivalry vanished, as snow
melts before the sun. Mankind awoke as from a dream. They laughed
at themselves for having been so long imposed on by absurdity; and
wondered they had not made the discovery sooner. It astonished them
to find, that nature and good sense could yield a more exquisite entertainment, than they had ever derived from the most sublime phrenzies

of chivalry. For, that this was indeed the case: that *Don Quixote* was more read, and more relished, than any other romance had ever been, we may infer, from the sudden and powerful effects it produced on the sentiments of mankind; as well as from the declaration of the author himself; who tells us, that upwards of twelve thousand copies of the first part were sold, before the second could be got ready for the press: —an amazing rapidity of sale, at a time when the readers and purchasers of books were but an inconsiderable number compared to what they are in our days. 'The very children,['] (says he) [']handle it, boys read it, men understand, and old people applaud, the performance. It is no sooner laid down by one, than another takes it up; some struggling, and some entreating, for a sight of it. In fine,['] (continues he) [']this history is the most delightful, and the least prejudicial, entertainment, that ever was seen; for, in the whole book, there is not the least shadow of a dishonourable word, nor one thought unworthy of a good catholick.'[11]

Don Quixote occasioned the death of the Old Romance, and gave birth to the New. Fiction henceforth divested herself of her gigantick size, tremendous aspect, and frantick demeanour; and, descending to the level of common life, conversed with man as his equal, and as a polite and chearful companion. Not that every subsequent Romance-writer adopted the plan, or the manner, of Cervantes: but it was from him they learned to avoid extravagance, and to imitate nature. And now probability was as much studied, as it had been formerly neglected.

But before I proceed to the New Romance, on which I shall be very brief, it is proper just to mention a species of Romantick narrative, which cannot be called either Old or New, but is a strange mixture of both. Of this kind are the *Grand Cyrus*, *Clelia*, and *Cleopatra*; each consisting of ten or a dozen large volumes, and pretending to have a foundation in antient history. In them, all facts and characters, real and fabulous; and all systems of policy and manners, the Greek, the Roman, the Feudal, and the modern, are jumbled together and confounded: as if a painter should represent Julius Cesar drinking tea with Queen Elizabeth, Jupiter, and Dulcinea del Toboso, and having on his head the laurel wreathe of antient Rome, a suit of Gothick armour on his shoulders, laced ruffles at his wrist, a pipe of tobacco in his mouth, and a pistol and tomahawk stuck in his belt. But I should go beyond my depth, if I were to criticize any of those enormous compositions. For, to confess the truth, I never had patience to read one half of one of the volumes; nor met with a person, who could give me any other account of them, than that they are intolerably tedious, and unspeakably absurd.

The New Romance may be divided into the *Serious* and the *Comick*: and each of these kinds may be variously subdivided.

I. 1. Of *Serious* Romances, some follow *the historical arrangement*; and, instead of beginning, like Homer and Virgil, in the middle of the subject,[12] give a continued narrative of the life of some one person, from his birth to his establishment in the world, or till his adventures may be supposed to have come to an end. Of this sort is *Robinson Crusoe*. The account commonly given of that well-known work is as follows.

Alexander Selkirk, a Scotch mariner, happened, by some accident which I forget, to be left in the uninhabited island of Juan Fernandes in the South Seas. Here he continued four years alone, without any other means of supporting life, than by running down goats, and killing such other animals as he could come at. To defend himself from danger during the night, he built a house of stones rudely put together, which a gentleman, who had been in it, (for it was extant when Anson arrived there) described to me as so very small, that one person could with difficulty crawl in. and stretch himself at length. Selkirk was delivered by an English vessel, and returned home. A late French writer says, he had become so fond of the savage state, that he was unwilling to quit it. But that is not true. The French writer either confounds the real story of Selkirk with a fabulous account of one Philip Quarl,[13] written after *Robinson Crusoe*, of which it is a paltry imitation; or wilfully misrepresents the fact, in order to justify, as far as he is able, an idle conceit, which, since the time of Rousseau, has been in fashion amongst infidel and affected theorists on the continent, that savage life is most natural to us, and that the more a man resembles a brute in his mind, body, and behaviour, the happier he becomes, and the more perfect.—Selkirk was advised to get his story put in writing, and published. Being illiterate himself, he told every thing he could remember to Daniel Defoe, a professed author of considerable note; who, instead of doing justice to the poor man, is said to have applied these materials to his own use, by making them the groundwork of *Robinson Crusoe*; which he soon after published, and which, being very popular, brought him a good deal of money.[14]

Some have thought, that a lovetale is necessary to make a romance interesting. But *Robinson Crusoe*, though there is nothing of love in it, is one of the most interesting narratives that ever was written; at least in all that part which relates to the desert island: being founded on a passion still more prevalent than love, the desire of self-preservation; and therefore likely to engage the curiosity of every class of readers, both old and young, both learned and unlearned.

I am willing to believe, that Defoe shared the profits of this publication with the poor seaman: for there is an air of humanity in it, which one would not expect from an author who is an arrant cheat. In the preface to his second volume, he speaks feelingly enough of the harm done him by those who had abridged the first, in order to reduce the price. 'The injury,['] says he, [']which these men do to the *proprietors* of works, is a practice all honest men abhor: and they believe they may challenge them to show the difference between that, and robbing on the highway, or breaking open a house. If they cannot show any difference in the crime, they will find it hard to show, why there should be any difference in the punishment.'[15] Is it to be imagined, that any man of common prudence would talk in this way, if he were conscious, that he himself might be proved guilty of that very dishonesty which he so severely condemns?

Be this however as it may, for I have no authority to *affirm* any thing on either side, *Robinson Crusoe* must be allowed, by the most rigid moralist, to be one of those novels, which one may read, not only with pleasure, but also with profit. It breathes throughout a spirit of piety and benevolence: it sets in a very striking light, as I have elsewhere observed, the importance of the mechanick arts, which they, who know not what it is to be without them, are so apt to undervalue: it fixes in the mind a lively idea of the horrors of solitude, and, consequently, of the sweets of social life, and of the blessings we derive from conversation, and mutual aid: and it shows, how, by labouring with one's own hands, one may secure independence, and open for one's self many sources of health and amusement. I agree, therefore, with Rousseau, that this is one of the best books that can be put in the hands of children.[16]—The style is plain, but not elegant, nor perfectly grammatical: and the second part of the story is tiresome.

2. A second species of the Modern Serious Romance is that, which follows *the poetical arrangement*; and, in order to shorten the time of the action, begins in the middle of the story. Such, partly, are *Sir Charles Grandison*, and *Clarissa Harlowe*, by Mr. Richardson. That author has adopted a plan of narrative of a peculiar kind: the persons, who bear a part in the action, are themselves the relaters of it. This is done by means of letters, or epistles; wherein the story is continued from time

to time, and the passions freely expressed, as they arise from every change of fortune, and while the persons concerned are supposed to be ignorant of the events that are to follow. And thus, the several agents are introduced in their turns, speaking, or, which is the same thing in this case, writing, suitably to their respective feelings, and characters: so that the fable is partly Epick, and partly Dramatick. There are some advantages in this form of narrative. It prevents all anticipation of the catastrophe; and keeps the reader in the same suspense, in which the persons themselves are supposed to be: and it pleases further, by the varieties of style, suited to the different tempers and sentiments of those who write the letters. But it has also its inconveniencies. For, unless the fable be short and simple, this mode of narration can hardly fail to run out into an extravagant length, and to be encumbered with repetitions. And indeed, Richardson himself, with all his powers of invention, is apt to be tedious, and to fall into a minuteness of detail, which is often unnecessary. His pathetick scenes, too, are overcharged, and so long continued, as to wear out the spirits of the reader. Nor can it be denied, that he has given too much prudery to his favourite women, and something of pedantry or finicalness to his favourite men.—Clementina was, no doubt, intended as a pattern of female excellence: but, though she may claim veneration as a saint, it is impossible to love her as a woman. And Grandison, though both a good and a great character, is in every thing so perfect, as in many things to discourage imitation; and so distant, and so formal, as to forbid all familiarity, and, of course, all cordial attachment. Alworthy is as good a man as he: but his virtue is purely human; and, having a little of our own weakness in it, and assuming no airs of superiority, invites our acquaintance, and engages our love.

For all this, however, Richardson is an author of uncommon merit. His characters are well drawn, and distinctly marked; and he delineates the operation of the passions with a picturesque accuracy, which discovers great knowledge of human nature. His moral sentiments are profound and judicious; in wit and humour he is not wanting; his dialogue is sometimes formal; but many of his conversation-pieces are executed with elegance and vivacity. For the good tendency of his writings he deserves still higher praise; for he was a man of unaffected piety, and had the improvement of his fellow-creatures very much at heart.

Yet, like most other novel-writers, he represents some of his wicked characters as more agreeable than was necessary to his plan; which may make the example dangerous. I do not think, that an author of fable, in either prose or verse, should make his bad characters completely bad: for, in the first place, that would not be natural, as the worst of men have generally some good in them: and, secondly, that would hurt his design, by making the tale less captivating; as the history of a person, so very worthless as to have not one good quality, would give disgust or horror, instead of pleasure. But, on the other hand, when a character, like Richardson's *Lovelace*, whom the reader ought to abominate for his crimes, is adorned with youth, beauty, eloquence, wit, and every other intellectual and bodily accomplishment, it is to be feared, that thoughtless young men may be tempted to imitate, even while they disapprove, him. Nor is it a sufficient apology to say, that he is punished in the end. The reader knows, that the story is a fiction: but he knows too, that such talents and qualities, if they were to appear in real life, would be irresistably engaging; and he may even fancy, that a character so highly ornamented must have been a favourite of the author. Is there not, then, reason to apprehend, that some readers will be more inclined to admire the gay profligate, than to fear his punishment?—Achilles in Homer, and Macbeth in Shakespeare, are not without great and good qualities, to raise out admiration, and make us take concern in what befals them. But no person is in any danger of being perverted by their example: their criminal conduct being described and directed in such a manner, by the art of the poet, as to show, that it is hateful in itself, and necessarily productive of misery, both to themselves, and to mankind.

I may add, that the punishment of Lovelace is a death, not of infamy, according to our notions, but rather of honour; which surely he did not deserve: and that the immediate cause of it is, not his wickedness, but some inferiority to his antagonist in the use of the small sword. With a little more skill in that exercise, he might, for any thing that appears in the story, have triumphed over Clarissa's avenger, as he had done over herself, and over the censure of the world. Had his crime been represented as the necessary cause of a series of mortifications, leading him gradually down to infamy, ruin, and despair, or producing by probable means an exemplary repentance, the fable would have been more useful in a moral view, and perhaps more interesting. And for the execution of such a plan the genius of Richardson seems to me to have been extremely well formed.—These remarks are offered, with a view rather to explain my own ideas of fable, than to detract from an author, who was an honour to his country, and of whose talents and virtues I am a sincere admirer.

His Epistolary manner has been imitated by many novel-writers; particularly by Rousseau in his *New Eloisa*; a work, not more remarkable for its eloquence, which is truly great, than for its glaring and manifold inconsistencies. For it is full of nature and extravagance, of sound philosophy and wild theory, of useful instruction and dangerous doctrine.

II. 1. The second kind of the New Romance is the *Comick*; which, like the first, may, with respect to the arrangement of events, be subdivided into the *Historical* and the *Poetical*.

Of the Historical form are the novels of Marivaux, and *Gil Blas* by M. le Sage. These authors abound in wit and humour; and give natural descriptions of present manners, in a simple, and very agreeable, style. And their works may be read without danger; being for the most part of a moral tendency. Only Le Sage appears to have had a partiality for cheats and sharpers: for these are people whom he introduces often; nor does he always paint them in the odious colours, that properly belong to all such pests of society. Even his hero Gil Blas he has made too much a rogue: which, as he is the relater of his own story, has this disagreeable effect, that it conveys to us, all the while we read him, an idea that we are in bad company, and deriving entertainment from the conversation of a man whom we cannot esteem.

Smollet follows the same historical arrangement in *Roderick Random* and *Peregrine Pickle*: two performances, of which I am sorry to say, that I can hardly allow them any other praise, than that they are humourous and entertaining. He excels, however, in drawing the characters of seamen; with whom in his younger days he had the best opportunities of being acquainted. He seems to have collected a vast number of merry stories; and he tells them with much vivacity and energy of expression. But his style often approaches to bombast; and many of his humourous pictures are exaggerated beyond all bounds of probability. And it does not appear that he knew how to contrive a regular fable, by making his events mutually dependent, and all co-operating to one and the same final purpose.—On the morality of these novels I cannot compliment him at all. He is often inexcusably licentious. Profligates, bullies, and misanthropes, are among his favourite characters. A duel he seems to have thought one of the highest efforts of human virtue; and playing dextrously at billiards a very genteel accomplishment. Two of his pieces, however, deserve to be mentioned with more respect. *Count Fathom*, though an improbable tale, is pleasing, and upon the whole not immoral, though in some passages very indelicate. And *Sir Launcelot Greaves*, though still more improbable, has great merit; and is truly original in the execution, notwithstanding that the hint is borrowed from *Don Quixote*.

2. The second species of the New Comick Romance is that which, in the arrangement of events, follows the poetical order; and which may properly enough be called the Epick Comedy, or rather the Comick Epick poem: *Epick*, because it is narrative; and *Comick*, because it is employed on the business of common life, and takes its persons from the middle and lower ranks of mankind.

This form of the Comick Romance has been brought to perfection in England by Henry Fielding; who seems to have possessed more wit and humour,[17] and more knowledge of mankind, than any other person of modern times, Shakespeare excepted; and whose great natural abilities were refined by a classical taste, which he had acquired by studying the best authors of antiquity: though it cannot be denied, that he appears on some occasions to have been rather too ostentatious, both of his learning, and of his wit.

Some have said, that *Joseph Andrews* is the best performance of Fielding. But its chief merit is parson Adams; who is indeed a character of masterly invention, and, next to *Don Quixote*, the most ludicrous personage that ever appeared in romance. This work, though full of exquisite humour, is blameable in many respects. Several passages offend by their indelicacy. And it is not easy to imagine, what could induce the author to add to the other faults of his hero's father Wilson the infamy of lying and cowardice; and then to dismiss him, by very improbable means, to a life of virtuous tranquillity, and endeavour to render him upon the whole a respectable character. Some youthful irregularities, rather hinted at than described, owing more to imprudence and unlucky accident than to confirmed habits of sensuality, and followed by inconvenience, perplexity, and remorse, their natural consequences, may, in a comick tale, be assigned even to a favourite personage, and, by proper management, form a very instructive part of the narration: but crimes, that bring dishonour, or that betray a hard heart, or an injurious disposition, should never be fixed on a character who them [*sic*] poet or novel-writer means to recommend to our esteem. On this principle, Fielding might be vindicated in regard to all the censurable conduct of Tom Jones, provided he had been less particular in describing it: and, by the same rule, Smollet's system of youthful profligacy, as exemplified in some of his libertines, is altogether without excuse.

Tom Jones and *Amelia* are Fielding's best performances; and the most perfect, perhaps, of their kind in the world. The fable of the latter is entirely poetical, and of the true epick species; beginning in the middle of the action, or rather as near the end as possible, and introducing the previous occurrences, in the form of a narrative episode. Of the former, the introductory part follows the historical arrangement; but the fable becomes strictly poetical, as soon as the great action of the piece commences, that is, if I mistake not, immediately after the sickness of Alworthy: for, from that period, the incidents proceed in an uninterrupted series to the final event, which happens about two months after.

Since the days of Homer, the world has not seen a more artful Epick fable. The characters and adventures are wonderfully diversified: yet the circumstances are all so natural, and rise so easily from one another, and co-operate with so much regularity in bringing on, even while they seem to retard, the catastrophe, that the curiosity of the reader is kept always awake, and, instead of flagging, grows more and more impatient as the story advances, till at last it becomes downright anxiety. And when we get to the end, and look back on the whole contrivance, we are amazed to find, that of so many incidents there should be so few superfluous; that in such variety of fiction there should be so great probability; and that so complex a tale should be so perspicuously conducted, with perfect unity of design.—These remarks may be applied either to *Tom Jones* or to *Amelia*: but they are made with a view to the former chiefly; which might give scope to a great deal of criticism, if I were not in haste to conclude the subject. Since the time of Fielding, who died in the year one thousand seven hundred and fifty-four, the Comick Romance, as far as I am acquainted with it, seems to have been declining apace, from simplicity and nature, into improbability and affectation.

Let not the usefulness of Romance-writing be estimated by the length of my discourse upon it. Romances are a dangerous recreation. A few, no doubt, of the best may be friendly to good taste and good morals; but far the greater part are unskilfully written, and tend to corrupt the heart, and stimulate the passions. A habit of reading them breeds a dislike to history, and all the substantial parts of knowledge; withdraws the attention from nature, and truth; and fills the mind with extravagant thoughts, and too often with criminal propensities. I would therefore caution my young reader against them: or, if he must, for the sake of amusement, and that he may have something to say on the subject, indulge himself in this way now and then, let it be sparingly, and seldom.

77 *The Lounger*, 20, Saturday June 18, 1785

by HENRY MACKENZIE

Henry Mackenzie (1745–1831), whom Sir Walter Scott called 'the Addison of the North', was author of three novels: *The Man of Feeling* (1771), *The Man of the World* (1773) and *Julia de Roubigné* (1777). He conducted two periodicals, *The Mirror* (1770) and *The Lounger* (1785–6).

Decipit exemplar vitiis imitabile.—
HOR.[1]

No species of composition is more generally read by one class of readers, or more undervalued by another, than that of the Novel. Its favourable reception from the young and the indolent, to whom the exercise of imagination is delightful, and the labour of thought is irksome, needs not to be wondered at; but the contempt which it meets from the more respectable class of literary men, it may perhaps be entitled to plead that it does not deserve. Considered in the abstract, as containing an interesting relation of events, illustrative of the manners and characters of mankind, it surely merits a higher station in the world of letters than is generally assigned it. If it has not the dignity, it has at least most of the difficulties, of the Epic or the Drama. The conduct of its fable, the support of its characters, the contrivance of its incidents, and its development of the passions, require a degree of invention, judgment, taste, and feeling, not much, if at all, inferior to those higher departments of writing, for the composition of which a very uncommon portion of genius is supposed to be requisite. Those difficulties are at the same time heightened by the circumstance, of this species of writing being of all others the most open to the judgment of the people; because it represents domestic scenes and situations in private life, in the execution of which any man may detect errors and discover blemishes, while the author has neither the pomp of poetry, nor the decoration of the stage, to cover or to conceal them.

To this circumstance, however, may perhaps be imputed the degradation into which it has fallen.—As few endowments were necessary to judge, so few have been supposed necessary to compose a novel; and all whose necessities or vanity prompted them to write, betook themselves to a field, which, as they imagined, it required no extent of information or depth of learning to cultivate, but in which a heated imagination, or an excursive fancy, were alone sufficient to succeed; and men of genius and of knowledge, despising a province in which such competitors were to be met, retired from it in disgust, and left it in the hands of the unworthy.

The effects of this have been felt, not only in the debasement of the Novel in point of literary merit, but in another particular still more material, in its perversion from a moral or instructive purpose to one directly the reverse. Ignorance and dulness are seldom long inoffensive, but generally support their own native insignificance by an alliance with voluptuousness and vice.

Even of those few novels which superior men have written, it cannot always be said, that they are equally calculated to improve as to delight. Nor is this only to be objected to some who have been professedly less scrupulous in that particular; but I am afraid may be also imputed to those whose works were meant to convey no bad impression, but, on the contrary, were intended to aid the cause of virtue, and to hold out patterns of the most exalted benevolence.

I am not, however, disposed to carry the idea of the dangerous tendency of all novels quite so far as some rigid moralists have done. As promoting a certain refinement of mind, they operate like all other works of genius and feeling, and have indeed a more immediate tendency to produce it than most others, from their treating of those very subjects which the reader will find around him in the world, and their containing those very situations in which he himself may not improbably at some time or other be placed. Those who object to them as inculcating precepts, and holding forth examples, of a refinement which virtue does not require, and which honesty is better without, do not perhaps sufficiently attend to the period of society which produces them. The code of morality must necessarily be enlarged in proportion to that state of manners to which cultivated eras give birth. As the idea of property made a crime of theft; as the invention of oaths made falsehood perjury; so the necessary refinement in manners of highly-polished nations creates a variety of duties and of offences, which men in ruder, and, it may be (for I enter not into that question), happier periods of society, could never have imagined.

The principal danger of novels, as forming a mistaken and pernicious system of morality, seems to me to arise from that contrast between one virtue or excellence and another, that war of duties which is to be found in many of them, particularly in that species called the *Sentimental*. These have been chiefly borrowed from our neighbours the French, whose style of manners, and the very powers of whose language, give them a great advantage in the delineation of that nicety, that subtilty of feeling, those entanglements of delicacy, which are so much interwoven with the characters and conduct of the chief personages in many of their most celebrated novels. In this rivalship of virtues and of duties, those are always likely to be preferred which in truth and reason are subordinate, and those to be degraded which ought to be paramount. The last, being of that great cardinal sort which must be common, because they apply to the great leading relations and circumstances of life, have an appearance less dignified and heroic than the others, which, as they come forth only on extraordinary occasions, are more apt to attract the view and excite the admiration of beholders. The duty to parents is contrasted with the ties of friendship and of love; the virtues of justice, of prudence, of economy, are put in competition with the exertions of generosity, of benevolence, and of compassion: and even of these virtues of sentiment there are still more refined divisions, in which the overstrained delicacy of the persons represented always leads them to act from the motive least obvious, and therefore generally the least reasonable.

In the enthusiasm of sentiment there is much the same danger as in the enthusiasm of religion, of substituting certain impulses and feelings of what may be called a visionary kind, in the place of real practical duties, which, in morals, as in theology, we might not improperly denominate good works. In morals, as in religion, there are not wanting instances of refined sentimentalists, who are contented with talking of virtues which they never practise, who pay in words what they owe in actions; or perhaps what is fully as dangerous, who open their minds to impressions which never have any effect upon their conduct, but are considered as something foreign to, and distinct from, it. This separation of conscience from feeling is a depravity of the most pernicious sort; it eludes the strongest obligation to rectitude, it blunts the strongest incitement to virtue; when the ties of the first bind the sentiment and not the will, and the rewards of the latter crown not the heart but the imagination.

That creation of refined and subtile feeling, reared by the authors of the works to which I allude, has an ill effect, not only on our ideas of virtue, but also on our estimate of happiness. That sickly sort of refinement creates imaginary evils and distresses, and imaginary blessings and enjoyments, which imbitter the common disappointments, and depreciate the common attainments of life. This affects the temper doubly, both with respect to ourselves and others: with respect to ourselves, from what we think ought to be our lot; with regard to others, from that we think ought to be their sentiments. It inspires a certain childish pride of our own superior delicacy, and an unfortunate contempt of the plain worth, the ordinary but useful occupations and ideas of those around us.

The reproach which has been sometimes made to novels, of exhibiting 'such faultless monsters as the world ne'er saw,'[2] may be just on the score of entertainment to their readers, to whom the delineation of uniform virtue, except when it is called into striking situations, will no doubt be insipid. But in point of moral tendency, the opposite character is much more reprehensible; I mean that character of mingled virtue and vice which is to be found in some of the best of our novels. Instances will readily occur to every reader, where the hero of the performance has violated, in one page, the most sacred laws of society, to whom, by the mere turning of the leaf, we are to be reconciled, whom we are to be made to love and admire, for the beauty of some humane, or the brilliancy of some heroic, action. It is, dangerous thus to bring us into the society of Vice, though introduced or accompanied by Virtue. In the application to ourselves, in which the moral tendency of all imaginary characters must be supposed to consist, this nourishes and supports a very common kind of self-deception, by which men are apt to balance their faults by the consideration of their good qualities; an account which, besides the fallacy of its principle, can scarcely fail to be erroneous, from our natural propensity to state our faults at the lowest, and our good qualities at their highest rate.

I have purposely pointed my observations, not to that common herd of novels (the wretched offspring of circulating libraries) which are despised for their insignificance, or proscribed for their immorality; but to the errors, as they appear to me, of those admired ones which are frequently put into the hands of youth for imitation as well as amusement. Of youth it is essential to preserve the imagination sound as well as pure, and not to allow them to forget, amidst the intricacies of Sentiment, or the dreams of Sensibility, the truths of Reason, or the laws of Principle.—Z.

78 From *The Observer*, 27, 1785

by RICHARD CUMBERLAND

Richard Cumberland (1732–1811), dramatist, diplomatist, essayist, novelist and translator, was active in many fields of literature for over half a century. His best plays (he wrote at least fifty) are *The Brothers* (1769), *The West Indian* (1771), *The Jew* (1794) and *The Wheel of Fortune* (1795). He wrote three novels: *Arundel* (1789), *Henry* (1795; see below, No. 96) and *John de Lancaster* (1809). *The Observer* was an essay series in book form which was originally published in 1785 and later greatly expanded; the essays are not separately dated.

A novel, conducted upon one uniform plan, containing a series of events in familiar life, in which no episodical story is interwoven, is, in effect, a protracted comedy, not divided into acts. The same natural display of character, the same facetious turn of dialogue and agreeable involution of incidents are essential to each composition. Novels of this description are not of many years' standing in England, and seem to have succeeded after some interval to romance, which, to say no worse of it, is a most unnatural and monstrous production. The *Don Quixote* of Cervantes is of a middle species; and the *Gil Blas*, which the Spaniards claim, and the French have the credit of, is a series of adventures rather than a novel, and both this and *Don Quixote* abound in episodical stories, which separately taken are more properly novels than the mother work.

Two authors of our nation began the fashion of novel-writing, upon different plans indeed, but each with a degree of success, which perhaps has never yet been equalled: Richardson disposed his fable into letters, and Fielding pursued the more natural mode of a continued narration, with an exception however of certain miscellaneous chapters, one of which he prefixed to each book in the nature of a prologue, in which the author speaks in person: he has executed this so pleasantly, that we are reconciled to the interruption in this instance; but I should doubt if it is a practice in which an imitator would be wise to follow him.[1]

I should have observed, that modern novelists have not confined themselves to comic fables, or such only as have happy endings, but sometimes, as in the instance of 'The Clarissa,' wind up their story with a tragical catastrophe; to subjects of this sort, perhaps, the epistolary mode of writing may be best adapted, at least it seems to give a more natural scope to pathetic descriptions; but there can be no doubt that fables replete with humorous situations, characteristic dialogue, and busy plot, are better suited to the mode which Fielding has pursued in his inimitable novel of 'The Foundling,' universally allowed the most perfect work of its sort in ours, or probably any other language.

There is a something so attractive to readers of all descriptions in these books, and they have been sought with such general avidity, that an incredible number of publications have been produced, and the scheme of circulating libraries lately established, which these very publications seem to have suggested, having spread them through the kingdom, novels are now become the amusing study of every rank and description of people in England.

Young minds are so apt to be tinctured by what they read, that it should be the duty of every person who has the charge of education, to make a proper choice of books for those who are under their care: and this is particularly necessary in respect to our daughters, who are brought up in a more confined and domestic manner than boys. Girls will be tempted to form themselves upon any characters, whether true or fictitious, which forcibly strike their imaginations, and nothing can be more pointedly addressed to the passions than many of these novel heroines. I would not be understood to accuse our modern writers of immoral designs; very few I believe can be found of that description; I do not therefore object to them as corrupting the youthful mind by pictures of immorality, but I think some amongst them may be apt to lead your female readers into affectation and false character by stories where the manners, though highly charged, are not in nature: and the more interesting such stories are, the greater will be their influence: in this light, a novel heroine, though described without a fault, yet if drawn out of nature, may be a very unfit model for imitation.

The novel, which of all others is formed upon the most studied plan of morality, is *Clarissa*, and few young women I believe are put under restriction by their parents or others from gratifying their curiosity with a perusal of this author: guided by the best intentions, and conscious that the moral of his book is fundamentally good, he has taken all possible pains to weave into his story incidents of such a tragical and affecting nature, as are calculated to make a strong and lasting impression on the youthful heart. The unmerited sufferings of an innocent and beautiful young lady, who is made a model of patience and purity; the unnatural obduracy of her parents; the infernal arts of the wretch who violates her, and the sad catastrophe of her death, are incidents in this affecting story better conceived than executed: failing in this most essential point, as a picture of human nature, I must regard the novel of *Clarissa* as one of the books, which a prudent parent will put under interdiction; for I think I can say from observation, that there are more artificial pedantic characters assumed by sentimental Misses, in the vain desire of being thought *Clarissa Harlows* [sic], than from any other source of imitation whatsoever: I suspect that it has given food to the idle passion for those eternal scribblings, which pass between one female friend and another, and tend to no good point of education. I have a young lady in my eye, who made her will, wrote an inscription for the plate of her own coffin, and forswore all mankind at the age of sixteen. As to the characters of Lovelace, of the heroine herself, and the heroine's parents, I take them all to be beings of another world. What Clarissa is made to do, and what she is allowed to omit, are equally out of the regions of nature. Fathers and mothers who may oppose the inclinations of their daughters, are not likely to profit from the examples in this story, nor will those daughters be disposed to think the worse of their own rights, or the better of their parents, for the black and odious colours in which these unnatural characters are painted. It will avail little to say that Clarissa's miseries are derivable from the false step of her elopement, when it is evident that elopement became necessary to avoid compulsion. To speak with more precision my opinion in the case, I think Clarissa dangerous only to such young persons whose characters are yet to be formed, and who from natural susceptibility may be prone to imitation, and likely to be turned aside into errors of affectation. In such hands, I think a book so addressed to the passions and wire-drawn into such prolixity, is not calculated to form either natural manners or natural style; nor would I have them learn of Clarissa to write long pedantic letters 'on their bended knees,' and beg 'to kiss the hem of their ever-honoured Mamma's garment,' any more than I would wish them to spurn at the addresses of a worthy lover, with the pert insult of a Miss Howe.

The natural temper and talents of our children should point out to our observation and judgment the particular mode in which they ought to be trained; the little tales told to them in infancy, and the books to be put into their hands in a forwarder age, are concerns highly worth attending to. Few female hearts in early youth can bear being softened by pathetic and affecting stories without prejudice. Young people are all imitation, and when a girl assumes the pathos of Clarissa without experiencing the same afflictions, or being put to the same trials, the result will be a most insufferable affectation and pedantry.

[. . . . .]

79 From *A Commentary Illustrating the Poetics of Aristotle*, 1786

by HENRY PYE

Henry Pye (1745–1813), poet and dramatist, was Poet Laureate from 1790. The passages reproduced below (selected from the many in which Pye refers to prose fiction), are as follows: (*a*) From Chapter VI, Note 1, 'Tragedy is an imitation, in ornamented language, of an action important and complete …'; (*b*) Chapter VIII, Note 1, 'The Unity of a Fable does not depend upon its relating to one person only'; (*c*) Chapter XV, Note 1, 'In forming the Manners four things are to be alluded to. The first and most essential is, that they should be good'; (*d*) Chapter XV, Note 2, 'A Woman, or even a slave may be drawn with this excellence of character, though it is probable that a woman should be worse than a man, and that a slave should be absolutely bad'; (*e*) Chapter XV, Note 5, 'The Fourth [element of Manners] is Consistency'. In each of these cases the chapter reference is to the *Poetics*; the title in inverted commas a quotation from the relevant chapter.

(*a*)

As we can only judge of the opinion of Aristotle, and how far it is really founded on nature, by our own sensations, or our observation of the sensations of others, we are much at a loss where to look for these means of decision. Dramatic representation, we have already observed, neither occupies the time or attention enough to have any great, or permanent energy, on our passions; and the perusal of tragedies, or other compositions of a congenial cast, is considered in general as the amusement of an idle hour, ready to be thrown aside in a moment on the arrival of the newspaper, or the summons to the card table. The only persons of the present day, who at all devote their attention with ardor and perseverance to the reading compositions of fictious distress, (and I believe their number, especially among the higher ranks, decreases every day,) are those usually called romantic young women, who dedicate much of their time to the study of the numerous tales, with which the press continually furnishes our circulating libraries. It is not my business here to enquire how this kind of application may influence their opinions, and conduct in life; but it certainly seems likely to throw some light on the influence a serious attention to scenes of imitated passion, may have on the force of real passion. And here we must confess, the first appearance is against the doctrine of the critic; the general effect of novel-reading on the gentler sex is too obvious to be doubted; it excites and inflames the passion which is the principal subject of the tale, and the susceptibility of the female votary of the circulating library, is proverbial. But we must, in the first place, recollect, that the passion of love is very different in itself from terror and pity, though it may be the cause of circumstances replete with both; and it is the tendency to this passion, and not to those of pity and terror, which is encreased by this kind of reading. Beside, it is not perhaps so much the passion itself that is enflamed, as the wish to feel it is created by this study. A desire of resembling the fictious heroine of a novel, has often induced a young mind to enquire for those sensations, which, without such a search, might have continued for some time dormant in the bosom. So far, therefore, is love from being blunted by imitative fiction, that such fiction is often an efficient cause of its being first excited.

[. . . . .]

(b)

If this rule is applied to the inimitable comic epopees of Fielding, and especially to *Tom Jones*, how many of the essential parts will be found so wonderfully connected, that even circumstances, apparently the most trifling, have consequences so interwoven with the plot, and so conducive to the solution of it, that they cannot be taken away, or altered, without changing and injuring the whole composition. And yet there are many episodic parts, which, though highly ornamental, may be removed without at all interfering with the general effect of the action. (I do not call the History of the Man of the Hill an episode; it is a separate tale.)

That in all fictitious narrative, whose aim is to affect the passions, the poetical arrangement is naturally and obviously preferable to the historical, may be fairly inferred, from the universal adoption of it by all the novel-writers, good and bad: a description of authors not very likely to be influenced in their choice by the rules of Aristotle. Indeed, the historic form, though it may succeed in humorous compositions, is almost incompatible with a pathetic tale; since to be interesting, the circumstances must be particularly related, which would either swell the work to an enormous size, or break it so into parts, as must be disagreeable to every reader. For this reason the extent of the dramatic action is naturally more confined than the epic, both from the interest being stronger, and, consequently, its going more into detail, and the division of the fable into parts being more obvious, and on that account more disgusting to the spectator, and hence the unity of time, though not carried to the excess prescribed by the French critics, is a necessary consideration in the drama. Shakespear, it is true, reconciles us to the breach of it; but what modern poet would presume to follow his example?

(c)

In the old and middle comedy, the manners, like those in modern farce when it keeps its true character, and in the burlesque epopee, such as *Hudibras*, are represented as devoid of this poetic goodness. But in what we call genteel comedy, and the comic epopee, the manners of the principal characters at least, though drawn in general conformity to those of the age, partake of this goodness in some degree. Though Tom Jones is not drawn different from other men as Achilles is, though he is not drawn as a perfect character, and therefore as a monster, like Grandison and Clarissa, every reader will see he has no foibles that disgrace him, one only excepted, his venal amour with Lady Bellaston. And there Fielding has committed an error, and every reader feels it, against this rule which Aristotle has given, or rather transcribed from the volume of nature. I have mentioned this as relative only to the principal characters. The subordinate ones may be purely burlesque even in comedy and the comic epopee.

(d)

The qualities that raise men in the esteem of the world, that render them in the general opinion of mankind great and respectable, on which poetical goodness of character depends, are often not connected, but frequently even in opposition to what may strictly be called moral virtue. That a degree of this poetical goodness is not incompatible even with atrocious crimes, has already been observed; and we may add, that in modern times it frequently depends on acknowledged vices, as a certain degree of gallantry and duelling. In regard to the first, how nearly has Fielding made Joseph Andrews an object of ridicule; and what pains is he obliged to employ to excuse him, by his violent attachment to another woman. The same may be observed as to duelling, in the character of Sir Charles Grandison, who, after all the trouble Richardson has taken to draw him perfect, is neither the object of our love or our respect. Indeed the poet's pencil is not always true to his intention.[1] I have no doubt that Rowe, in *The Fair Penitent*, meant to make Altamont the object of our esteem, and Lothario of our detestation. But he has so contrived in the execution, that we despise Altamont, and the gallant gay Lothario is the favorite of the spectators, though he is an unprincipled, and in one instance a despicable villain, for no crime can be more truly despicable than boasting of a woman's favors. The same may be said of two other characters in different works, Lovelace and Sir Charles Grandison. But a woman may be drawn perfectly good, and at the same time perfectly interesting, for there is no virtue in the catalogue of moral or christian duties that is not becoming, and does not both give and receive additional lustre, when possessed by that amiable sex. The utmost exertions of patience, and meekness, which at least sink the dignity of the tragic hero, raise the tragic heroine in our esteem. The characters of Imogen, of Desdemona, and of Cordelia, are as nearly patterns of perfection as human nature will admit, erring only as to those passions which we have already mentioned as furnishing that [. . .[2]] great frailty which causes the distress of virtuous characters without awakening our disgust, or sinking them in our esteem.

(e)

I will now produce three instances from works of narrative imitation, and those justly in the highest class of estimation. To begin with *Don Quixote*. In the part first published by Cervantes, and his subsequent addition in consequence of a spurious attempt by another hand, he has two distinct characters. 'In the first part it is true he is not drawn as an absolute maniac, when he is not discoursing of knight errantry, but all his conversation is tinged with singularity; and the pertinent things he says are incoherently arranged, and themselves out of place; as for instance, his long speech to the goatherds about the golden age: but in the second part he is made a man of sound judgment and elegant literature when the immediate subject of his madness is not touched upon.'[1]

My next instance is from a work which is of undoubted excellence indeed, leaving every work of the same nature far behind. I mean the character of Allworthy in *Tom Jones*. He has always appeared to me a striking instance of a character at opposition with himself, though more perhaps in general with that which the author tells you in his own person he is, than with his own conduct in those parts where the author suffers him to act from himself. The author is at great pains to inform us frequently that he is, though no scholar, a man of sense and discernment, with a benevolence almost angelic; and to press this more forcibly on our minds, he has given him a name strongly expressive of his moral goodness, though all his other characters have common names. But how is he really drawn? He is the dupe of every insinuating rascal he meets; and a dupe not of the most amiable kind, since he is always led to acts of justice and severity. The consequence of his pliability is oftener the punishment of the innocent than the acquittal of the guilty; and in such punishment he is severe and implacable. As in the case of Jones himself, his supposed father and mother, and black George. He suffers his adopted son and his foundling to be ill treated by an imperious pedagogue, whose whole character and conversation is a satire on christianity, and to have their principles corrupted by a hypocritical infidel.

The third instance is not so striking, but is I think to be found in a character, whose singularity as well as general uniformity with itself is universally and deservedly admired, and was a particular favorite with its author on this very account. I mean Sir Roger de Coverly in the *Spectator*. But is his conduct throughout the work consonant with the original delineation of his character? Or can his singularities, however amiable and however entertaining, be at all said to 'proceed from his good sense, and be contradictions to the manners of the world, only as he thinks the world is in the wrong?'[2]

80 *The Microcosm*, 26, Monday, May 14, 1787

by GEORGE CANNING

George Canning (1770–1827), statesman and author, was Tory Prime Minister from April 12, 1827, until his death on August 8 of the same year. In 1797 he collaborated with others in writing the *Anti-Jacobin*, a satirical periodical to which he contributed poems and articles. When Canning founded *The Microcosm* he was seventeen and still at Eton; the periodical ran from November 1786 to July 1787.

> *Fabula nullius veneris, sine pondere, et arte.*
> HOR.[1]

A silly story, without weight, or art.

Novel-writing has by some late authors been aptly enough styled the younger sister of Romance. A family likeness indeed is very evident; and in their leading features, though in the one on a more enlarged, and in the other on a more contracted scale, a strong resemblance is easily discoverable between them.

An eminent characteristic of each is Fiction; a quality which they possess, however, in very different degrees. The fiction of romance is restricted by no fetters of reason, or of truth; but gives a loose to lawless imagination, and transgresses at will the bounds of time and place, of nature and possibility. The fiction of the other, on the contrary, is shackled with a thousand restraints; is checked in her most rapid progress by the barriers of reason; and bounded in her most excursive flights by the limits of probability.

To drop our metaphors: we shall not indeed find in novels, as in romances, the hero sighing respectfully at the feet of his mistress, during a ten years' courtship in a wilderness; nor shall we be entertained with the history of such a tour, as that of Saint George; who mounts his horse one morning at Cappadocia, takes his way through Mesopotamia, then turns to the right into Illyria, and so, by way of Grecia and Thracia, arrives in the afternoon in England. To such glorious violations as these of time and place, romance writers have an exclusive claim. Novelists usually find it more convenient to change the scene of courtship from a desert to a drawing-room; and far from thinking it necessary to lay a ten years' siege to the affections of their heroine, they contrive to carry their point in an hour or two; as well for the sake of enhancing the character of their hero, as for establishing their favourite maxim of love at first sight; and their hero, who seldom extends his travels beyond the turnpike-road, is commonly content to choose the safer, though less expeditious, conveyance of a post-chaise, in preference to such a horse as that of Saint George.

But, these peculiarities of absurdity alone excepted, we shall find, that the novel is but a more modern modification of the same ingredients which constitute the romance; and that a recipe for the one may be equally serviceable for the composition of the other.

A Romance (generally speaking) consists of a number of strange events, with a hero in the middle of them; who, being an adventurous knight, wades through them to one grand design, namely, the emancipation of some captive princess, from the oppression of a merciless giant; for the accomplishment of which purpose he must set at nought the incantations of the caitiff magician; must scale the ramparts of his castle; and baffle the vigilance of the female dragon, to whose custody his heroine is committed.

Foreign as they may at first sight seem from the purposes of a novel, we shall find, upon a little examination, that these are in fact the very circumstances upon which the generality of them are built; modernized indeed in some degree, by the transformations of merciless giants into austere guardians, and of she-dragons into maiden aunts. We must be contented also that the heroine, though retaining her tenderness, be divested of her royalty; and in the hero we must give up the knight-errant for the accomplished fine gentleman.

Still, however, though the performers are changed, the characters themselves remain nearly the same. In the guardian we trace all the qualities which distinguish his ferocious predecessor; substituting only, in the room of magical incantations, a little plain cursing and swearing; and the maiden aunt retains all the prying vigilance, and suspicious malignity, in short, every endowment but the claws, which characterize her romantic counterpart. The hero of a novel has not indeed any opportunity of displaying his courage in the scaling of a rampart, or his generosity in the deliverance of enthralled multitudes; but as it is necessary that a hero should signalize himself by both these qualifications, it is usual, to manifest the one by climbing the garden wall, or leaping the park-paling, in defiance of 'steel-traps and spring-guns;' and the other, by flinging a crown to each of the post-boys, on alighting from his chaise and four.

In the article of interviews, the two species of composition are pretty much on an equality; provided only, that they are supplied with a 'quantum sufficit' of moonlight, which is indispensably requisite; it being the etiquette for the moon to appear particularly conscious on these occasions. For the adorer, when permitted to pay his vows at the shrine of his divinity, custom has established in both cases a pretty universal form of prayer.

Thus far the writers of novel and romance seem to be on a very equal footing; to enjoy similar advantages, and to merit equal admiration. We are now come to a very material point, in which romance has but slender claims to comparative excellence; I mean the choice of names and titles. However lofty and sonorous the names of Amadis and Orlando; however tender and delicate may be those of Zorayda and Roxana, are they to be compared with the attractive alliteration, the seducing softness, of Lydia Lovemore, and Sir Harry Harlowe; of Frederic Freelove, and Clarissa Clearstarch? Or can the simple *Don Belianis, of Greece*, or the *Seven Champions of Christendom*, trick out so enticing a title-page, and awaken such pleasing expectations, as the *Innocent Adultery*, the *Tears of Sensibility*, or the *Amours of the Count de D******, and L——y —————————?[2]

It occurs to me while I am writing this, that as there has been of late years so considerable a consumption of names and titles, as to have exhausted all the efforts of invention, and ransacked all the alliterations of the alphabet; it may not be amiss to inform all novelists, male and female, who under these circumstances must necessarily wish, with Falstaff, to know 'where a commodity of good names may be bought,'[3] that at my warehouse for wit, I have laid in a great number of the above articles, of the most fashionable and approved patterns. Ladies may suit themselves with a vast variety, adapted to every composition of the kind; whether they may choose them to consist of two adjectives only, as the 'Generous Inconstant,'—the 'Fair Fugitive,'—or the name of a place, as 'Grogram Grove,' 'Gander Green,' or whether they prefer the still newer method of coupling persons and things with an 'or,' as 'Louisa; or, the Purling Stream,'—'Estafina; or, the Abbey in the Dale,' —'Eliza; or, the Little House on the Hill.' Added to these, I have a complete assortment of names for every individual that can find a place in a novel; from the Belviles and Beverleys of high life, to the Humphreyses and Gubbinses of low; suited to all ages, ranks, and professions; to persons of every stamp, and characters of every denomination.

In painting the scenes of low life, the novel again enjoys the most decisive superiority. Romance indeed sometimes makes use of the grosser sentiments, and less refined affections of the squire and the confidant, as a foil to the delicate adoration, the platonic purity, which make the love of the hero, and suits the sensibility of his mistress. But where shall we find such a thorough knowledge of nature, such an insight into the human heart, as is displayed by our novelists; when, as an agreeable relief from the insipid sameness of polite insincerity, they condescend to portray in coarse colours, the workings of more genuine passions in the bosom of Dolly, the dairy-maid, or Hannah, the house-maid?

When on such grounds and on a plan usually very similar to the one I have here endeavoured to sketch, are founded by far the greater number of those novels, which crowd the teeming catalogue of a circulating library; is it to be wondered at, that they are sought out with such avidity, and run through with such delight, by all those (a considerable part of my fellow-citizens) who cannot resist the impulse of curiosity, or withstand the allurements of a title-page? Can we be surprised, that they look forward, with expecting eagerness, to that inundation of delicious nonsense, with which the press annually over-flows; replete as it is with stories without invention, anecdotes without novelty, observations without aptness, and reflections without morality?

Under this description come the generality of these performances. There are, no doubt, a multitude of exceptions. The paths which a Fielding and a Richardson have trodden, must be sacred. Were I to profane these by impertinent criticism, I might with justice be accused of avowed enmity to wit; of open apostacy from true feeling, and true taste.

But let me hope to stand excused from the charge of presumption, if even here I venture some observations, which I am confident must have occurred to many; and to which almost every body, when reminded of them, will be ready to give a hearty concurrence.

Is not the novel of *Tom Jones*, however excellent a work of itself, generally put too early into our hands, and proposed too soon to the imitation of children? That it is a character drawn faithfully from nature, by the hand of a master, most accurately delineated, and most exquisitely finished, is indeed indisputable. But is it not also a character, in whose shades the lines of right and wrong, of propriety and misconduct, are so intimately blended, and softened into each other, as to render it too difficult for the indiscriminating eye of childhood to distinguish between rectitude and error? Are not its imperfections so nearly allied to excellence, and does not the excess of its good qualities bear so strong an affinity to imperfection, as to require a more matured judgment, a more accurate penetration, to point out the line where virtue ends and vice begins? The arguments urged in opposition to this are, that it is a faithful copy of nature.—Undoubtedly it is—but is nature to be held up to the view of childhood, in every light, however unamiable; to be exhibited in every attitude, however unbecoming? the hero's connexion with Miss Seagrim, for instance, and the supposed consequences of it are very natural no doubt; are they therefore objects worthy of imitation? But that a child must admire the character, is certain; that he should wish to imitate what he admires, follows of course; and that it is much more easy to imitate faults than excellences, is an observation too trite, I fear, not to be well founded. A character virtuous and amiable in the aggregate, but vicious in particular parts, is much more dangerous to a mind, prone to imitation, as that of youth naturally is, than one wicked and vicious in the extreme. The one is an open assault of an avowed enemy, which every one has judgment to see, and consequently fortitude to resist; the other is the treacherous attack of an insidious invader; who makes the passions his agents to blind the judgment, and bribes the understanding to betray the heart.— Such is the character of Jones. He interests our affections at the moment that his actions revolt against our ideas of propriety; nor can even his infidelity to Sophia, however ungrateful, nor his connexion with Lady Bellastone [*sic*], though perhaps the most degrading situation in which human nature can be viewed, materially lessen him in our esteem and admiration. On these grounds therefore, though there cannot be a more partial admirer of the work itself, I cannot hesitate a moment to consider that 'faultless monster'[4] Sir Charles Grandison, whose insipid uniformity of goodness it is fashionable to decry, far the more preferable to be held up to a child as an object of imitation. The only objection urged to this is, that Grandison is too perfect to be imitated with success. And to what does this argument amount? truly this, it tends to prove, that an imitator cannot come up to his original; consequently, the surest way to become a Jones, is to aim at being a

Grandison: for according to that argument, let a man rate his virtues at the highest price, and the natural bias of his passions will make him bate something of his valuation.—Hence therefore the character of Grandison is assuredly the properer pattern of the two. An attempt at the imitation of that, must necessarily be productive of some attainment in virtue. The character of Jones can neither operate as an incitement to virtue, or a discouragement from vice. He is too faulty for the one, and too excellent for the other. Even his good qualities must, on an undiscerning mind, have a bad effect; since, by fascinating its affections, they render it blind to his foibles; and the character becomes the more dangerous, in proportion as it is the more amiable.

But to return from this long digression, to the consideration of novels in general. Some of my fellow-citizens may perhaps conjecture, that I have affected to undervalue them from interested motives; and that I would wean them from their study of them, for the purpose only of increasing the demand for my own lucubrations. To wipe off any suspicions of the kind, and to prove to them that my only motives are a view to their advantage, I promise, in the course of a few numbers, to point out to the observation, and recommend to the perusal of professed novel readers, a set of books, which they now treat with undeserved contempt, but from which I will prove, that they may derive at least as much entertainment, and certainly much more useful instruction, than from the dull details of unmeaning sentiment, and insipid conversation; of incidents the most highly unnatural, and events the most uninteresting.[5]—B.

81 *Olla Podrida*, 15, Saturday, June 23, 1787

by THOMAS MONROE

Olla Podrida was founded in March 1787 by Thomas Monroe (or Munro) (1764–1815), and ran until January 1788. Monroe is also known as the translator (with William Beloe), of Alciphron's *Epistles* (1791).

> ———*Nimis alta sapit,*
> *Bellua multorum capitum.*[1]

In a society, instituted for the purpose of amicable disputation, to which I once found means to obtain admittance, the following question was proposed for discussion:—'Which circumstances would be more irksome to a gentleman of delicate feelings; the reflection that he had killed another in a duel, or had been himself pulled by the nose from Penzance in Cornwall to our town of Berwick-upon-Tweed, by way of London.' That his audience might have as clear a comprehension as possible of the subject to be discussed, the leader of the debate thought it necessary to specify to them the distance between the two places mentioned, in which his accuracy was questioned by a gentleman with his handkerchief under his wig. The contest was carried on with violence and acrimony, but was at length somewhat appeased by means of a third person, who, upon bringing the parties to explain, discovered that they had made their calculations upon different principles, the one having consulted Paterson's book of roads, the other, Ogilby's.[2]

It was on all sides sagaciously concluded upon that one must be wrong: but it was impossible to ascertain which, without examining the comparative excellencies of Messrs. Paterson and Ogilby, each of whom was extolled by either party as a literary Colossus. This gave the debate another interesting turn; and as I found the heat of the room and the contest likely to endanger my welfare, and produce something more than a war of words, I made as precipitate a retreat as the nature of the case would admit; but before I could gain the door, I found the amicable disputants had laid aside their rhetoric and their coats, and

347

exchanged the fanciful and ideal shafts of wit for the material weapons of pewter pots and oaken sticks. Never was that happy comparison of the grammarians more thoroughly illustrated, by which they liken logic to the clenched fist! My escape from these logicians was a source of comfortable contemplation, yet I could not lay aside all my fears for the safety of those I had left behind; however, I had the satisfaction to find the next morning, that no material injury had been sustained. Upon turning into a shop, I bought a pair of gloves of the Patersonian; and soon after discovered the follower of Ogilby mending the clubroom windows.

These, and a few other circumstances, which I need not, perhaps, enumerate, have induced me to offer to my patient readers a few observations on that great love of refinement and sentimentality which is daily gaining ground among the lower orders of our fellow-countrymen, of which nothing can I believe radically cure them but a Dutch war. The grand causes of this mischief, I am inclined to suppose, are the above-mentioned pewter-pot spouting clubs, and those rhapsodies of nonsense which are so liberally poured upon the public, under the title of Sentimental Novels, utterly subversive of common sense, and not very warm friends to common honesty. There is a fascinating power in nonsense, which may sometimes afford relaxation, if not amusement, to a man of sense; but which always meets with something congenial to itself in meaner capacities. For such capacities such compositions are well adapted; and for these the furrow is left unfinished, and 'the hammers miss their wonted stroke.'[3]

Some of my readers may, perhaps, be not only readers of novels, but writers of them. Though I do not consider myself as qualified in any particular to dictate to so respectable a part of the community, yet I cannot forbear offering a few, perhaps erroneous, remarks upon them and their productions.

While the writers of novels have so many admirable models, upon which their style might be formed, it is not without regret that we turn over the insipid pages which are thrust into our sight in every bookseller's shop. They seem to have forgotten that there are writers better than themselves; that if we wish for delicate and refined sentiment, we can recur to *Grandison* and *Clarissa*; if we would see the world more perhaps as it is, than as it should be, we have *Joseph Andrews* and *Tom Jones*; or that we can find the happy mixture of satire and moral tendency in the *Spiritual Quixote* and *Cecilia*.[4]

I cannot help noticing the glaring impropriety they are guilty of, who make their nobility and their peasants speak the same language. They defend themselves, no doubt, by the authority and example of Virgil's Shepherds, Sanazarius's Fishermen,[5] and the rustics of Mr. Pope. But when they are told, that to copy the deformities of good writers will be no embellishment to bad ones, they may perhaps cease to overwhelm us with the sentimentality of their Abigails, the heroic gallantry of their footmen, and the rhetorical flourishes of their shoemakers. These are more particularly the characters which do a material injury to that part of the nation, who, when they have shut up shop, wet their thumbs and spell through a novel. A love-sick chambermaid is enough to ruin half the sisterhood; an intriguing apprentice is the torment of master tradesmen; and the high-flown notions of honour, which are inculcated by 'Johnny with his shoulder-knot,' will set a couple of tailors a duelling. If the rapid course of these grievances be not checked, we shall have the epicure justly complaining that he can get no lamb to eat with his asparagus, from the sensibility of the Leadenhall-butchers; or that the melting tenderness of the cooks prevents the eels from being skinned, or the lobsters boiled alive. Should delicacy of thinking become too common, we may drive the lawyers from their quibbles, and how then are we to get those little odd jobs done for ourselves and our estates, so convenient for our families, and so beneficial to our landed interests? Suppose, moreover, the Jews (I do not mean particularly those to whom Dr. Priestley's invitation is directed),[6] but the money-lenders and the proprietors of the crucible, should be infected with this growing sense of honour; the gaming-table must be deserted; there would be no market for stolen watches; and the triumph of sentiment would be the downfal of the nation.

There is much perhaps to be complained of in other publications which tend to disseminate the glare and tinsel of false sentiment; I mean the works of those imitators of Sterne, whose pages are polluted with ribaldry and dashes; and those compilers of modern tragedies, at which no man weeps, unless in pure friendship for the author.

If I in the playhouse saw a huge blacksmith-like looking fellow blubbering over the precious foolery of *Nina*,[7] I should immediately take it for granted he came in with an order, and look upon his iron tears as a *forgery*. Indeed, might I be allowed to dictate upon such an occasion, no man should be permitted to moisten a white handkerchief at the *ohs* and the *ahs* of a modern tragedy, unless he possessed an estate of seven hundred a year, clear of mortgage, and every other encumbrance. Such people have a right to fling away their time as they please;

the works of the loom receive no impediment from their idleness, and it is at least an innocent though insipid amusement.

While I seem endeavouring to harden the hearts of my country against those attacks which are made upon them from the stage, I am far from wishing to rob them of that prompt benevolence which is a leading feature in our national character. But I am afraid of refinement even in our virtues. I am afraid lest the same eye which is so prone to give its tributary tear to the well-told history of fancied woe, should be able to look upon real misery without emotion, because its tale is told without plot, incident, or ornament. I would only therefore remind those fair ladies and well-dressed gentlemen who frequent our theatres because they have nothing else to do, or that they may enjoy the luxury of shedding tears with Mrs. Siddons,[8] that if they will look round among their fellow-creatures, they will find their time rather too short, than too long, for the exercise of their compassion in alleviating the distresses of their neighbours: and they may, by these means be supplied with luxuries, which will never reproach them with time squandered away, or mispent in idleness or vice.

MONRO.

82 From the *Gentleman's Magazine*, LVII, December 1787

This article is signed R.R.E.

[. . . . .]
It is reported, that a tax is to be imposed, during the ensuing session of parliament, on shoes and boots. Though the people of this country have given sufficient proofs of their disposition to acquiesce in any burthens which the state of the Government may make it necessary to lay upon them; yet, if such assistance can be derived from the superfluities, rather than from the necessaries, of life, Ministers will not, I hope, be above adopting an hint, though from an unknown pen.

Novels have been long and frequently regarded not as being merely useless to society, but even as pernicious, from the very indifferent morality, and ridiculous way of thinking, which they almost generally inculcate. Why then, in the name of common sense, should such an useless and pernicious commodity, with which we are over-run, go duty-free, while the really useful necessary of life is taxed to the utmost extent? A tax on books of this description only (for books of real utility should ever be circulated free as air) would bring in a very considerable sum for the service of Government, without being levied on the poor or the industrious.

[. . . . .]

83 From *Winter Evenings, or, Lucubrations on Life and Letters*, 115, 1788

by VICESSIMUS KNOX

Winter Evenings . . ., like *The Observer* (see above, No. 78), was an essay series in volume form, published in two volumes in 1788. For Knox, see above, No. 74, headnote.

On multiplying Books by the Publication of trifling and useless Works. Ev[ening] 115

Majoragius, abounding in leisure, and abusing that happy circumstance, is said to have written an oration in praise of mud or clay; Puteanus, in the same situation, celebrated an egg; one has written a panegyric on drunkenness; and others on a louse, a flea, the itch, and the ague.[1] They might, it is certain, write what they pleased, and it is happy for us that there is no compulsion to read what they have thus wantonly composed.

There are already more books than can be used by any man, or to any good purpose. To increase their number by writing mere nonsense and insipid bagatelle, is certainly improper. And it is to be wished that they who are so fond of scribbling to spoil paper, without the least idea of advantage to science or morals, would be contented with the amusement they derive from the employ, and forbear publication.

The love of novelty is indeed so powerful, that it will often recommend to notice books which have nothing else to recommend them. But it is to be wished, that as the love of novelty may certainly as well be gratified by good performances as by bad ones, it would give itself the trouble to exercise the powers of judgment and selection.

The most trifling compositions of the present age are novels, poems, and miscellanies.

There are, however, many novels of real and substantial value, such as appear to have owed their origin to true genius and to classical taste. Wherever they exhibit genuine pictures of life and manners; and wherever they furnish matter for reflection, they certainly constitute some of the most useful books for the instruction of young persons. They are so pleasing that the mind is gradually allured by them to virtue and wisdom, which it would perhaps never have duly considered and fully adopted had they been recommended solely by dull argumentation.

But it is a misfortune, that among the great variety and multitude of novels with which the world abounds, very few are capable of teaching morality. Their authors are found for the most part to lean to the side of vice; or if any begin with a sincere purpose of instructing the rising generation in real goodness, they are so injudicious in the conduct of their work, as to enter into such warm descriptions and narratives as conduce rather to inflame than to allay the fury of the passions.

There are three kind of novels; those which are really good, and have nothing in them of a corrupting nature; those which are extremely excellent, considered only as compositions, but of a bad tendency; and those which are almost insipid, which possess nothing striking in the story, nor elegant in the language, but are formed merely to amuse minds of an effeminate and inconsiderate turn.

The first sort ought to be read in youth, as they are peculiarly fitted to improve the mind. They are such as *Don Quixote*, if any such can be found. The second are certainly to be laid aside till the student has passed the dangerous age of early youth. The last are never to be read at all, but to be classed with Majoragius *De Luto*.

Poems, without any pretensions to poetry beyond a smoothness of versification and good rhymes, greatly abound in the present age. Every newspaper has its poet's corner. Now, as Horace has justly said, and as thousands have said since Horace, there is no possibility of tolerating mediocrity in poetry.[2] Poetry is not one of the necessaries of life. The information it conveys may be conveyed in prose. It is sought only as an excellence, a refinement, an elegance. If therefore it is not excellent, refined, and elegant, it may be dispensed with. We shall be better pleased with a plain good dinner, than with a dessert of pretended sweetmeats, in which there is nothing truly delicious. Almost all the versification which obtrudes itself on the public eye in public papers, is useless and superfluous. It proceeds from those who, with little learning or genius, are smitten by the sweets of poetical fame, and are desirous of making an appeal to the world, and trying whether or not they shall be judged worthy of the laurel. Among the trifling and useless poetry may certainly be classed all rebuses and acrostics, and most of the modern pastorals.

It will perhaps be said, if these silly sports of ingenuity amuse the idle innocently, they are useful. But I ask whether, if the idle were to lay aside such unimproving works, they might not probably find more pleasure, together with improvement, in works of sound judgment, taste, and knowledge?

[. . . . .]

84 From a review of *Emmeline, the Orphan of the Castle* (1788), *The Analytical Review*, 1, July 1788

The *Analytical Review* was founded and conducted for the greater part of its life (1788–99) by Thomas Christie (1701–96). According to the *Dictionary of National Biography* (IV, 1908), '. . . though not displaying any extraordinary ability, and now utterly forgotten, the review was a great advance upon anything that had up to that time appeared, and has served as the model of many other periodicals'.

Charlotte Smith (1749–1806) wrote several novels after *Emmeline* . . .: *Ethelinde, or the Recluse of the Lake* (1790), *Desmond* (1792), *Celestina* (1792), *The Old Manor House* (1793) and *Marchmont* (1796).

[. . . . .]
Few of the numerous productions termed novels, claim any attention; and while we distinguish this one, we cannot help lamenting that it has the same tendency as the generality, whose preposterous sentiments our young females imbibe with such avidity. Vanity thus fostered, takes deep root in the forming mind, and affectation banishes natural graces, or at least obscures them. We do not mean to confound affectation and vice, or allude to those pernicious writings that obviously vitiate the heart, while they lead the understanding astray. But we must observe, that the false expectations these wild scenes excite, tend to debauch the mind, and throw an insipid kind of uniformity over the moderate and rational prospects of life, consequently *adventures* are sought for and created, when duties are neglected, and content despised.

We will venture to ask any young girl if Lady Adelina's theatrical contrition did not catch her attention, while Mrs. Stafford's rational resignation escaped her notice? Lady Adelina is indeed a character as absurd as dangerous. Despair is not repentance, nor is contrition of any use when it does not serve to strengthen resolutions of amendment. The being who indulges useless sorrow, instead of fulfilling the duties of life, may claim our pity, but should never excite admiration; for in such characters there is no true greatness of soul, or just sentiments of religion; indeed this kind of sorrow is rather the offspring of romantic notions and false refinement, than of sensibility and a nice sense of duty. Mrs. Stafford, when disappointed in her husband, turned to her children. We mention this character because it deserves praise.

We have not observed many touches of nature in the delineation of the passions, except the emotions which the descriptions of romantic views gave rise to; in them the poetrical talents of the author appear, as well as in some sonnets interspersed in the work. Indeed some of the descriptions are so interesting and beautiful that we would give a specimen if they could be separated from the woven web without injuring them, and if we have not already exceeded the bounds prescribed.

M.

85 Two Essays from *Variety: A Collection of Essays, written in the Year 1787*, 1788

by ANNA SEWARD

The two Essays reproduced below appeared as Nos. XXV and XXVI in *Variety* . . .; they are on the same subject, under the title, 'On the *Clarissa* of Richardson and Fielding's *Tom Jones*', and were written in answer to Richard Cumberland's paper in *The Observer* (see above, No. 79). *Variety* . . . was edited by H. Repton (1752–1818), well known as the author of several works on landscape gardening: *Letter to Uvedale Price* (1794), *Sketches of Hints on Landscape Gardening* (1795) and *An Enquiry into the changes in Landscape Gardening* (1806). Another of his works on this subject, *Observations on the Theory and Practice of Landscape Gardening* (1803), is alluded to in *Mansfield Park*, chapter vi. Repton appears as Marmaduke Milestone in T. L. Peacock's *Headlong Hall* (1816).

Anna Seward (1747–1809), the 'Swan of Lichfield', was an intimate of Erasmus Darwin and Samuel Johnson, and did not publish much during her life, in spite of her reputation for wit and learning. Her poems and miscellaneous works were published by Sir Walter Scott in 1810; her letters were given to the world in 1811.

'Tis hard to say if greater want of skill
Appears in *writing*, or in *judging* ill;
But, of the two, least dangerous is th' offence
To tire our patience, than mislead our sense.

PoPE.[1]

It cannot be doubted that the understanding, and virtue, the safety and happiness, of those branches of Society which are raised above the necessity of mechanic toil, depend much upon the early impressions they receive from books which captivate the imagination, and interest the heart. Consequently a writer is much their foe, who seeks to throw contempt upon any work which is eminently calculated to inspire

357

delicacy, and discretion of conduct, purity of morals, tenderness, generosity, and piety of heart,—while he recommends another composition, possessing allurement, too well calculated to make it recommend *itself*; but which has a demonstrable tendency to encourage libertinism in our young men; and, in our young women, an infatuated propensity to bestow their affections, and even esteem upon men of profligate habits.

That an author capable of writing agreeably upon many subjects, who must have observed with what difficulty vicious habits, contracted in early life, are laid aside as it advances; and that *continued*, how fatal they prove to domestic comfort, that a man who is himself a father, should avow such a preference, and employ his oratory, and aim at wit in its defence, may well awaken the wonder and disdain of thinking minds.

A paper in Mr. Cumberland's *Observer*, on the subject of Novels, suggested these reflections. It points out, in that large range of fashionable reading, which are the paths to be *interdicted*, and which *chosen* for young people by their Parents, and Guardians. From the praise which its author lavishes upon *Fielding's Tom Jones*, and from his affected contempt of the *Clarissa of Richardson*, he seems to recommend the former to our youths as forcibly, by implication, as he reprobates the latter, in direct and positive terms. Men eminent for piety, wisdom, and virtue, have recommended Richardson's *Clarissa* from the pulpit;[2] a work which Dr. Johnson, (so generally unwilling to praise) has been often heard to pronounce, 'not only the first *novel*, but perhaps the first *work* in our language, splendid in point of genius, and calculated to promote the dearest interests of religion and virtue.'[3]

Those who have ability to perceive the riches of that work in every varied excellence of beautiful composition, will not be insensible to the merit of the *Tom Jones*, as a fascinating performance, whose situations are interesting, whose characters display the hand of a master, whose humour is pointed and natural, whose style is easy, and to whose powers of engaging, the pathetic graces have not been wanting.

But while they acknowledge all these agreeable properties, they will feel it amongst the most striking instances of human absurdity, that a serious writer should recommend it to the libraries of the rising generation by unqualified praise, while he condemns the *Clarissa* as a ridiculous romance, inimical to good sense, discretion, and morality.

A lady of wit and spirit has been heard to declare, that she was once compleatly silenced by a very stupid personage, in the midst of a declamation, and encircled by a large party of ladies and gentlemen. She was haranguing upon the preference she should feel of Tom Jones, to Sir Charles Grandison, as a brother, a friend, a lover, or an husband. The *silly* gentlewoman, in the meer desire of prating, and perfectly unconscious of the power of what she was going to utter, interrupted the Lady Orator with, 'Ladies and gentlemen, *I* am reading *Tom Jones*, but I have not finished it. I have just left him in bed with another man's wife.'

Perhaps it is not impossible, though very uncommon, that bravery, ingenuousness, compassion, and generosity, should exist in the mind of a young man, who is indiscriminately licentious respecting women; but it is ill for morals when such a character is thus indirectly held up to imitation by an author professing morality.

Beneath this splendid veil of engaging qualities, a vicious character loses all its deformity in the easily dazzled eyes of youth. In Sophia's character, her sex find their sanction for attaching themselves to a libertine; that rock, on which female happiness is so often wrecked.

Having thus enforced the obvious bad tendency of the work, over which Mr. Cumberland pours so much applause, let us turn to the volumes he *interdicts*, to the *Clarissa* of Richardson. It is no where that Morality is more powerfully enforced; it is no where that Piety is more exquisitely lovely. Every individual in that large Dramatis Personae, is drawn with such distinctness, such characteristic strength, that not a letter, a single speech in the whole work, but so peculiarly belongs to the nature of that spirit, which is supposed to have dictated it; that it is needless to cast the eye back to the name of the speaker, or to look at the signature.

Amongst the stately family at Harlow-Place, we do indeed perceive more precise, and solemn ceremony than we find in the houses of country gentlemen at *this* period, when Gallic ease has stolen upon the self-importance of the British '*Squirality*'; but every body knows that such *were* the manners of opulent country families, some forty years back, where the master chose to be the gentleman, rather than the toping and riotous Foxhunter. Let it also be remembered, that the Harlowes were a *new-raised* family, that wanted to establish their *questionably* [*sic*] dignity.

As to the persisting authority, unjustly exercised upon young women in the article of marriage, *that* feature of probability in this charming work, is still ascertained by a variety of examples every year, at least, in *wealthy*, and still oftener in *high* life; though, because ceremony is not the *fashion*, there may be less *parade* in the *manner* of enforcing it.

> For rich-ones, with unfather'd eyes,
> As Pride, or thirst of gold assail,
> Attend their human Sacrifice,
> Without the Grecian Painter's veil.[4]

The author meant to hold up the portraits of Clarissa, and Grandison, to each sex, as models of male, and female virtue. It has been truly said, that whatever be our aim, whether the attainment of an art, of science, or of virtue, the model, from which we copy, cannot be too *perfect*. We might as well blame the transcendant sculptor, as the moralist; as rationally prefers less exquisite, less beautiful statues, to the Venus de Medicis, and the Apollo Belvidere, because they may be nearer resemblances of the human form; as chuse to contemplate a Jones, and a Sophia, rather than a Grandison, and a Clarissa.

If worn and hacknied in the tainted mazes of Society, *our* ardor for Virtue is grown palled, and sick, so that we behold representations of consummate excellence without delight, let us not seek to deprive the generous credulity, and hoping sensibility of youth, of the noblest patterns our language affords (without the scriptural pale) of moral virtue, and piety; adorned and graceful in the charms of youth and beauty; in the splendor of elevated intellect; in the utmost elegance of style, and in all the interest of trying situations.

An accurate observer of life and manners, must have many times beheld very exact resemblances of every character in *Clarissa*; the glorious maid, and her profligate ravisher alone excepted.

To form a bright example of female virtue, superior to temptation in the great essential *chastity*; and in whom every lesser consideration of worldly fame and prosperity should be subordinate to the delicacy of exalted principle; it was necessary to draw the character of *Lovelace*, exactly as he *is* drawn. Less accomplished, less brave, less bountiful, less estimable in all respects, (where his darling vice did not interfere) he could not have obtained the degree of interest he possessed in the heart of a Clarissa; and without which, her resistance had lost all its merit. Less hardened by the power of this absorbing vice, less determined, less cruelly persisting, she could not have sustained from him those wrongs from which she rises so far above the Lucretian-chastity; evincing by her conduct the superior excellence of the Christian principles to those which hurried into suicide the injured Roman matron.

As the *worst* possible moral results from the character of Tom Jones, so does the *best* result from that of Lovelace. By the former, our youth are taught to believe that they may be very noble fellows, whom every body will love, and yet indulge their criminal appetites in the seduction of what they *believe* to be rustic innocence, as in Jones's amour with Molly Seagrim; and plunge into *known* adultery, as in his connection with Mrs. Waters; and this, even though they are in love with an amiable woman, as Jones with Sophia. A situation, which infinitely enhances, and indeed renders wholly unpardonable the gross, and brutal guilt of profligacy. While by the character of Lovelace, as by that of Macbeth, we are taught, that gallant courage, and brilliant talents, form no security against a man's becoming darkly villainous, if he deliver himself up, without restraint, to the influence of his consitutional vice.

While the eye of sensibility streams over the suffering, and over the dying Clarissa, there is a 'secret, stern, vindictive, yet not unjust pleasure, that brightens those tears,'[5] and which always arises in the generous bosom upon the punishment of treachery, like that of Lovelace, and of inflexibility like that of the Harlow-family.

Cold to the sense of devotion, dead to the hope, and trust of a blessed immortality, must be that heart, which does not triumph, and delight (however the eyes may overflow) in the death of Clarissa, in the everlasting rest of a broken heart, in the emancipation of an oppressed, an injured, and angelic spirit, soaring above all its cruel persecutors, to unfading light, and ever-during felicity.

* *

Mr Cumberland accuses this work of tedious prolixity, and the accusation is pretty general. It cannot be denied that even ingenious minds capable of perceiving its various excellences, the graces of its eloquence, the powers of its pathos, and the brilliance of its wit, may, on a *first* perusal, find themselves so anxiously interested in the events, as to become impatient of any pause in the story.

But *recurring* to these volumes, (to which the sensible reader *will* recur as to Shakespear, to Milton, or the *Rambler*[6]) when satisfied curiosity leaves the mind calm enough to remark, and enjoy at leisure their innumerable beauties; something will be found in *every* letter, which is highly curious and entertaining. In the master-strokes of truth, and nature, do they delineate the mind, and the manners of the supposed writer; besides throwing strong collateral light, and colouring, upon *other* characters in the work. This excellence of appropriation pervades all the epistles, even those, in which elegance of style is judiciously abated, as in the letters of the proud, unyielding Harlowes; or wholly thrown aside, as in those of the proverbial Lord M——, the pedant Brand, and the menial personages; while, on this recurrent perusal, the characteristic graces of the more *eloquent* epistles shine out, in Variety inexhaustible.

The letters of *Lovelace* exhibit every gay attraction of peerless wit, picturesque description, classic allusion, and universal knowledge, without any affectation in its display; a style unrivalled in its easy flow, and fascinating harmony; and, what strikingly evinces the address, and virtuous design of the author, the epistles of this seducing libertine, even more forcibly than any of the others, warn the youthful female against the designs of the opposite Sex, by the startling axioms they contain, respecting the conduct of women. It is from the letters of *Lovelace*, that they learn how inevitably despicable they become in the eyes of those very men, to whose solicitations they are beginning to make sacrifices, (apparently trivial) of that delicacy and purity so lovely in the sex; sacrifices that generally end in the utter loss of honour from libertine encroachment.

In Colonel *Morden*'s letters, and in those of Lovelace, and Belford, which describe the colonel's person, his air, his manners, and his conduct, we see a perfect fine gentleman, intrepid and accomplished as the former, benevolent as the latter, and more virtuous; while beneath the dignity which that virtue confers, the dazzling *Lovelace* sinks into visible and conscious inferiority.

We find, in the touching epistles of the matchless Heroine of this work, the most complete powers of imagery and description, shaded over by that soft veil of distress, thro' which they appear with heightened grace, and dearer interest; the importance of every duty that blesses society; the danger and misery of every deviation from the path of rectitude, enforced with the eloquence of angels,—her character rising amidst her severe trials, her deep distresses, and remorseless injuries, into unrivalled magnanimity;—while in its noblest elevation, the charm of female softness is never for a single moment lost.

Mr. JEPHSON (perhaps our best Tragedy-writer since Shakespear)[7] has availed himself, in his poetic and spirited tragedy *Julia*, of the penknife-scene in *Clarissa*. Deprived of the preparatory circumstances that constitute a large part of its transcendant sublimity in the *original* situation, it could not but lose extremely by the transposition; but to those who do not perfectly recollect the pages from whence it is taken, the effect in the Tragedy is very fine.

Mr. CUMBERLAND tells the public, that he knew a young female, whose head was turned by reading Clarissa; and who, in the rage of imitation, insisted upon having her coffin in her bed-chamber!

Insane people have always some reigning idea. That the coffin of Clarissa should once have proved that reigning idea, is surely a very contemptible reason for interdicting this noble composition, as inimical to the morals, and discretion of youth.

Many religious enthusiasts have fancied they had prophetic and apostolic inspiration. At the Cathedral of one of our celebrated provincial towns, some twenty years ago, I often used to see a man, whom many of the present inhabitants remember. It was his custom to stand, during service, before the rails of the altar. He had read about our Saviour, till he fancied himself that sacred character, and a native resemblance of face, and figure to the prints of Jesus, aided the phrenzy. He had trained the growth of his dark beard in the Jewish fashion, and his hair, parted upon his forehead, hung in equal ringlets down each side the front part of his neck. He was thin, and pale, with a remarkable air of placid dignity. The mildness this maniac constantly preserved, rendered him inoffensive.

With the same reason might the SCRIPTURES be censured as a dangerous study upon that instance, as this admirable work, because one romantic delirious fool bespoke her coffin, without the reasons which impelled Clarissa to take that singular step.

It is curious to hear the author of our most sentimental comedies, speak with contempt over the unerring sentiments which enrich these volumes. It would be happy for the rising, and for the future generation, if our young women would imitate the principles, and the conduct of Clarissa, though not perhaps in bespeaking their coffin: a circumstance for which she apologizes, confessing it a sally of mournful enthusiasm, and too scrupulous delicacy; excusable only from the peculiarity of her situation, and from being obliged to chuse a male executor. Recommending Clarissa's conduct as an example, I desire it may be remembered that her flight with Lovelace was involuntary, and that her meeting and corresponding with him, was merely from the persecutions she endured, and in the hope of preventing the most fatal mischiefs between him and her brother. She, however, repents of the two last circumstances, as forming a deep error, imploring Heaven that its consequences may warn her sex against being rash enough to repose the smallest degree of confidence in a libertine; who, as she says, to *be* a libertine must have got over and defied all moral restraints.

Is it from the pen of a *father* that we see the unfeeling, the pointless sneer upon the exemplary duty, the contrite affection of a dying daughter, because she writes *on her knees* to supplicate pardon for what she considers a great fault, that prohibited correspondence (though she had been impelled into the commission of it by the cruelty of her family) and to invoke blessings upon them, who had shewn no mercy to her!

In contradiction to experience, and with great illiberality, Mr. CUMBERLAND asserts, that encouraging young women to correspond with each other, tends to no good point of education. *Every* good habit is capable of being perverted to bad uses. Because numerous books of evil tendency are extant, we might as wisely resolve that our daughters should not learn to *read*, as that, because they *may* write frivolous, and improper letters, they should be precluded from the *certain* advantages of a well-regulated epistolary intercourse with their young friends. Discreet parents will, in a great degree, suggest the subjects of these letters, and invite from time to time, a communication of their contents, by expressing pleasure in their perusal. Such an intercourse forms the style of young people, gives them habits of reflection, awakens intellectual emulation, and supplies them with resources, which have an inevitable tendency to abate the desire of dissipation, enables them to be rational and pleasing companions to men of sense when they marry, to fill the parental and monitory duties with dignity and delight, to the certain improvement of the future generation.

If women intrigue more in France than in England, though their understandings are generally better cultivated, it is because their inclinations are never consulted in their marriage engagements: and because infamy is less consequent than it is *here*, upon a violation of those engagements. But the French women are Lucretias compared to the Italians; a superiority which arises from the companionable qualities of the former, and the unlettered ignorance of the latter, that delivers up all the powers of their imagination to the influence of one reigning idea. Whoever has successfully studied the nature of the human mind, knows, that to store it with a *variety* of ideas, to render it capable of perceiving the value of knowledge, and the charms of genius, is to render it less subservient to the influence of the senses.

After Mr. CUMBERLAND has expressed his desire of banishing the finest moral work of this age, from the libraries of our youth, and the pen from the fingers of our women; he proceeds to inveigh more justly against that mode of education, too prevailing within these last twenty years, which can never enlarge the flock of ideas, or inspire any taste for intellectual pleasures. Upon this plan, a girl's time, in that important period, which divides infancy from womanhood, is every hour of it engrossed by the French grammar, the harpsichord, the dancing, and the drawing-master.

When young ladies *thus*, and *only* thus accomplished, becomes mistresses, in any degree of their own time, whether single, or married, there is no probability, alas! that they will devote it to the voluminous pages of the moral, the *pious* RICHARDSON. They have no imaginations that can awaken to a perception of his genius—no hearts that can soften at his pathos—no understanding to perceive the undeviating truth, and good sense of his observations.

The *Female Quixotte* [sic] is an admirable satire upon the *now* totally exploded study of the old romances, and gave the death's wound to that declining taste. But to satirize, with any probability of *good* effect, the CLARISSA, or the GRANDISON, is impossible. People of judgment will not attempt it, and injudicious people will attempt it in *vain*.

To read novels frequently, and indiscriminately, is a most pernicious habit. There are no means so effectual of rendering them distasteful as an early familiarity with the effusions of RICHARDSON'S genius. They will exalt the understanding above *endurance* of the trash, daily pouring out from the circulating libraries. Who that has read MILTON wastes the midnight taper over the vapid fustian of Sir RICHARD BLACKMORE?[8]

Mr. CUMBERLAND does not want genius, though he will permit nobody to be *sentimental* but himself. His *very* sentimental comedies have considerable merit, and though too little humorous for the comic line of writing, they are pathetic and agreeable. Morals are more likely to suffer from our despising, than from our admiring them.

His tragedies have incurred more contempt than they deserve. Amidst frequent plagiarisms, and much turgid writing, there are speeches of unborrowed beauty, and striking imagery, both in the *Battle of Hastings* and in the *Carmelite*.[9] Whole scenes in the latter have the true dramatic spirit.

Judgment is this author's great desideratum. We perceive the want of that power in his own writings, and therefore need not wonder at its absence, when he decides upon the writings of others.

Under the influence of perpetually recurring insanity, the heroine of his *Carmelite* preserves an important secret through twenty years, adheres to a regular plan of future enterprize, which is never interrupted by this intermitting madness, nor in the least degree partakes of its influence. The author, who could draw a character so utterly out of nature, and probability, is likely enough to fancy that RICHARDSON's works may be injurious to the good sense, the manners, and the morals of our youth.

86 From a letter entitled 'Sentiments of eminent writers in Honour of the Female Sex', *Gentleman's Magazine*, LVIII, November, 1788

The letter from which the following passage is reproduced was addressed to Mr. Urban, dated November 13, and signed R.O.P.

[. . . . .]

Though in romance the heroines are frequently represented in terms so extravagant as to provoke the ridicule of Cervantes, yet is this species of writing, as executed by authors of the middle centuries, infinitely preferable to modern novels. Better is it for young minds to be conversant with patterns of superior virtues, and with actions of extraordinary merit, than to dwell on examples and scenes of vice. In romance, the female sex is eminently good; in novels, for the most part, corruptly bad: so that novels not only enervate the mind, by super-inducing an affectation of sentimental feeling; they not only render it incapable of acting with fortitude and propriety in cases of REAL distress, which short experience of life will shew to be more abundant than to need the addition of imaginary evils; but they have a tendency still more fatal, they bring young readers acquainted with the worst part of the female sex, habituate them to loose principles and immodest practices, and thus send them into the world debauched, at least in heart, at an age which should be adorned with simplicity and inno-cence. Concern for the female character makes this remark not foreign to our subject.

[. . . . .]

The Child of Woe. A Novel. By Mrs. Elizabeth Norman. 1789.[1]

The Child of Woe having no marked features to characterize it, we can only term it a truly feminine novel. Indeed, the generality of them, in which improper descriptions are not introduced, are so near akin to each other, that with a few very trifling alterations, the same review would serve for almost all of them. More or less emphasis might be laid on the particular ingredients which compose the following receipt for a novel. Unnatural characters, improbable incidents, sad tales of woe rehearsed in an affected, half-prose, half-poetical style, exquisite double-refined sensibility, dazzling beauty, and *elegant* drapery, to adorn the celestial body, (these descriptions cannot be too minute) should never be forgotten in a book intended to amuse the fair.

This account will be a just one of ninety-nine novels out of a hundred; our readers must, then, excuse us, if we use the same words when we speak of productions in which we find so little variety; immoral ones we shall censure, and praise the *good*; the intermediate tribe which only infuse vanity and affectation into the minds of young readers, we shall not attempt so nicely to discriminate, as to point out the different shades of merit. Let not the female novelist be offended, who rises a tint above her contemporaries, if her darling is confounded with performances of the same complexion; for *scrupulous* exactness is never expected in any kind of classing.

W.

Mount Pelham. A Novel. By the Author of *Rosa de Montmorien*. 1788.[2]

Much ado about nothing. We place this novel without any reservation, at the bottom of the second class. The language is affected; and is has all the faults we have before enumerated. The morality is rather lax; for the author, a female, says, 'so gentle, so forgiving, is the nature of a virtuous female; and so prone are we to love the offender, yet detest the offence.' This is the varnish of sentiment to hide sensuality.

W.

The Ill Effects of a rash Vow. A Novel. In a Series of Letters. 1788.[3]

The style of this novel is tolerable; and some characters and incidents rather interesting: but the catastrophe, which turns on the absurd rash vow, is so *ridiculously* dreadful, that we smiled at the numbers death swept away; and quietly place this sad tale in the numerous class of middling performances, except the conclusion, which deviating so widely from nature, sinks below mediocrity.

W.

88 Review of *The Denial; or, The Happy Retreat* (1790); *The Monthly Review*, Series 2, III, December 1790

The Denial ... was by the Reverend James Thomson, who also wrote *The History of Major Piper* ... (1793) and *Winifred, a tale of wonder* (1803). The review was by Mrs. Elizabeth Moody, with some contribution by Ralph Griffiths.

Of the various species of composition that in course come before us, there are none in which *our* writers of the male sex have less excelled, since the days of Richardson and Fielding, than in the arrangement of a novel. Ladies seem to appropriate to themselves an exclusive privilege in this kind of writing; witness the numerous productions of romantic tales to which female authors have given birth. The portraiture of the tender passions, the delicacy of sentiment, and the easy flow of style, may, perhaps, be most adapted to the genius of the softer sex: but however that may be, politeness, certainly, will not suffer us to dispute this palm with our fair competitors. We, though of the harder sex, as men, and of a still harder *race as critics*, are no enemies to an affecting well-told story: but as we are *known* not to be very *easily pleased*, it may be imagined that those performances only will obtain the sanction of our applause, which can stand the test of certain criteria of excellence.

The story of a novel should be formed of a variety of interesting incidents; a knowledge of the world, and of mankind, are essential requisites in the writer; the characters should be always natural; the personages should talk, think, and act, as becomes their respective ages, situations, and characters; the sentiments should be moral, chaste, and delicate; the language should be easy, correct, and elegant, free from affectation, and unobscured by pedantry; and the narrative should be as little interrupted as possible by digressions and episodes of every kind: yet if an author chuses to indulge, occasionally, in moral reflections, in the view of blending instruction with amusement, we would not wish, altogether, to frustrate so good a design:—but, that his precepts may obtain the utmost efficacy, we would recommend them to be inserted in those periods of the history, where the reader's curiosity can most patiently submit to suspense.

Having thus given a sketch of what a novel should be to *please us*, we proceed to the work which has given occasion to these remarks.

This novel, then, consists of a series of letters between the Hon. Mr. Wilton and his friend Mr. Benfield. Mr. Wilton is the son of Lord Wilton, a cruel, avaritious, despotic parent, who wishes to force his son into a marriage, (extremely against his inclinations,) with Miss Silvertop, a young lady of large fortune: the parties are introduced to each other, and are left alone for the purpose of *making love*; when, unluckily, the gentleman begins by asking the young lady, *which are her favourites among the dramatic authors*. Miss Silvertop, not having been instructed in her literary catechism, stares, and seems not to comprehend him. He is not, however, discouraged: but pursues his *learned inquiries*, till at last the young lady betrays such a total *want of erudition*, that Mr. Wilton, completely disgusted, resolves, in defiance of all paternal injunctions, to decline the marriage. Lord Wilton is in great wrath, utters dreadful imprecations, and even curses his son, who runs out of the house, gets into a stage coach, and arrives at Morpeth in Northumberland; where he becomes enamoured of a beautiful young lady, named Olivia. Mr. Fennel, one of Olivia's lovers, is jealous of Mr. Wilton, and sends him a challenge; a duel ensues—Mr. W. disarms and wounds his antagonist; who is so enraged, that he *insists on being dead*, that Mr. W. may be *hanged*:—the latter is therefore, with all due formality, ushered into a prison: but Mr. Fennel, having reported *falsely of himself that he was* DEAD, and being *taken alive*, Mr. Wilton is released from his confinement, and marries Olivia; who proves to be another Miss Silvertop. The old Lord, who had determined on an alliance with the family of the Silvertops, recalls his curses, and changes them into blessings; and a happy union likewise takes place, with regard to an episodical pair, whose adventures serve to diversify the work:—which here naturally concludes.

In regard to the general character of Mr. Thomson's performance, it certainly is not void of merit. The volumes abound with pious and moral reflections, not unworthy the pen of a clergyman: but we should have admired this piety and this morality still more, had the language (especially of the earlier letters), been less verbose, and the style less stiffened with hard words. Terms of the same signification are frequently coupled together:* a mode of writing rather suitable to an

* For instance, 'black criminality,' pref. p. 7.; 'Wanton lasciviousness,' ib. p. 9.; 'mutual reciprocation,' ib. p. 16.; 'cautious timidity;' p. 32.—Other expressions, which we have remarked, seem much too stiff and pedantic for the characters

indenture than a book of entertainment; and peculiarly inconsistent with the natural ease and freedom of the epistolary style.

Notwithstanding the impropriety of the language of some parts of this work, for it is not uniformly thus censurable, the story has not failed to interest us in the persual; and it would be great injustice to the sensible writer, if we did not speak of his performance as entitled to a considerable degree of distinction above the common crowd—the *canaille* of modern romances and novels.

The leading moral purpose of this work, is to expose the unreasonableness, absurdity, and tyranny, of parents who usurp an absolute authority over their children, in respect of their matrimonial engagements; forcing all natural affection, and every prospect of happiness from that source, to give way to the calls of avarice or ambition.—This is a beaten path, which has been trodden by almost every novellist and dramatic writer;—who, we are happy to think, have successively encountered a monster which is now seldom seen but in their performances.

---

that use them—as, 'Pray, Madam,' answers Mr. Wilton to a question from his lady mother, 'what prompts the interrogation?'—'My dear Henry,' says the countess, 'I am afraid the air of your native country, after so long an absence in the warmer climates of France and Italy, is not *congenial* to your health, as you seem to have *acquired* a slight indisposition this morning,' p. 33.; and the Hon. Mr. W. is, in like manner, accosted by his honourable sister, with 'Pray, Henry, if our native air be more *salubrious* than that of the continent'—p. 36. With equal solemnity does the young nobleman answer his Right Hon. father's haughty commands to marry the lady *not* of his choice: 'The will hath a certain prerogative, in the exercise of which it admits of no compulsory methods to corrode its happiness. It thinks, it acts with *spontaneity*; and when opposed, suffers a diminution of its pleasure.' p. 37, &c. &c.

We would just observe, also, that the hero of this piece is said to be the only son of the *Earl* Wilton, and yet he is merely styled the *Hon. Mr.* Wilton. Every Earl has a secondary title, which, by courtesy, is borne by his eldest son; and his daughters are addressed as *Lady Ann, Lady Mary.* &c.

89 From a review of *The Labyrinths of Life* (1791); *The Monthly Review*, Series 2, V, July 1791

The Labyrinths of Life was by Mrs. Thomson (d. unknown), who also wrote *Excessive Sensibility* . . . (1787), *Fatal Follies* . . . (1788), *The Pride of Ancestry* . . . (1804) and *Laurette* . . . (1807). The review was by John Noorthouck.

When a manufacture has been carried on long enough for the workmen to attain a general proficiency, the uniformity of the stuffs will render it difficult to decide on the preference of one piece beyond another; and this must be our apology for not entering into a discussion of the merits of the novel now before us, which, at the same time that it exhibits nothing to shock our feelings, affords nothing to attract particular attention, either as to materials or workmanship.[1] Two of the earliest fabricators of this species of goods, the modern novel, in our country, were Daniel Defoe, and Mrs. Haywood; the success of *Pamela* may be said to have brought it into fashion; and the progress has not been less rapid than the extension of the use of tea, to which a novel is almost as general an attendant, as the bread and butter, especially in a morning. While we are on this subject, it is also to be noted, that nothing is more common than to find hair-powder lodged between the leaves of a novel; which evinces the corresponding attention paid to the inside as well as to the outside of a modern head. Richardson, Fielding, Smollet, and Sterne, were the Wedgwoods of their days;[2] and the imitators that have since started up in the same line, exceed all power of calculation! When an art becomes general, then is the time for the invention of engines to facilitate the operations, as in the cotton manufacture. Swift's machine for the composition of books, described in his *Gulliver*, like most other first attempts, has not been found to answer.[3] It was reserved for us to publish a scheme for the easy multiplication of novels, cheap in its execution, and certain in its operation, so long as not only our presses, but those of Germany and France, will furnish raw materials to work up; and before they can fail, we may hope to import ample supplies from America. Here then we disinterestedly offer it *pro bono publico*; and expect the thanks of the whole body of frizeurs, for our assistance toward relieving them from a multitude of impatient exclamations, and profane oaths.

RECIPE FOR DRESSING UP NOVELS *ad libitum*.

Go to Middle Row, Holborn; where, since mankind have discovered that their own hair is sufficiently capable of distortion, the sellers of old cast-off wigs have given place to the dealers in cast-off books; there on the bulks, from among the classes of a groat or sixpence *per* volume, buy any old forgotten novel, the older the better; give new names to the personages and places, reform the dates, modernize such circumstances as may happen to be antiquated, and, if necessary, touch up the style a little with a few of those polite cant words and phrases that may be in fashion at the time. All this may done with a pen, in the margin of the printed book, without the trouble of transcribing the whole, unless it is to be carried to a bookseller for sale; for then you must shew a manuscript. In either case, it may be boldly sent to the printer; for printers, like surgeons and lawyers, are bound to keep the secrets of their employers.[4]

To a publisher, there are many advantages attending this mode of proceeding; and the saving of copy-money is to be reckoned as the chief. A novel of two or three volumes, that could not be purchased under four or five guineas, may be thus new vamped from an old one, by a compositor who dabbles a little with his pen, for perhaps half a guinea; and if the alterations be skilfully performed, they will confound the judgment, so that, neither author nor bookseller knowing his own book again, a prosecution for copy-right need not be apprehended. The most that even a reader with a good memory could say, would be, that there is nothing new in it; and though we have so expressed ourselves a hundred times, novels are pouring forth as fast as ever! We are therefore not without suspicions that this our scheme has been anticipated, and is already in practice; for, as far as recollection can reach, the characters, situations, plots, and catastrophes, are, with very few exceptions, still the same.

[. . . . .]

90 From a review of *Theological, philosophical, and moral Essays, on the following Subjects: Celibacy, Wedlock, Seduction, Pride, Duelling, Self-murder, Lying* [etc., etc.], (1791); *The Analytical Review*, XI, December 1791

This forbidding work was written by the Reverend Edward Barry.

[. . . . .]

In the next essay, which is 'on wedlock', we find our author very strenuously recommending 'chastity in marriage', as a 'very salutary prescription'; and gravely asserting from the testimony of 'fathers and divines of old, yea, philosophers', that marriage should be 'serious, seasonable, circumspect, and mixed with severity, and that an intemperate man in wedlock, differs but little from an adulterer'.

Seduction is defined to be 'the art of tempting, deceiving, and corrupting', and early marriage is pointed out as the best preventive against this crime, but from the present state of society it is lamented, that 'the most lovely part of creation, by some means or other, are virtually defrauded of this natural, this moral, and this sacred remedy'!

As a specimen of the style and manner of the author we shall give a few extracts on this subject.

'Among the many incentives to seduction, that of novel reading most assuredly ranks as one; not but flowers may sometimes be selected—but weeds, pernicious fatal weeds, too often choak up the garden;—the greater part of such writings are studiously contrived to interest, to agitate, and to convulse the passions, already but too prone, by a sympathy of sentiment, to lead the mind astray. The very mummery of tale, which *swindled* tears from the eyes, and transport from the heart, which gave sensations it could not relieve, has left a train of gunpowder in the soul, and in such a posture, that one chance spark of fire might be sufficient to blow up reputation, and make a bankrupt of virtue. Obscene books and prints create and inflame, in no small degree, impure desires; and to guard against other causes of seduction, it should be the serious attention of those who preside over the seminaries of female education, that not only the lessons, but the strictest examples of chastity should be enforced: for this purpose, the conduct of masters should be seasonably watched, and the accustomed familiarity of servants with such pupils, ought to be more than scrupulously eyed, and religiously avoided.'

[. . . . .]

91 From *The Analytical Review*, XVI, May 1793, August 1793 and Appendix

The four sections reproduced below contain the following material: (*a*) from a review of *The Old Manor House. A Novel* (1793), by Charlotte Smith; (*b*) four short reviews; (*c*) from a review of *Letters and Essays, Moral and Miscellaneous* (1793), by Mary Hays; (*d*) from a review of *The Wandering Islander . . .* (1792), by Charles Henry Wilson.

Mary Hays, author of the book reviewed in (*c*), seems to have been a very minor novelist and contributor to the miscellanies. She also wrote *The Hermit, an Oriental Tale* (1786), *Memoirs of Emma Courtney* (1796) and *The Victim of Prejudice* (1799).

(a)

If it were inquired what is the principal excellence of novel writing, the greater number of readers would perhaps place it in novelty of story, variety of incident, and an arrangement happily contrived to awaken, and to keep alive curiosity. Others, who have naturally a high degree of sensibility, or who are at that period of life in which the heart is most susceptible of tender emotions, would be inclined to pronounce those the best novels, which most successfully touch the strings of sentiment and passion; and would estimate the merit of a story, by its power of calling forth the sympathetic tear. Whilst a third class of readers, who, even in the perusal of a novel, look further than to the present momentary amusement of fancy or gratification of feeling, will value a fictitious tale in proportion as it exhibits a true picture of men and manners; and, in judging of the merit of any work of this kind, will, first of all, inquire what characters it describes, and with what degree of accuracy and strength it delineates them.

Disposed as we are to rank ourselves in the last class of novel readers, we give the ingenious author of the *Old Manor House*, to whom the public has been indebted for some other similar productions, great credit for her talents as a novelist. In the present novel, she has not,

indeed, been particularly fortunate in her story. Some leading circumstances are scarcely reconcileable with probability; particularly the
daily and nightly interviews of the two lovers, residing so long in the
same mansion, all the while kept secret from the rest of the family.
Sometimes the narrative is clogged by collateral incidents, which produce little effect: the whole amour of the old general with the sister of
Orlando might have been omitted without much loss. With respect to
sentiment and passion, the reader's mind is throughout agreeably
interested, rather than powerfully agitated. But, as an exhibition of
characters, the piece has considerable merit. They are taken from
different classes of life, marked with distinct features, illustrated by
happily associated incidents, and furnished with suitable sentiments and
language. Among these, the principal persons, Orlando and Monimia,
are patterns, the former of ardent and unalterable affection, courage,
generosity, and gratitude, the latter of simplicity, modesty, and tenderness. Mrs. Rayland, the mistress of the mansion, is family-pride, personified. Her old *femme de charge*, Mrs. Lennard, is a starch prude,
severe and suspicious with respect to others, but very indulgent to
herself. General Tracy is a great master of the polite art of appearing
to be what a man is not. Dr. Hollybourn is a pompous, but fawning,
canting priest, capable of any meanness, or baseness, to serve his
interest. Several of the less important characters, both in high and low
life, are equally well drawn; and the piece, on the whole, is a gallery of
portraits, of which it would not be difficult to find the originals in real
life.

[. . . . .]

(*b*)

Argal; or the Silver Devil, being the Adventures of an Evil Spirit, comprising
a Series of interesting Anecdotes in public and private Life, with which the
Demon became acquainted in various Parts of the World, during his Con-
finement in the Metalline Substance to which he was condemned. Related
by himself. In Two Volumes.[1]

Divested of it's [sic] fictitious dress, this work is little more than a relation of loose intrigues of gallantry, and plots of knavery. The demon
Ashtaroth, condemned to be confined within a piece of silver which
passes through various hands, becomes acquainted with many characters,
and a witness of many adventures; but the author has contrived to

introduce his demon every where into bad company, and consequently to relate stories which, if they convey to the reader any knowledge of the world, only teach us to know the worst part of mankind. The title will perhaps put the reader in mind of the *Devil upon Two Sticks*, or of the *Adventures of a Guinea*; but upon the comparison, the work will be found far inferiour to those celebrated productions in wit and satire, as well as in correctness and elegance of style.

Simple Facts; or the History of an Orphan. In Two Volumes. By Mrs. Matthews.[2]

A few *simple facts* are in this little novel made the grounds of a natural and easy tale, which, if not wrought up with sufficient skill, or protracted to a sufficient length, to make any very deep impression upon the heart, may however afford in the perusal an agreeable amusement of the fancy, and will encourage no sentiments inconsistent with honour and virtue. The orphan, of whom the tale is related, becomes an early object of tender attachment to the son of her kind patroness; and, though many obstacles arise to their union, and many enticements are presented to alienate their affections, they exhibit an example of invincible constancy, and at last, in reward for their fidelity, are led to the altar amidst the smiles of fortune, and the congratulations of friendship. The writer is too busy in conducting her lovers to the temple of Hymen, to find leisure for stepping aside out of the straight path of narrative, to gather the flowers of description, or to pluck the fruit of instruction.

Elizabeth Percy; a Novel, founded on Facts. Written by a Lady.[3]

In constructing the story of a novel, next to the difficulty of inventing incidents, is that of connecting them by such a skilful arrangement, as to afford the reader a pleasing perception of uniformity amidst variety. We cannot compliment the author of this novel with having executed this part of her task with any great degree of success. A sufficient number of people are, it is true, brought together; many fine feelings and passions are put into motion; and, before the novel is half finished, we have six tender attachments, and two marriages. But the general effect is that of a confused picture, where the figures, however pleasing or striking, considered individually, produce on the whole an indistinct impression, for want of being properly grouped. In the style of the piece, there is more vivacity than correctness.—'A sister, *who* miss P. did not fail to invite;—had grown in friendship as they *grew in nature*;—

lord Carey solemnly *aver*;—who in a generous fit may behave *hand-some*;' are a few of the peculiarities of expression to be found in these volumes.

The Conflict, a Sentimental Tale, in a Series of Letters. In Two Volumes.[4]

The reader should be left to find out from the perusal of a novel, and not be told in the title page, that it is a sentimental tale. In the present case, however, the author's word may be taken. The tale is full of tender sentiments, and, if not written with superior elegance, may afford a few hours agreeable amusement to the sentimental reader.

(c)

The rights of woman, which have been of late so ably asserted by an enlightened female philosopher,[1] have been very successfully exercised by the writer of these papers. Taking encouragement from the doctrine and the example of the justly admired advocate for her sex, miss H. ventures beyond the boundaries which the tyranny of example and custom has prescribed to female writers; and while, in some of her pieces, she amuses her readers with pleasing and instructive moral tales, in others, she carries them out of the flowery path of fiction into the sober walks of reason, and leads them to inquiry and reflection on various subjects of political, metaphysical, and theological speculation. If the work be less distinguished by the elegance of composition than the productions of some other female pens, the deficiency is, in a great measure, compensated by the just and useful observations which she makes on moral conduct; and by the perspicuity with which she explains to her female readers some of the leading arguments on philosophical or theological subjects.

Of the fictitious tales contained in this volume two only are works of fancy, enlivened by poetical imagery; the first, a fragment, in the manner of the old romances; the second, the hermit, an eastern tale: the rest are simple domestic narratives, chiefly intended, and very well adapted, to guard young females against the contagion of fashionable frivolousness; to teach them the great importance of improving their understandings; to warn them of the pernicious consequences of early indulgence; and to guide their judgment respecting the connexions they may form in life. Religious sentiments are interspersed through all these pieces, as well as through those which are written in the form of essays, on the topics of female character, the choice of books, conversation, and friendship, and the like; but these sentiments are not of the fanatical or superstitious kind, but such as appear to have arisen from rational inquiry. In some of these letters are discussed, in the way of easy argumentation, several of those topics which have lately engaged the attention of the public, particularly the controversy concerning the utility and obligation of worship, and those concerning materialism and necessity. But these subjects, as may be easily supposed, are treated rather in a loose and general way, than in the style of close reasoning, or deep investigation. The system of Dr. Priestley on these subjects is pretty closely followed.[2] Referring to the volume itself for what miss H. has advanced on these topics, we shall quote, as a specimen, her remarks in a letter to a friend on a more general subject, that of reading novels. P. 86.

'Be not too much alarmed, my friend, at your daughter's predilection for novels and romances; nor think of restraining her by authority from this her favourite pursuit; as by so-doing, you would probably lose her confidence, without correcting her taste; in which case the mischief might indeed become serious. She is now advancing towards woman-hood, and will expect to be treated no longer as a child, but as a reasonable being; and this expectation is just. The reciprocal duties between parents and children, though they ought never to cease, yet change their nature at different periods of life. A good mother, who has both by example and precept trained her offspring in the principles and practice of virtue, will have nothing to fear from this change. While she proves herself by her whole conduct the friend of her children, and entitles herself to their love and reverence, her influence will be unbounded, because the habits of obedience, which were required in childhood, will be strengthened by reason and affection; and her empire will be over the heart and understanding. A disposition to act in opposition to coercive and arbitrary measures, has been frequently attributed to a perverseness in human nature: this appears to me a false and injurious notion. Does it not rather indicate that love of freedom, and generous disdain of imposition, that ever glow in an elevated and noble mind? I should tremble for the future moral conduct of the child, whom force and blows only could restrain from doing what was wrong; should he ever arrive at maturity, if he break not the laws of his country, it will be merely because he is withheld by sordid and selfish motives.

'I have scarce ever known an amiable young mind that has not been a little tinctured, with what "the sons of interest deem romance". If the first steps into life are marked by coldness and caution, such a character will never possess any other than negative virtues, though it may incur few hazards.

Youth's the lovely source of generous foibles.[3]

Where nothing is risqued, nothing can be gained. We shall certainly be subjected to disappointment, by forming flushed and ardent expectations; and find perhaps a brake of thorns, where we expected a parterre of flowers. Yet, "the exertion of our own faculties (says a sensible writer) will be the blessed fruit of disappointed hope."

'My revered, and deceased friend Mr. Robinson, of Cambridge, writing to me on the advantages of early affliction, observes, that before he met with it in Shakespear, he had been convinced that—

There was some soul of good, in things evil,
Would men observingly distil it out.[4]

He goes on to add,—"I am of opinion, that if it be good for mankind to bear the yoke, it is chiefly so by bearing it in their youth. Notice the most of those who have grown to maturity without any exercises of this kind! Absolute strangers to themselves, and to the world in which they live! The latent powers of their own minds unknown, diamonds in rocks unconvulsed! Strangers to the feelings of others, and never impregnated with sympathy, the ferment of the soul! Nothing is so conducive to the knowledge of God, to the dignity of man, to the world in which we live, to that to which we are going, as a smarting course of providential discipline."

'But the age of chivalry (as a certain rhetorician laments) is no more![5] The present race of young people are too vapid and too dissipated to be captivated by sublime descriptions of heroic virtue; and too much engrossed by the important pursuit, of varying their outward appearance with the constant fluctuation of mode, to have leisure to attend to the dangerous refinements of sentiment. Yet do not mistake me, nor suppose that I mean to recommend the indiscriminate perusal of romances and novels; on the contrary, I think with you, that the generality of works of this kind are frivolous, if not pernicious; though there are undoubtedly, many exceptions. But the love of the marvellous, or of extraordinary, and unexpected coincidencies, is natural to young minds, that have any degree of energy and fancy. I would only wish them to be fond of books, and I should have no doubt of being able to lead their taste, from the pursuit of mere amusement, to solid improvement. Awaken but the desire of information, and the gradation from pursuing "the mazes of some wondrous tale", up to the highest degree of interesting and useful knowledge, is easy and natural. Accustom your daughters by a cheerful and amiable frankness, to do nothing without consulting you; let them read with you, and let the choice of their books be free. Converse with them on the merits of the various authors, and accustom them to critical and literary discussions. They will soon be emulous of gaining your approbation by entering into your ideas, and will be ashamed of being pleased with what you ridicule as absurd, and out of nature, or disapprove, as having an improper and immoral tendency. You have only to persuade them that you have a confidence in their principles and good sense, and they will be eager to justify your favourable opinion. The human heart in early life, before the world, the mean, unfeeling, selfish world, breaks in upon its gay mistakes, is naturally grateful, and susceptible of lively impressions from kind and generous treatment. This sensibility properly cherished, and cultivated, may be made to produce the noblest fruits. I often shudder, when I observe in large families the little attention that is paid to the minds of the children, because by an education equally defective, the parents are themselves incapacitated for this most important charge. "How should a woman unused to reflection, be capable of educating her children? How will she be able to discern what is proper for them? How shall she train them to virtues to which she is herself a stranger, or to any kind of merit of which she has no idea? She will only know how to sooth, or to menace them; to render them either insolent or timorous; she will either make them mannerly monkeys, or wild idle boys; but they never will shew any marks of good sense, or behave as amiable children." Rousseau.'[6]

Some small pieces of poetry are annexed. We regret that these letters and essays, which are in many respects valuable, were not carefully revised by some learned friend, who might have prevented such errours as the following:—the general tendency of the scriptures militate against this idea—ideas that harmonize best with the general tenure of revelation—have stimulas to mental improvement—when *suitability* is wanting.

D. M.

(d)

The Wandering Islander; or, the History of Mr. Charles North. In Two Volumes.

Novel-writing is become so much the art of trifling, or more properly of money-catching, that we are not apt to be over sanguine when we hear of new publications of this kind. In general, if a moderate degree of entertainment be derived, the reader should be content to retire, *uti conviva satur*.[1]

With respect to the work before us, it answers very well, in our opinion, to the character of a novel. It possesses much original humour, many just and liberal sentiments, pertinent reflections on life and manners, and incidents, that have a sufficient degree of novelty to keep up the attention of the reader. It is too in the main, well written, though the style in a few instances is a little incorrect, and the quotations in two or three places not quite accurate. The following privileges of a novel-writer are laid down by Mr. North in his own humorous manner. p. xiii.

'A novel-writer may be as profuse of titles, as any monarch in Europe.

'——————— may lay all his or her scenes in high life, provided he or she live in a garret.

'——————— may break a promise as well as any lord in the kingdom.

'——————— not bound to spell words according to Johnson, Sheridan,[2] &c.

'——————— if a female, at full liberty to break Priscian's head,[3] as often as she does her husband's; and if her novel does not succeed, may hang or drown herself—why not, as well as poets and painters?

'——————— entitled to prose licence as well as poetic, and to eat and drink at pleasure—in imagination.

'——————— at full liberty to seize on all French prizes, provided they understand a few words of the language.

'——————— entitled to disemvowel, or rather, as *Tom Brown* expresses it, to *disembowel* any word or words, in the English or any other language.[4]

'——————— always permitted to throw the one half of their faults on the *unfortunate* press, and the other on the bad taste of the public.'

[. . . . .]

Passage (*a*) consists of a review of *Memoirs of Mary* (1793), by Susannah Gunning, who wrote ten novels between 1764 and 1799; she is not to be confused with Elizabeth Gunning, whose six novels were published between 1794 and 1812. Passage (*b*) is taken from a review of *Essay on Novels; a poetical Epistle. Addressed to an ancient and to a modern Bishop. With six Sonnets, from Werter* (1793), by Alexander Thompson, who also wrote *Whist, a Poem* (1791) and the *German Miscellany* (1796).

(*a*)

One of the principal reasons why so many writers of novels fail of success is, that they attempt to exhibit scenes, and describe characters, with which they have not been conversant. Not choosing to confine themselves, in their narrative, to those humble walks, in which nature has placed them in real life, they take upon them to represent manners, which they have had no opportunity of observing. Hence their *lords* and *ladies* are often no more like the people of fashion at the west end of the town, than the waxen figures in Fleet-street are like the illustrious personages whom they are said to represent.[1] Mrs. G., the author of the story before us, has an advantage over most other novelists, in having been intimately acquainted with the scenes and characters, from which she professes to draw her materials! And as far as reviewers can be supposed capable of judging, we give it as our opinion, that she draws a very natural and lively picture of what passes in high life. Her design appears to have been, not to astonish by improbable incidents, or to harrow up the soul by scenes of distress which can barely be supposed to exist, but to interest and instruct, by representing persons, manners, and events, as they are exhibited in real life. And she has, we think, executed this design very successfully. The incidents of the novel are natural; the characters are marked with that peculiarity of feature, which shows that they have been drawn from actual observation; and the language possesses the ease and vivacity, though in some instances the negligence too, of polite conversation.

Mary, the principal person in the piece, is not like the heroine of many a novel, all made up of sentiment and passion. After having been educated under the eye of an excellent grandmother, she enters into the great world, not only with the simplicity of innocence, but with the dignity of a mind well instructed; and passes through many trying situations, with a degree of firmness, which renders her respectable as well as amiable. The grandmother is an exalted character, with no other foible than that of being too fond of praising the fine eyes, and the white hands of her Mary. The lovers of Mary are natural characters, and therefore not perfect; but the hero, to whom her heart remains unalterably attached, approves himself worthy of her love. In her intercourse with the great world, she suffers much from envy and malignity; but at last escapes, and arrives at the full possession of domestic felicity.

We do not meet with any passage in this novel, which will be read with advantage detached from the narrative, and we shall not disgust our readers with an inanimate skeleton of the story. We shall therefore only remark further, that the piece would have appeared to more advantage if it had been *throughout* in the form of letters; without putting the writer to the aukward necessity of making her appearance to inform the reader of the contents of certain letters or papers, which had unfortunately been mislaid.

D. M.

(*b*)

Prevalent as is the present rage for novel reading, we apprehend there are few of the admirers of this species of literary entertainment, who will not be surprised to be told, that novel writing is entitled to the highest place in the scale of poetry, and that Milton and Shakespeare, Virgil and Homer, must bow the knee to Richardson and Fielding, Rousseau and Goethe. This, however, is the opinion seriously maintained in the poetical essay now before us. Nay, Mr. T. goes so far as to assert, that if he were doomed to be deprived of all the works of art that were ever produced, and only allowed to choose one precious fragment, it should be—*nine pages of the Sorrows of Werter*. Though we cannot suppose that many of our readers will be inclined to adopt this opinion, they may perhaps wish to see in what manner so pleasing a writer as the author of *Whist*, a poem, treats the subject; we shall therefore add a short extract.

After paying due honour to bishop Heliodorus, the author of the first novel, *The Loves of Theagenes and Chariclea*, our poet thus expostulates with bishop Hurd on his general censure of this class of literary productions. P. 6.

> Ask thy own heart; for to that honest judge
> Still lies, on points like these, the last appeal.
> What epic song, though glitt'ring with the pomp
> Of heav'nly vision, strengthen'd by the force
> And magic splendour of poetic phrase,
> Conjoin'd with all the fascinating pow'r
> Of tuneful sound, was ever yet perus'd
> With half that eagerness, which ev'n the worst,
> (What then the best?) of these domestic tales,
> Scarce ever fails to raise? But let us call
> More special proof. Does Virgil's pious prince,
> When by the will divine, constrain'd to quit
> His fair Phœnician queen, inspire the soul
> With such emotion, as when Grandison,
> (Tho' sore the conflict) at religion's call,
> Resigns Bologna's maid? Can all the craft
> Of shy Ulysses, or the craftier wiles
> Of Milton's subtle fiend, so much amuse
> The curious mind as that exhaustless store
> Of treach'rous arts by Lovelace us'd, to gain
> His cruel purpose? Or the fate of Troy,
> (Tho' hosts of heroes fight on either side,
> And all Olympus in the cause contend),
> Awake those energies of hope and fear,
> Which still attend on each important step
> That hastens or retards Clarissa's fall?
> Say, does the mind of true unbiass'd taste,
> Free from the trammels of scholastic rule,
> With half that pleasure Milton's page peruse;
> That labour'd page, where all the pomp of words,
> And each ungraceful and pedantic aid
> Of foreign hues, and mythologic lore,
> Essays to paint the charm of Eden's bow'rs
> As when that simple page attracts the view,
> In which Geneva's animated son

His Julia's garden paints, and fills each line
With native beauty, and unborrow'd grace?
Or say, by bigot prejudice unsway'd,
Did ever genuine feeling's eye survey,
That rich effusion of pathetic song,
By far the fairest of the Mantuan muse,
Where hapless Dido's melancholy care,
Perhaps the pomp of voluntary death,
With half that luxury of pleasing woe
As when his art, who ev'ry passion sway'd,
And made them move at virtue's fair command,
Presents Clarissa to the weeping view;
Triumphant rising from her shameful wrongs,
Above relentless kindred's rude neglect,
With firm unshaken soul preparing all
The mournful requisites of fun'ral pomp,
And fondly placing in her dauntless view
The sable colour'd chest, so soon to prove
The last sad mansion of her lovely frame?

93 From a review of *The Mysteries of Udolpho, a Romance; interspersed with some Pieces of Poetry* (1794), *The Critical Review*, Series 2, XI, August 1794

Mrs. Ann Radcliffe had already published two novels when *The Mysteries of Udolpho* . . . appeared—*A Sicilian Romance* (1790) and *The Romance of the Forest* (1791). See also below, Nos. 94 and 98.

> Thine too these golden keys, immortal boy!
> This can unlock the gates of joy,
> Of horror, that and thrilling fears,
> Or ope the sacred source of sympathetic tears.[1]

Such were the presents of the Muse to the infant Shakspeare, and though perhaps to no other mortal has she been so lavish of her gifts, the keys referring to the third line Mrs. Radcliffe must be allowed to be completely in possession of. This, all who have read the *Romance of the Forest* will willingly bear witness to. Nor does the present production require the name of its author to ascertain that it comes from the same hand. The same powers of description are displayed, the same predilection is discovered for the wonderful and the gloomy—the same mysterious terrors are continually exciting in the mind the idea of a supernatural appearance, keeping us, as it were, upon the very edge and confines of the world of spirits, and yet are ingeniously explained by familiar causes; curiosity is kept upon the stretch from page to page, and from volume to volume, and the secret, which the reader thinks himself every instant on the point of penetrating, flies like a phantom before him, and eludes his eagerness till the very last moment of protracted expectation. This art of escaping the guesses of the reader has been improved and brought to perfection along with the reader's sagacity; just as the various inventions of locks, bolts, and private drawers, in order to secure, fasten, and hide, have always kept pace with the ingenuity of the pickpocket and housebreaker, whose profession it is to unlock, unfasten, and lay open what you have taken so much pains to conceal. In this contest of curiosity on one side, and invention on the other, Mrs. Radcliffe has certainly the advantage. She delights in concealing her plan with the most artificial contrivance, and seems to amuse herself with saying, at every turn and doubling of the story, 'Now you think you have me, but I shall take care to disappoint you.' This method is, however, liable to the following inconvenience, that in the search of what is new, an author is apt to forget what is natural; and, in rejecting the more obvious conclusions, to take those which are less satisfactory. The trite and the extravagant are the Scylla and Charybdis of writers who deal in fiction. With regard to the work before us, while we acknowledge the extraordinary powers of Mrs. Radcliffe, some readers will be inclined to doubt whether they have been exerted in the present work with equal effect as in the *Romance of the Forest*.—Four volumes cannot depend entirely on terrific incidents and intricacy of story. They require character, unity of design, a delineation of the scenes of real life, and the variety of well supported contrast. *The Mysteries of Udolpho* are indeed relieved by much elegant description and picturesque scenery; but in the descriptions there is too much of sameness: the pine and the larch tree wave, and the full moon pours its lustre through almost every chapter. Curiosity is raised oftener than it is gratified; or rather, it is raised so high that no adequate gratification can be given it; the interest is completely dissolved when once the adventure is finished, and the reader, when he is got to the end of the work, looks about in vain for the spell which had bound him so strongly to it. There are other little defects, which impartiality obliges us to notice. The manners do not sufficiently correspond with the æra the author has chosen; which is the latter end of the sixteenth century. There is, perhaps, no direct anachronism, but the style of accomplishments given to the heroine, a country young lady, brought up on the banks of the Garonne; the mention of botany; of little circles of infidelity, &c. give so much the air of modern manners, as is not counterbalanced by Gothic arches and antique furniture. It is possible that the manners of different ages may not differ so much as we are apt to imagine, and more than probable that we are generally wrong when we attempt to delineate any but our own; but there is at least a style of manners which our imagination has appropriated to each period, and which, like the costume of theatrical dress, is not departed from without hurting the feelings.—The character of Annette, a talkative waiting-maid, is much worn, and that of the aunt, madame Cheron, is too low and selfish to excite any degree of interest, or justify the dangers her niece exposes herself to for her sake. We must likewise observe, that the adventures do not sufficiently point to one centre: we do not, however, attempt to analyse the story; as it would have no other effect than destroying the pleasure of the reader, we shall content ourselves with giving the following specimen of one of those picturesque scenes of terror, which the author knows so well to work up.

[. . . . .]²

94 From a review of *The Mysteries of Udolpho, a Romance; interspersed with some pieces of Poetry* (1794), *The Monthly Review*, Series 2, XV, November 1794

This review was by William Enfield.

If the merit of fictitious narratives may be estimated by their power of pleasing, Mrs. Radcliffe's romances will be entitled to rank highly in the scale of literary excellence. There are, we believe, few readers of novels who have not been delighted with her *Romance of the Forest*;[1] and we incur little risque in predicting that the *Mysteries of Udolpho* will be perused with equal pleasure.

The works of this ingenious writer not only possess, in common with many other productions of the same class, the agreeable qualities of correctness of sentiment and elegance of style, but are also distinguished by a rich vein of invention, which supplies an endless variety of incidents to fill the imagination of the reader; by an admirable ingenuity of contrivance to awaken his curiosity, and to bind him in the chains of suspence; and by a vigour of conception and a delicacy of feeling which are capable of producing the strongest sympathetic emotions, whether of pity or terror. Both these passions are excited in the present romance, but chiefly the latter; and we admire the enchanting power with which the author at her pleasure seizes and detains them. We are no less pleased with the proofs of sound judgment, which appear in the selection of proper circumstances to produce a distinct and full exhibition, before the reader's fancy, both of persons and events; and, still more, in the care which has been taken to preserve his mind in one uniform tone of sentiment, by presenting to it a long continued train of scenes and incidents, which harmonize with each other.

Through the whole of the first volume, the emotions which the writer intends to excite are entirely of the tender kind. Emily, the heroine of the tale, early becomes familiar with sorrow, through the death of her parents; yet not before the reader is made acquainted with their characters and manners, and has accompanied them through a number of interesting circumstances, sufficient to dispose him to the exercise of tender sympathy. At the same time, her heart receives, by slow and imperceptible degrees, the soft impressions of love; and the reader is permitted, without the introduction of any dissonant feelings, to enjoy the luxury of observing the rise and progress of this passion, and of sympathizing with the lovers in every diversity of sentiment, which an uncommon vicissitude of events could produce; till, at last, Emily is separated from her Valancourt, to experience a sad variety of woe. With the interesting narrative of this volume, are frequently interwoven descriptions of nature in the rich and beautiful country of the South of France, which are perfectly in unison with the story; at the same time that they display, in a favourable light, the writer's powers of fancy and of language, and afford no small addition to the reader's gratification. We should have great pleasure, would our limits permit, in giving to our readers some specimens of these descriptions.

Something of the marvellous is introduced in the first volume, sufficient to throw an interesting air of *mystery* over the story; and the reader feels the pleasing agitation of uncertainty concerning several circumstances, of which the writer has had the address not to give a glance of explanation till toward the close of the work. In the remaining volumes, however, her genius is employed to raise up forms which chill the soul with horror; and tales are told that are no less fitted to 'quell each trembling heart with grateful terror', than those with which, 'by night,

> The village matron round the blazing heart
> Suspends her infant audience.'²

Without introducing into her narrative any thing really supernatural, Mrs. Radcliffe has contrived to produce as powerful an effect as if the invisible world had been obedient to her magic spell; and the reader experiences in perfection the strange luxury of artificial terror, without being obliged for a moment to hoodwink his reason, or to yield to the weakness of superstitious credulity. We shall not forestall his pleasure by detailing the particulars: but we will not hesitate to say, in general, that, within the limits of nature and probability, a story so well contrived to hold curiosity in pleasing suspense, and at the same time to agitate the soul with strong emotions of sympathetic terror, has seldom been produced.

Another part of the merit of this novel must not be overlooked. The characters are drawn with uncommon distinctness, propriety, and boldness. Emily, the principal female character, being naturally possessed of delicate sensibility and warm affection, is early warned by her father against indulging the pride of fine feelings,—(the romantic error of amiable minds,)—and is taught that the strength of fortitude is more valuable than the grace of sensibility. Hence she acquires a habit of self command, which gives a mild dignity to her manners, and a steady firmness to her conduct. She is patient under authority, without tameness or cunning. Desirous, in the first place, of her own approbation, she is equally unaffected by the praise and the censure of fools. In love, she is tender and ardent without weakness, and constant notwithstanding every inducement, from interest or terror, to abandon the object of her affection. Good sense effectually fortifies her against superstitious fear; and a noble integrity and sublime piety support her in the midst of terrors and dangers. In the character and fortunes of Emily's aunt, Madame Cheron, to whom her sufferings are solely owing, is exhibited an example of the mischief which silly pride brings on itself and others. Dazzled with shew, she wants the sense both to discern merit and to detect imposture: supercilious in her condescension, and ostentatious in her pity, she inflicts cruel wounds without intention; she admires and despises by turns, and equally without reason: she neither bears injuries with meekness nor resents them with dignity; and her exasperated pride vents itself in feeble lamentation, and prevents her from using the necessary means for her safety, till at length it exposes her to cruel insults, and precipitates her destruction.——Montoni, her second husband, is an Italian of strong talents, but of an abandoned character and desperate fortune: he is unprincipled, dauntless, and enterprising; reserved through pride and discontent, deep craft conceals all his plans: wild and various in his passions, yet capable of making them all bend to his interest, he is the cause of cruel wretchedness and infinite terror to those who are under his power. The gleams of comic humour play through the gloom of the story, in the character and conversation of the faithful servant Annette, who has an insuperable propensity to credulity, and an irresistible impulse to communication: but whose *naïveté*, simple honesty, and affection, render her character interesting. Several other portraits are drawn with equal strength; for which we must refer to the volumes.

The numerous mysteries of the plot are fully disclosed in the conclusion, and the reader is perfectly satisfied at finding villainy punished, and steady virtue and persevering affection rewarded. If there be any part of the story which lies open to material objection, it is that which makes Valancourt, Emily's lover, fall into disgraceful indiscretions during her absence, and into a temporary alienation of affection. This, in a young man of noble principles and exalted sentiments, after such a long intimacy, and such a series of incidents tending to give permanency to his passion and stability to his character, we must think *unnatural*. The performance would in our opinion have been more perfect, as well as more pleasing, if Du Pont, Emily's unsuccessful admirer, had never appeared; and if Valancourt had been, as Emily expected, her deliverer from the Castle of Udolpho. The story, we apprehend, might have been easily brought to its present termination on this supposition.

The embellishments of the work are highly finished. The descriptions are rich, glowing, and varied: they discover a vigorous imagination, and an uncommon command of language; and many of them would furnish admirable subjects for the pencil of the painter. If the reader, in the eagerness of curiosity, should be tempted to pass over any of them for the sake of proceeding more rapidly with the story, he will do both himself and the author injustice. They recur, however, too frequently; and, consequently, a similarity of expression is often perceptible. Several of the pieces of poetry are elegant performances, but they would have appeared with more advantage as a separate publication.

[. . . . .]

95 From a review of *Things as they are, or, the Adventures of Caleb Williams* (1794), *The Analytical Review*, XXI, February 1795

Caleb Williams was William Godwin's (1756–1836) first novel, though he had already published his *Enquiry concerning Political Justice* (1793); he followed it with *St Leon* (1799), *Fleetwood* (1805), *Faulkener* (1807), *Cloudesly* (1830) and *Deloraine* (1833).

We are somewhat at a loss how to introduce our readers to an acquaintance with this singular narrative. Of incident it presents little, of character and situation much. The power of genius is often seen in these pages to give efficacy to scenes and reflections, little calculated in their own nature to affect the human mind. Strong feeling, and a depth of reflection on the state and habits of society, claim our attention, and lead us forward at the will of the writer, while an almost total want or disregard of the rules of composition have betrayed him into faults of the first magnitude. We will first analyze the story, and then proceed to make a few remarks on the whole.

The story is written in the first person. 'My life,' says the imaginary writer, p. 1, 'has been for several years a theatre of calamity. I have been a mark for the vigilance of tyranny, and I could not escape. My fairest prospects have been blasted. My enemy has shown himself inaccessible to intreaties, and untired in persecution. My fame as well as my happiness has become his victim. Every one, as far as my story has been known, has refused to assist me in my distress, and has execrated my name. I have not deserved this treatment. My own conscience witnesses in behalf of that innocence, my pretentions to which are regarded in the world as incredible. There is now, however, little hope that I shall escape from the toils that universally beset me. I am incited to the penning of these memoirs, only by a desire to divert my mind from the deplorableness of my situation, and a faint idea that posterity may by their means be induced to render me a justice, which my contemporaries refuse. My story will at least appear to have that consistency, which is seldom attendant but upon truth.'

Caleb Williams was born in an humble sphere, in a remote county of England. His education was confined, but the activity of his mind prompted him to neglect no means of information from men and books. The residence of his parents was within the manor of Ferdinando Falkland, esq., whose steward, Mr. Collins, being a favourable observer of the acquisitions of young Williams, made such a report of his progress to his patron, that the youth, at the period of eighteen years of age, when he had the misfortune to lose his only parent, was received into the family, at the mansion house, as secretary and librarian to Mr. F.

[. . . . .]

Such are the plan, execution, and effect of the novel, written by the author of the Inquiry concerning political Justice.[1] The two great objects of fictitious narrative are entertainment and instruction. For mere entertainment it may be said, that intellectual relaxation or amusement is of more value, and attended with better effects, than any other employment commonly taken up as a relief from the more fatiguing duties of life: and in defence of the other object, instruction, nothing need be urged. The greatest sources of entertainment are those, on which the powers of intellect are most ardently employed. What are these? Universal benevolence on the ground of moral principle in the individual; and particular benevolence, on which the natural arrangements of society depend. Hence flow the duties of friendship, sexual attachment, parental love, filial affection, protection, gratitude, and every other object of amiable emotion. Will Mr. G.'s system of morality overthrow any or all of these? If it should, still they will remain as the beloved sources of exquisite enjoyment, capable of bringing forth all the powers of the understanding, and affording the most sublime entertainment. Whatever may be the portion of errour attached to the present state of society, still the errours in these great departments are as worthy the attention of the novelist, as the admiration of chivalry, the love of reputation, or the fatal effects of indiscreet curiosity. To us it appears, that the author is not sufficiently aware of the necessity of drawing a general outline of the plot of any work of imagination, before the narrative is entered upon; and that from this cause, as well as from a wish to avoid common place subjects, he has greatly restricted his power, and the effect of his composition. He has no tale of rational love, no marked instance of personal attachment, no fondly anxious parent, or child devoted to filial duty, in the developement of his story; but by the exertion of genius, which is indeed astonishing, he rivets our attention to a minute dissection of the characters, feelings, and emotions, of three insulated men, in a great measure confined to their own individual ease and comfort. Hence he was reduced to fill his third volume with a series of incidents similar to those of the *Newgate Calendar*,[2] though every where related with the imagination of a poet, and the discriminating spirit of a philosopher. If we were to give a character of this performance in few words, we should say, that it equals the *Eloise* of Rousseau in depth and accuracy of dissertation; approaches the *sorrows of Werter* in the gigantic energy of mental picture; but falls far beneath them both in felicity of subject.

We will not enter more minutely into the discussion of a plot so imperfect; or inquire into the degree of probability, that such characters should act as they are made to do. It does not appear to us, that any entire moral pervades this narrative. The author's occasional deductions, on the state of society, are but too well founded. The character of Tyrrel is not very uncommon, but his fate teaches us nothing. Falkland is extremely singular in his motives, his actions, and his wretched end; and this singularity pervades and governs the adventures of Williams. The adaptation of the causes to the effects, the merits or demerits of the personages, and the whole contexture of the story, apply too little to any thing within the ordinary course of observation, to afford any general moral.

X.

For Cumberland see above, No. 78 and headnote.

BOOK I, CH. I

The high Dignity, Powers, and Prerogatives of the Novel-Writer

All the world will acknowledge the superiority of works of invention over those of compilation. The writer of novels, therefore, will take rank before the writer of matter-of-fact, and rest his title to precedence upon his proofs of originality. Possibly this may be ill relished by the historian, who holds himself as an author of a high class; and, indeed, it seems to bear a little hard upon his prerogatives, who, generally speaking, can boast as good a share of invention as those who more immediately profess it.

The accounts which historians favour us with, of the early ages and origin of nations, would be novels, if fiction alone could make them such; but having only the improbabilities, without the amusing properties, of Fairy Tales and Arabian Nights, they cannot rank even with the lowest works of fancy.

The histories of the heroic ages are better entitled to be considered as romances; the adventures of a Hercules, a Theseus, and a Jason, afford some little entertainment to the reader, but it is a compliment to call them the *Quixotes* of antiquity.

The writers of the lives of illustrious persons, like the novelists, generally make their own hero; but not often with the same attention to nature; the lying legends of Pythagoras, Abaris, and Apollonius, would not pass upon the world in any fiction, that did not avowedly bid defiance to credibility.[1]

The liberty some writers take, of embellishing their histories with florid speeches and declamations, put into the mouths of people, who, probably, never uttered a single sentence as it is set down in their parts, is a palpable intrusion on the province of the dramatist or novelist, who, building fables upon old foundations, with the help of a few historic characters and facts, give an air of truth to fiction. Here I might instance those amusing fabrications in our own times, entitled Parliamentary Debates, where truth and short-hand have no share with invention, and the senator's best historian is he that is least faithful to his words.

In short, there have been, and still are, many more novelists in the world of letters, than have taken credit to themselves for it, or perhaps ever suspected they were entitled so to do.

After all, it is only in the professed department of the novel that true and absolute liberty is enjoyed. If I was now writing the history of Alexander the Great, who, as everybody believes, died of a drunken fit, let me do what I will with him in the career of his victories, drunk he must be at last, and drunk he must die. With the hero of my novel it is otherwise; over him I have despotic power; his fate and fortune, life or death, depend on my will; and whether I shall crown him with length of days and prosperity, or cut short his thread by an untimely stroke, is a question within my own choice to determine; and though I must account to nature and probability for the regularity of my proceedings, no appeal lies to truth and matter-of-fact against my positive decision in the case. I have those powers in my hand which the historian, properly so called, hath not; I am not tied down to any incidents and events which I cannot over-rule; I may deal punishment to the evil, and reward to the good, which he whose pen must record the dispensations of Providence rarely hath in his power to do. For the moral of my story, therefore, I am fairly responsible, and no less for the purity of the narrative; for, though the real scenes of life can hardly fail to contaminate the page that records them, the writer who invents impurities is without excuse.

I know that the privileges of the novelist are more than can well be defined, and his range wider than that portion of created nature which is known to us; yet I do not meditate to stretch my rights so far, nor shall put my privileges to their full exertion: it is not my ambition to run truth out of sight, or put credulity out of breath by following me; I do not propose to make any demands upon my hero that he cannot reasonably fulfil, or press him into straits from which virtue, by its native energy, cannot extricate herself with ease; I shall require of him no sacrifices for the sake of public fame, no pedantic, ostentatious apathy, for his lot is humble, and his feelings natural; I shall let him swim with the current, and not strive to tow him against the stream of probability.

I know that I could play my puppets after my own fancy, for the wires are in my hand; that I could make them declaim like heroes in a tragedy, or gabble like a gang of gipsies under a hedge; that I could weave my fable, as the Turks do carpets, without counterfeiting the likeness of any one thing in earth, sea, or air; produce beings out of nature, that no sober author ever dreamt of, and force beings into nature, that no well-bred reader ever met with; but I have lived long enough to see wonderful revolutions effected by an intemperate abuse of power, and shall be cautious how I risk privileges so precious upon experiments so trivial.

I am not sure that I shall make my leading characters happy enough to satisfy the sanguine, serious enough to suit the sentimental, or beautiful enough to warm the imagination of the animated reader. Some may think I have not been sufficiently liberal to them in point of fortune, others may wish I had favoured them with a few more casualties and misadventures. I am aware that, in a novel, travelling the road is very hazardous, that even taking the air does not secure the company from a sudden overturn in their carriage, and that few adventurers ever set foot in a boat without a soaking in the water; but I have not yet found out the wit of being mischievous. I perceive that broken bones are considered as becoming appendages to young gentlemen when in love; that faintings and hysterics are expected of young ladies upon all tender occasions; and that a burning hot fever, with a high delirium, is one of the warmest topics we can strike upon, and heightens the charms of a heroine beyond any other expedient that can be started for the purpose. All these weapons I know are within my reach, and the use of them I know; but it is a cut-finger business at best, and I think them safest in the sheath.

One thing, however, there is for me to do, that cannot be dispensed with, though I shall, probably, hold it off as long as I can—I must make love, and I am far from sure I shall make it in a style to please my readers. I wish to my heart I knew what sort of love they best like; for there are so many patterns, I am puzzled how to choose what shall please them. I have been sometimes told, that the author of *Arundel* was not far from the butt; if so, I hope I am as good a marksman as he is. His, if I rightly remember, was rather point-blank firing; now I am inclined to think I shall give my piece a certain elevation that will send the shot upon a range; but it is no matter how I manage it, so it does but reach the heart at last.

Precedents in plenty are before me; heroes and heroines of all tempers, characters, and descriptions; love-suits as long as Chancery-suits;

hearts conquered at a glance, surprised by treachery, or stormed by impudence—yet where to fix I know not.

I will ask advice of Nature, and rule myself by her report.

Reasons for writing as fast as we can

Those rules which a well-bred man lays down for himself, when he engages in the difficult task of telling a long story about persons unknown to the circle he is in, may with equal propriety be adopted by an author in the conduct of a novel; both pursue the same object, and both incur the same risk of failing in the pursuit, which certainly requires a considerable share of management and address to succeed in.

A story will infallibly disgust, if it is told in vulgar and ill-chosen language; if interlarded with affected phrases, or florid descriptions, that advance no interest; if it is delivered in a pedantic, laboured style, unsuitable to characters in familiar life; if it substitutes dull jokes and ribaldry in the place of wit and pleasantry; if the teller either digresses too often from the main subject, or dwells too long and circumstantially upon matters not sufficiently important or amusing; in short, if it fails in any of those requisites that should keep the attention wakeful and alert, it is a bad story, and the teller has wilfully brought himself into disgrace with his hearers, by cheating them of their expectations and abusing their indulgence.

So is it with the novel-writer; the same faults will be punished with the same contempt.

Be the matter ever so interesting, which falls to the task of any one man to relate in public company, he will naturally be ashamed of keeping their attention too long upon the stretch; and if he cannot prevail upon other tongues to move, yet, in good manners and common delicacy, he will contrive to make some breaks and pauses in his narrative, which may give relief to the ear, and some degree of relaxation to the mind. This seems generally understood by the novel-writer, who, by the distribution of his matter into books and chapters, tenders to the reader, in his several stages, so many inns or bating-places by the way, where he hangs out a sign that there is rest at least to be had for the weary traveller.

An eminent author, whose talent for novel-writing was unequalled, and whose authority ought greatly to weigh with all who succeed him in the same line, furnished his baiting-places with such ingenious hospitality, as not only to supply his guests with the necessary remissions from fatigue, but also to recruit them with viands of a very nutritive, as well as palatable quality. According to this figure of speech, (which cannot be mistaken, as alluding to his prefatory chapters,) he was not only a pleasant, facetious companion by the way, but acted the part of an admirable host at every one of the inns. Alas! it was famous travelling in his days. I remember him full well, and despair of ever meeting his like again, upon that road, at least.

Others there have been, and one there was, of the same day, who was a well-meaning, civil soul, and had a soft simpering kind of address, that took mightily with the ladies, whom he contrived to usher through a long, long journey, with their handkerchiefs at their eyes, weeping and wailing by the way, till he conducted them, at the close of it, either to a ravishment, or a funeral, or perhaps to a mad-house, where he left them to get off as they could. He was a charming man, and had a deal of custom; but the other's was the house that I frequented.

There was a third, somewhat posterior in time, not in talents, who was indeed a rough driver, and rather too severe to his cattle; but, in faith, he carried us on at a merry pace over land or sea; nothing came amiss to him, for he was up to both elements, and a match for nature in every shape, character, and degree: he was not very courteous, it must be owned, for he had a capacity for higher things, and was above his business; he only wanted a little more suavity and discretion to have figured with the best.[2]

With these I shall stop; for another step would bring me into company with the living, and of my partiality for my contemporaries I am too conscious to put my judgment to the risk of criticism, which may not be over-indulgent to mistakes of the heart. Them and myself I implicitly resign to the favour and protection of those public-spirited inspectors of literature, who undertake the laborious task of reviewing everything we write, and who understand so well the policy of the wise Lacedæmonians, that no sooner do they light upon a deformed or ricketty bantling, but they charitably strangle it outright, and don't let it survive to disgrace us with posterity. This is mercy to the age at large, though any one of us, upon whom it falls, is apt to call it cruelty, when we are sent to the trunk-maker and the pastry-cook to drive the best bargain we can for our property,[3] before it is turned over to the worms, who then only take us into reading when nobody else will; but such is our obstinacy notwithstanding, that it seems as if we spitefully wrote the more, in contradiction to our real friends, who fairly tell us we cannot write at all.

However, at the very worst, we can always draw this consolation from our faults, that our kind correctors have had infinite pleasure in finding them out; for surely if the discovery gave pain, no man would voluntarily engage in the search.

There is also another cheering reflection we have to feed upon, which is, that those authors who shall follow us in point of time, will fall short of us in point of merit. Homer himself tells us this, who, as an epic poet, was surely interested to hold up his heroes as high as he could, and yet is compelled to confess, that the pelting they bestowed upon each other was but children's play, compared to what their fathers could do at that sport.[4] Now it is clear, that, from Homer's day to the present hour, there has been a gradual falling-off in the human powers, mental and bodily, from which I infer, that the novel last written may always be presumed the worst that ever was written; and therefore that it behoves every writer, and myself amongst the rest, to write as fast as ever we can, for the longer we are about it the worse it will be. And this reminds me that I ought to bring this chapter to a conclusion, and attend to the history, which, in the meantime, has been standing still, and cannot profit by a pause.

BOOK III, CH. I

A Dissertation, which our Readers will either sleep over, or pass over, as best suits them

An author will naturally cast his composition in that kind of style and character where he thinks himself most likely to succeed; and in this he will be directed by considering, in the first place, what is the natural turn of his own mind, where his strength lies, and to what his talents point; and secondly, by the public taste, which, however much it is his interest to consult, should not be suffered to betray him into undertakings he is not fitted for.

Novels, like dramas, may certainly be composed either in the tragic or comic cast, according to the writer's choice and fancy. Tales of fiction, with mournful catastrophes, have been wrought up with very considerable effect. I could name some of the pathetic sort, which are uncommonly beautiful, and deeply interesting; their success might well encourage any author who has powers and propensities suitable, to copy the attempt; on the other hand, examples muster strongest for the story with a happy ending: middle measures have also been struck upon by some, and novels of the tragi-comic character aptly and ingeniously devised, which, after agitating the passions of terror and pity, allay them with the unexpected relief of happiness and good fortune in the concluding scenes.

By all or any of these channels, the author may shape his course to fame, if he has skill to shun the shoals of insipidity on the one hand, and the rocks of improbability on the other; in one word, if he will keep the happy mean of nature. Exquisitely fine are those sensations which the well-wrought tale of pity excites; but double care is required to guide them to the right point, because they are so penetrating; whoever stirs those passions in a guilty cause, may do infinite mischief, for they sink into young and tender hearts, and where they sink, they leave a deep and permanent impression; they are curious instruments in the hand of the artist, but murderous weapons in the possession of the assassin.

Cheerful fictions, with happy endings, are written with more ease, and have less risk as to the moral; they play about the fancy in a more harmless manner; the author is seldom so careless of his characters as not to deal out what is termed poetical justice, amongst them, rewarding the good, and punishing the unworthy; pride and oppression are rarely made to triumph ultimately; engaging libertinism, seldom fails to reform; and true love, after all its trials, is finally crowned with possession.

The mixt, or composite sort, which steer between grave and gay, yet are tinctured with each, deal out terror and suspense in their progress, artfully interwoven into the substance of the fable, for the purpose of introducing some new and unforeseen reverse of fortune at the story's close, which is to put the tortured mind at rest. This demands a conduct of some skill; for if the writer's zeal for the introduction of new and striking incidents, wherein consists the merit of this species of composition, be not tempered by a due attention to nature, character, and probability, the whole web is broken, and the work falls to the ground: in good hands it becomes a very pleasing production, for the curiosity is kept alive through the whole progress of the narrative, and the mind that has been suspended between hope and fear, at last subsides in perfect satisfaction with the just and equitable event of things.

A novel may be carried on in a series of letters, or in regular detail; both methods have their partisans, and in numbers they seem pretty equally divided; which of the two is the more popular, I cannot take upon myself to say; but I should guess that letters give the writer most amusement and relief, not only from their greater diversity of style, but from the respite which their intermissions afford him. These advantages, however, have a counterpoise, for his course becomes more circuitous and subject to embarrassment, than when he takes the narrative wholly into his own hands. Without great management and address in keeping his dates progressive, and distinctly methodized, his reader is exposed to be called back and puzzled; and, as the characters who conduct the correspondence must be kept asunder, the scene is oftentimes distracted where we wish it to be entire, or else the intercourse of letters is made glaringly unnatural and pedantic, by compressing the distances from which they are dated, and putting two people to the ridiculous necessity of writing long narratives to each other when conversation was within their reach.

For myself, having now made experiment of both methods, I can only say, that, were I to consult my own amusement solely, I should prefer the vehicle of letters. This, however, must be acknowledged, that all conversations, where the speakers are brought upon the scene, are far more natural when delivered at first hand, than when retailed by a correspondent; for we know that such sort of narratives do not commonly pass by the post, and the letter, both in style and substance, appears extremely stiff, tedious, and pedantic. Upon the whole, I should conjecture that the writer is best accommodated by the one, and the reader most gratified by the other. I hope I am right in my conjecture as to the reader's preference of the method I am now pursuing, else I have chosen ill for myself, and gained no credit by the sacrifice.

BOOK IV, CH. I

The Author appeals to his Readers

I shall now put in a few words, whilst my history pauses, touching what I claim from my readers as a right, and what I hope and expect from them as a favour.

My claim is briefly this, credit in all cases for an honest meaning, or, in other words, the best sense that a doubtful passage will bear: it is thus I have treated others; the same treatment I have a right now to claim from them.

On the score of favour, I am their suitor in the humblest sense; for

I see so many imperfections starting up in my performance, which I cannot cure, and suspect there may be so many more, which possibly I shall not discover, that I have no notion of sending my sins into the world without one apology; I am not hardy enough to give in the account between my readers and myself, without the usual salvo of *errors excepted.*—Take Nature for your guide, says the critic; follow her, and you can't go wrong.—True, most sagacious critic, I reply; but what is so difficult? Does the tragic poet always find her out? Does the comic writer never miss her haunts? Yet they profess to paint from Nature, and, no doubt, they do their best: the outline may be true, but the least slip in filling it up mars the portrait; it demands a steady hand, a faithful eye, a watchful judgment, to make the likeness perfect; and, grant it perfect, the author's work will gain no praise, unless it be pleasing also; for who opens a novel but in the expectation of being amused by it?

Let it be merry, says one, for I love to laugh.—Let it be pathetic, says a second, for I have no objection to the melancholy tale that makes me weep.—Let your characters be strongly marked, cries a third, your fable well imagined, and work it up with a variety of new and striking incidents, for I like to have my attention kept alive.—These, and a hundred more, are the demands which one poor brain is to satisfy in a work of fancy; wit, humour, character, invention, genius, are to be set to work together; fiction is to be combined with probability, novelty with nature, ridicule with good-humour, passion with morality, and pain with pleasure; everything is to be natural, yet nothing common; animating, but not inflammatory; interesting, but not incredible; in short, there must be everything that judgment can plan, and genius execute, to make the composition perfect. No man has done all this; and he who has done most towards it, has still fallen very short of the whole.

With all this consciousness about me, I yet do not despair but that the candid reader will find something in this fable to overbalance its miscarriages. I shall proceed as one who knows his danger, but is not discouraged from his duty. These children of my fancy, whom I have brought into existence, I shall treat as they deserve, dealing out their portions of honour and dishonour as their conduct seems to call for it; and though some amongst them will probably persist in acting an evil part to the last, yet, collectively, they will leave no evil lesson behind them.

As to our hero, if he has been so fortunate as to gain an interest in the good opinion of the reader in this period of his history, I am bold to hope he will not forfeit it in the succeeding occurrences of his life, but that he shall preserve a consistent character to the end; that so, when his part is finished, be it happy or unhappy, he may earn a plaudit as the curtain drops.

I do not aim to draw a perfect character; for, after a pretty long acquaintance with mankind, I have never met with any one example of the sort. How then shall I describe what I have not seen? On the contrary, if I wish to form a character, like this of Henry, in which virtue predominates, or like that of Blachford, where the opposite qualities prevail, I have nature before me in both cases; but if, in the former instance, I will not suffer a single shade to fall upon my canvass, and in the latter, do not let one tint of light appear, what do I present to the spectator, but a confused and shapeless mass, here too glaring, and there too opaque, to preserve any outline that can give to view the form and fashion of a man?—The brightest side of human nature is not without a spot, the darkest side is not without a spark.

For my own part, as I am not apt to be amused with stories told to the discredit of mankind, I should be sorry if this of mine appeared to any of my readers to have that tendency in the general. A contrast of character there will be in all histories, true or feigned; but when an author is the biographer of men and women of his own making, he has it in his power, without losing sight of nature, to let the prevailing impression of his fable be favourable or unfavourable, and indulge his own propensities to a certain degree, whichever way they point. Now I know not why we should studiously put forward none but the worst features of the time we live in; yet I think this has been done by some novelists of great celebrity, in whom there reigns a spirit of satire, that, in my opinion, neither adds to their merit nor our amusement. A pedant, who secludes himself from society, may nourish a cynical humour; but a writer, who gives the living manners of the age, is supposed to live amongst men, and write from the crowd rather than the closet; now, if such a man runs about from place to place, with no cleanlier purpose than to search for filth and ordure, I conceive his office to be that of a scavenger rather than a scholar. An honest man, as I take it, will always find honesty enough, and a friendly man meet friendship enough, in his contemporaries, to keep him in good humour with them. Something, indeed, may be found to reprehend in all times; as the manners and the morals fluctuate, the mirror that reflects them faithfully will give to objects as they pass their proper form and feature. In the time I am now writing, the national character shews itself in so bright a point of view, that the author must be harsh in the extreme, who holds up fictions of depravity as exemplars of the era in which he lives.

I think I may promise myself, therefore, that the general spirit of my history will not be thought morose. I have, indeed, taken occasion, in the character of Jemima Cawdle, to make free with enthusiasm; but I have at the same time exhibited it in contact with a virtuous principle, under the auspices of my worthy friend Ezekiel Daw. I have described a domestic tyrant in the person of Lord Crowbery; but I did not give him a title, because I thought that pride was attached to a peerage, or that the cruel and overbearing part which my fable assigns to him, was characteristic of nobility, the very contrary of which I hold for doctrine; neither did I locate Blachford in Jamaica, as favouring an invective against our countrymen in the West Indies; no man, I believe, can be found less inclined to be a convert to that groundless prejudice, which vain and shallow heads have been hatching for purposes no less fatal to the interests of the public, than to the reputations of individuals.

To represent scenes of familiar life in an elegant and interesting manner, is one of the most difficult tasks an author can take in hand; for of these, every man is a critic: Nature is, in the first place, to be attended to, and probability is not to be lost sight of; but it must be nature strongly featured, and probability closely bordering on the marvellous; the one must touch upon extravagance, and the other be highly seasoned with adventures—for who will thank us for a dull and lifeless journal of insipid facts? Now every peculiarity of humour in the human character is a strain upon nature, and every surprising incident is a degree of violence to probability: how far shall we go then for our reader's amusement? how soon shall we stop in consideration of ourselves? There is undoubtedly a land-mark in the fields of fancy, *suntcerti denique fines*,[5] but it requires a nice discernment to find them out, and a cautious temper not to step beyond them.

Here, then, I will rest my cause, and conclude my chapter. My readers have my best endeavours to amuse them: I have devoted very many hours to the composition of these volumes, and I am beholden to them for beguiling me of many a care; if they retain their property when they shall pass into the hands of those who peruse them, it will be everything I can hope for from them.

BOOK V, CH. I

A short Treatise upon Love, Ancient and Modern

Love, as a deity, was invested, by those who made him such, with the most contradictory attributes: they feigned him blind, yet called him an unerring marksman; gave him wings, yet allowed that constancy was his best qualification; described him as an infant, yet were not to learn that infancy alone is exempted from his power.

These are contrarieties, which none but the initiated can reconcile. They justify his blindness, when, hurried on by the impetuosity of passion, they espy no danger in the precipice before them; they acknowledge he is swift of wing, when the minutes they devote to his enjoyments fly so quickly; and they cannot but regard him as an infant, when one short honeymoon begins and terminates his date of life.

A thousand ingenious devices have been formed to suit the various properties of this fabulous divinity, and every symbol has its moral; he had been allegorized and enigmatized in innumerable ways; the pen, the pencil, and the chisel, have been worn out in his service; floods of ink, looms of canvass, and quarries of marble, have been exhausted in the boundless field of figurative description. The lover, who finds out so many ways of torturing himself, cannot fail to strike out symbols and devices to express the passion under which he suffers; then the verse flows mournfully elegiac, and the bleeding heart, transfixed with an arrow, is emblematically displayed; thus, whilst the poet varies his measure, the painter and the sculptor vary their devices, as joy or sorrow, success or disappointment, influence their fancy. One man's Cupid is set astride upon a lion, to exemplify his power; another places his upon a crocodile, to satirize his hypocrisy; here the god is made to trample upon kingly crowns, there to trifle with a wanton sparrow; the adamantine rock now crumbles at his stroke, anon we see him basking on the bosom of Chloe, his arrows broken, and his pinions bound.

The Greeks, who had more caprice in their passions than either nature or morality can excuse, nevertheless bequeathed their *Cupid* to posterity, with a considerable stock in hand; but the moderns added more, from funds of their own, and everything they bestowed was honestly appropriated to the only sex that has any claim upon the regular and solid firm of *Venus, Cupid,* and *Co.*

When superstition met its final overthrow, and the heathen temples were dismantled of their images and altars, Love alone, the youngest

of the deities, survived the disaster, and still holds his dignities and
prerogatives by Christian courtesy; and, though modern ingenuity has
not added much to his embellishments, yet, in the ardour and sincerity
of our devotion, we do not yield to the ancients: the whole region of
romance has been made over to him; our drama, tragic as well as comic,
has gone far beyond that of the ancients in building its fable and character upon the passion of love. Last, in point of time, but not of
allegiance, comes the fraternity of novelists, who are his clients to a
man. Love is the essence of every tale; and so studious are our authors
not to let the spirit of that essence become vapid, that few, if any, fail
to conclude with the event of marriage; connubial love is of a quality
too tame for their purpose.

As the majority of our novels are formed upon domestic plots, and
most of these drawn from the very times in which they are written, the
living manners must be characterized by the authors of such fables, and
we must of course make our love of such materials as the fashion of the
age affords; it will not, therefore, resemble the high-flown passion of
the Gothic knights and heroes of the old romance, neither will it
partake of those coarse manners and expressions which our old comic
writers adopt; it will even take a different shade from what a novelist
would have given it half a century ago; for the social commerce of the
sexes is now so very different from what it was then, that beauty is no
longer worshipped with that distant respect which our antiquated
beaux paid to their mistresses.

As the modern fine gentleman studies nothing but his ease, and aims
only to be what he terms *comfortable*, regarding all those things, that
used to be considered as annoyances and embarrassments, with cool
indifference and contempt, even love in him is not an active passion; he
expresses no raptures at the sight of beauty, and, if he is haply provoked
to some slight exertion out of course, it must be some new face just
launched upon the public, that can fan his languid spirit into any
emotion approaching towards curiosity. Nothing is an object of
admiration with him; he covets no gratifications that are to be earned
by labour, no favours that are to be extorted by assiduity; his pleasures
must court him, and the fair one he affects must forget that she is a
divinity, and banish from her thoughts the accustomed homage of
sighs and tears and bending knees, for all these things give trouble to the
performer, and on that account are, by general consent, exploded and
abolished.

Now, the writer of novels has not the privilege which the painter of portraits has, of dressing modern characters in antique habits; so that some of our best productions in this class are already become, in some particulars, out of fashion; even the inimitable composition of *The Foundling*, is fading away in some of its tints, though the hand of the master, as a correct delineator of nature, will be traced to all posterity, and hold its rank amongst the foremost of that class, which enrols the names of Cervantes, Rabelais, Le Sage, Voltaire, Rousseau, Richardson, Smollet [*sic*], Johnson, Sterne, and some others, whose pens Death hath not yet stopped, and long may it be ere he does!

Having now allowed the historic muse her customary bait, we shall soon urge her to fresh exertions, by which a certain young lady, who as yet has barely stepped upon the stage, will begin to support a more important interest in the business of this drama. Isabella Manstock, in the bloom of youth and beauty, cannot long remain an idle character; though she has flattered herself that filial affection will keep possession of her heart, to the exclusion of that intruding passion we have been speaking of, yet nature and experience will compel me to exhibit that lovely recusant as one amongst many, who have been fain to truckle to the tyrant they abjure. The time is drawing near when impressions, which she never felt before, will force their way; when the merits, the misfortunes, the attentions of our hero, will take hold upon her heart; when her eyes will dwell upon his person with delight, her ear listen to his praises with rapture, to his sighs with pity, to his suit with favour. Then, if Love, who is not to be affronted with impunity, gives a loose to his revenge, and makes her feel the full terrors of his power, the reader will be pleased to bear in mind, that I have not taken my lovers from the inanimate groups that form the circle of fashion, but sought them in the sequestered walks of rural life, where the senses are not deadened by variety, nor indifference become habitual by the affectation of it.

BOOK VI, CH. I

The Author hints at a Reform in the Constitution of a Novel

It is my wish to devote these short prefatory Essays to our fraternity of Novelists, if haply my good-will can strike out anything for their use and profit; it is, therefore, in the friendly spirit of criticism, that I protest against a practice, which some few of the corps have lately taken up, of adulterating their compositions with a dash of politics, which I conceive to be a kind of fraud upon their customers, that not only brings disgrace and loss upon themselves individually, but is injurious to the trade in general. I shall not point out the particular offenders, as they are sufficiently noted by those who have read their productions; and, if they have but wisdom enough to reform, I should be loath that past errors should be remembered to the prejudice of their future fortune.

I trust, they need not be told, that there are clubs and coffee-houses in this free country, where nonsense may be talked with impunity; but it is a serious risk to print it. Round their own fire-sides their zeal may boil over without scalding their fingers; but when they cater for the public, they should be warned how they mix up any such inflammatory materials, as temperate stomachs will not bear; our only aim should be to refresh our friendly visitors with an exhilarating wholesome draught, not to disturb their reason with an intoxicating nauseous drug.

All that I am bound to do as a story-maker, is, to make a story; I am not bound to reform the constitution of my country in the same breath, nor even (Heaven be thanked!) to overturn it, though that might be the easier task of the two, or, more properly speaking, one and the same thing in its consequences. Nature is my guide; man's nature, not his natural rights: the one ushers me by the straightest avenue to the human heart, the other bewilders me in a maze of metaphysics.

Doubtless, it becomes the gentle nature of a female votary of the Muse, and of every author soft as females, to let no occasion slip for making public such their amiable propensity, through every channel that the press affords; the poor African is therefore fair game for every minstrel that has tuned his lyre to the sweet chords of pity and con- dolence; whether he *builds immortal verse* upon his loss of liberty, or weaves his melancholy fate into the pathos of a novel, in either case he finds a mine of sentiment, digs up enthusiasm from its richest vein, and gratifies at once his spleen and his ambition. The happy virtuous negro, torn from his own fine temperate climate, and transported into the torrid heats of our inhospitable islands, there to sweat and bleed beneath the lash of barbarous task-masters, inspires so fine a rhapsody, and gives so touching a display of British cruelty that, against the force of truth, the unguarded reader credits it, and blushes for the country that he lives in. No matter that the world at large bears testimony to the charities of our land, to her magnanimity, her honour, her benevo- lence; though thousands of the persecuted sufferers for conscience sake, fly to Britain as the universal philanthropist, in whose arms there is a sure asylum for the wretched, still the degrading fiction bears down truth; black troops of savages are raised to cast a nation's character in shade; the African lives free and happy under the mild government of his native princes; he never licks the dust in their presence, nor loads the gibbet to adorn their palaces, and, though snatched from death by his purchaser, yet, not emancipated from slavery by his employer, he must be taught to murmur, and the sigh, which he cannot draw from his own bosom, must be inspired into him by the breath of others, till, urged by these incendiary condolences, he shakes off his contentment, rises terrible in his enthusiasm, and, though redeemed from death by those whom he destroys, sates himself with carnage, and, ripping forth the heart of his benefactor, shews the trophy of his freedom, and gloriously asserts the Rights of Man. Cast your eyes towards those blood-besprinkled islands, which ye have conspired to illuminate, ye merciful reformers, and glory in your doctrines, if your consciences will let you. I blush to think, that folly can effect such mischief.[6]

A fast friend to the interests of the press, and a great authority in point, who vends our wares to the amount of one hundred thousand volumes annually, Heaven augment his little modicum of trade![7] ingenuously acquaints us with those honest arts, by which he rose to eminence so justly earned; of these, one trifling requisite, amongst many more noble acquirements, he mentions to be, that of keeping himself always *pretty well informed of the state of politics in Europe*, not exactly by the reading of novels, nor purposely for the writing of them, but for reasons much more wise and weighty; namely, because he has *always found, that bookselling is much affected by the political state of affairs.* May the secrets of all the cabinets in Europe be ever open to a politician, who makes so good an use, and draws such worthy profit from his information; and I would to Heaven, those wrong-headed zealots of our fraternity above alluded to, had his political knowledge for our edification, or would copy his prudence for their own amendment.

This experienced personage further observes, that *the best time for bookselling is, when there is no kind of news stirring*: it is a little mortifying, I must own, but his authority is conclusive, for he tells us, that *then many of those, who for months would have done nothing but talk of war or peace, revolutions and counter-revolutions, &c. &c. for want of other amusements, will have recourse to books.* If this observation be true, (and who can doubt that men love talking better than reading?) the author's golden age is that of public tranquillity; how ill then does he employ his talents, who, instead of exerting them for the peace and quiet of mankind, turns them to the purposes of discontent, *of revolutions and counter-revolutions*, writing the world into such a temper, that no readers are left in it? The true patriot in the republic of letters is he, who, in times of war and tumult, can so write as to invite the world's attention to his peaceful studies, and divert it from its sanguinary politics; the incendiary author, on the contrary, is a fool and a *felo de se*.

If men, therefore, have so little disposition towards the purchasing of books, when there is *so much news stirring* abroad, let him who writes at such a moment give double diligence to what he writes; let him so manage it as to contrast the tædium of the politician's task, and not revolt him with a double dose of what he is weary of. Strong efforts will succeed, when feeble ones must fail; novelty and surprise will ever attract admiration, the most enthusiastic passion of the human mind; and though the philosophy of Rome cried it down, Plato himself confesses it to have been the moving spring of the philosophy of Greece.[8]

Here, then, we discern the proper province of works of fiction for *novelty and surprise* (as Bishop Warburton defines them) *are the insepable attendants of imposture*;[9] and the very time, when strong attractions are required to draw men to their books, is the time for such productions to appear, and the strength of their attraction will depend upon the writer's care and talents. Now, though *novelty and surprise* are what we aim to treat our readers with, we are no otherwise *impostors*, than those fair-dealing jugglers are, who candidly warn their spectators beforehand, that their tricks are nothing more than mere slight of hand, the effect of nimble art and practised adroitness, by which they cheat the sight, but aim not to impose upon the understanding; like them, the novelist professes to deal in ingenious deceptions, but deceptions so like truth and nature, that, whilst his performances have all the vivacity of a romance to excite admiration, they have the harmony of a history to engage approbation. Monsters, and prodigies, and every species of unnatural composition, are not to be admitted into a novel; for these tend only to raise wonder in the ignorant and superstitious, and are a sort of black art, now universally exploded. A writer of romances, in the present age, cannot make so free with the credulity of the readers, as Herodotus or even Livy did with theirs, though professed historians.

A novel may be considered as a dilated comedy; its plot, therefore, should be uniform, and its narrative unbroken: episode and digression are sparingly, if at all, to be admitted; the early practice of weaving story within story should be avoided; the adventures of *the Man of the Hill*, in *The Foundling* is an excrescence that offends against the grace and symmetry of the plot: whatever makes a pause in the main business, and keeps the chief characters too long out of sight, must be a defect. In all histories, whether true or fictitious, the author cannot too carefully refrain from speaking in his own person; and this is yet another reason to be added to those already given, why political discussions should never be admitted in a novel, as they are sure to be set down to the author's account, let him assign them as he will. It is not necessary that the leading character of a novel should be honest and amiable, but it is indispensable it should be interesting and entertaining; and every writer, who wishes to endear man to man by pleasing pictures of human nature, or, in other words, by presenting virtuous characters in amiable lights, will let the good preponderate over the evil; he will not take his maxims from Rochfoucault,[10] nor shape his fellow-creatures after the models of Hobbes or Swift; the spirit of the author will be seen in the general moral and tendency of the piece, though he will allot to every particular character its proper sentiment and language; the outline will be that of nature, and fancy will dispose the group into various attitudes and actions; but the general colouring and complexion of the whole will reflect the peculiar and distinguishing tints of the master.

BOOK VII, CH. I

An humble Apology for Authors in general, with some modest Hints at their peculiar Usefulness

I hope the candid reader now and then calls to mind how much more nimbly he travels over these pages, than the writer of them did. When our dulness is complained of, it would be but charity in him to reflect how much pains that same dulness has cost us; more, he may be assured, than our brighter intervals, where we sprung nimbly forward with an easy weight, instead of toiling like a carrier's horse, whose slow and heavy pace argues the load he draws, and the labour he endures: Alas for us poor novelists, if there were no mercy for dull authors, and our countrymen, like the barbarous Libethrians of old, should take it into their minds to banish music and the muses out of the land, and murder every Orpheus that did not fiddle to their taste![11] They should consider, that the man who makes a book, makes a very pretty piece of furniture; and if they will but consign us to a quiet station on a shelf, and give us wherewithal to cover us in a decent trim, the worst amongst us will serve to fill up the file, and stop a gap in the ranks.

'Tis hard indeed to toil, as we sometimes do, to our own loss and disappointment; to sweat in the field of fame, merely to reap a harvest of chaff, and pile up reams of paper for the worm to dine upon. It is a cruel thing to rack our brains for nothing, run our jaded fancies to a stand-still, and then lie down at the conclusion of our race, a carcase for the critics. And what is our crime all the while? A mere mistake between our readers and ourselves, occasioned by a small miscalculation of our capacities and their candour; all which would be avoided, if, happily for us, they had not the wit to find out our blunders, or, happily for them, had all that good-nature for us, that we generously exercise towards ourselves. If once they could bring their tempers to this charming complacency, they might depend upon having books in plenty; authors would multiply like polypusses, and the press would be the happiest mother in the kingdom.

How many worthy gentlemen are there in this blessed island of ours, who have so much time upon their hands, that they do not know what to do with it? I am aware how large and respectable a portion of this enlightened nation centre their delights in the chase, and draw an elegant resource from the sagacity of the hound, and the vigour of the horse: but they cannot always be on the saddle; the elements they cannot command; and frost and snow will lock them up within their castle walls: there it is possible that solitude may surprise them, and dismiss them for a time to the solace of their own lucubrations; now, with all possible respect for these resources, I should think it may sometimes be worth their while to make experiment of other people's lucubrations, when they have worn out their own, for those must be but sorry thoughts, which are not better than not thinking at all; and the least they can gain by an author is a nap.

The ingenuity of man has invented a thousand contrivances for innocently disposing of idle time; let us, therefore, who write books, have only the idlers on our side, in gratitude for the amusement we give them, and let the rest of the world be as splenetic as they will, we may set their spleen at naught; the majority will be with us.

If a querulous infant is stilled by a rattle, the maker of the rattle has saved somebody's ears from pain and persecution; grant, therefore, that a novel is nothing better than a toy for children of a larger growth and more unruly age, society has some cause to thank the writer of it; it may have put an aching head to rest; it may have cheered the debtor in his prison, or the country squire in a hard frost. Traders will cry up the commodity they deal in, therefore I do not greatly insist on the praises which some that write books have bestowed on book-writing; but I do observe, that great respect is paid to an author by those who cannot read him, wherefore, I conclude, those who can read, and do not praise him, are only silent because they want words to express their admiration and gratitude; whilse those sanguine flatterers, who, in the excess of their respect for our persons, cry down our performances, give evident proof how much higher they had pitched their expectations of what our talents would produce, than our productions could make good; but though, in their zeal for our reputations, they tell us how ill we write, they seldom neglect at the same time to shew us how we might have written still worse.

Some over-wise people have pretended to discover, that this altercation between author and critic, is nothing more than a mere plot and contrivance to play into each other's hands, like Mountebank and Zany; but this is over-acted sagacity, and an affectation of finding more mysteries in the art of authorship, than really belong to it; for my part, I believe it is a business of a more simple nature, than most which can be taken up, and that authors in general require nothing more than pen, ink, and paper, to set up with. In ancient times, the trade was in few hands, and the work seems then to have been composed with much pains and forethought; materials were collected with great care, and put together with consummate accuracy and attention; every part was fitted to its place, polished to the heighth, and finished to perfection; there were inspectors on the part of the public, men of sound judgment, and fully competent to the office, who brought the work to a standard of rule and measure, and insisted upon it, that every whole should have *a beginning, a middle, and an end.* Under these strict regulations the ancients wrote; but now that practice has made us perfect, and the trade is got into so many hands, these regulations are done away, and so far from requiring of us a *beginning, middle, and end,* it is enough if we can shew a head and a tail; and it is not always that even these can be made out with any tolerable precision. As our authors write with less labour, our critics review with less care, and for every one fault that they mark in our productions, there probably might be found one hundred that they overlook. It is an idle notion, however, to suppose, that therefore they are in league and concert with the authors they revise; for where could that poor fraternity find a fund to compensate them for suffering a vocation, once so reputable, to fall into such utter disgrace under their management, as to be no longer the employ of a gentleman? As for our readers, on whom we never fail to bestow the terms of candid, gentle, courteous, and others of the like soothing cast, they certainly deserve all the fair words we can give them; for it is not to be denied, but that we make occasionally very great demands upon their candour, gentleness, and courtesy, exercising them frequently and fully with such trials as require those several endowments in no small proportion. The farther I advance, therefore, in this work, the civiller I will be; and to those readers who shall follow me into this third volume, I may with justice apply the epithets of patient, persevering, faithful, and so on, with a *crescendo* in my strain, till the piece is concluded.

But are there not also fastidious, angry, querulential readers? readers with full stomachs, who complain of being surfeited and overloaded with the story-telling trash of our circulating libraries? It cannot be altogether denied, but still they are readers: if the load is so heavy upon them as they pretend it is, I will put them in the way of getting rid of it, by reviving the law of the ancient Cecertæans, who obliged their artists to hawk about their several wares, carrying them on their backs, till they found purchasers to ease them of the burden. Were this law put in force against authors, few of us, I doubt, would be found able to stand under the weight of our own unpurchased works.

But whilst the public is contented with things as they are, where is the wonder if the reform is never made by us till they begin it in themselves? Let their taste lead the fashion, and our productions must accord to it. Whilst the Cookeries of Hannah Glass outcirculate the Commentaries of Blackstone,[12] authors will be found, who prefer the compilation of receipts to that of records, as the easier and more profitable task of the two. If puerilities are pleasing, men will write *ut pueris placeant.*

When Demosthenes was engaged in the defence of a certain citizen of Athens, who was brought to trial upon a charge of a capital nature, neither the importance of the cause, nor the eloquence of the pleader, could fix the attention of the judges who were sitting on the trial; the orator, observing their levity, on a sudden stopped short in the midst of his harangue, and addressing himself to the court,—'Listen to me,' he cried, 'ye venerable judges, for a few moments, and I will tell you a merry tale:—A certain young man, having occasion to take a journey from this city of ours to Megara, hired an ass for the job; but being extremely incommoded on the way by a scorching sun, which smote him with intolerable heat at noon, he dismounted from his beast, and made free to take post under the shade of his carcase; upon this, the

ass-owner who accompanied him, remonstrated with great vehemence contending that his ass was let for the journey simply and precisely, and that the service now required of him was extra-conditional and illegal; the traveller, with equal vehemence, maintained, that he was warranted in the use he made of him, and that having hired the ass in substance, he was entitled to the benefit of his shadow into the bargain; the question was open to controversy, and the parties went to trial on the case.'
—Here Demosthenes ceased, and taking up his brief, prepared to leave the court; the judges, seeing this, called out to him to return and go on with his pleading.—'For shame, ye men of Athens,' cried the indignant orator, 'ye can lend your ears to the story of an ass, but will not bestow your attention upon a trial that involves the life or death of a fellow-citizen!'[13]

BOOK VIII, CH. I

An Old Man's Prattle in a Wintry Night

As the state of society becomes more refined, eccentricity of character wears away; a writer, therefore, of the present age, who aims to give amusing pictures of the humours of the times, finds nature less favourable to him in that respect than she was to those who resorted to her for the like purposes a century or two ago. This cannot be denied; but nature still is inexhaustible, and there is no need to emigrate from her domain in search of novelty and entertainment.

Originality of humour, or, as it is more commonly called, a new character, in play or novel, is the writer's first aim, as it is sure to be the first in request by every spectator and critic, and the chief test by which his genius will be tried; but when we use the term originality, as applied to the human character, we cannot be understood to mean a new creature, a being formed by fancy, and not to be found in nature, but simply a close copy, a happy likeness, of some striking character, whose peculiarities have a strong effect, either in the moral or the humour of our composition. The old drama abounds with personages of this sort, and as the moulds in which they were cast are now destroyed by time, we gaze upon them with surprise and delight, regarding them as non-descripts, or creatures of a separate species, though, at the time of their production, they were doubtless sketched from nature; and it is possible that the authors of that era were not more applauded for their originality, than we of the present time are by our contemporaries. When the critics, therefore, cry against the stage as fallen off in its spirit

from the old masters, and seem to think we ought to exhibit as much
novelty, and produce as much surprise, by living characters, as they do
by raising the dead, who are out of memory, and forgotten, they
require of us a power, which, though the Witch of Endor had, no
modern poet now can boast;[14] hence it follows, that some amongst us,
who are indignant of reproach, however unreasonable, being hurried
upon rash attempts, either spend their talents in copying after copies,
whilst they aim to paint the manners as they were in times past, or,
endeavouring to create the same surprise by modern novelties, find
themselves carried out of nature and probability into the visions of
extravagance and romance. This in its consequence brings disgrace upon
the stage, by reducing comedy into farce, and farce into puppet-show
and pantomime: the novelist, in the meantime, breaking loose from
society, runs wild into forests and deserts, in search of caves and uninhabited castles, where, forgetting every law of nature, and even every
feature of the human countenance, he paints men and women such as
never were in existence, and then, amidst the shades of night and
horror, rattles his chains, and conjures up his ghosts, till, having
frightened his readers out of their senses, he vainly supposes he has
charmed them into applause.

But the evil does not stop here; for, as a man who runs mad about
the streets, will be followed by a mob, in like manner the rhodo-
montade of the novel is copied by the nonsense of the opera; and whilst
ghosts glide over the stage, thunders roll, and towers tumble, to the
amusement of the galleries, the carpenter plays off his machinery to the
roar of applauding crowds, and the author, if he has any feeling for the
dignity of his profession, blushes at his triumphs, when he reflects that
they are founded on the disgrace of the theatre.

Let the author then beware how he is piqued into absurdities by his
own vanity, or the false taste of the public: if the genius that God has
given him, and the matter that nature supplies him with, will not serve
the purpose, let him drop the undertaking. If his imagination can frame
incidents, combine them well, and weave them naturally into a pleasing
fable, he has gained his point; but an over-anxiety to produce some
striking novelty will most likely end in producing some striking
absurdity. All ranks of life are open to his choice, and he has a right
to select the strongest humours he can find; but if he does not find what
suits his purpose in nature, he has no excuse for going out of it, whilst
he professes to be a delineator of the living manners: fancy may ramble
as she likes, if she avowedly beats about for imaginary beings; but if

she produces her own creations, and calls them men and women, or paints characters out of date, and passes them upon us for contemporaries, she does more than she has fair warrant and authority to do.

What I have here said of character is applicable to incident: the writers of fiction are generally actuated by so strong a passion for the marvellous, that they seem to throw everything off the hinges, merely to alarm us with the din and clatter they make. Of all wretched expedients which barren genius can resort to, the abrupt introduction of casualties is one of the meanest. In the novels of the present day, we encounter them at every turn, yet they never impose upon credulity; for when the sick heroine at death's door, threatens us with an exit, we are convinced she does not mean to favour us with the performance of it. Surely there is no occasion for all this; neither is the impression very pleasing which it conveys.

If that originality of character, which we have been speaking of, is now become hardly attainable, discrimination is yet within reach; and by a happy contrast of leading characters, although they shall not be really new, yet all the best effects of novelty may be obtained by an alternate play on each other's humours, by the means of which very comic and amusing situations may be struck out. Amongst our countrymen, the great masters of contrast in our own day are Fielding and Sterne: Square and Thwackum, Western and his sister, the father and the uncle of Tristram Shandy, are admirable instances: Shakespeare had it from nature, Johnson caught it from Aristophanes; Socrates and the Clown Strepsiades, in the comedy of *The Clouds*, is, perhaps, the most brilliant contrast of comic humour in the now-existing records of the stage, ancient or modern.

Let me suppose I am now speaking to a young author, sitting down for the first time to his maiden work. The first thing necessary is to understand himself; the next, to know the age in which he writes: when his nerves are fortified with a proper confidence in his own powers, let that confidence be tempered with all the respect which is due to people of an enlightened understanding, who are to be his examiners and judges. It is a very sacred correspondence that takes place between the mind of the author and the mind of the reader; it is not like the slight and casual intercourse we hold with our familiars and acquaintance, where any prattle serves to fill up a few social minutes, and set the table in a roar; what we commit to our readers has no apology from hurry and inattention; it is the result of thought well digested, of sentiments by which we must stand or fall in reputation, of principles for which we must be responsible to our contemporaries and to posterity.

In the degree of entertainment our productions may have the fortune to afford, our expectations may be pardonably mistaken; but in what offends good morals, or sins against the truth of nature, we err without excuse; self-love cannot blind us in these respects, because it is not a matter of talents, but of rectitude and common sense. We talk of critics as of men set apart on purpose to annoy and censure us; whereas every reader is a critic, and publishes his opinion of us wherever he goes; we ourselves are critics in our turn, and what we complain of in our own persons we do to others; and though few think it worth their while to publish their criticisms, let it be remembered, that some men's voices circulate farther than other men's publications.

Let us, therefore, who write, weigh well the duty of the task we engage in, and let the puerile practice of invoking the mercy of our readers be no more thought of; for, generally speaking, we are entitled to no more mercy than liberal-minded men will give us without our begging for it: I am aware of some exceptions, and am, I hope, as sensitive towards such cases as I ought to be; but I am now speaking generally of authors, who write for fame and not for bread. If these had all the diffidence they affect to have, how came it not to stand in their way when they resorted to the press? And why this terror of the critics? An author cannot be harmed by a bad critic; and why should he be afraid of being benefited [sic] by a good one?

BOOK IX, CH. I

A short Interlude between the Acts

Whilst the dramatic author cheers his audience with a tune between the acts, I am forced to fill up my intervals with a treatise, and, what is still worse, with a treatise of my own making, which is not quite the case with his tune. His spectators are regaled with harmony in a brilliant theatre, amidst a blaze of lights; my reader, in his solitary chair, sits moping over the dull strain of an uninteresting dissertation, which probably has little other merit but of putting him to sleep; what inspires his critics with good humour, only stupifies mine.

But if these are his advantages in the periods of suspension, many more, and much greater are they, when he returns to the stage, and I to my history. The actor before the curtain, and the scenist behind it, conspire to lift him into fame, almost without any effort of his own;

he is upheld by the charms of spectacle, I am loaded with the drudgery of detail; he has castles in the clouds, that drop down at the word of command, we are forced to labour late and early, till our brains are well nigh beaten into brick and mortar, with the slavery of building them. A nimble scene-painter will dash off a cataract in full froth and foam, that will cost us twenty pages of hard pumping, before we can get a single drop to flow; how many pens do we split in conjuring up a storm of thunder and lightning, whilst he, by one mark in the margin of his manuscript, sets all the elements in a roar; we find it a very troublesome job to furnish horses and carriages for the conveyance of our company, his characters are wafted from scene to scene by a whistle; when his heroine is in a crisis, some one cries,—*Hah! she faints!*—and the inimitable Siddons dies away; another cries,—*Hah! she revives!*—the inimitable Siddons is alive again. We cannot do this without salts and hartshorn, at the least, and in an obstinate fit, hardly with the help of burnt feathers, an unsavoury experiment he is never driven to.

Let us put the case, that the author of a novel shall lay his scene in the house of some abandoned strumpet, where a set of cut-throats resort for the plotting of some murderous conspiracy, and let the hero of his story, for whom our pity is to be interested, enlist himself in this gang, and let him introduce a virtuous wife, the darling of his heart, and the faithful partner of his bed, into this house of ill-fame, and assembly of villains, there to be left in the hands of these miscreants as a hostage for his good faith, telling her withal, that he is sworn to assassinate her father that very night,—who but would cry out against the conduct of such a fable? but let Otway's fascinating muse put this into melodious metre, let the bell toll for execution, bring forth the rack, send the actress on the stage, with hair dishevelled, cheeks of chalk, and eyes wildly staring—no matter why so mad at once, nor what she talks of, (be it of *seas of milk*, or *ships of amber*,)—all hearts bow down to her resistless energy; she takes her poet on her wings, and soars to fame.[15]

Wonderful in all ages, and honoured by all enlightened nations, hath been the actor's magic art; the theatres and forums of Greece were embellished with his statues; they gazed upon him *like a descended god*; their greatest poets, down to Æschylus and Aristophanes, trod the stage in person: Rome also honoured her actors, and they, in return, were the grace and ornament of all societies; their sayings were re-corded, and collections of their apothegms have come down to our times; Cæsar, in all his power, made suit to them, and even knights of Rome did not revolt from the profession. It remained for modern times to complete their triumphs, by admitting female candidates into the lists; from that moment Nature took possession of her rights; the finest feelings were consigned to the fairest forms; the very Muse herself appeared in her own sex and person; beauty, that gives being to the poet's rapturous vision, a voice that guides his language to the heart, smiles that enchant, tears that dissolve us, with looks that fascinate, and dying plaintive tones that sink into the soul, are now the appropriate and exclusive attributes of that all-conquering sex; in short, they bind our nobles in chains, and our princes in links—of love.

BOOK X, CH. I

In which the Author confutes himself

Having been so long employed in finding words, according to rule and method, for others, I begin to think I have a right to bestow some according to my own fancy; and that just now prompts me to write without any rule or method whatsoever.

In the first place, then, permit me to say, that I do not allow any man can have a fair excuse for not reading these volumes once, at least, in his life, provided he can read at all. For what is the plea, I would fain know, that he can set up for refusing them a perusal? Is he too wise to be taught anything new?—They do not pretend to have any new thing in them or about them; they boast themselves to be as old as nature; and, as for instruction, if he is too wise to want it, they are not so foolish as to force it upon him against his wishes.

Is he too lazy to be amused by any reading? then let him employ a toad-eater to recite them in his ears till he falls asleep; he cannot purchase a cheaper or more harmless narcotic in his apothecary's shop.

Is he too proud to stoop his genius to the perusal of a trivial novel? my life upon it, his genius is oftentimes more trivially employed. Is truth his constant study and pursuit? and has he not yet found out that there is truth in fiction; that, by the device of fable, (as the philosopher Saint Pierre well observes,) the soul gradually opens itself to truth? I am vain enough to think there may be many more truths in this poor fable, than he will discover or comprehend in all his metaphysics.[16]

But some may plead business, and business must be followed.— True! and so must hounds; but the man who follows either, be it ever so closely, will still find that he has gone many miles out of his way. Let the man of business recollect how much of his life is spent in being busy about nothing, and he cannot but acknowledge he has had time to bestow upon the reading of these little books, and a hundred others. But all this while he has been accumulating money; if he dies to-morrow, he will die worth one hundred thousand pounds; and if he does, *is he any whit wiser*, (I put the question in the words of the inimitable author of *The Serious Call*,) *is he any whit wiser*, I demand, *than he who has taken the same pains to have a hundred thousand pair of boots and spurs when he leaves the world?*[17]

But hark ye, Mr. Novelist, the fastidious philosopher will say, my studies do not lie your way. To him I could answer—then are my studies, learned sir, more complaisant than yours; for, as far as you yourself participate of human nature, so far you come within the scope of my researches; why then may not you deign to read me, though I do not aspire to copy you? Though your proud castle is barred against my approach, my humble cottage is the seat of general hospitality, and open to you in common with the rest of my fellow-creatures. The simple goose-quill, that can fan one spark of pure benevolence into activity, by the playfulness of its motion, has done more for mankind than the full-plumed philosopher, who, with the strut of the goose itself, cackles out his despicable spleen, and hisses at each passenger as he goes regardless by him.

If but one of all my readers has felt the sympathy of a generous sentiment, if another has experienced the conscious sense of self-reproaching turpitude, and blushed at the discovery, I think I have thrown more light into the world, than the philosopher can dig out of the bowels of the earth, though he may thereby affect to decide upon the world's age, as jockeys do upon horses, by looking in their mouths. What if philosophers have now found out that water is no element? they have neither added to its uses, nor taken any away; and as for me, though, for peace sake, I will forbear to say it is an element, I will not promise them to rest my faith so far upon their dogma, as to say that it is not. The Author of Nature seems graciously to have ordained, that in searching after things without use, our inquiries should be pursued without success, so that no labour might be wasted upon things that cannot profit us: but it is only after these curious nothings that our philosopher is ever on the quest; and yet he pretends to say, that he has no leisure to bestow upon my men and women! Why will he not rather study to be informed of what would profit him to know, and submit to be ignorant of what the Great Disposer of the Universe hath, in tender consideration of his short-lived creatures, buried out of sight?

As much truth as man's intellect can admit, is accessible to man's inquiries, but ignorance is given to the soul, as the lid is bestowed upon the eye; it lets in all the light it can usefully dispense with, and shuts out what it cannot bear.[18] And now, no more of the philosopher; whilst I am contemplating the statue, let him hunt after the beetle that crawls at the base of it.

There is, notwithstanding, more for me to do; and as these volumes are my clients, so am I their advocate, and must be prepared for all that may oppose me; the next, however, is a gentle caviller, and approaches in a form that challenges my respect; it is a reader I would not offend and shock for all that fame could give me; she comes with modest blushes on her cheeks, and points to certain pages doubled down in my offending work, too highly coloured for her chaste revolting eye to rest upon. What shall I reply to this appellant? How defend myself from one, who comes into the lists with all the virtues armed in her support? Where now is my impure Jemima? where is Fanny Claypole? where even my benevolent Susan May? Fled out of sight, abashed and self-condemned! What avails it to me to say that they are Nature's children? My reproving critic does not wish to make acquaintance with the profligates of her family. In vain I urge, that contrast is the soul of composition; that joy and sorrow, health and sickness, good and evil, chequer life itself through every stage; that even virtue wants an opposite to give its lustre full display; she does not think that scenes, which address themselves to the passions, can be defended by arguments that apply to the judgment: I may be justified by the rules of composition; she is trying me by those of decorum. If I shelter myself in the plea, that temptations are the test of an heroic spirit; that I cannot *make bricks without straw*; and that although the said straw be of an inflammable quality, yet I must work with such materials as I have: she will not hesitate to admit the necessity of temptations, but she will resolutely condemn the too profuse and prominent display of them; she would work her shades more tender; mine are too bold: If I say, wait for the moral, she replies, that it is the nature of susceptibility not to wait; the mischief is in the front, the moral is in the rear; the remedy cannot always overtake the disease; and she asks, where is the wit in voluntarily provoking the fang of the viper, because, forsooth, we have a medicine in our closet that will stanch the position, if we do not slip the time of applying it?

Mark now, candid reader, if I have not wove a hedge about myself, which I have neither cunning to creep through, nor agility to climb;

but it is ever thus when I argue with the ladies. If their modesty is of so touchy a temper, as to accuse me of impudence, I know no better way to convince them of their mistake, than by copying that modesty, and making no defence; and sure I am, that such would be their conduct in the case of real attack, when the relation of it only stirs them into such tremors and palpitations; I fear, therefore, that their extreme susceptibility proves too much; those must ride their palfreys with a very loose rein, who are so soon thrown out of their seat upon every little start or stumble that they make.

What I have written, I have written in the hope of recommending virtue by the fiction of a virtuous character, which, to render amiable, I made natural, and to render natural, I made subject to temptations, though resolute in withstanding them: in one instance only my hero owes his victory to chance, and not to his own fortitude; if virtue, therefore, cannot read her own encomium, without catching fire at the allurements of her antagonist, she is not that pure and perfect virtue I was studious to pay court to, but some hypocrite, who has basely tricked herself out in the uniform of the corps, for the opportunity of deserting over to the enemy with her arms and accoutrements.

BOOK XI, CH. I

Describes what our Heroine is, and what we wish our Virgin Readers to be

The time is so nearly approaching, when I must close this history, that I am now in the situation of a man, who, being on the point of parting from friends, in whose company he has taken a long and pleasant tour, is anxious to call to mind any faults or omissions he may have fallen into, that he may explain such as will bear a justification, and ask pardon for what demands an apology.

To enter on a review of all my errors, is a task above my hands; but there is one, I apprehend, apparently too gross to be overlooked by any of my readers; I mean that of neglecting to describe the person of my heroine. If this is a crime, it is the more unpardonable, forasmuch as I cannot plead oversight and inadvertency in excuse of it; I have kept her portrait wilfully in its case, and not disclosed even the colour of her eyes, or set to view a single locket of her hair. Fielding's Sophia had locks of glossy black, more modern novels give their heroines flaxen tresses and azure eyes; there is a fashion in beauty; perhaps my Isabella had neither the jet of the raven, nor the ivory of the swan: I would prefix to these volumes an engraving from her portrait, but Henry would not let it out of his hands; and our great artists are so fully employed, that not one was at leisure to go down to Manstock-house to take the copy.

Now, as I have not the vanity to attempt an undertaking, which I believe no author has yet succeeded in, I will not aim to describe what will not bear a description: singularity or deformity may be delineated by the vehicle of words; perfect beauty eludes the power of language. Let it suffice for me to say, upon the faith of an historian, that my heroine was all the most doting lover, when dreaming of his mistress, fancies her to be, and something more than the self-admiring beauty beholds, when she examines herself in the glass. Yet in many things she fell short of some, whom I have heard extolled above the modesty of praise: her eyes could not express what theirs excel in; when they sparkled, it was with benevolence; when they languished, it was with pity; they were not repulsive enough to look a modest man out of countenance, nor attractive enough to inspire an impudent man with hope; good nature dimpled round her lips, that encased two rows of purest pearls, but scorn never pouted in the one, and the grin of folly never was put on to disclose the other: her voice was melody that kept the middle tones, for it could neither sound the pitch of an affected scream, nor grumble in the base note of a sullen murmur: her motions were the expressive marks that charactered her mind; composed and temperate, rage never agitated them; pride never distorted them; light and elastic when she hastened to the succour of the wretched, she neither aped the languor of sickliness, nor the mincing step of affectation: she danced gracefully, but not like a professor; loved music, but was no performer; had an eye for nature, but never libelled a single feature of it by pen or pencil: she had read sufficiently for her years, and profitably for her instruction; she could express her thoughts, in speaking or in writing, elegantly, and without embarrassment; but she possessed in its perfection, the still happier gift of a patient ear whilst others were speaking, and of a polite attention to what they spoke. Being the only child of her parents, the little bickerings of brothers and sisters never irritated her temper, nor did the triumphs of a rival ever fan one spark of envy in her breast: educated entirely by an excellent mother, she had no communication with governesses and servants, nor any friendships with caballing misses. That she was deceived in supposing her heart so pre-occupied by filial affection, as to be unassailable by love, these sheets have sufficiently evinced; but when she found herself surprised into a tender attachment, and fully understood the merits of the person who inspired it, she scorned to mask herself in false appearances, played off no vain coquetries to teaze and tantalize her lover by affected scruples and counterfeited fears, but with a candour, that resulted from her purity of thought, gave him to know the interest he had gained, justly conceiving artifice need not be used to smother a confession, which honour dictated, and delicacy might avow.

If I offend against refinement, by describing an ingenuous nature, I make no other answer but by an appeal to the hearts of my readers, as in like cases I have done to those of my spectators: let them decree! when men of doubtful characters, for doubtful purposes, approach the fair, let the fair resort to their defences; I am no casuist in a case of cunning, nor am I fond of working to my point by crooked paths, or describing the base properties of degenerated nature. If any of my female readers has been taught to think hypocrisy a virtue, by the necessity she had been under of resorting to it, I will not argue against her prejudices for a friend that has been so useful to her; I can only say it is not a virtue I am studious to bestow upon the character of Isabella.

BOOK XII, CH. I

The Author's last Address to his Readers

We are now drawing nigh to the conclusion of our history, and if my kind reader has found amusement in his task, I shall not regret the toil and labour of mine. Great must be that author's mortification, who miscarries in a trivial undertaking; and certain it is, that small matters should never be attempted without strong presumption of success. Something there must be in every man's view, who commits himself to the press; and as all speculations upon profit are now becoming more and more precarious, there seems little left to animate the adventurer, but a disinterested passion for fame; I think it is, therefore, to the credit of the corps, that we still continue to volunteer it with such spirit, that no abatement is yet discernible either in our numbers or exertions. When I search my own heart for the motives that have operated with such activity upon me, for resorting to my pen, I find myself impelled by a principle I am not ashamed of, since it has been uniformly that of doing everything in my power, for keeping alive a general spirit of good humour, and endearing man to man, by bringing characters under review, which prejudice has kept at distance from the mass of society; I have never failed to lend my feeble hand to theirs, who are benevolently employed in recommending love and harmony to mankind: I love my contemporaries, and detest that language so much in use, which tends to sink the present age on a comparison with ages past; and as I hold this to be an illiberal and ungenerous propensity, I thank God I have reached that time of life when it is chiefly prevalent, and yet perceive myself more than ever abhorrent from the practice of it.

I must now send my hero into the world to shift for himself; I have done what I could for him whilst he was under my care, and have bequeathed him nature for his guide at parting. The trials and temptations I have exposed him to, are such as might befall any person in his situation, and not greater than every man of steady principles, without any romantic strain of virtue or courage, may resolutely meet. I have not set his character upon stilts, for sentimental enthusiasts to gaze at, but kept him on the plain ground with nature's common stock, studying to endow him with the patient virtues rather than the proud.

To my heroine, I have given as many charms as the reader's imagination shall be disposed to afford her, without being indebted to descriptions, which I reject upon conscience, having so often read them in other novelists with satiety and disgust; and I flatter myself, my Isabella will appear not the less attractive for the very few and slight demands I have made upon her health and constitution, not having been able to discover, amongst all the numerous examples of sickly and tormented heroines, any peculiar delicacy in their diseases, or much amusement in their casualties; in one instance only I have fallen in with the fashion.

I have kept my narrative free from the perplexities of episode and digression, and given the scene to my characters without any intrusion of my own person, which I hold to be an unpardonable impertinence. Of poetry I have made no use, and of quotation, so very sparingly, as scarce to be perceptible. The incidents, I trust, are in no case improbable; and, as to that combination of circumstances, which appears to criminate my hero in the second book, I have, since the writing of it, been told of a case upon record, which so nearly resembles it, as to give my narrative the air of being founded upon fact in that particular, which, in reality, it was not. In point of style, I flatter myself the critic will not find much to reprehend; but in that and every other particular, I am fairly before him; let him strike with justice, and I will not murmur at the stroke.

And now, if this page shall meet the eyes of a certain lady, not less distinguished for her many amiable qualities, than for her exalted rank, she will perceive that I have fulfilled her instructions, and composed a novel, to the best of my ability, in the form she recommended and prescribed. Uncertain of its fate, I forbear to make known whose commands I have been honoured with, content if she alone is satisfied with my obedience, and not entirely disappointed with the execution of a work, which, but for her, I never should have undertaken.

97 From a review of *Camilla: or, a Picture of Youth* (1796), *The British Critic*, VIII, November 1796

The British Critic was founded in 1793 by Robert Nares (1753–1829), philologist and divine, in collaboration with William Beloe (1756–1817), who edited the first forty-two numbers.

Camilla . . . was by Mme. D'Arblay (Frances Burney; see above, No. 73 and headnote).

To the old romance, which exhibited exalted personages, and displayed their sentiments in improbable or impossible situations, has succeeded the more reasonable, modern novel; which delineates characters drawn from actual observation, and, when ably executed, presents an accurate and captivating view of real life. To excel in this species of composition are required all the powers of the dramatic writer; an extensive acquaintance with human nature, an acute discernment, and exact discrimination of characters, a correct judgment of probability in situations, an active imagination in devising and combining incidents, with command of language for describing them. There is no species of composition that more forcibly attracts and irresistibly detains attention; and, though the regular manufacture, and regular sale of the most imperfect attempts, by very incompetent writers, are by no means creditable to the taste that encourages so idle a traffic; yet may the better class of novels be allowed to maintain their dignity, and demand a particular examination.

To astonish by the marvellous, and appal by the terrific, have lately been the favourite designs of many writers of novels; who, in pursuit of those effects, have frequently appeared to desert, and sometimes have really transgressed the bounds of nature and possibility. We cannot approve of these extravagances. The artful conduct of an interesting plot, and the dramatic delineation of character, are certainly the features that give most dignity to this species of fiction; these are found in great perfection in those English novels which are admitted as models; those of Richardson, Fielding, and Smollet: and their merits cannot be rivalled by any thing imported from the regions of fairy tale.

Of the requisites above enumerated, Mrs. D'Arblay (formerly Miss Burney) possesses evidently the greater part. They were evinced abundantly in her former novels of *Evelina* and *Cecilia*; nor do we think them (whatever may have been the effect of an expectation too highly raised) less conspicuous in *Camilla*. An inexhaustible fund of characters appears to be treasured in her mind, which she produces with a copiousness almost without example. No author, unless supported by a very decided genius for such delineations, could venture to bring forward so great a number of distinctly characterized personages, or succeed so well in making them act consistently, in such a variety of situations. But here we must admit a distinction. Her characters of a higher stamp are usually drawn with exact propriety and truth; but those either of lower life, or of a ridiculous cast, are, for the most part, strong caricatures. They are related more to farce than to comedy. Such are Mr. Briggs, more especially, in *Cecilia*; and Mr. Dubster, Mrs. Mitten, and Dr. Orkborne, in the present novel. Even the good and well drawn Sir Hugh must be thought, in some instances, rather too strongly touched. His various and entire settlement of his fortune, and his late attempt to learn Latin, are surely traits of this cast.

Among the numerous characters displayed in this novel, the most original and highly finished are those of Mrs. Arlbery, Sir Hugh Tyrold, and Camilla herself. Sir Sedley Clarendel is skilfully drawn, and has some new features of discrimination; but he is rather (so quickly do fashions pass) an obsolete coxcomb, than one of the present hour. Mrs. A., a widow of vivacity, wit, and considerable remains of beauty, rich and gay, contrives to live according to her own fancy, merely by disregarding the common opinions of the world, but observing the rules of propriety in all essential matters. A real benevolence of heart and soundness of understanding, are so hidden under external levity of manners, that they do not appear till discovered by more intimate approach.

[. . . . .]

98 From a review of *The Italian, or the Confessional of the Black Penitents. A Romance* (1797), *The Monthly Review*, Series 2, XXII, March 1797

The Italian . . . was the last novel published during Mrs. Radcliffe's life; but *Gaston de Blondeville, or the Court of Henry III. Keeping Festival in Ardenne, A Romance* was published in 1826, three years after her death. This review was by Arthur Aikin (1773–1854), younger brother of John and Anna Laetitia (see above, No. 69 and headnote).

The most excellent, but at the same time the most difficult, species of novel-writing consists in an accurate and interesting representation of such manners and characters as society presents; not, indeed, every-day characters, for the interest excited by *them* would be feeble; yet so far they ought to be common characters, as to enable the reader to judge whether the copy be a free, faithful, and even improved sketch from Nature. Such is the *Clarissa* of Richardson, and such is the *Tom Jones* of Fielding. Miss Burney's *Cecilia* is also a striking instance of the higher novel; the more remarkable, indeed, as it displays a knowledge of the world which the forms of society rarely allow to women an opportunity of attaining.

Next comes the modern Romance; in which, high description, extravagant characters, and extraordinary and scarcely possible occurrences combine to rivet the attention, and to excite emotions more thrilling than even the best selected and best described natural scene. This species of fiction is perhaps more imposing than the former, on the first perusal: but the characteristic which distinguishes it essentially from, and shews its vast inferiority to, the genuine novel, is that, like a secret, it ceases to interest after it can no longer awaken our curiosity; while the other, like truth, may be reconsidered and studied with increased satisfaction. Whatever is perfect in its kind is better than an imperfect and unsuccessful attempt at any thing higher; and, judging by this maxim, we consider the present romance as occupying a very distinguished rank among the modern works of fiction. We discern much more unity and *simplicity* in this than in the former publications of the fair writer; the attention never flags in the perusal; nor do inferior interests engage the reader, to the prejudice of the chief characters. The impetuous Marchesa, the stern, intriguing, terrific Schedoni, and the amiable, pensive Olivia, interesting as they are of themselves, become doubly so by their connection with Vivaldi and Ellena. The consultation in the church of San Nicolo between the Marchesa and Schedoni is a most striking and impressive scene; and the examination of Vivaldi at the Tribunal of the Inquisition is wrought up with great spirit and address. The part, however, which displays the greatest genius, and the most force of description, is the account of the scenes which passed in the lone house on the shore of the Adriatic, between Schedoni, Ellena, and Spalatro:—the horrible sublimity which characterizes the discovery made by the former that Ellena was his daughter,[1] at the instant in which he was about to stab her, is perhaps unparalleled.

[. . . . .]

99 From *A view of the Commencement and Progress of Romance*, 1797

by JOHN MOORE

John Moore (1729–1802), doctor of medicine, wrote several novels and miscellaneous works: *A View of Society and Manners in France, Switzerland and Germany* (1779), *Zeluco* (1786), *Journal during a Residence in France* . . . (1792), *Edward* (1796) and *Mordant* (1800). Moore's essay on romance has a confused history and a complex relationship with Robert Anderson's *Memoir* of Tobias Smollett prefixed to his edition of *The Miscellaneous Works of Tobias Smollett* (1796). Anderson's essay was first published in an edition of the *British Poets* (1795) and expanded for inclusion in the *Memoir*; it was further enlarged for the edition of 1800, published separately in 1803 and enlarged still further for the edition of 1806. Moore's essay was published in his edition of the works of Smollett (1797), but seems to have been written very much earlier. It was edited by Anderson in his edition of *The Works of John Moore* (1820), and heavily borrowed from by him for the later editions of *The Miscellaneous Works of Tobias Smollett*.

[. . . . .]

Richardson introduced a new species of romance, wherein the persons concerned are supposed to be the relaters of what passes; and the sentiments are expressed as they arise on the first impression, and while the relater is still ignorant of the events that are to follow.

This method certainly has the advantage of affording the author the opportunity of varying his style, by adapting it to the characters of the different persons he introduces; an advantage of which Richardson avails himself very successfully; which was by no means the case with Rousseau; for although his *Eloisa* is written in letters, in imitation of *Clarissa*, he has failed in adapting the style of the letters to the characters of the supposed writers, in the same happy manner that is executed by Richardson. Through the whole of the [N]ew *Eloisa*, whether Julia, St. Preux, Clara, or any other name be attached to the letter, you always perceive that Jean Jacques is the real writer.

This manner of giving the whole story by letters is liable to the inconveniencies of producing repetitions, and of drawing out the story to a tiresome length; which inconveniencies Richardson has not always had the address to avoid. His favourite character of Grandison is much too formal to be a favourite with the women in general; and there is somewhat of prudery in his heroines that prevents them from being favourites with the men: but he describes the operation of the passions with a truth and minuteness that evinces a great knowledge of human nature. The madness of Clementina is delineated with the pencil of a great master. Nothing can be more affecting than the distresses of Clarissa. He was conscious that his strength lay in the pathetic, and by this perhaps he was led to prolong scenes of sorrow till the spirits of the reader are fatigued, and the luxury of sympathy is overpowered.

The striking and animated character of Lovelace is supported to the last, with wonderful spirit. It is easy for an author to declare, that his hero is possessed of an infinite deal of wit and pleasantry, invention and eloquence: To make him display those qualities through a great variety of scenes, is very difficult, yet it has been executed by this author in the most successful manner. Richardson himself was undoubtedly convinced, that all those accomplishments, with the addition of youth, beauty, and the most undaunted intrepidity, would not prevent the profligacy, perfidy, and shocking cruelty of Lovelace from rendering him odious to every reader. In this, perhaps, he was mistaken. The brilliant colours in which Lovelace is painted are too apt to fascinate the imagination, and may have secured him a corner in the hearts even of some young women of character, in spite of his crimes. As for the young men, if none of them had ever attempted to imitate the profligacy of Lovelace, but those who possessed his accomplishments, the exhibition of his portrait would do little harm: but there is reason to fear, that some with the first only, and but a slender portion of the second, have sometimes attempted to pass for complete Lovelaces.

The late Henry Fielding, in the romance of *Joseph Andrews*, written in imitation of the style and manner of Cervantes, displayed much of the spirit and humour of his model; and he afterwards gave the world a still stronger proof of his knowledge of human nature, and the powers of his invention, by the publication of *Tom Jones*; a work wherein, after the imagination of the reader has been gratified by the exhibition of a variety of interesting scenes and characters, and his heart warmly engaged in the fortunes of her hero, his mind is agitated and alarmed by a series of incidents which seem to cross and obstruct the schemes and blast the hopes of him for whom he is now deeply interested, and whom he sees involved in unmerited disgrace, and threatened with ruin. At this point, when the whole horizon is covered with darkness, and hardly one faint ray of light darts from any quarter, the clouds gradually begin to disperse, obscurity disappears, the intricacies become plain, the impediments that oppose the desired catastrophe are removed by means quite natural, though unforeseen, and the story flows clearly and delightfully to a conclusion; 'like a river,' to adopt the eloquent illustration of an ingenious writer of the present age, 'which in its progress foams among fragments of rocks, and for a while seems pent up by insurmountable oppositions, then angrily dashes for a while, then plunges under ground into caverns, and runs a subterraneous course, till at length it breaks out again, meanders round the country, and with a clear placid stream flows gently to the ocean.'[1]

Dr. Smollett, in the *Continuation of his History of England*, observes, that towards the end of the reign of George II, and about the beginning of that of his present majesty, 'genius in writing spontaneously arose; and though neglected by the great, flourished under the culture of a public which had pretensions to taste, and piqued itself on encouraging literary merit.' He proceeds to enumerate the most distinguished writers in the various branches of literature at that period, and gives his suffrage to the great talents of one who pursued the same line with himself, in the following words.—'The genius of Cervantes was transfused into the novels of Fielding, who painted the characters and ridiculed the follies of life with equal strength, humour, and propriety.'[2]

The romances of Dr. Smollett are not so much distinguished for the invention of the story, as for strong masculine humour, just observations on life, and a great variety of original characters. In *Humphry Clinker* he hardly attempts any story; it is a mere vehicle for characters and remarks on life and manners. The characters of the different correspondents are supported throughout with the utmost propriety, and the peculiar style suitable to each writer is maintained with more precision than in any romance in the epistolary form with which I am acquainted.

If we except the character of Lismahago, some features of which, though highly comic, are extravagantly stretched, Dr. Smollett has avoided the marvellous, and adhered more closely to nature and to familiar life in *Humphry Clinker* than in any of his other romances. It is justly observed by Dr. Anderson, in his life of Smollett,[3] that this performance has all the spirit of his former works, and is the production of a mind mellowed by experience, and softened, not soured, by misfortune: it is peculiarly entertaining to observe his address and attention to nature, in the different representations of the same places and people, and transactions by the different characters.

Many useful lessons are given for the conduct of life, particularly in the story of Mr. Baynard, who is brought to the brink of ruin by the vanity of his wife and the good-natured facility of his temper. The whole of Bramble's account of the Temple of Cold Reception is admirably taken from nature.

The letters of Tabitha Bramble and Winifred Jenkins are pleasingly characteristic, and capable of surprising the most solemn of mankind into laughter, if their features be not kept steady by stupidity as well as pride.

From the assemblies of high life Dr. Smollett thought that humour was banished by ceremony, affectation, and cards; *that nature being castigated almost to still life, mirth never appeared but in an insipid grin.* His extreme fondness for humour therefore led him to seek it where it was to be found, namely, in the inferior societies of life, which, in despite of the acuteness with which he seized and described it, has exposed him to the censure of the fastidious.

The success of Richardson, Fielding, and Smollett, in this species of writing, produced, what great success generally does produce, a prodigious number of imitators: but by far the greatest part of them, like Hamlet's players, imitated abominably;[4] and instead of representing the manners of the age, exhibited men and women, neither having the manners of Christians nor Pagans, and who seemed to have been made by the least expert of nature's journeymen.

There were, for a considerable time, so many novels written of this description, and with so few exceptions, that the very words Romance or Novel conveyed the idea of a frivolous or pernicious book. Even this, however, did not diminish the number, though it made many people at pains to declare, that for their part they never read novels; a declaration sometimes made by persons of both sexes, who never read any thing else. This is being by much too cautious. They might, with equal prudence, declare, that they never would read any book, because many books are silly or pernicious. The truth is, that the best romances always have been, and always will be, read with delight by men of genius; and with the more delight, the more taste and genius the reader

440

happens to have. Nothing can be so interesting to men as man. The modern romances are or ought to be a representation of life and manners in the country where the scene is placed. Had works of this nature existed in the flourishing ages of the Greek and Roman republics, and had some of the best of them been preserved, how infinitely would they be relished at present! as they would give a much more minute and satisfactory picture of private and domestic life than is found in history, which dwells chiefly on war and affairs of state. This species of writing may also be made most subservient to the purposes of instruction; but even those which afford amusement only, provided they contain nothing immoral, are not without utility, and deserve by no means to be spoken of with that contempt which they sometimes are, by their most intimate acquaintance. These gentlemen ought to recollect in what manner they usually employ that portion of their time which they do not pass in reading what they so much affect to despise: they ought to recollect how many languid intervals there are in their journey through life; how often they fill them up in a more pernicious way; and if a novel or romance should now and then help them to jog along with more innocence and less yawning, they ought to be a little more grateful.

It may be said, that such people had much better study books of science, or read moral essays or sermons. Unquestionably they had: but unfortunately they will not; for although some authors have shewn that it is possible to write sermons so that they shall be as much or more read than the best romance, yet this talent is extremely rare; and it is often lamented that sermons and moral essays, containing much good instruction, are less universally perused than many novels, more inelegantly written. What does this prove, but that there is something so peculiarly attractive in this species of writing, that performances, which would have been neglected in any other form, find readers in this?

Some very respectable authors have even insinuated, that romances are more entertaining than history itself, and that they thereby breed a dislike to that useful study.[5] I fear this is not a likely argument to prevail on mankind to quit romances for history; and therefore, even if I were of that opinion, which is not the case, I should not publish it.

But it is universally known, that books of pure science and instruction, which require much thought, are not studied spontaneously by any but those who have already a considerable degree of steadiness of mind and desire of knowledge. Persons of dissipated minds, incapable of attention, who stand most in need of instruction, are the least willing to receive it; they throw such books down the moment they perceive their drift. But a romance in the highest degree entertaining, may be written with as moral an intention, and contain as many excellent rules for the conduct of life, as any book with a more solemn and scientific title. This, however, not being suspected by the persons above alluded to, they continue to read in the confidence of meeting with amusement only, and fearless of any plot or plan for their instruction of improvement; they find folly ridiculed in a pleasant manner, vice placed in a degrading light, and a variety of instructive lessons so inter-woven with an interesting story, that they cannot satisfy their curiosity until they have received impressions of a useful or virtuous nature, and thus acquire something infinitely more valuable than what they were in pursuit of.

Isabinda of Bellefield, a Sentimental Novel, in a Series of Letters. By Mrs. Courtney (1796).[1]

The rapid increase which this class of publications has acquired, and is daily acquiring, renders this part of the critic's task a work of increased difficulty. Our shelves are groaning with the weight of novels which demand a hearing; and before we can disengage ourselves from the perusal of more important matter, in order to deliberate upon their respective merits, half the number have done their duty at the Circulating Libraries, and found a quiet repose in the records of the catalogue. So much we thought it necessary to premise, in order to account for our giving, as we purpose now to do, a sort of gaol-delivery to these trembling expectants; and making a general clearance of those novels whose dates are expiring.

Isabinda is evidently the production of a writer not unacquainted with the more familiar scenes of life and manners. It appears to aim, in some parts, at a resemblance with *Evelina*; but stands indisputably below the object of its imitation. The characters are such as to excite an interest in the event of the novel; and the tendency, so far as we can discover, both of the facts and sentiments, is such as to throw the balance of advantage into the scale of virtue.

Family Secrets; Literary and Domestic. By Mr. Pratt (1797).[2]

We have often commended the ingenuity of Mr. Pratt, and his diligence may be truly said to be indefatigable. They, who are partial to this kind of reading, will not be displeased at the protracted extent of these volumes, while they, who take up such publications, to amuse a few passing intervals of leisure, will regret, that they were not comprised in a smaller compass. Perhaps, in this observation, we have expressed the true character of the work, very amusing for ordinary readers, but not of adequate importance, to detain those engaged in superior pursuits. The title seems a misnomer; we looked in vain for the literary secrets, but literature is an indefinite expression, and of infinite gradation, from the Problems of Newton's Philosophy, to the *Lessons* of Mrs. Barbauld.[3] The work also commences with an inaccuracy; we are told of the Honourable and Reverend Armine Fitzorton, who, in the next page, is denominated Sir Armine.—Yet the work abounds with a variety of characters, exceedingly well delineated, with many scenes and descriptions, happily imagined, and successfully introduced, and will considerably add to the fame which Mr. Pratt has already obtained in this species of writing.

Laura; or, the Influence of a Kiss. By A. H. Gezner. Translated from the German (1797).[4]

This is a whimsical publication, and does not add much to the stock, even of literary entertainment. If it can be read without injury, it is as much as we can say; and the plates which accompany it, some of them at least, are borrowed from the French Edition of the Translation from the Greek Romance of *Daphnis and Chloe*.

The Neapolitan; or the Test of Integrity, a Novel, in Three Volumes. By Ellen of Exeter (1796).[5]

These volumes present an agreeable and diversified history of events not altogether fictitious. For so much as belongs not to herself, the writer has made her acknowledgments to Mr. Cumberland, from whose narrative, in some periodical publication, the ground-work of the novel was derived. With this deduction, the author is entitled to much praise. Her scenes are painted with the useful colouring of chaste description, and rational sentiment. The mind is excited to attention, and kept alive, by the general thread of the narrative; and the affections occasionally impressed with much effect, by the energy and pathos which animate the style. If the novel be deficient in those important requisites which lead to the highest fame, it is by no means destitute of those lesser ornaments, which, by promoting the innocent amusement of the public, entitle the writer to an honourable reputation.

The Abbey of Clugny. A Novel. By Mrs. Meeke, Author of Count St. Blanchard (1796).[6]

The narrative part of this novel, comprehends the history and adventures of French personages, with manners nearly, if not altogether, English. The story is, however, varied by the usual and necessary expedients of novel writers, to render it amusing. There is nothing in the descriptions of scenery, or expressions of sentimemt, which will attract the critic's notice, or extort the reader's praise. If the author's ambition be, indeed, limited to the view expressed at the close of the novel, we think she will not be disappointed in her hope, that this history 'will amuse, for a few hours, those who may deign to peruse it.'

101 From a review of *Santa Maria; or, The Mysterious Pregnancy*, 1798; *Gentleman's Magazine*, LXVIII, September 1798

Santa Maria . . . was by J. Fox, who also wrote *Tancred. A Tale of Ancient Times* (1791). The review may be by James Peller Malcolm.

Santa Maria; or, The Mysterious Pregnancy: a Romance. In Three Volumes. By J. Fox.

Whatever objection may be made, in this philosophical age, to *mysteries* in religion, they are acknowledged to be excellences in novels and romances. The wonderful and miraculous is the *forte* of our modern novel-writers, and a most singular revolution has taken place in this department of literature. Instead of pictures sketched from Nature, and portraits drawn from Life, 'catching the Manners living as they rise,'[1] we have narrations of haunted towers, old Blue Beards and Red Beards, spectres, sprites, apparitions, black banners waving on the battlements of castles, strange voices, tapers burning one moment and extinguished by some unknown hand the next, clandestine noises, flashing of lightning, and howling of winds. The 'Old Wives' Fables,' and legendary tales of old, are vamped up afresh, and put into a modern dress, to spread terror throughout all the nurseries and boarding-schools of the metropolis. To be serious; we know of no useful purpose novels of such a nature can produce. They can only tend to infuse the most wild and ridiculous ideas into the minds of young people; fill them with groundless fears; make them imagine every *dark chamber* to be haunted, and even to be startled at their own shadows. Mr. Fox has very justly named his novel 'The *Mysterious* Pregnancy;' but it is too mysterious even for *romance*. The idea of a woman being pregnant, and yet totally ignorant of the *cause* of it, pertinaciously persisting in asserting her *virgin innocence*, when she had actually been ravished, is so abominably absurd and *outré* as to bid defiance to all probability. We have also to object to Mr. Fox's novel the history of Father Conrad the monk, which seems purposely introduced (to ape the present unhappy custom of our romance-writers) to cast an odium upon religion and its ministers. We are willing to allow that, in those monastic societies which are now nearly abolished throughout Europe, there were to be found men of the most profligate and licentious manners; but we think it unfair to throw an odium upon any *collective* body of men on account of the nefarious conduct of a *few individuals* belonging to that body. If the ministers of religion are intended to be aspersed in the person of Father Conrad, or if the grand body of the Roman Catholic clergy *only* are designed by Mr. Fox to be held up to view as base and profligate men, we abhor the idea. Had Mr. F. exercised the least candour and liberality of sentiment, he would have disdained to have joined in the ungenerous and insidious attempts to render religion odious, by drawing the characters of its ministers in the most degrading and contemptible point of view imaginable. With respect to the other characters introduced, that of 'Dros' appears to most advantage. But the everlasting repetition of 'Lachryma Christi' is intolerably disgusting. The style is often turgid and rough; frequently bombast, and sometimes obscure. The following sentences are justly reprehensible: Vol. I. p. 23, 'If thou hast ever seen thy dearest bosom friend *topping* headlong into the dreary recess of the grave.' '*Topping* into the grave' is an entire new phrase; perhaps it has an allusion to the bathing-machines, and the *manner* in which the *visitors* at Brighton are *dipped*.—P. 153, 'The Count, on this, proceeded to the other chest, and likewise found *all empty* there.'—P. 202, 'The sounds, so heavenly and attractive, *perched them* immediately on the stair, which they were preparing to quit.'—P. 206, 'Here, however, I arrived at last, covered with bruises from head to foot, and, what is more extraordinary, *soberer* than ever I was in my life.' We might point out several similar inaccuracies in the remaining volumes, but we forbear.—We think Mr. F. might have selected a female name more grateful to the ear than *Mopso*, who is occasionally introduced. While we thus honestly give our sentiments on the execution of this romance, we are far from viewing Mr. Fox as incapable of furnishing the publick with a good novel; and, amidst the absurdities that are here noticed, have occasionally met with a passage composed in a masterly manner; such is the description of the storm at Naples, and the eruption of Mount Vesuvius, and of the last moments of Father Conrad. This romance is dedicated to the Duke of Marlborough.

There are thousands of melancholy stories might be furnished from real life affording instruction, nay, every species of moral. Let those be the foundation of our tragedies, together with the numberless traits of heroism to be found, independent of death, revenge, and suicide, in our history, for serious dramas. Connected in some degree with this subject are the detestable novels poured forth on every side, teeming with hidden murders, spectres, vaults, skeletons, putrid carcases, and dungeons. Good Heaven! to what a pitch of deformity have the times led the studies of the first work of Creation, soft and *tender*-passioned females! The worst passions of the worst of men, poison, daggers, fire, and lust, horror, dismay, and the Inquisition, are dragged before us in every shape that can be thought of. It must be acknowledged due care hath been taken that the poison should not lose its effect; for, our most gloomy and horrific Novels have been, and are, working into plays; and he or she that escapes the Book will hardly fail to meet its Hero or its Devil on the Stage. How much is it to be lamented, that our writers will not turn their thoughts to such scenes as Fielding, Richardson, Smollet, and Cumberland, have done! In the name of humanity, let us leave carcases to decay in the earth, and the spirit to the Almighty's good direction; and in future let the principal persons of our works of fancy be more like men and women of this earth than demons of the infernal regions. I think it would be well if some worthy persons were to engage in a review of all the Novels of the year in a monthly publication, pointing out such as were of an improper tendency with candour, and recommending those of merit. From such a work parents and guardians might select profit and entertainment for their pupils, and prevent their taste from being vitiated by scenes of depravity and wickedness too often to be found pourtrayed by the hand of real Genius.

J. P. Malcolm.[2]

Notes

1 Rejection of the neo-classic idea of fiction, with its highly artificial concept of resemblance and propriety, did not, of course, involve a rejection of Aristotelean principles. On the contrary, Aristotle's work continued to be treated as a primary critical text.

2 Preface to *Ibrahim* . . ., trans. by Henry Cogan (1652). Because the degree to which Georges de Scudéry was responsible for this Preface or for any part of his sister's work remains doubtful, I have written throughout as if she worked completely independently.

3 Translator's Preface to *Cassandre* (1703); see below, No. 4.

4 The reference here is to Sir William Davenant's Preface to *Gondibert* (1650); see J. E. Spingarn, *Critical Texts of the Seventeenth Century* (1908), II, 1–53. The debate between Davenant and Hobbes, both of whom assume that 'the description of Great Men and Great Actions is the constant designe of a Poet . . .' is very close in terminology to the discussions of the romance-writers.

5 Charles Gildon, *An Essay at a Vindication of Love in Tragedies, against Rapin and Mr. Rymer. Directed to Mr. Dennis*, published in *Miscellaneous Letters and Essays on Several Subjects, Philosophical, Moral, Historical, Critical, Amorous &c. in Prose and Verse. By Several Gentlemen and Ladies* (1694).

6 Clara Reeve, *The Progress of Romance* (1785), Facsimile Text ed. (1930), I, 69: 'You remind me of what my good Aunts have often told me, that they, my Mother, and a select party of relations and friends, used to meet once a week at each other's houses, to hear these stories;—one used to read, while the rest ply'd their needles.'

7 Clara Reeve, op. cit., 111.

8 Lord Shaftesbury, *Advice to an Author* (1710), III; see *Characteristics* . . ., ed. J. M. Robertson (new ed., 1963), 220–5. Shaftesbury is actually discussing traveller's tales, but his remarks apply equally to several categories of prose fiction common at the time.

9 John Clarke, *An Essay upon Study. Wherein Directions are given for the Due Conduct thereof, and the Collection of a Library* . . . (2nd ed., 1737), 250–1.

10 *Remarks on Clarissa, Addressed to the Author* . . . (1749), 55.

11 Denis Diderot published his *Eloge de Richardson* in 1761; Rousseau praised the novelist in his *Confessions*, Book IX (1788).

12 See below, No. 85, n. 3.

13 The text of Fielding's letter was published by E. L. McAdam, Jr., in an article entitled 'A New Letter from Fielding', *Yale Review* (1948), XXXVIII, 33–9.

14 *Works of Pope* (1751), IV, 169; see below, No. 62, n. 6.

15 Quoted from the text in *Ballantyne's Novelist's Library*, VIII (1824).

16 It was not only the moralists who were of this opinion. Henry Pye, for example, who had no moral axe to grind, assumed that the degree to which young women read novels and the extent to which they were influenced by them were the same as was suggested by writers more involved in the situation.

17 See J. Dryden, *Dedication of the Aeneid* (1697); and A. Pope, Note to the *Iliad* (1715–20), I, 155.

18 Early attempts at classification of the new form were often on the lines suggested by Fielding's statement that he was writing biography. Cleland, however, objected to this method as inaccurate and detracting from the proper dignity of composition; see below, Nos. 35 and 36.

19 Murphy's account was very widely read and frequently echoed; it even attracted the attentions of a plagiarist, who reproduced it, with some cutting of its less essential parts, in *Town and Country Magazine* for July 1777 under the title 'A Short View of the Celebrated Mr. Fielding's Moral Romances'. R. D. Mayo mentions this article (*The English Novel in the Magazines*, 1962, 267), but does not refer to its origin.

20 *Tatler*, 117, Saturday, January 7, 1709–10.

2: PREFACE TO 'INCOGNITA'

1 Horace, *Ars Poetica*, 180–2: 'Less vividly is the mind stirred by what finds entrance through the ears than by what is brought before the trusty eyes, and what the spectator can see for himself'.

3: 'ATHENIAN MERCURY'

1 Quintus Curtius Rufus (first or second century A.D.), author of a history of Alexander the Great in ten books. Xenophon (d. 359 B.C.) wrote *Anabasis*, an account of the expedition of Cyrus the Younger against Artaxerxes, and *Cyropaedia*, a life of Cyrus, accounted by Plato and Cicero a moral romance.

2 Mazares and Artamen are characters in Madeleine de Scudéry's *Artamène* . . .

5: PREFACE TO 'QUEEN ZARAH . . .'

1 The 'little histories' which Mrs. Manley mentions correspond to novels as Lord Chesterfield defines them (see below, No. 24); the word 'novel' as they knew it referred to short love-stories, *romans à clef*, secret histories and scandalous chronicles.

2 That is, of course, not exactly in the modern sense, but rather as 'novels with a basis in true history'—which might be thought to include the heroical romances.

3 Presumably Asians (?).

4 This is not an original remark; cf. Boileau's *L'Art Poetique*, Chant III: '. . . D'un seul nom quelquefois le son dur ou bizarre/Rend un Poëme entier, ou burlesque ou barbare.'

5 That is, feasible.

6 Crispus Sallustius (d. 35 B.C.), whose only extant work is a history of the Cataline Conspiracy and of the wars of Jugurtha, King of Numidia.

7 Cornelius Tacitus (A.D. *c.* 55–*c.* 117), author of *Vita Agricolae*, *Germanica*, *Annales*.

6(b): JOHN DENNIS

1 That is, *Othello*.

8: 'ORIGIN OF ROMANCES'

1 Horace, *Epistulae*, I, 2, 3–4: 'Who tells us what is fair, what is foul, what is helpful, what not, more plainly and better than Chrysippus or Chantor.'

2 Virgil, *Georgics*, 4, 6, 7: 'Slight is the field of toil; but not slight the glory, if adverse powers leave one free, and Apollo hearkens to the prayer.'

3 Several English writers had already tried before the time when Lewis was writing: Roger Boyle, Lord Broghill (1621–79), with *Parthenissa* (1655); Sir George Mackenzie (1637–91) with *Aretina, the Serius Romance* (1660); Nathaniel Ingelo (d. 1683) with *Bentivolio and Urania* (1660); and Robert Boyle (1626–91) with *Theodora and Didymus* (1687).

4 Horace, *Ars Poetica*, 343: '. . . he has blended profit and pleasure'.

5 Giovanni Battista Giraldi (1504–73), *Discorsi intorno al comporne di romanzi . . .* (1554). Giovanni Battista Pigna (1530–75), *Giudizio intorno al romanzi* (1554).

6 That is, Matteo Maria Boiardo (1441–94) author of the unfinished *Orlando Innamorato*, and Ludovico Ariosto (1475–1533), author of *Orlando Furioso* (1532).

7 Aristotle, *Poetics*, III and VI; e.g. 'From all this it is manifest that a poet should be a maker of fables rather than of verses . . .'

8 Titus Petronius Arbiter (d. A.D. c. 65), *Satyricon*, 118: 'It is not a question of recording real events in verse; histories can do that far better. The free spirit of genius must plunge headlong into allusion and divine interpositions, and rack itself for epigrams coloured by mythology, so that what results seems rather the prophecies of an inspired seer than the exactitude of a statement made on oaths before witnesses.' Trans. M. Heseltine (1913), 253.

9 The Paladins were the Twelve Peers of Charlemagne the Great, of whom the Count Palatine was the foremost.

10 Herodotus of Halicarnassus (c. 480–c. 425 B.C.), Greek historian. Hanno, a Carthaginian navigator of the sixth century B.C., whose account of his voyages survives in a Greek translation known as the *Periples of Hanno*. Philostrates (d. A.D. 244) wrote a *Life of Apollonius of Tyana*.

11 *Poetics*, II, 12 and 13 and II, 6.

12 Giovanni Nanni or Nannius, known as Annius Viterbensis (c. 1432–1502) wrote *De futuris Christianorum Triumphis in Turcos . . .* (1486) and *Antiquitatum variorum volumina xvii, cum commentariis* (1498).

13 I have omitted a long passage at this point, in which Huet discusses the ultimate origins of the practice of romance-writing, tracing it from the Egyptians, through the Greek Milesian tales, the 'barbarous' poetry of Northern Europe, to the troubadours of Provence. Huet's definition of 'romance' is very loose and has no relationship to prose fiction.

14 *Poetics*, I, 5: 'All men likewise, naturally receive pleasure from imitation. This is evident from what we experience in viewing the works of imitative art; for in them we contemplate with pleasure, and with the more pleasure the more exactly they are imitated, such objects as, if real, we could not see without pain . . .'

15 Plato, *Laws*, VI, 773.

abridgement of the *Letters* of Publius Caecilius Secundus (the Younger, A.D. 61–115), published in 1329.

13: PREFACE TO 'A SELECT COLLECTION . . .'

1 That is, Huet's; see above, No. 8.
2 This is a point made by Huet; see above, No. 8.

15: PREFACE TO 'MOLL FLANDERS'

1 That is, the city of Bath; the article is not unusual at this period and later—Beau Nash, 'King of Bath', had gone to the city as recently as 1705.
2 This word is being used in its earlier sense (for which *O.E.D.* gives 1585), of sifted or cleansed.

18: FROM 'THE TEA-TABLE . . .'

1 Marie Catherine le Jumel de Barneville (*c.* 1650–1705), Baronne D'Aulnoy. For one English version of her *contes* and tales see *The Diverting Works of the Countess D'Anois* . . . (1707). Matteo Bandello (1480?–1562) wrote a series of *novella* or short romances in the style of Boccaccio. Bonaventure des Perriers (late fifteenth century–1544), wrote *Novelles récréations et joyeux devis* (1558).
2 The passage concludes with a dramatization of the deterioration of conversation which follows the entrance of the fashionable lady.

22: PREFACE TO '. . . MR. CLEVELAND'

1 Cf. Proverbs xxxi, 1 and 4: 'The words of King Lemuel, the prophecy that his mother taught him . . .'
2 *Paradise Lost*, VIII, 532–3.
3 Edward Hyde (1609–74), Earl of Clarendon, *The True Historical Narrative of the Rebellion and Civil Wars in England* (1702–4), XV: 'Without doubt, no man with more wickedness ever attempted anything, or brought to pass what he desired more wickedly, more in the face and contempt of religion and moral honesty; yet wickedness as great as his could never have accomplished these trophies without the assistance of a great spirit . . .'
4 Sir John Chardin (1642–1713), French traveller, knighted by Charles II, published accounts of his travels in 1686 and 1711.
5 William Camden (1551–1623), *Britannia* . . . (1586), 'Darbyshire', 314: '. . . *ad quod specus sive subterraneus meatus* (*honorem praefabor*) *Diaboli Podex dictu, magno hiatu patet, multiplicesq; recessus habet* . . .' Philemon Holland's translation (1610), reads; 'Under which, there is a cave or hole within the ground, called, saving your reverence, *The Devils Arse*, that gapeth with a wide mouth, and hath in it many turnings and retyring roomes . . .' (557), which reveals an unusual manifestation of delicacy on Prévost's part.
6 La Rochelle, long a Protestant stronghold in the religious wars of France, was forced to surrender after a three-month siege in 1628.
7 *Les Aventures de Télémaque* (1699), were by François de Salignac de la Motte

Fénelon (1651–1715), tutor to the Royal Dukes of Burgundy, Anjou and Berry, author of *Traité de l'Education des Filles* (1687), created Archbishop of Cambrai in 1694, and condemned as a heretic by Innocent XII in the same year.

24: FROM A LETTER OF PHILIP DORMER STANHOPE . . .

1 *Don Carlos: An Historical Novel* (1672), was by César Vichard de Saint-Réal (1639–92); the work was translated in Samuel Croxall's *A Select Collection . . .*, but as this letter was written in French it is presumed that the novel was read in the same language.

2 *Amadis de Gaul* is a Spanish or Portuguese romance by Garcia de Montalva (second half of fifteenth century), from the original of Johan de Lobeira (1261–1325), or Vasco de Lobeira (d. 1403).

25: INTRODUCTORY . . . TO 'PAMELA' (1740)

1 This sentence was chosen by Fielding for indecent parody; see *Joseph Andrew and Shamela* (1965), ed. M. C. Battestin, 305.

2 Longinus, *On the Sublime*, VII. 'But when a passage is pregnant in suggestion, when it is hard, nay impossible, to distract the attention from it, and when it takes a strong and lasting hold on the memory, then we may be sure that we have lighted on the true Sublime.'

3 Untraced, but cf. *Sermones*, I, iv, 43–4.

4 That is, in the early sense of 'innocent'.

5 Marcia is a character in Addison's *Cato* (1713), and does compassionate the two youths, her brothers, concerning their rivalry for the affections of Lucia; but this phrase does not seem to relate to any phrase in the play.

6 The Reverend Mr. Peters is a character in *Pamela*.

7 Richardson hoped to obtain Hogarth as engraver, but failed; eventually the illustrations were done by Francis Hayman and Hubert Gravelot.

26: PREFACE TO 'CLARISSA . . .' (1747)

1 This isolated sentence stands, in the original, at the head of a description of the characters.

27: PREFACE TO 'RODERICK RANDOM'

1 Alain René Le Sage (1668–1747) published *Les Aventures de Gil Blas de Santillane* between 1715 and 1735. Equally popular was his *Diable boiteaux* (1707), translated into English as *The Devil on Two Sticks* as early as 1708. His last novel, *Le Bachelier de Salamanque* (1736), was not well received.

28: PREFACE TO '. . . CLARISSA . . .' WARBURTON

1 That is, dregs.

30: FROM A REVIEW OF 'TOM JONES'

1 The original has a note at this point, giving publisher and price of *Tom Jones*.

2 The whole of this review, with the exception of the short passages reproduced above and below, is taken up with a 'Plan of the Novel'.

31: 'THE FOOL, NO. 422'

1 Horace, *Carminum*, III, 6, 19: '. . . derived from this source disaster has overflowed the homeland and the people'.

2 Armand Jean de Plessis (1585–1642), Cardinal and Duc de Richelieu under Louis XIII.

3 Widely used, of course, to designate a meaningless and trivial relation before and after Ben Jonson took it for the title of his play (1633) and Swift for his satire (1704).

4 See an account of it in our *Mag.* for February last, pp. 51, &c. [o.n.]

32: AN ACCOUNT OF 'CLARISSA'

1 S. Richardson, printer. The foreign writers frequently mistake English names. [o.n.]

2 That is, in Madeleine de Scudéry's *Artemène ou le Grand Cyrus*.

3 Pierre Carlet de Chamblain de Marivaux (1688–1763), dramatist, essayist and novelist, author of two unfinished novels, *Marianne* (1731–41) and *Le Paysan Parvenu* (1734–6).

4 *Ariane* (1632) was by Jean Desmarets de Saint-Sorlin (1595–1676); *La Princess de Clèves* (1678) was by Marie Madeleine de Vergne, Comptesse de La Fayette (1634–93).

5 The fate of Corneille's Théodore in the play of that title (1645) was prostitution and ultimate death.

33: 'RAMBLER', 4

1 Horace, *Ars Poetica*, 334: '. . . to say [what is] at once pleasing and helpful to life'. Thomas Creech (1659–1700) published many translations, including several versions of Lucretius.

2 Giovanni Giovanno Pontanus (1425–1503), an Italian poet, was criticized by Julius Caesar Scaliger (1484–1558) in his *Poetics* (*ante* 1581), V, iv.

3 Horace, *Epistulae* 2, 1, 170: '. . . a heavier burden as much as the indulgence is less'.

4 Apelles (fourth century B.C.), most famous of the painters of ancient Greece, painted a picture of Venus rising from the sea. His encounter with the shoemaker who correctly criticized his depiction of a sandal and then presumed to criticize the leg gave rise to the proverb, '*Ne sutor ultra crepidam*': 'Let not the shoemaker go beyond the shoe' (see Pliny, 35, 10).

5 Juvenal, XIV, 48–9: '. . . disregard not your boy's tender years, and let your infant son stand in the way of the sins that you propose'.

6 Untraced.

7 Gaius Caligula, quoting from the tragedian, L. Accius; see Suetonius, IV, XX, 10.

34: FROM A LETTER OF MRS. DONELLAN

1 Juba is a Numidian prince in Addison's *Cato* (1713) and Bevil the hero of Steele's last play, *The Conscious Lovers* (1722).

35: FROM 'AN ESSAY ON THE NEW SPECIES . . .'

1 *The Life and Adventures of Joe Thompson* (1750) was by Edward Kimber (d. 1769). *The History of Charlotte Summers, the Fortunate Parish Girl* (1750) was published anonymously and its author remains unknown. *Peregrine Pickle* (1751) was Tobias Smollett's second novel (see also above, No. 27, and below, No. 36).

2 The *Examen of the History of Tom Jones* (1750) was published anonymously—and the author does not deserve the name of critic. It has been conjectured that he is the same person who wrote *The Apology for the Life of Mr. Bamfylde Moore Carew* (1749), to the second edition of which were added some remarks hostile to Fielding.

3 Oroondates and Statira appear in La Calprenède's *Cassandre* (see above, No. 4).

4 In George Villiers, Duke of Buckingham's burlesque, *The Rehearsal* (1671), I.

5 *Tom Jones*, XVI, 1: 'I have heard of a dramatic writer who used to say, he would rather write a play than a prologue; in like manner, I think, I have with less pains written one of the books of this history, than the prefatory chapter to each of them.'

6 Horace, *Carminum*, 4, 12, 28. '. . . it is sweet at the fitting time to cast serious thoughts aside'.

7 Horace, *Sermones*, 1, 3, 6; '. . . from the egg-course to the fruit'.

8 *Spectator*, 40. 'Whatever crosses and disappointments a good man suffers in the body of the tragedy, they will make but a small impression on our minds, when we know that in the last act he is to arrive at the end of his wishes and desires.'

9 The passage omitted at this point consists of a rather unimpressive digression on imitation and originality.

10 [*sic*] Cf. Horace, *Ars Poetica*, 360. '. . . *operi longo fas est obreperi somnum*'. Philip Francis (1708–73) published his translation of Horace's *Satires* in 1746.

11 William Shirley (fl. 1739–80). The phrase occurs in his *Edward the Black Prince; or, The Battle of Poictiers: An Historical Tragedy. Attempted after the Manner of Shakespeare* (1750), I, 1.

12 Horace, *Ars Poetica*, 338–9.

13 *Othello*, IV, 2.

36: FROM A REVIEW OF 'PEREGRINE PICKLE'

1 Horace, *Ars Poetica*, 338.

2 Cornelius Nepos, historian of the Augustan Age, wrote an account of the Greek and Roman generals. *David Simple* (1744) was by Sarah Fielding (1710–1768).

3 That is, Fielding, in *Joseph Andrews*, III, i.

4 Horace, *Ars Poetica*, 343. '. . . the useful with the pleasing'.

5 The remainder of this article is taken up with plot summary, as was usual

with the monthly reviewers; this explanation will not be made again below, but it may be assumed that it holds good for later omissions from reviews.

37: FROM A REVIEW OF 'AMELIA'

1 This word is spelt 'Libercy' in the original.
2 Samuel Butler, *Hudibras* (1663–78), Part I, Canto 1.

38: FROM THE PREFACE TO 'CLARISSA HARLOWE' (1751)

1 See above, Nos. 26 and 28.
2 The concluding note to which Richardson refers is not reprinted in this volume, but is available to most readers in the Everyman edition of the novel.

39: FROM A LETTER OF PHILIP SKELTON

1 Plato, *Apology*, 28: '. . . the envy and detraction of the world, which has been the death of many good men, and will probably be the death of many more . . .', Lucius Caecilius Firmianus Lactantius (d. A.D. 325); see *The Divine Institutes*, trans. Sister F. McDonald (1964), V, 22, and VI, 17, pp. 386–7 and 442–3. The first passage describes the good man, the second quotes Seneca on the inevitability of his sufferings. The description coincides closely with Grandison's character.

40: FROM A REVIEW OF 'AMELIA'

1 Marie Catherine Hortense Desjardins, Dame de Villedieu (*c.* 1640–83), to whom Louis XIV gave a pension of 1,500 crowns. Voltaire said of her, '. . . *elle a fait perdre le gôut des longs romans*' (see J. M. Quérard, *La France Littéraire* . . . (1839), X, 171–2). Of her several works of prose fiction only one seems to have met with English translation (*Les Exiles* . . ., 1675, in 1679 and 1726), and as there does not seem to be a translation of this in Great Britain I do not know where this quotation occurs.
2 Cf. *Epistulae*, VI, 5: '*deinde quia largum iter est per praecepta, breve et efficax per exempla*': '. . . and then, because the way is long if you follow precept, but short and helpful, if you follow examples'.

41: FROM A LETTER OF SAMUEL RICHARDSON

1 *Covent Garden Journal*, 8, January 28, 1752, 'Proceedings at the Court of Censorial Enquiry'. Fielding says: '. . . I do, therefore, solemnly declare to you, Mr. Censor, that I will trouble the World no more with any Children of mine by the same Muse.'
2 William Young (b. 1702); see W. C. Cross, *The History of Henry Fielding* (1918), I, 175 and 344–5.

42: DEDICATION TO '. . . POMPEY THE LITTLE'

1 William Warburton, *Works of Pope* (1751), IV, 169. See above, No. 28, headnote, and below, No. 62, nn. 5 and 6.

2 Probably Coventry is referring to Claude-Prosper Jolyot de Crebillon (1707–1777), author of the light-hearted and licentious novels, *L'Ecumoire* (1734) and *Le Sopha* (1745), for which he was banished from Paris.

43: FROM 'THE FEMALE QUIXOTE'

1 This list, with that in n. 2, below, is formidable; all the names relate to the heroic romances. Clelia appears in the romance of that title by de Scudéry; Cleopatra, Candace and Elisa all appear in La Calprenède's *Cléopatre*.

2 Olympia and Arsinoe belong to *Cléopatre*; Parisatis, Berenice, Deidamia and another Arsinoe belong to *Cassandre* (see above, No. 4); Albysinda and Placidia may be found by the curious reader in La Calprenède's *Pharamond*. To the other three illustrious Sufferers I am an absolute Stranger.

3 *Macbeth*, IV, 3.

4 Richardson. [o.n.]

5 *Clarissa*. [o.n.]

6 The author of the *Rambler*. [o.n.] See above, No. 33, headnote.

7 Lokman the Wise was an Arabian fabulist who lived before King David, and author of a collection of fables published in Arabic with a Latin translation by Erpenius (1615).

44: 'THE ADVENTURER', 4

1 Horace, *Ars Poetica*, 338. Wenstworth Dillon (1633–85), Fourth Earl of Roscommon, published his translation of Horace in 1680.

46: 'THE ADVENTURER', 16

1 *Aeneid*, V, 344.

2 See above, No. 44.

3 Presumably these are cited as typical phrases rather than as quotations.

4 Merchant Taylors' School was set up in Suffolk Lane, Cannon St. in 1561. The building was destroyed by fire and replaced in 1675, and the school remained in this building until 1875. Among the many famous pupils of the school were Titus Oates, Lord Clive and Vicessimus Knox.

5 Matthew xxv, 21, 23.

6 *Essay on Man* (1733–4), II, 217.

47: 'THE ADVENTURER', 18

1 Phaedrus, a Thracian slave, became a freedman of the Emperor Augustus and translated Aesop's fables into iambic verse in the reign of Tiberius.

2 See Aristotle, *Rhetorics*, II, 20.

48: 'THE WORLD', 19

1 Adam Fitzadam was the editorial *persona* from behind which Moore conducted *The World*.

2 Thomas Otway (1652–85), *The Orphan* (1680), I, 351.

3 *Iliad*, IV: 'As when some stately trappings are decreed / To grace a monarch on his bounding steed, / A nymph in Caria . . . bred, stains the pure ivory . . .' (Pope's translation).

4 This title is untraced, if it is a title (it is unitalicized in the original); but cf. Nathaniel Ingelo's *Bentivolio and Urania* (1660).

5 That is, Minerva, so called from the Greek word for 'virgin'.

6 Presumably a reference to works like Mrs. Haywood's *Betsy Thoughtless* (1751) and the anonymous *Charlotte Summers* (1750), rather than a reference to specific novels.

7 I have not identified the persons referred to under this title.

49: DEDICATION TO 'FERDINAND COUNT FATHOM'

1 Maskwell is the villain of William Congreve's *The Double Dealer* (1694), Bevil appears in Steele's *The Conscious Lovers* (1722), and Edward is victorious in William Shirley's *Edward the Black Prince . . .* (1750).

51: 'THE WORLD', 79

1. Cf. *Paradise Lost*, IV, 756: 'Relations dear, and all the Charities / of Father, Son, and Brother . . .'

2 Moorfields was a district of London in which, during the eighteenth century, two converted hospitals for the insane were situated in the old Bedlam or Bethlehem and St. Luke's. Later, in 1790, Bedlam was removed to Old Street.

52: A LETTER . . . OF LIEN CHI ALTANGI . . .

1 Cantharides was used medically as a diuretic or an aphrodisiac and asafoetida as an anti-spasmodic.

2 Tom Durfey (1653–1723), dramatist and song-writer.

3 This seems to be a fabricated reference: Durfey published many works, but the *Oylet Hole* does not seem to have been among them.

53: DIALOGUE XXVIII FROM 'DIALOGUES OF THE DEAD'

1 Solon (*c.* 638–558 B.C.) was an Athenian legislator and poet. Numa was the legendary second King of Rome after Romulus and founder of a system of religion under divine guidance. L. Furius Camillus (d. 365 B.C.), called the second Romulus, saved Rome from the Gauls. The lives of all three are told in Plutarch.

2 See, for example, No. 5. Secret histories were fast being superseded at this date by novels written according to the design of the four great novelists of the mid-century.

3 Lucretia, wife of Tarquinius Collatinus, was raped and mutilated by Sextus, son of King Tarquin; see, for example, Shakespeare, *The Rape of Lucrece* (1594).

4 Portia, wife of Marcus Junius Brutus, murderer of Caesar, who killed herself by swallowing live coals when she heard of her husband's death.

5 Georges de Scudéry, under whose name some of his sister's romances were published.

6 Astrea, during the Golden Age, brought blessings to mankind, but retreated to the heavens before their wickedness and became the constellation Virgo. Pandora, the first woman, was owner of the famous box which, when opened, released all the ills of the human race, leaving Hope at the bottom as a sole consolation.

7 The Danaides were forty-nine of the fifty daughters of Danaus, King of Argus (grandfather of Perseus), who were ordered by their father to kill their husbands on their wedding night. Only one, Hypermnestra, allowed her husband to escape and so avoided the fate of her sisters—to spend eternity filling a sieve with water.

54: FROM A REVIEW OF '. . . TOM FOOL'

1 Information concerning this performer may be obtained from *Studies in Philology*, XVIII, July 1921, 313–16, and XX, January 1923, 58 and 68. He does not seem to have been a Turk, but rather of non-European extraction, born in Great Britain. His astounding feats on the high and low wires (including a vertical descent down a rope head-first and dancing with a boy suspended from one foot), made him extremely popular during the Commonwealth. Evelyn went to see him in 1657 and watched 'even to astonishment'. One of the contemporary ballads made about him ran as follows: 'A Wight there is come out of the East, / A mortal of great fame; / He looks like a man, for he is not a beast, / Yet he has never a Christian name: / Some say he's a Turk, Some call him a Jew, / For ten that belie him, scarce one tells true, / Let him be what he will, 'tis all one to you; / But yet he shall be a Turk.'

57: FROM A REVIEW OF '. . . TRISTRAM SHANDY'

1 Lucian: 'To one who said, "You're a Prometheus in Words." '

2 In the fragments of Ctesias we find the description of an Indian animal called 'martichora', with the face of a man, and a tail that serves both for a bow and a quiver full of arrows. He expressly says he saw such an animal at the court of Persia. He moreover mentions the king's guard, consisting of 6,000 men, each having eight fingers and eight toes on every hand and foot. Lucian likewise lashes Herodotus as an historian who had imposed upon mankind and tells us plainly that Thucydides means Herodotus when he complains of the insincerity of the historians who wrote before him. [o.n.]

3 Jambolus is unidentified.

4 Plato, *Symposium*, 215. The comparison actually made by Plato was between Socrates and a bust of Silenus set up in a statue-maker's shop. The reviewer seems to be referring rather to Rabelais, who himself refers to the passage in Plato's work.

5 This may be a quotation from Rabelais, but if so, it is untraced.

6 Lord Foppington is a character in Sir John Vanbrugh's *The Relapse* (1697), in R. B. Sheridan's *A Trip to Scarborough* (1777) and in Colley Cibber's *The*

Careless Husband (1705). A Jack Pudding is a clown, or 'merry droll'; see *Spectator*, 47.

7 Cf. Horace, *Ars Poetica*, 247 and 270: *'aut immunda crepent ignominosaque dicta'* ('... or cracking their bawdy and shameless jokes'), and *'at vestri proavi Plautinos et numeros et / laudavere sales ...'* ('... but your forefathers praised the measures and the wit of Plautus').

8 Cf. *Pantagruel*, Book I, chapter ii: 'The Nativity of the redoubtable Pantagruel.... And because in that very day Pantagruel was born, his father gave him that name; ... For when his mother Badabec was in the bringing of him forth, and that the midwives did wait to receive him, there came first out of her belly three score and eight tregeneers, that is, salt-sellers, every one of them leading in a halter, a mule heavy laden with salt; after whom issued forth nine dromedaries, with great loads of gammons of bacon, and dried neats' tongues on their backs. Then followed seven camels loaded with links and chitterlings, hogs' puddings and sausages. After them came out five great wains, full of leeks, garlick, onions, and chibots, ... As they were tattling this together after their own manner of chat, behold, out comes Pantagruel all hairy like a bear, whereupon one of them inspired with a prophetical spirit, said, This will be a terrible fellow, he is born with all his hair, he is undoubtedly to do wonderful things, and, if he live, he shall have age' (Sir Thomas Urquart's translation, 1653–93).

9 'Doglike hunger.'

10 I do not know where the *Critical* reviewers were reviled; it does not seem to have been in the *Monthly*.

11 In a bull published against the Emperor Lewis in the year 1346 by Pope Clement VI, we find the following imprecation: 'May the wrath of God, of St. Peter and St. Paul crush him in this world and that which is to come. May the earth open and swallow him alive: may his memory perish, and all the elements be his enemies: and may his children fall into the hands of his adversaries, even in the sight of their father.' [o.n.]

58: FROM A REVIEW OF 'ALMORAN AND HAMET'

1 Jean de La Fontaine (1621–95), *Le Pourvoir Des Fables*; see Fable IV, *Œvres* ..., ed. H. Regnier (1884), II, 234.

2 Some say that he made choice of five beautiful damsels of Croton for this purpose. Cicero tells us that the picture was painted for the Crotonians; but Pliny says it was for the people of Agrigentum, who sent him their most beautiful virgins for that purpose. [o.n.] Zeuxis flourished in the later part of the fifteenth century B.C.

3 William Lowndes, father of the bibliographer, was the second of that name to keep a bookshop in the Strand; his father, referred to here, was the original of Mr. Briggs in Fanny Burney's *Cecilia*.

4 As they will find, it is implied in *Tristram Shandy*. Three months before he wrote this review Ruffhead had been responsible for a savage attack on *Tristram Shandy*; see, *The Monthly Review*, XXIV, January 1761.

59: FROM A REVIEW OF 'ELOISA'

1 *Vide The Critical Review* [XI] for January 1761. [o.n.]

2 Part I, Letter XIII, and Part I, Letter XI.

60: 'ON FICTITIOUS HISTORY'

1 Andrew Fletcher of Saltoun (1655–1716) in *Letter to the Marquis of Montrose* (1704).

2 'Accommodating the appearances of things to the desires of the mind, not bringing down the mind, as history and philosophy do, to the course of events. [o.n.] Francis Bacon, *De Dignitate et Augmentis Scientarum* . . . (1623), II, 13.

3 See above, No. 8, n. 13.

4 Turpin (d. *c.* 800), Archbishop of Rheims, is supposed to be the author of *De Vita et Gestis Carolii Magni*.

5 See above, No. 59.

6 This is one of the earliest references to Defoe's technique as a writer of fiction, clearly separable from comment on subject-matter or literal truth, or its virtue as an improving book.

61: FROM AN 'ESSAY ON POETRY AND MUSIC . . .'

1 Horace, *Ars Poetica*, 15, etc. [o.n.]

2 Sir John Vanbrugh (1664–1726), dramatist and architect.

62: FROM THE INTRODUCTION TO 'THE WORKS OF . . . FIELDING'

1 That is, Fielding's activities as a magistrate and his publication of *A Charge to the Grand Jury* . . . (1749) and *An Enquiry into the Causes of the late Increase of Robbers* . . . (1751).

2 Marc-Jérôme Vida (1490–1566), *Poeticorum* (1527), II, 151–5, with a slight change of punctuation: 'So, to the trav'ller, as he journeys on / To reach the walls of some far distant town. / If, high in air, the dubious turrets rise, / Peep o'er the hills, and dance before his eyes; / Pleas'd the refreshing prospect to survey, / Each stride he lengthens, and beguils the way. / More pleas'd (the tempting scene in view) to goe, / Than pensively to walk the gloomy vales below.' *Vida's Art of Poetry*, trans. Rev. Mr. Christoph Pitt (1725), 49–50.

3 *Jonathan Wild* (1743), Book IV, chapter 13.

4 Horace, *Ars Poetica*, 86: '. . . to retain the fitting shades of the work.'

5 William Warburton; see above, No. 28, headnote.

6 *Works of Pope* (1751), IV, 169; see above, No. 42, n. 1.

7 Jean de La Bruyère (1645–96) published a translation of the *Characters* of Theophrastus in 1688, and followed it with an imitation of his own. He was elected to the Academy in 1695. Marivaux achieved the same honour in 1736.

8 'One better than the best.' This seems to be a common tag rather than a quotation.

9 'He did not know what it was well to leave out.' Again a tag rather than a quotation.

10 Alexander Pope, *Moral Essays* (1731–5), I, 29.

11 Untraced; but cf. *Romans de Marivaux*, ed. M. Arland (1957), *La Vie de Marianne*, 82–3 and *Le Paysan Parvenu*, 568.

12 Alexander Pope, *Essay on Man* (1732–4), IV, 364.

13 *Vide* the Preface to *Joseph Andrew*. [o.n.]

14 *Tom Jones* was published in 1749; *Amelia* in 1751.

15 Longinus, *On the Sublime*, IX: 'When we turn to the *Odyssey* we find occasion to observe that a great poetical genius in the decline of power which comes with old age naturally turns towards the fabulous. . . . The *Odyssey* is, in fact, a sort of epilogue to the *Iliad* . . .'

63: THE PREFACES TO 'THE CASTLE OF OTRANTO . . .'

1 Untraced.

2 The following remark is foreign to the present question, yet excusable in an Englishman, who is willing to think that the severe criticisms of so masterly a writer as Voltaire on our immortal countryman, may have been the effusions of wit and precipitation, rather than the result of judgement and attention. May not the critic's skill in the force and powers of our language have been as incorrect and incompetent as his knowledge of our history? Of the latter his own pen has dropped glaring evidence. In his preface to Thomas Corneille's *Earl of Essex*, monsieur de Voltaire allows that the truth of history has been grossly perverted in that piece. In excuse he pleads, that when Corneille wrote, the noblesse of France were much unread in English story; but now, says the commentator, that they study it, such misrepresentation would not be suffered—Yet forgetting that the period of ignorance is lapsed, and that it is not very necessary to instruct the knowing, he undertakes from the overflowing of his own reading to give the nobility of his own country a detail of Queen Elizabeth's favourites—of whom, says he, Robert Dudley was the first, and the earl of Leicester the second.—Could one have believed that it could be necessary to inform monsieur de Voltaire himself, that Robert Dudley and the earl of Leicester were the same person? [o.n.] Voltaire's *Commentary* was published in 1764.

3 *L'Enfant Prodigue* (1736), Preface: '. . . we find a mixture of the grave and of the gay, the comic and the pathetic [the life of man is chequer'd in this manner,] and a simple adventure is very often productive of these contrasts. Nothing is more easy to be met with, than a family where a father scolds, the daughter, distractedly in love, weeps, the son makes a jest of both, and the relations all act different parts in the scene. . . . We do not infer from this, that in every comedy there should be some scenes of buffoonery, and others pathetic; there are many excellent pieces, where gaiety alone predominates; others, which are wholly serious; others, which have a mixture of both, and others, affecting enough to excite tears. We ought not to exclude any species; and if my opinion were to be asked, which species is the best, I should answer, that which is treated in the most masterly manner' (*The Dramatic Works of M. de Voltaire*, trans. Rev. D. Williams (1781), II, 107–8.

4 *Lettre à Monsieur le Marquis Scipion Maffei*, prefixed to *Mérope* (1743). Allesandro Maffei (1622–1730) also wrote a play with this title (1713).

5 *Lettre à . . . Maffei;* slightly altered in quotation: 'All these characteristics are

ingenuous: everything in it is fitting to those whom you introduce on the scene, and to the customs which you give them. These natural familiarities would have been, as I believe, well received in Athens; but Paris and our *parterre* want a different kind of simplicity' (my translation).

6 See above, n. 2.

7 Not, it seems, a quotation, 'difficult trifles'.

8 The quotation comes from Racine's *Bérénice*, I, i, 7–8, and is made in Voltaire's *Remarques sur 'Bérénice', Tragédie de Racine* (1764). Voltaire comments: '*Ce détail n'est point inutile: il fair voir clairment combien l'unité de lieu est observée: il met le spectateur au fait tout d'un coup. On pourrait que* la pompe de ces lieux, et ce cabinet superbe, *paraissent des expressions peu convenables à un prince, que cette pompe ne doit point du tout éblouir, et qui est occupé de toute autre chose que des ornements d'un cabinet. J'ai toujours remarqué que la douceur des vers empêchait qu'on ne remarquât ce défaut.*'

64: FROM 'DISSERTATION ON THE IDEA OF UNIVERSAL POETRY'

1 Hurd has been arguing for the separation of the idea of poetry from the idea of verse.

2 That is, Fénelon, author of *Télémaque*.

3 Alexander Pope, *Essay on Criticism* (1711), 43.

65: FROM THE 'GENTLEMAN'S MAGAZINE', XXXVII

1 *Polly Honeycombe* (1760), a farce based on the antics of a daughter whose head has been turned by novels, was by George Colman the Elder (1732–94).

66: FROM THE 'GENTLEMAN'S MAGAZINE', XL

1 *La Jolie Femme, ou la Femme du jour* (1769) was by Nic.-Th. Barthe.

2 This was translated into English under the title of *Memoirs of the Marquis de Bretagne* in 1745, and printed for Edward Cave, and just reprinted for the Publisher of this Magazine. The other two have also been translated, and received with applause. [o.n.] At this date the *Gentleman's Magazine* was held jointly by Richard Cave and David Henry. For Prévost see above, No. 22, headnote.

3 The Heroine of the *History of the Chevalier de Grieux*, translated into English, in 1767, and printed for White. [o.n.]

4 Improperly styled in English, *The Devil upon Two Sticks*, and on the last translation *The Devil upon Crutches*. Sage's *Bachelor of Salamanca* is much inferior to his other works, and therefore probably is omitted here. [o.n.]

5 Not the *Protector* surely, but rather the *Destroyer*. [o.n.]

6 This will scarce be allowed by the admirers of Richardson, nor does it seem true. [o.n.]

7 This too will not be allowed. [o.n.]

8 Cf. first Preface to *Julie ou la Nouvelle Héloise:* '*Que si, après l'avoir lû tout entier, quelqu'un m'osoit blamer de l'avoir publié; qu'il le dise, s'il veut, à toute la terre, mais qu'il ne vienne pas me le dire: je sens que je ne pourrois de ma vie estimer cet homme-là.*'

67: FROM 'SOMETHING NEW'

1 In the previous chapter Griffiths had disposed of miscellanies—one of which he was writing.

2 Françoise d'Aubigné, Marquise de Maintenon (1635–1719), second wife of Louis XIV, whose period of influence saw an increase in religious persecution and moral restraint.

3 *Measure for Measure*, I, 4.

4 *The Triumvirate.* [o.n.] That is, *The Triumvirate: Or The Authentic Memoirs of A, B and C* (1764).

68: FROM A REVIEW OF 'DE L'HOMME, ET DE LA FEMME . . .

1 Simon-André Tissot (1728–97) wrote numerous books on medicine and health, particularly *Onanisme, Dissertation sur les malades produites par le masturbation* (1760) and *Avis aux gens de lettres et aux personnes sédentaires sur leur santé* (1768).

69: THREE ESSAYS FROM 'MISCELLANEOUS PIECES . .'

(a)

1 That is, assumed, adopted from without, additional.

(b)

1 *Macbeth*, III, 5.

2 Jaffeir and Belvidera are the hero and heroine of Otway's *Venice Preserved . .* (1682), Wolsey falls in Shakespeare's *Henry VIII*, and Jane Shore's death occurs in Nicholas Rowe's play named after the heroine (1714).

3 William Collins, *Ode to Fear* (1747), 74–5.

4 *Il Penseroso*, 119.

5 Ibid., 109–10.

6 *Henry V*, IV, 9.

7 Robert François Damiens (1714–57) attempted the life of Louis XV and was executed only after a series of hideous tortures.

8 Untraced.

9 *Ferdinand Count Fathom* (1753), chapter 21.

(c)

1 Alexander Pope, *Oddysey*, IX (slightly misquoted) and XII.

2 That is, Henry Fielding in *Amelia*.

3 This is a reference to a famous statue discovered during the excavations at Pompeii; it represents a young woman suckling an old man, presumed to be her father, and is generally called the Roman charity.

4 Belisarius (527–63), a famous general in the reign of the Emperor Justinian, of whom it is reported by a twelfth-century monk, Tzetzes, that he wandered about for some time as a blind beggar.

5 Thomas Otway, *The Orphan* (1690), II, 246–53, with slight misquotation.

6 That is, in *Venice Preserved . . .*

7 This reference is untraced.

8 That is, in Addison's play of that name (1713).

9 The paper ends with a short allegorical tale, the action of which is placed in the Golden Age, after the departure of Astrea from the earth. The tale deals with the issue of Pity from the union of Love and Sorrow. Pity weeps into Helicon, 'and ever since the Muses' spring has retained a strong taste of the infusion'. Jove orders Pity to follow his mother, Sorrow, and decrees that they die together, when Love will be reunited with Joy, 'his immortal and long-betrothed bride'.

70: FROM 'THE ORIGIN AND PROGRESS OF LANGUAGE'

(b)

1 *Ars Poetica*, 241: '. . . may sweat much, but toil in vain when attempting the same'.

(c)

1 P. 110. [o.n.]

2 Book IV, chapter 8. [o.n.]

3 *Ars Poetica*, 15–16, with *assuiter* for *adsuiter*: '. . one or two [purple] patches stitched in to glitter far and wide'.

71: PREFACE TO 'LIBERAL OPINIONS', V

1 Mentor—Athene in disguise—accompanied Telemachus in his search for Ulysses.

2 Alexander Pope, *Essay on Man* (1733–4), II, 217–18.

3 *Paradise Lost*, II, 113–14.

73: PREFACE TO 'EVELINA'

1 However superior the capacities in which these great writers deserve to be considered, they must pardon me that, for the dignity of my subject, I have to rank the authors of *Rasselas* and *Eloise* as Novelists. [o.n.]

2 John Sheffield, First Duke of Buckingham (1648–1721), *An Essay on Poetry* (1682), 235.

74: 'ON NOVEL READING'

1 Juvenal, XIV, 48–9: '. . . disregard not your boy's tender years, and let your infant son stand in the way of the sin that you propose'.

2 Presumably William Lily (1468?–1522), author of a Latin grammar, *Grammatices Rudimenta* (1527).

3 Charles Rollin (1661–1741) published his popular *Histoire ancienne* between 1730 and 1738.

76: FROM 'ON FABLE AND ROMANCE'

1 John Gay (1685–1732) published his *Fables* in 1727 and 1738, Sir Roger Lestrange (1616–1704) translated Aesop's *Fables* (1692 and 1699), Jean de La

Fontaine (1621–95) published his *Fables* in 1668 and Bracciolini Poggio (1380–1459) was author of *Liber Facetiarum* (1438–52).

2 Cebes was a Theban philosopher (fl. 405 B.C.), a disciple of Socrates famous for his dialogues and for his *Tables*, which give an account of human life. The fable of the attempt of pleasure and virtue to win the loyalty of Hercules was the work of Prodicus (*c.* 396 B.C.), sophist and rhetorician.

3 Cicero, *de Officiis*, Lib. i, cap. 32. [o.n.]

4 Antoine Gallande (1646–1715) translated *The Arabian Nights* (1704–17).

5 The 'History of the Barber and his six brothers' is contained within the 'History of the Little Hunchback'.

6 See the Preface to his *Voyages*. [o.n.] The volume referred to is that in which Hawkesworth gave the official account of the voyages of discovery made at the command of George III (1772); Beattie's objection was one commonly made.

7 *The History of John Bull* (1712), a collection of pamphlets by John Arbuthnot (1667–1735), was included in Pope and Swift's *Miscellanies* (1727).

8 That is, Giovanni Battista Andrieno (1578–?), author of *Adam or Original Sin* (1613); see Voltaire, *The Epick Poetry of the European Nations* (1727).

9 The *Imprimatur* prefixed to Patrick's *Pilgrim* is dated April 11, 1665. Bunyan's *Progress* was written while he was in Bedford prison, where he lay twelve years, from 1660 to 1672; but I cannot find in what year it was first printed. [o.n.] For a more detailed discussion of the relationship between Patrick's allegory and Bunyan's, see *Sir Walter Scott on Novelists and Fiction* (1968), 392–5.

10 I know not whether this author is not the only human being, who ever presumed to speak in ludicrous terms of the Last Judgment. His profane verses on that tremendous subject were not published, so far as I know, till after his death: for Chesterfield's Letter to Voltaire, in which they are inserted, and spoken of with approbation (which is no more than one would expect from such a critick), and said to be copied from the original in Swift's hand-writing, is dated in the year one thousand seven hundred and fifty-two. But this is no excuse for the Author. We may guess at what was in his mind, when he wrote them; and at what remained in his mind, while he could have destroyed them, and would not. Not is it any excuse to say, that he makes Jupiter the agent: a Christian, granting the utmost possible favour to Poetick licence, cannot conceive a heathen idol to do that, of which the only information we have is from the word of God, and in regard to which we certainly know, that it will be done by the Deity himself. That humourous and instructive allegory of Addison, (*Spectator*, 558, 559) in which Jupiter is supposed to put it in every person's power to choose his own condition, is not only conformable to antient philosophy, but is actually founded on a passage of Horace.

I mean not to insinuate, that Swift was favourable to infidelity. There is good reason to believe he was not; and that, though too many of his levities are inexcusable, he could occasionally be both serious and pious. In fact, an infidel clergyman would be such a compound of execrable impiety and contemptible meanness, that I am unwilling to suppose there can be such a monster. The profaneness of this author I impute to his passion for ridicule, and rage of witticism; which, when they settle into a habit, and venture on liberties with what is sacred, never fail to pervert the mind, and harden the heart. [o.n.]

11 Third volume of *Don Quixote*, near the beginning. [o.n.]

12 *Essay on Poetry and Musick*, Part i, chap. 5. [o.n.] See above, No. 61.
13 *The Adventures of Philip Quarll* (1727) is attributed to Edward Dorrington. Selkirk was rescued by Woodes Rogers (d. 1732), in 1709. The visit of George, Baron Anson (1697–1762), was made during his voyage round the world, 1740–4.
14 This story about the relationship between *Robinson Crusoe* and the adventures of Selkirk persisted throughout the eighteenth century into the nineteenth; its pointlessness was neatly demonstrated by Sir Walter Scott in his essay on Defoe, *Sir Walter Scott on Novelists and Fiction* (1968), 181–2.
15 See above, No. 11.
16 Jean-Jacques Rousseau, *Emile* (1762) III; see trans., B. Foxley (1911), 147.
17 The great Lord Lyttleton, after mentioning several particulars of Pope, Swift, and other wits of that time, when I asked some question relating to the Author of *Tom Jones*, began his answer with these words, 'Henry Fielding, I assure you, had more wit and humour than all the persons we have been speaking of put together.' This testimony of his Lordship, who was intimately acquainted with Fielding, ought not to be forgotten. [o.n.]

77: 'THE LOUNGER', 20

1 'The example, that is imitable in its faults, takes in the ignorant.' [o.n.] Horace, *Epistulae*, I, 19, 17.
2 John Sheffield, *An Essay on Poetry*, 235.

78: FROM 'THE OBSERVER', 29

1 Cf. below, No. 96. Cumberland seems to have changed his mind.

79: FROM 'A COMMENTARY ILLUSTRATING THE POETICS . . .'

(d)

1 Massinger has succeeded in this in his *Fatal Dowry*, from which Rowe entirely borrowed his plot, though without any acknowledgement. See a comparison between these plays in the *Observer*, Nos. 89, 90, 91. [o.n.]
2 The Greek phrase for 'that great faculty' has been omitted at this point.

(e)

1 See Andrew's *Anecdotes*, p. 31. Article 'Books'. [o.n.] James Pettit Andrews (1737?–97), *Anecdotes antient and modern* (1789).
2 Slightly misquoted from *Spectator*, 2, March 2, 1711.

80: 'THE MICROCOSM', 26

1 *Ars Poetica*, 320: '. . . though a play without force and art'.
2 *Don Belianis* (date uncertain) was by Feliciana da Silva; the *Famous History of the Seven Champions of Christendom* (c. 1597), was by R. Johnson (1573–1659?). *L'adultère innocent* was by Paul Scarron and appeared in his *Nouvelles tragi-comiques* (1655); a translation was included in *A Select Collection of Novels* (1720),

Volume IV. *Tears of Sensibility* (1773) was a translation by J. Murdock from the French of Françoise Marie de Baculard d'Arnauld. I have not traced a title exactly corresponding to the *Amours of the Count D*****, and L——y——*, but it would be possible to cite several which correspond closely. Roxana belongs to La Calprenède's *Cassandre*; Zorayde perhaps to *Don Quixote*; Sir Harry Harlowe either to David Garrick's *Neck or Nothing* (1766) or Richard Cumberland's *The Mysterious Husband* (1783). The other characters remain untraced.

3 1 *Henry IV*, I, 2.

4 John Sheffield, *An Essay on Poetry*, 235.

5 See *The Microcosm*, 30, Monday, June 14, 1787. 'On Mr. Newbery's Little Books'.

81: 'OLLA PODRIDA', 15

1 Horace, *Epistulae*, I, 1, 76: 'You are a many-headed monster-thing.' The first line is untraced.

2 Daniel Patterson (1739–1825) wrote *A New and Accurate Description of all the Direct and Principal Cross Roads in Great Britain* . . . (1771); his rival, John Ogilby (1600–76), produced *Britannia, Volume the first, or an Illustration of the Kingdom of England and Dominion of Wales, by a Geographical and Historical Description of the principal Roads thereof* . . . (1675).

3 Untraced.

4 *The Spiritual Quixote* (1772) was by Richard Graves (1715–1804). *Cecilia* was by Frances Burney.

5 Jacopo Sannazaro (1458–1540), Italian poet and author of *Arcadia* (1481–96).

6 Joseph Priestley (1733–1804), scientist and theologian; the work referred to is *Letters to the Jews, inviting them to an Amicable Discussion of the Evidence of Christianity* (1787), which was followed in the same year by a second part, '. . . occasioned by Mr. David Levi's Reply'.

7 *Nina; or the madness of love: a comedy in two Acts, and in prose* (1787) was translated from the French of J. B. Marvolier de Vivetière by George Monk Berkeley.

8 Sarah Siddons (1755–1831), tragic actress and sister of the Kemble brothers, painted by Sir Joshua Reynolds as 'The Tragic Muse'.

83: FROM 'WINTER EVENINGS . . .'

1 Antoine-Marie, Conte Majoragius (1514–55), and Henri Dupuy, called Putaneus (1574–1646). I have found no reference to the works concerned.

2 *Ars Poetica*, 366–85.

85: TWO ESSAYS FROM 'VARIETY . . .'

1 *Essay on Criticism*, 1.

2 Perhaps a vague reference to Dr. Benjamin Slocock's reference to *Pamela* from the pulpit of St. Saviour's, Southwark.

3 Cf. 'Original Anecdotes of Dr. Johnson', *Boswell's Life of Johnson*, ed. J. W. Croker (1831), Appendix V. Croker reports Miss Reynold's recollections: 'He [Johnson] was a great admirer of Richardson's works in general, but of *Clarissa*

he always spoke with the highest enthusiastic praise. He used to say, that it was the first book in the world for the knowledge it displays of the human heart.'

4 Slightly misquoted from *Owen o Carron*, st. xviii, by John Langhorne (1735–79).

5 Untraced.

6 That is, Johnson's periodical; see above, No. 33.

7 Robert Jephson (1736–1803), dramatist and poet, who wrote, among other things, *Julia, or the Italian Love* (1787), *The Count of Narbonne* (1781) and *Conspiracy* (1796).

8. Sir Richard Blackmore (d. 1729), author of many voluminous works, including five epic poems.

9 Published in 1778 amd 1784 respectively.

87: THREE REVIEWS FROM 'THE ANALYTICAL REVIEW', III

1 This seems to have been Mrs. Norman's only attempt at prose fiction.

2 By Ann Hilditch.

3 This novel seems to remain anonymous.

89: FROM A REVIEW OF 'THE LABYRINTHS OF LIFE'

1 We cannot avoid remarking the dull uniformity of conclusion which this writer has given to the letters of his personages. From whomsoever, and to whomsoever, the epistles are written, the single word 'Your's,' suffices, nearly throughout all the volumes. [o.n.]

2 Josiah Wedgwood (1730–95), inventor of the type of pottery which bears his name, was plagued with imitators.

3 *Gulliver's Travels*, chapter v.

4 For evidence as to the seriousness of this charge, see Dorothy Blakey, *The Minerva Press 1790–1820* (1939).

91: FROM 'THE ANALYTICAL REVIEW', XVI

(b)

1 *Argal* . . . was by George Hadley.

2 Mrs. C. Matthews also wrote *Anecdotes of the Clairville Family* . . . (1802) and *Griffith Abbey* . . . (1807).

3 *Elizabeth Percy* remains anonymous.

4 *The Conflict* . . . was by M. Heron.

(c)

1 Mrs. Wollstonecraft. [o.n.] That is, Mrs. Mary Wollstonecraft Godwin (1759–97), author of *Vindication of the Rights of Women* (1792).

2 See above, No. 81, n. 6.

3 Untraced.

4 *Henry V*, IV.

5 Edmund Burke (1729–97) in *Reflexions on the Revolution in France* (1790).

6 Jean-Jacques Rousseau, *Emile* (1762); see trans., B. Foxley (1961), chapter v, 371.

(*d*)

1 Horace, *Sermones*, I, 1, 119.
2. Thomas Sheridan (1719–88) produced *A General Dictionary of the English Language* (1780; revised 1789).
3 Priscian (fifth–sixth centuries A.D.), a Roman grammarian. To break his head was to infringe the rules of grammar.
4 Tom Browne (1663–1704), satirist, wit and translator. I have not traced this reference.

92: TWO REVIEWS FROM 'THE ANALYTICAL REVIEW', XVIII

1 The waxworks at No. 17 Fleet Street, removed to Water Lane in 1812, was run by a Mrs. Salmon (d. 1812). Mrs. Salmon's exhibition was substantial, containing 150 items in the Royal Court of England alone. It may or may not be identical with earlier displays in the same neighbourhood—as, for example, the exhibitions of *Pamela* and *Pamela in High Life* advertised as 'at the Corner of the Shoe-Lane, facing Salisbury Court, Fleet-Street'.

93: FROM A REVIEW OF 'THE MYSTERIES OF UDOLPHO'

1 Thomas Gray, *The Progress of Poesy* (1754), 91–5.
2 The scene of terror chosen for illustration is that from *The Mysteries of Udolpho*, III, chapter 1, where Emily goes with the servant Barnadine to find her aunt.

94: FROM A REVIEW OF 'THE MYSTERIES OF UDOLPHO'

1 See our Rev. N. S. vol. viii. p. 82. [o.n.]
2 Untraced.

95: FROM A REVIEW OF 'THINGS AS THEY ARE .

1 See our Rev. Vol. xvi, p. 121 and 388. [o.n.]
2 *The Newgate Calendar or Malefactor's Bloody Register* (*c.* 1774).

96: THE INTRODUCTORY CHAPTERS FROM 'HENRY'

1 That is, presumably, the 'lying legends' accumulated around the name of Pythagoras (fifth century B.C.) after his death; Abaris, a Scythian in the age of the Trojan War, who gave oracles and claimed to transport himself wherever he pleased; and Apollonius Tyana, who claimed magic powers and whose biography by his friend Damis contains a variety of 'lying legends'.
2 Fielding, Richardson and Smollett respectively, in each of the three paragraphs.

3 A reference to the use of manuscript and printed sheets for wrapping and for the lining of trunks.

4 Cf. *Iliad* (Pope's translation), I, 345–55.

5 Horace, *Sermones*, I, i, 106: '. . . there are, in short, fixed bounds'.

6 This paragraph, referring to both prose and poetry, male and female authors, seems to be directed against poems like Cowper's 'The Negro's Complaint' and 'Pity for Poor Africans', and particularly against Anna Maria Mackenzie's *Slavery, or, The Times* (1792), as well as the rash of poems and pamphlets which broke forth at this time—such as, for example, *British Cruelty; or the Wrongs of Africa* (1792).

7 James Lackington (1744–1815), bookseller, who announced in his *Memoirs of the Forty-Five First Years of the Life of James Lackington* (1791) that he estimated his sales at 100,000 volumes a year and his profits at between £4,000 and £5,000.

8 Plato, *Theaetetus*, 155.

9 Untraced.

10 François, Duc de La Rochefoucauld (1613–80), author of *Réflexions ou sentences et maximes morales* (1665).

11 The citizens of Libethrus in Thrace claimed to possess the tomb of Orpheus.

12 Hannah Glasse (fl. 1747) wrote *The Art of Cookery made Plain and Easy* (1747). Sir William Blackstone (1723–80) was author of *Commentaries on the Laws of England* (1765–9).

13 For Demosthenes (382–22 B.C.) see Plutarch, Diodorus, 16, Pausanius, I, c. 8 and XII, c. 23.

14 II Samuel xii.

15 Thomas Otway, *Venice Preserved* (1682), V, 369: 'Lutes, Laurells, Seas of Milk, and ships of Amber'.

16 Jacques Henri Bernardin de Saint Pierre (1737–1814), engineer and romanticist, author of *Paul et Virginie* (1787). Cumberland's reference is to the introduction to the *Indian Cottage* (1791): ' 'Tis those nations that have approached the nearest to Nature, and consequently, such as are the most free, that display the strongest disposition to adore truth with fables: this proceeds from the love of truth itself, which is the sentiment of the laws of Nature. Truth is the light of the soul, as physical light is the truth of bodies. . . . Few men can bear the pure light of the sun. . . . In like manner, few are capable of comprehending truth purely metaphysical. 'Tis on account of the weakness of our understanding that Nature has given us ignorance, to serve as an eye-lid to the mind; by means of this the soul opens by degrees to truth, admits only so much as she can bear, and surrounds herself with fables, which are like groves, in whose shade she may contemplate it, and when she is desirous of soaring to the Deity himself, she veils him with allegories and mysteries that she may be able to endure his resplendence', *The Works of St. Pierre* . . . (1807), IV, 283–4.

17 William Law (1686–1761), precursor of Methodism, author of *The Serious Call to a Devout and Holy Life. Adapted to the State and Condition of All orders of Christians* . . . (1729); see chapter xiii, 218–19, concerning the character, Negotius.

18 See above, n. 16.

98: FROM A REVIEW OF 'THE ITALIAN . . .'

1 It afterward appears, indeed, that this idea was erroneous, and that Ellena was the daughter of Schedoni's brother. [o.n.]

99: FROM 'A VIEW OF THE COMMENCEMENT . . . OF ROMANCE'

1 *Essay on the Life and Genius of Henry Fielding, Esq.* by A. Murphy, Esq. [o.n.]
2 T. Smollett, *The History of England from the Revolution to the Death of George the Second. (Designed as a Continuation of Mr. Hume's History)* (1760–5), 1818 ed., 379–80 and 381. Smollett also said: 'The laudable aim of enlisting the passions on the side of virtue was successfully pursued by Richardson in his *Pamela, Clarissa,* and *Grandison*; a species of writing equally new and extraordinary, where, mingled with much superfluity, we find a sublime system of ethics, an amazing knowledge and command of human nature.' In the first edition of *Peregrine Pickle* (1751) Smollett had spoken very unfavourably of Fielding, though he excised the passages from the second and later editions.
3 *Life of Tobias Smollett, M.D., With Critical Observations on his Works* (1796), 50: 'It has all the spirit and vigour of his former works, and is evidently the production of a mind enriched and mellowed by experience, and softened, but not soured by misfortune.'
4 *Hamlet*, III, 2.
5 See, for example, Nos. 74 and 76.

100: FIVE REVIEWS FROM 'THE BRITISH CRITIC'

1 Mrs. Courtney does not seem to have written any other novels.
2 See above, No. 71.
3 *Lessons for Children, of three years old* (1779), later expanded and apparently very popular.
4 This work is not mentioned in B. Q. Morgann's *A Critical Bibliography o, German Literature in English Translation 1481–1927* (revised ed. 1965).
5 By Anna Maria Mackenzie; see also above, No. 96, n. 6.
6 Mrs. Meeke was responsible for a total of eighteen novels.

101: FROM A REVIEW OF 'SANTA MARIA . . .'

1 Alexander Pope, *Essay on Man*, I, 13.
2 Presumably James Peller Malcolm (1767–1815), engraver and miscellaneous writer, whose work appeared regularly in the *Gentleman's Magazine*.

Index of Titles

This index is selective.
Italic numerals refer to the notes.

Index of Names

This index is selective.
Italic numerals refer to the notes.